MW01174228

COLLECTED WORKS OF
GEORGE BERNARD SHAW

COLLECTED WORKS OF
GEORGE BERNARD SHAW

PERFECT WAGNERITE: COMMENTARY
ON THE RING, DARK LADY OF THE SONNETS,
MRS. WARREN'S PROFESSION AND
YOU NEVER CAN TELL

BIBLIOBAZAAR

COLLECTED WORKS OF
GEORGE BERNARD SHAW

CONTENTS

THE PERFECT WAGNERITE:
A COMMENTARY ON THE NIBLUNG'S RING

THE DARK LADY OF THE SONNETS

MRS WARREN'S PROFESSION

YOU NEVER CAN TELL

THE PERFECT WAGNERITE:
A COMMENTARY ON THE
NIBLUNG'S RING

PREFACE TO THE
FIRST GERMAN EDITION

In reading through this German version of my book in the Manuscript of my friend Siegfried Trebitsch, I was struck by the inadequacy of the merely negative explanation given by me of the irrelevance of Night Falls On The Gods to the general philosophic scheme of The Ring. That explanation is correct as far as it goes; but, put as I put it, it now seems to me to suggest that the operatic character of Night Falls On The Gods was the result of indifference or forgetfulness produced by the lapse of twenty-five years between the first projection of the work and its completion. Now it is clear that in whatever other ways Wagner may have changed, he never became careless and he never became indifferent. I have therefore inserted a new section in which I show how the revolutionary history of Western Europe from the Liberal explosion of 1848 to the confused attempt at a socialist, military, and municipal administration in Paris in 1871 (that is to say, from the beginning of The Niblung's Ring by Wagner to the long-delayed completion of Night Falls On The Gods), demonstrated practically that the passing away of the present order was going to be a much more complicated business than it appears in Wagner's Siegfried. I have therefore interpolated a new chapter which will perhaps induce some readers of the original English text to read the book again in German.

For some time to come, indeed, I shall have to refer English readers to this German edition as the most complete in existence.

My obligation to Herr Trebitsch for making me a living German author instead of merely a translated English one is so great that I am bound to point out that he is not responsible for my views or Wagner's, and that it is as an artist and a man of letters, and not as a propagandist, that he is conveying to the German speaking peoples political criticisms which occasionally reflect on contemporary authorities with a European reputation for sensitiveness. And as the very sympathy which makes his translations so excellent may be regarded with suspicion, let me hasten to declare I am bound to Germany by the ties that hold my nature most strongly. Not that I like the average German: nobody does, even in his own country. But then the average man is not popular anywhere; and as no German considers himself an average one, each reader will, as an exceptional man, sympathize with my dislike of the common herd. And if I cannot love the typical modern German, I can at least pity and understand him. His worst fault is that he cannot see that it is possible to have too much of a good thing. Being convinced that duty, industry, education, loyalty, patriotism and respectability are good things (and I am magnanimous enough to admit that they are not altogether bad things when taken in strict moderation at the right time and in the right place), he indulges in them on all occasions shamelessly and excessively. He commits hideous crimes when crime is presented to him as part of his duty; his craze for work is more ruinous than the craze for drink; when he can afford secondary education for his sons you find three out of every five of them with their minds lamed for life by examinations which only a thoroughly wooden head could go through with impunity; and if a king is patriotic and respectable (few kings are) he puts up statues to him and exalts him above Charlemagne and Henry the Fowler. And when he meets a man of genius, he instinctively insults him, starves him, and, if possible, imprisons and kills him.

Now I do not pretend to be perfect myself. Heaven knows I have to struggle hard enough every day with what the Germans call my higher impulses. I know too well the temptation to be moral, to be self-sacrificing, to be loyal and patriotic, to be respectable and well-spoken of. But I wrestle with it and—as far as human frailty will allow—conquer it, whereas the

German abandons himself to it without scruple or reflection, and is actually proud of his pious intemperance and self-indulgence. Nothing will cure him of this mania. It may end in starvation, crushing taxation, suppression of all freedom to try new social experiments and reform obsolete institutions, in snobbery, jobbery, idolatry, and an omnipresent tyranny in which his doctor and his schoolmaster, his lawyer and his priest, coerce him worse than any official or drill sergeant: no matter: it is respectable, says the German, therefore it must be good, and cannot be carried too far; and everybody who rebels against it must be a rascal. Even the Social-Democrats in Germany differ from the rest only in carrying academic orthodoxy beyond human endurance—beyond even German endurance. I am a Socialist and a Democrat myself, the hero of a hundred platforms, one of the leaders of the most notable Socialist organizations in England. I am as conspicuous in English Socialism as Bebel is in German Socialism; but do you suppose that the German Social-Democrats tolerate me? Not a bit of it. I have begged again and again to be taken to the bosom of my German comrades. I have pleaded that the Super-Proletarians of all lands should unite. I have pointed out that the German Social-Democratic party has done nothing at its Congresses for the last ten years except the things I told them to do ten years before, and that its path is white with the bones of the Socialist superstitions I and my fellow Fabians have slain. Useless. They do not care a rap whether I am a Socialist or not. All they want to know is; Am I orthodox? Am I correct in my revolutionary views? Am I reverent to the revolutionary authorities? Because I am a genuine free-thinker they look at me as a policeman looks at a midnight prowler or as a Berlin bourgeois looks at a suspicious foreigner. They ask "Do you believe that Marx was omniscient and infallible; that Engels was his prophet; that Bebel and Singer are his inspired apostles; and that Das Kapital is the Bible?" Hastening in my innocence to clear myself of what I regard as an accusation of credulity and ignorance, I assure them earnestly that I know ten times as much of economics and a hundred times as much of practical administration as

15

Marx did; that I knew Engels personally and rather liked him as a witty and amiable old 1848 veteran who despised modern Socialism; that I regard Bebel and Singer as men of like passions with myself, but considerably less advanced; and that I read Das Kapital in the year 1882 or thereabouts, and still consider it one of the most important books of the nineteenth century because of its power of changing the minds of those who read it, in spite of its unsound capitalist economics, its parade of quotations from books which the author had either not read or not understood, its affectation of algebraic formulas, and its general attempt to disguise a masterpiece of propagandist journalism and prophetic invective as a drily scientific treatise of the sort that used to impose on people in 1860, when any book that pretended to be scientific was accepted as a Bible. In those days Darwin and Helmholtz were the real fathers of the Church; and nobody would listen to religion, poetry or rhetoric; so that even Socialism had to call itself "scientific," and predict the date of the revolution, as if it were a comet, by calculations founded on "historic laws."

To my amazement these reasonable remarks were received as hideous blasphemies; none of the party papers were allowed to print any word of mine; the very Revisionists themselves found that the scandal of my heresy damaged them more than my support aided them; and I found myself an outcast from German Social-Democracy at the moment when, thanks to Trebitsch, the German bourgeoisie and nobility began to smile on me, seduced by the pleasure of playing with fire, and perhaps by Agnes Sorma's acting as Candida.

Thus you may see that when a German, by becoming a Social-Democrat, throws off all the bonds of convention, and stands free from all allegiance to established religion, law, order, patriotism, and learning, he promptly uses his freedom to put on a headier set of chains; expels anti-militarists with the blood-thirstiest martial anti-foreign ardor; and gives the Kaiser reason to thank heaven that he was born in the comparative freedom and Laodicean tolerance of Kingship, and not in the Calvinistic bigotry and pedantry of Marxism.

Why, then, you may ask, do I say that I am bound to Germany by the ties that hold my nature most strongly? Very simply because I should have perished of despair in my youth but for the world created for me by that great German dynasty which began with Bach and will perhaps not end with Richard Strauss. Do not suppose for a moment that I learnt my art from English men of letters. True, they showed me how to handle English words; but if I had known no more than that, my works would never have crossed the Channel. My masters were the masters of a universal language: they were, to go from summit to summit, Bach, Handel, Haydn, Mozart, Beethoven and Wagner. Had the Germans understood any of these men, they would have hanged them. Fortunately they did not understand them, and therefore only neglected them until they were dead, after which they learnt to dance to their tunes with an easy conscience. For their sakes Germany stands consecrated as the Holy Land of the capitalist age, just as Italy, for its painters' sakes, is the Holy Land of the early unvulgarized Renascence; France, for its builders' sakes, of the age of Christian chivalry and faith; and Greece, for its sculptors' sakes, of the Periclean age.

These Holy Lands are my fatherlands: in them alone am I truly at home: all my work is but to bring the whole world under this sanctification.

And so, O worthy, respectable, dutiful, patriotic, brave, industrious German reader, you who used to fear only God and your own conscience, and now fear nothing at all, here is my book for you; and—in all sincerity— much good may it do you!

London, 23rd. October 1907.

PREFACE TO THE SECOND EDITION

The preparation of a Second Edition of this booklet is quite the most unexpected literary task that has ever been set me. When it first appeared I was ungrateful enough to remonstrate with its publisher for printing, as I thought, more copies than the most sanguine Wagnerite could ever hope to sell. But the result proved that exactly one person buys a copy on every day in the year, including Sundays; and so, in the process of the suns, a reprint has become necessary.

Save a few verbal slips of no importance, I have found nothing to alter in this edition. As usual, the only protests the book has elicited are protests, not against the opinions it expresses, but against the facts it records. There are people who cannot bear to be told that their hero was associated with a famous Anarchist in a rebellion; that he was proclaimed as "wanted" by the police; that he wrote revolutionary pamphlets; and that his picture of Niblunghome under the reign of Alberic is a poetic vision of unregulated industrial capitalism as it was made known in Germany in the middle of the nineteenth century by Engels's Condition of the Laboring classes in England. They frantically deny these facts, and then declare that I have connected them with Wagner in a paroxysm of senseless perversity. I am sorry I have hurt them; and I appeal to charitable publishers to bring out a new life of Wagner, which shall describe him as a court musician of unquestioned fashion and orthodoxy, and a pillar of the most exclusive Dresden circles. Such a work, would, I believe, have a large sale, and be read with satisfaction and reassurance by many lovers of Wagner's music.

As to my much demurred-to relegation of Night Falls On The Gods to the category of grand opera, I have nothing to add or withdraw. Such a classification is to me as much a matter of fact as the Dresden rising or the police proclamation; but I shall not pretend that it is a matter of such fact as everybody's judgment can grapple with. People who prefer grand opera to serious music-drama naturally resent my placing a very grand opera below a very serious music-drama. The ordinary lover of Shakespeare would equally demur to my placing his popular catchpenny plays, of which As You Like It is an avowed type, below true Shakespearean plays like Measure for Measure. I cannot help that. Popular dramas and operas may have overwhelming merits as enchanting make-believes; but a poet's sincerest vision of the world must always take precedence of his prettiest fool's paradise.

As many English Wagnerites seem to be still under the impression that Wagner composed Rienzi in his youth, Tannhauser and Lohengrin in his middle age, and The Ring in his later years, may I again remind them that The Ring was the result of a political convulsion which occurred when Wagner was only thirty-six, and that the poem was completed when he was forty, with thirty more years of work before him? It is as much a first essay in political philosophy as Die Feen is a first essay in romantic opera. The attempt to recover its spirit twenty years later, when the music of Night Falls On The Gods was added, was an attempt to revive the barricades of Dresden in the Temple of the Grail. Only those who have never had any political enthusiasms to survive can believe that such an attempt could succeed. G. B. S.

London, 1901

PREFACE TO THE FIRST EDITION

This book is a commentary on The Ring of the Niblungs, Wagner's chief work. I offer it to those enthusiastic admirers of Wagner who are unable to follow his ideas, and do not in the least understand the dilemma of Wotan, though they are filled with indignation at the irreverence of the Philistines who frankly avow that they find the remarks of the god too often tedious and nonsensical. Now to be devoted to Wagner merely as a dog is devoted to his master, sharing a few elementary ideas, appetites and emotions with him, and, for the rest, reverencing his superiority without understanding it, is no true Wagnerism. Yet nothing better is possible without a stock of ideas common to master and disciple. Unfortunately, the ideas of the revolutionary Wagner of 1848 are taught neither by the education nor the experience of English and American gentlemen-amateurs, who are almost always political mugwumps, and hardly ever associate with revolutionists. The earlier attempts to translate his numerous pamphlets and essays into English, resulted in ludicrous mixtures of pure nonsense with the absurdest distortions of his ideas into the ideas of the translators. We now have a translation which is a masterpiece of interpretation and an eminent addition to our literature; but that is not because its author, Mr. Ashton Ellis, knows the German dictionary better than his predecessors. He is simply in possession of Wagner's ideas, which were to them inconceivable.

All I pretend to do in this book is to impart the ideas which are most likely to be lacking in the conventional Englishman's equipment. I came by them myself much as Wagner did, having learnt more about music than about anything else in my youth, and sown my political wild oats subsequently in the revolutionary school. This combination is not common in England; and as I seem, so far, to be the only publicly articulate result of it, I venture to add my commentary to what has already been written by musicians who are no revolutionists, and revolutionists who are no musicians.

G. B. S.

THE PERFECT WAGNERITE

PRELIMINARY ENCOURAGEMENTS

A few of these will be welcome to the ordinary citizen visiting the theatre to satisfy his curiosity, or his desire to be in the fashion, by witnessing a representation of Richard Wagner's famous Ring of the Niblungs.

First, The Ring, with all its gods and giants and dwarfs, its water-maidens and Valkyries, its wishing-cap, magic ring, enchanted sword, and miraculous treasure, is a drama of today, and not of a remote and fabulous antiquity. It could not have been written before the second half of the nineteenth century, because it deals with events which were only then consummating themselves. Unless the spectator recognizes in it an image of the life he is himself fighting his way through, it must needs appear to him a monstrous development of the Christmas pantomimes, spun out here and there into intolerable lengths of dull conversation by the principal baritone. Fortunately, even from this point of view, The Ring is full of extraordinarily attractive episodes, both orchestral and dramatic. The nature music alone—music of river and rainbow, fire and forest—is enough to bribe people with any love of the country in them to endure the passages of political philosophy in the sure hope of a prettier page to come. Everybody, too, can enjoy the love music, the hammer and anvil music, the clumping of the giants, the tune of the young woodsman's horn, the trilling of the bird, the dragon music and nightmare music and thunder and lightning music, the profusion of simple melody, the sensuous charm of the orchestration: in short, the vast extent of common ground between The Ring and the ordinary music we use for play and pleasure. Hence it is that the four separate music-plays of which it is built have become popular throughout Europe as operas. We shall presently see that one of them, Night Falls On The Gods, actually is an opera.

It is generally understood, however, that there is an inner ring of superior persons to whom the whole work has a most urgent and searching philosophic and social significance. I profess to be such a superior person; and I write this pamphlet for the assistance of those who wish to be introduced to the work on equal terms with that inner circle of adepts.

My second encouragement is addressed to modest citizens who may suppose themselves to be disqualified from enjoying The Ring by their technical ignorance of music. They may dismiss all such misgivings speedily and confidently. If the sound of music has any power to move them, they will find that Wagner exacts nothing further. There is not a single bar of "classical music" in The Ring—not a note in it that has any other point than the single direct point of giving musical expression to the drama. In classical music there are, as the analytical programs tell us, first subjects and second subjects, free fantasias, recapitulations, and codas; there are fugues, with counter-subjects, strettos, and pedal points; there are passacaglias on ground basses, canons ad hypodiapente, and other ingenuities, which have, after all, stood or fallen by their prettiness as much as the simplest folk-tune. Wagner is never driving at anything of this sort any more than Shakespeare in his plays is driving at such ingenuities of verse-making as sonnets, triolets, and the like. And this is why he is so easy for the natural musician who has had no academic teaching. The professors, when Wagner's music is played to them, exclaim at once "What is this? Is it aria, or recitative? Is there no cabaletta to it—not even a full close? Why was that discord not prepared; and why does he not resolve it correctly? How dare he indulge in those scandalous and illicit transitions into a key that has not one note in common with the key he has just left? Listen to those false relations! What does he want with six drums and eight horns when Mozart worked miracles with two of each? The man is no musician." The layman neither knows nor cares about any of these things. If Wagner were to turn aside from his straightforward dramatic purpose to propitiate the professors with correct exercises in sonata form, his music would at once become unintelligible to the unsophisticated spectator, upon whom the familiar and dreaded "classical" sensation would descend like the influenza. Nothing of the kind need be dreaded. The unskilled, untaught musician may approach Wagner boldly; for there is no possibility of a misunderstanding between them: The Ring music is perfectly single and simple. It is the adept musician of the old school who has everything to unlearn: and him I leave, unpitied, to his fate.

THE RING OF THE NIBLUNGS

The Ring consists of four plays, intended to be performed on four successive evenings, entitled The Rhine Gold (a prologue to the other three), The Valkyries, Siegfried, and Night Falls On The Gods; or, in the original German, Das Rheingold, Die Walkure, Siegfried, and Die Gotterdammerung.

THE RHINE GOLD

Let me assume for a moment that you are a young and good-looking woman. Try to imagine yourself in that character at Klondyke five years ago. The place is teeming with gold. If you are content to leave the gold alone, as the wise leave flowers without plucking them, enjoying with perfect naivete its color and glitter and preciousness, no human being will ever be the worse for your knowledge of it; and whilst you remain in that frame of mind the golden age will endure.

Now suppose a man comes along: a man who has no sense of the golden age, nor any power of living in the present: a man with common desires, cupidities, ambitions, just like most of the men you know. Suppose you reveal to that man the fact that if he will only pluck this gold up, and turn it into money, millions of men, driven by the invisible whip of hunger, will toil underground and overground night and day to pile up more and more gold for him until he is master of the world! You will find that the prospect will not tempt him so much as you might imagine, because it involves some distasteful trouble to himself to start with, and because there is something else within his reach involving no distasteful toil, which he desires more passionately; and that is yourself. So long as he is preoccupied with love of you, the gold, and all that it implies, will escape him: the golden age will endure. Not until he forswears love will he stretch out his hand to the gold, and found the Plutonic empire for himself. But the choice between love and gold may not rest altogether with him. He may be an ugly, ungracious, unamiable person, whose affections may seem merely ludicrous and despicable to you. In that case, you may repulse him, and most bitterly humiliate and disappoint him. What is left to him then but to curse the love he can never win, and turn remorselessly to the gold? With that, he will make short work of your golden age, and leave you lamenting its lost thoughtlessness and sweetness.

In due time the gold of Klondyke will find its way to the great cities of the world. But the old dilemma will keep continually reproducing itself. The man who will turn his back on love, and upon all the fruitful it, and will set himself single-heartedly to gather gold in an exultant dream of wielding its Plutonic powers, will find the treasure yielding quickly to his touch. But few men will make this sacrifice voluntarily. Not until the Plutonic power is so strongly set up that the higher human impulses are suppressed as rebellious, and even the mere appetites are denied, starved, and insulted when they cannot purchase their satisfaction with gold, are the energetic spirits driven to build their lives upon riches. How inevitable that course has become to us is plain enough to those who have the power of understanding what they see as they look at the plutocratic societies of our modern capitals.

First Scene

Here, then, is the subject of the first scene of The Rhine Gold. As you sit waiting for the curtain to rise, you suddenly catch the booming ground-tone of a mighty river. It becomes plainer, clearer: you get nearer to the surface, and catch the green light and the flights of bubbles. Then the curtain goes up and you see what you heard—the depths of the Rhine, with three strange fairy fishes, half water-maidens, singing and enjoying themselves exuberantly. They are not singing barcarolles or ballads about the Lorely and her fated lovers, but simply trolling any nonsense that comes into their heads in time to the dancing of the water and the rhythm of their swimming. It is the golden age; and the attraction of this spot for the Rhine maidens is a lump of the Rhine gold, which they value, in an entirely uncommercial way, for its bodily beauty and splendor. Just at present it is eclipsed, because the sun is not striking down through the water.

Presently there comes a poor devil of a dwarf stealing along the slippery rocks of the river bed, a creature with energy enough to make him strong of body and fierce of passion, but with a brutish narrowness of intelligence and selfishness of imagination: too stupid to see that his own welfare can only be compassed as part of the welfare of the world, too full of brute force not to grab vigorously at his own gain. Such dwarfs are quite common in London. He comes now with a fruitful impulse in him, in search of what he lacks in himself, beauty, lightness of heart, imagination, music. The Rhine maidens, representing all these to him, fill him with hope and longing; and he never considers that he has nothing to offer that they could possibly desire, being by natural limitation incapable of seeing anything from anyone else's point of view. With perfect simplicity, he offers himself as a sweetheart to them. But they are thoughtless, elemental, only half real things, much like modern young ladies. That the poor dwarf is repulsive to their sense of physical beauty and their romantic conception of heroism, that he is ugly and awkward, greedy and ridiculous, disposes for them of his claim to live and love. They mock him atrociously, pretending to fall in love with him at first sight, and then slipping away and making game of him, heaping ridicule and disgust on the poor wretch until he is beside himself with mortification and rage. They forget him when the water begins to glitter in the sun, and the gold to reflect its glory. They break into ecstatic worship of their treasure; and though they know the parable of Klondyke quite well, they have no fear that the gold will be wrenched away by the dwarf, since it will yield to no one who has not forsworn love for it, and it is in pursuit of love that he has come to them. They forget that they have poisoned that desire in him by their mockery and denial of it, and that he now knows that life will give him nothing that he cannot wrest from it by the Plutonic power. It is just as if some poor, rough, vulgar, coarse fellow were to offer to take his part in aristocratic society, and be snubbed into the knowledge that only as a millionaire could he ever hope to bring that society to his feet and buy himself a beautiful and refined wife. His choice is forced on him. He forswears love as thousands of us forswear it every day; and in a moment the gold is in his grasp, and he disappears in the depths, leaving the water-fairies vainly screaming "Stop thief!" whilst the river seems to plunge into darkness and sink from us as we rise to the cloud regions above.

And now, what forces are there in the world to resist Alberic, our dwarf, in his new character of sworn plutocrat? He is soon at work wielding the power of the gold. For his gain, hordes of his fellow-creatures are thenceforth condemned to slave miserably, overground and underground, lashed to their work by the invisible whip of starvation. They never see him, any more than the victims of our "dangerous trades" ever see the shareholders whose power is nevertheless everywhere, driving them to destruction. The very wealth they create with their labor becomes an additional force to impoverish them; for as fast as they make it it slips from their hands into the hands of their master, and makes him mightier than ever. You can see the process for yourself in every civilized country today, where millions of people toil in want and disease to heap up more wealth for our Alberics, laying up nothing for themselves, except sometimes horrible and agonizing disease and the certainty of premature death. All this part of the story is frightfully real, frightfully present, frightfully modern; and its effects on our social life are so ghastly and ruinous that we no longer know enough of happiness to be discomposed by it. It is only the poet, with his vision of what life might be, to whom these things are unendurable. If we were a race of poets we would make an end of them before the end of this miserable century. Being a race of moral dwarfs instead, we think them highly respectable, comfortable and proper, and allow them to breed and multiply their evil in all directions. If there were no higher power in the world to work against Alberic, the end of it would be utter destruction.

Such a force there is, however; and it is called Godhead. The mysterious thing we call life organizes itself into all living shapes, bird, beast, beetle and fish, rising to the human marvel in cunning dwarfs and in laborious muscular giants, capable, these last, of enduring toil, willing to buy love and life, not with suicidal curses and renunciations, but with patient manual drudgery in the service of higher powers. And these higher powers are called into existence by the same self-organization of life still more wonderfully into rare persons who may by comparison be called gods, creatures capable of thought, whose aims extend far beyond the satisfaction of their bodily appetites and personal affections, since they perceive that it is only by the establishment of a social order founded on common bonds of moral faith that the world can rise from mere savagery. But how is this order to be set up by Godhead in a world of stupid giants, since these thoughtless ones pursue only their narrower personal ends and can by no means understand the aims of a god? Godhead, face to face with Stupidity, must compromise. Unable to enforce on the world the pure law of thought, it must resort to a mechanical law of commandments to be enforced by brute punishments and the destruction of the disobedient. And however carefully these laws are framed to represent the highest thoughts of the framers at the moment of their promulgation, before a day has elapsed that thought has grown and widened by the ceaseless evolution of life; and lo! yesterday's law already fallen out with today's thought. Yet if the high givers of that law themselves set the example of breaking it before it is a week old, they destroy all its authority with their subjects, and so break the weapon they have forged to rule them for their own good. They must therefore maintain at all costs the sanctity of the law, even when it has ceased to represent their thought; so that at last they get entangled in a network of ordinances which they no longer believe in, and yet have made so sacred by custom and so terrible by punishment, that they cannot themselves escape from them. Thus Godhead's resort to law finally costs it half its integrity—as if a spiritual king, to gain temporal power, had plucked out one of his eyes—and it finally begins secretly to long for the advent of some power higher than itself which will destroy its artificial empire of law, and establish a true republic of free thought.

This is by no means the only difficulty in the dominion of Law. The brute force for its execution must be purchased; and the mass of its subjects must be persuaded to respect the authority which employs this force. But how is such respect to be implanted in them if they are unable to comprehend the thought of the lawgiver? Clearly, only by associating the legislative power with such displays of splendor and majesty as will impress their senses and awe their imaginations. The god turned lawgiver, in short, must be crowned Pontiff and King. Since he cannot be known to the common folk as their superior in wisdom, he must be known to them as their superior in riches, as the dweller in castles, the wearer of gold and purple, the eater of mighty feasts, the commander of armies, and the wielder of powers of life and death, of salvation and damnation after death. Something may be done in this way without corruption whilst the golden age still endures. Your gods may not prevail with the dwarfs; but they may go to these honest giants who will give a day's work for a day's pay, and induce them to build for Godhead a mighty fortress, complete with hall and chapel, tower and bell, for the sake of the homesteads that will grow up in security round that church-castle. This only, however, whilst the golden age lasts. The moment the Plutonic power is let loose, and the loveless Alberic comes into the field with his corrupting millions, the gods are face to face with destruction; since Alberic, able with invisible hunger-whip to force the labor of the dwarfs and to buy the services of the giants, can outshine all the temporal shows and splendors of the golden age, and make himself master of the world, unless the gods, with their bigger brains, can capture his gold. This, the dilemma of the Church today, is the situation created by the exploit of Alberic in the depths of the Rhine.

Second Scene

From the bed of the river we rise into cloudy regions, and finally come out into the clear in a meadow, where Wotan, the god of gods, and his consort Fricka lie sleeping. Wotan, you will observe, has lost one eye; and you will presently learn that he plucked it out voluntarily as the price to be paid for his alliance with Fricka, who in return has brought to him as her dowry all the powers of Law. The meadow is on the brink of a ravine, beyond which, towering on distant heights, stands Godhome, a mighty castle, newly built as a house of state for the one-eyed god and his all-ruling wife. Wotan has not yet seen this castle except in his dreams: two giants have just built it for him whilst he slept; and the reality is before him for the first time when Fricka wakes him. In that majestic burg he is to rule with her and through her over the humble giants, who have eyes to gape at the glorious castles their own hands have built from his design, but no brains to design castles for themselves, or to comprehend divinity. As a god, he is to be great, secure, and mighty; but he is also to be passionless, affectionless, wholly impartial; for Godhead, if it is to live with Law, must have no weaknesses, no respect for persons. All such sweet littlenesses must be left to the humble stupid giants to make their toil sweet to them; and the god must, after all, pay for Olympian power the same price the dwarf has paid for Plutonic power.

Wotan has forgotten this in his dreams of greatness. Not so Fricka. What she is thinking of is this price that Wotan has consented to pay, in token whereof he has promised this day to hand over to the giants Fricka's sister, the goddess Freia, with her golden love-apples. When Fricka reproaches Wotan with having selfishly forgotten this, she finds that he, like herself, is not prepared to go through with his bargain, and that he is trusting to another great worldforce, the Lie (a European Power, as Lassalle said), to help him to trick the giants out of their reward. But this force does not dwell in Wotan himself, but in another, a god over whom he has triumphed, one Loki, the god of Intellect, Argument, Imagination, Illusion, and Reason. Loki has promised to deliver him from his contract, and to cheat the giants for him; but he has not arrived to keep his word: indeed, as Fricka bitterly points out, why should not the Lie fail Wotan, since such failure is the very essence of him?

The giants come soon enough; and Freia flies to Wotan for protection against them. Their purposes are quite honest; and they have no doubt of the god's faith. There stands their part of the contract fulfilled, stone on stone, port and pinnacle all faithfully finished from Wotan's design by their mighty labor. They have come undoubtingly for their agreed wage. Then there happens what is to them an incredible, inconceivable thing. The god begins to shuffle. There are no moments in life more tragic than those in which the humble common man, the manual worker, leaving with implicit trust all high affairs to his betters, and reverencing them wholly as worthy of that trust, even to the extent of accepting as his rightful function the saving of them from all roughening and coarsening drudgeries, first discovers that they are corrupt, greedy, unjust and treacherous. The shock drives a ray of prophetic light into one giant's mind, and gives him a momentary eloquence. In that moment he rises above his stupid gianthood, and earnestly warns the Son of Light that all his power and eminence of priesthood, godhood, and kingship must stand or fall with the unbearable cold greatness of the incorruptible law-giver. But Wotan, whose assumed character of law-giver is altogether false to his real passionate nature, despises the rebuke; and the giant's ray of insight is lost in the murk of his virtuous indignation.

In the midst of the wrangle, Loki comes at last, excusing himself for being late on the ground that he has been detained by a matter of importance which he has promised to lay before Wotan. When pressed to give his mind to the business immediately in hand, and to extricate Wotan from his dilemma, he has nothing to say except that the giants are evidently altogether in the right. The castle has been duly built: he has tried every stone of it, and found the work first-rate: there is nothing to be done but pay the price agreed upon by handing over Freia to the giants. The gods are furious; and Wotan passionately declares that he only consented to the bargain on Loki's promise to find a way for him out of it. But Loki says no: he has promised to find a way out if any such way exist, but not to make a way if there is no way. He has wandered over the whole earth in search of some treasure great enough to buy Freia back from the giants; but in all the world he has found nothing for which Man will give up Woman. And this, by the way, reminds him of the matter he had promised to lay before Wotan. The Rhine maidens have complained to him of Alberic's theft of their gold; and he mentions it as a curious exception to his universal law of the unpurchasable preciousness of love, that this gold-robber has forsworn love for the sake of the fabulous riches of the Plutonic empire and the mastery of the world through its power.

No sooner is the tale told than the giants stoop lower than the dwarf. Alberic forswore love only when it was denied to him and made the instrument for cruelly murdering his self-respect. But the giants, with love within their reach, with Freia and her golden apples in their hands, offer to give her up for the treasure of Alberic. Observe, it is the treasure alone that they desire. They have no fierce dreams of dominion over their superiors, or of moulding the world to any conceptions of their own. They are neither clever nor ambitious: they simply covet money. Alberic's gold: that is their demand, or else Freia, as agreed upon, whom they now carry off as hostage, leaving Wotan to consider their ultimatum.

Freia gone, the gods begin to wither and age: her golden apples, which they so lightly bargained away, they now find to be a matter of life and death to them; for not even the gods can live on Law and Godhead alone, be their castles ever so splendid. Loki alone is unaffected: the Lie, with all its cunning wonders, its glistenings and shiftings and mirages, is a mere appearance: it has no body and needs no food. What is Wotan to do? Loki sees the answer clearly enough: he must bluntly rob Alberic. There is nothing to prevent him except moral scruple; for Alberic, after all, is a poor, dim, dwarfed, credulous creature whom a god can outsee and a lie can outwit. Down, then, Wotan and Loki plunge into the mine where Alberic's slaves are piling up wealth for him under the invisible whip.

Third Scene

This gloomy place need not be a mine: it might just as well be a match-factory, with yellow phosphorus, phossy jaw, a large dividend, and plenty of clergymen shareholders. Or it might be a whitelead factory, or a chemical works, or a pottery, or a railway shunting yard, or a tailoring shop, or a little gin-sodden laundry, or a bakehouse, or a big shop, or any other of the places where human life and welfare are daily sacrificed in order that some greedy foolish creature may be able to hymn exultantly to his Platonic idol:

> Thou mak'st me eat whilst others starve,
> And sing while others do lament:
> Such untome Thy blessings are,
> As if I were Thine only care.

In the mine, which resounds with the clinking anvils of the dwarfs toiling miserably to heap up treasure for their master, Alberic has set his brother Mime—more familiarly, Mimmy—to make him a helmet. Mimmy dimly sees that there is some magic in this helmet, and tries to keep it; but Alberic wrests it from him, and shows him, to his cost, that it is the veil of the invisible whip, and that he who wears it can appear in what shape he will, or disappear from view altogether. This helmet is a very common article in our streets, where it generally takes the form of a tall hat. It makes a man invisible as a shareholder, and changes him into various shapes, such as a pious Christian, a subscriber to hospitals, a benefactor of the poor, a model husband and father, a shrewd, practical independent Englishman, and what not, when he is really a pitiful parasite on the commonwealth, consuming a great deal, and producing nothing, feeling nothing, knowing nothing, believing nothing, and doing nothing except what all the rest do, and that only because he is afraid not to do it, or at least pretend to do it.

When Wotan and Loki arrive, Loki claims Alberic as an old acquaintance. But the dwarf has no faith in these civil strangers: Greed instinctively mistrusts Intellect, even in the garb of Poetry and the company of Godhead, whilst envying the brilliancy of the one and the dignity of the other. Alberic breaks out at them with a terrible boast of the power now within his grasp. He paints for them the world as it will be when his dominion over it is complete, when the soft airs and green mosses of its valleys shall be changed into smoke, slag, and filth; when slavery, disease, and squalor, soothed by drunkenness and mastered by the policeman's baton, shall become the foundation of society; and when nothing shall escape ruin except such pretty places and pretty women as he may like to buy for the slaking of his own lusts. In that kingdom of evil he sees that there will be no power but his own. These gods, with their moralities and legalities and intellectual subtlety, will go under and be starved out of existence. He bids Wotan and Loki beware of it; and his "Hab' Acht!" is hoarse, horrible, and sinister. Wotan is revolted to the very depths of his being: he cannot stifle the execration that bursts from him. But Loki is unaffected: he has no moral passion: indignation is as absurd to him as enthusiasm. He finds it exquisitely amusing—having a touch of the comic spirit in him—that the dwarf, in stirring up the moral fervor of Wotan, has removed his last moral scruple about becoming a thief. Wotan will now rob the dwarf without remorse; for is it not positively his highest duty to take this power out of such evil hands and use it himself in the interests of Godhead? On the loftiest moral grounds, he lets Loki do his worst.

A little cunningly disguised flattery makes short work of Alberic. Loki pretends to be afraid of him; and he swallows that bait unhesitatingly. But how, enquires Loki, is he to guard against the hatred of his million slaves? Will they not steal from him, whilst he sleeps, the magic ring, the symbol of his power, which he has forged from the gold of the Rhine? "You think yourself very clever," sneers Alberic, and then begins to boast of the enchantments of the magic helmet. Loki refuses to believe in such marvels without witnessing them. Alberic, only too glad to show off his powers, puts on the helmet and transforms himself into a monstrous serpent. Loki gratifies him by pretending to be frightened out of his wits, but ventures to remark that it would be better still if the helmet could transform its owner into some tiny creature that could hide and spy in the smallest cranny. Alberic promptly transforms himself into a toad. In an instant Wotan's foot is on him; Loki tears away the helmet; they pinion him, and drag him away a prisoner up through the earth to the meadow by the castle.

Fourth Scene

There, to pay for his freedom, he has to summon his slaves from the depths to place all the treasure they have heaped up for him at the feet of Wotan. Then he demands his liberty; but Wotan must have the ring as well. And here the dwarf, like the giant before him, feels the very foundations of the world shake beneath him at the discovery of his own base cupidity in a higher power. That evil should, in its loveless desperation, create malign powers which Godhead could not create, seems but natural justice to him. But that Godhead should steal those malign powers from evil, and wield them itself, is a monstrous perversion; and his appeal to Wotan to forego it is almost terrible in its conviction of wrong. It is of no avail. Wotan falls back again on virtuous indignation. He reminds Alberic that he stole the gold from the Rhine maidens, and takes the attitude of the just judge compelling a restitution of stolen goods. Alberic knowing perfectly well that the judge is taking the goods to put them m his own pocket, has the ring torn from his finger, and is once more as poor as he was when he came slipping and stumbling among the slimy rocks in the bed of the Rhine.

This is the way of the world. In older times, when the Christian laborer was drained dry by the knightly spendthrift, and the spendthrift was drained by the Jewish usurer, Church and State, religion and law, seized on the Jew and drained him as a Christian duty. When the forces of lovelessness and greed had built up our own sordid capitalist systems, driven by invisible proprietorship, robbing the poor, defacing the earth, and forcing themselves as a universal curse even on the generous and humane, then religion and law and intellect, which would never themselves have discovered such systems, their natural bent being towards welfare, economy, and life instead of towards corruption, waste, and death, nevertheless did not scruple to seize by fraud and force these powers of evil on presence of using them for good. And it inevitably happens that when the Church, the Law, and all the Talents have made common cause to rob the people, the Church is far more vitally harmed by that unfaithfulness to itself than its more mechanical confederates; so that finally they turn on their discredited ally and rob the Church, with the cheerful co-operation of Loki, as in France and Italy for instance.

The twin giants come back with their hostage, in whose presence Godhead blooms again. The gold is ready for them; but now that the moment has come for parting with Freia the gold does not seem so tempting; and they are sorely loth to let her go. Not unless there is gold enough to utterly hide her from them—not until the heap has grown so that they can see nothing but gold—until money has come between them and every human feeling, will they part with her. There is not gold enough to accomplish this: however cunningly Loki spreads it, the glint of Freia's hair is still visible to Giant Fafnir, and the magic helmet must go on the heap to shut it out. Even then Fafnir's brother, Fasolt, can catch a beam from her eye through a chink, and is rendered incapable thereby of forswearing her. There is nothing to stop that chink but the ring; and Wotan is as greedily bent on keeping that as Alberic himself was; nor can the other gods persuade him that Freia is worth it, since for the highest god, love is not the highest good, but only the universal delight that bribes all living things to travail with renewed life. Life itself, with its accomplished marvels and its infinite potentialities, is the only force that Godhead can worship. Wotan does not yield until he is reached by the voice of the fruitful earth that before he or the dwarfs or the giants or the Law or the Lie or any of these things were, had the seed of them all in her bosom, and the seed perhaps of something higher even than himself, that shall one day supersede him and cut the tangles and alliances and compromises that already have cost him one of his eyes. When Erda, the First Mother of life, rises from her sleeping-place in the heart of the earth, and warns him to yield the ring, he obeys her; the ring is added to the heap of gold; and all sense of Freia is cut off from the giants.

But now what Law is left to these two poor stupid laborers whereby one shall yield to the other any of the treasure for which they have each paid the whole price in surrendering Freia? They look by mere habit to the god to judge for them; but he, with his heart stirring towards higher forces than himself, turns with disgust from these lower forces. They settle it as two wolves might; and Fafnir batters his brother dead with his staff. It is a horrible thing to see and hear, to anyone who knows how much blood has been shed in the world in just that way by its brutalized toilers, honest fellows enough until their betters betrayed them. Fafnir goes off with his booty. It is quite useless to him. He has neither the cunning nor the ambition to establish the Plutonic empire with it. Merely to prevent others from getting it is the only purpose it brings him. He piles it in a cave; transforms himself into a dragon by the helmet; and devotes his life to guarding it, as much a slave to it as a jailor is to his prisoner. He had much better have thrown it all back into the Rhine and transformed himself into the shortest-lived animal that enjoys at least a brief run in the sunshine. His case, however, is far too common to be surprising. The world is overstocked with persons who sacrifice all their affections, and madly trample and batter down their fellows to obtain riches of which, when they get them, they are unable to make the smallest use, and to which they become the most miserable slaves.

The gods soon forget Fafnir in their rejoicing over Freia. Donner, the Thunder god, springs to a rocky summit and calls the clouds as a shepherd calls his flocks. They come at his summons; and he and the castle are hidden by their black legions. Froh, the Rainbow god, hastens to his side. At the stroke of Donner's hammer the black murk is riven in all directions by darting ribbons of lightning; and as the air clears, the castle is seen in its fullest splendor, accessible now by the rainbow bridge which Froh has cast across the ravine. In the glory of this moment Wotan has a great thought. With all his aspirations to establish a reign of noble thought, of righteousness, order, and justice, he has found that day that there is no race yet in the world that quite spontaneously, naturally, and unconsciously realizes his ideal. He himself has found how far short Godhead falls of the thing it conceives. He, the greatest of gods, has been unable to control his fate: he has been forced against his will to choose between evils, to make disgraceful bargains, to break them still more disgracefully, and even then to see the price of his disgrace slip through his fingers. His consort has cost him half his vision; his castle has cost him his affections; and the attempt to retain both has cost him his honor. On every side he is shackled and bound, dependent on the laws of Fricka and on the lies of Loki, forced to traffic with dwarfs for handicraft and with giants for strength, and to pay them both in false coin. After all, a god is a pitiful thing. But the fertility of the First Mother is not yet exhausted. The life that came from her has ever climbed up to a higher and higher organization. From toad and serpent to dwarf, from bear and elephant to giant, from dwarf and giant to a god with thoughts, with comprehension of the world, with ideals. Why should it stop there? Why should it not rise from the god to the Hero? to the creature in whom the god's unavailing thought shall have become effective will and life, who shall make his way straight to truth and reality over the laws of Fricka and the lies of Loki with a strength that overcomes giants and a cunning that outwits dwarfs? Yes: Erda, the First Mother, must travail again, and breed him a race of heroes to deliver the world and himself from his limited powers and disgraceful bargains. This is the vision that flashes on him as he turns to the rainbow bridge and calls his wife to come and dwell with him in Valhalla, the home of the gods.

They are all overcome with Valhalla's glory except Loki. He is behind the scenes of this joint reign of the Divine and the Legal. He despises these gods with their ideals and their golden apples. "I am ashamed," he says, "to have dealings with these futile creatures." And so he follows them to the rainbow bridge. But as they set foot on it, from the river below rises the wailing of the Rhine maidens for their lost gold. "You down there in the water," cries Loki with brutal irony: "you used to bask in the glitter of your gold: henceforth you shall bask in the splendor of the gods." And they reply that the truth is in the depths and the darkness, and that what blazes on high there is falsehood. And with that the gods pass into their glorious stronghold.

WAGNER AS REVOLUTIONIST

Before leaving this explanation of The Rhine Gold, I must have a word or two about it with the reader. It is the least popular of the sections of The Ring. The reason is that its dramatic moments lie quite outside the consciousness of people whose joys and sorrows are all domestic and personal, and whose religions and political ideas are purely conventional and superstitious. To them it is a struggle between half a dozen fairytale personages for a ring, involving hours of scolding and cheating, and one long scene in a dark gruesome mine, with gloomy, ugly music, and not a glimpse of a handsome young man or pretty woman. Only those of wider consciousness can follow it breathlessly, seeing in it the whole tragedy of human history and the whole horror of the dilemmas from which the world is shrinking today. At Bayreuth I have seen a party of English tourists, after enduring agonies of boredom from Alberic, rise in the middle of the third scene, and almost force their way out of the dark theatre into the sunlit pine-wood without. And I have seen people who were deeply affected by the scene driven almost beside themselves by this disturbance. But it was a very natural thing for the unfortunate tourists to do, since in this Rhine Gold prologue there is no interval between the acts for escape. Roughly speaking, people who have no general ideas, no touch of the concern of the philosopher and statesman for the race, cannot enjoy The Rhine Gold as a drama. They may find compensations in some exceedingly pretty music, at times even grand and glorious, which will enable them to escape occasionally from the struggle between Alberic and Wotan; but if their capacity for music should be as limited as their comprehension of the world, they had better stay away.

And now, attentive Reader, we have reached the point at which some foolish person is sure to interrupt us by declaring that The Rhine Gold is what they call "a work of art" pure and simple, and that Wagner never dreamt of shareholders, tall hats, whitelead factories, and industrial and political questions looked at from the socialistic and humanitarian points of view. We need not discuss these impertinences: it is easier to silence them with the facts of Wagner's life. In 1843 he obtained the position of conductor of the Opera at Dresden at a salary of L225 a year, with a pension. This was a first-rate permanent appointment in the service of the Saxon State, carrying an assured professional position and livelihood with it In 1848, the year of revolutions, the discontented middle class, unable to rouse the Churchand-State governments of the day from their bondage to custom, caste, and law by appeals to morality or constitutional agitation for Liberal reforms, made common cause with the starving wage-working class, and resorted to armed rebellion, which reached Dresden in 1849. Had Wagner been the mere musical epicure and political mugwump that the term "artist" seems to suggest to so many critics and amateurs—that is, a creature in their own lazy likeness—he need have taken no more part in the political struggles of his day than Bishop took in the English Reform agitation of 1832, or Sterndale Bennett in the Chartist or Free Trade movements. What he did do was first to make a desperate appeal to the King to cast off his bonds and answer the need of the time by taking true Kingship on himself and leading his people to the redress of their intolerable wrongs (fancy the poor monarch's feelings!), and then, when the crash came, to take his side with the right and the poor against the rich and the wrong. When the insurrection was defeated, three leaders of it were especially marked down for vengeance: August Roeckel, an old friend of Wagner's to whom he wrote a well-known series of letters; Michael Bakoonin, afterwards a famous apostle of revolutionary Anarchism; and Wagner himself. Wagner escaped to Switzerland: Roeckel and Bakoonin suffered long terms of imprisonment. Wagner was of course utterly ruined, pecuniarily and socially (to his own intense relief and satisfaction); and his exile lasted twelve years. His first idea was to get his Tannhauser produced in Paris. With the notion of explaining himself to the Parisians he wrote a pamphlet entitled Art and Revolution, a glance through which will show how thoroughly the socialistic side of the revolution had his sympathy, and how completely he had got free from the influence of the established Churches of his day. For three years he kept pouring forth pamphlets—some of them elaborate treatises in size and intellectual rank, but still essentially the pamphlets and manifestoes of a born agitator— on social evolution, religion, life, art and the influence of riches. In 1853 the poem of The Ring was privately printed; and in 1854, five years after the Dresden insurrection, The Rhine Gold score was completed to the last drum tap.

These facts are on official record in Germany, where the proclamation summing up Wagner as "a politically dangerous person" may be consulted to this day. The pamphlets are now accessible to English readers in the translation of Mr. Ashton Ellis. This being so, any person who, having perhaps heard that I am a Socialist, attempts to persuade you that my interpretation of The Rhine Gold is only "my socialism" read into the works of a dilettantist who borrowed an idle tale from an old saga to make an opera book with, may safely be dismissed from your consideration as an ignoramus.

If you are now satisfied that The Rhine Gold is an allegory, do not forget that an allegory is never quite consistent except when it is written by someone without dramatic faculty, in which case it is unreadable. There is only one way of dramatizing an idea; and that is by putting on the stage a human being possessed by that idea, yet none the less a human being with all the human impulses which make him akin and therefore interesting to us. Bunyan, in his Pilgrim's Progress, does not, like his unread imitators, attempt to personify Christianity and Valour: he dramatizes for you the life of the Christian and the Valiant Man. Just so, though I have shown that Wotan is Godhead and Kingship, and Loki Logic and Imagination without living Will (Brain without Heart, to put it vulgarly); yet in the drama Wotan is a religiously moral man, and Loki a witty, ingenious, imaginative and cynical one. As to Fricka, who stands for State Law, she does not assume her allegorical character in The Rhine Gold at all, but is simply Wotan's wife and Freia's sister: nay, she contradicts her allegorical self by conniving at all Wotan's rogueries. That, of course, is just what State Law would do; but we must not save the credit of the allegory by a quip. Not until she reappears in the next play (The Valkyries) does her function in the allegorical scheme become plain.

One preconception will bewilder the spectator hopelessly unless he has been warned against it or is naturally free from it. In the old-fashioned orders of creation, the supernatural personages are invariably conceived as greater than man, for good or evil. In the modern humanitarian order as adopted by Wagner, Man is the highest. In The Rhine Gold, it is pretended that there are as yet no men on the earth. There are dwarfs, giants, and gods. The danger is that you will jump to the conclusion that the gods, at least, are a higher order than the human order. On the contrary, the world is waiting for Man to redeem it from the lame and cramped government of the gods. Once grasp that; and the allegory becomes simple enough. Really, of course, the dwarfs, giants, and gods are dramatizations of the three main orders of men: to wit, the instinctive, predatory, lustful, greedy people; the patient, toiling, stupid, respectful, money-worshipping people; and the intellectual, moral, talented people who devise and administer States and Churches. History shows us only one order higher than the highest of these: namely, the order of Heroes.

Now it is quite clear—though you have perhaps never thought of it—that if the next generation of Englishmen consisted wholly of Julius Caesars, all our political, ecclesiastical, and moral institutions would vanish, and the less perishable of their appurtenances be classed with Stonehenge and the cromlechs and round towers as inexplicable relics of a bygone social order. Julius Caesars would no more trouble themselves about such contrivances as our codes and churches than a fellow of the

Royal Society will touch his hat to the squire and listen to the village curate's sermons. This is precisely what must happen some day if life continues thrusting towards higher and higher organization as it has hitherto done. As most of our English professional men are to Australian bushmen, so, we must suppose, will the average man of some future day be to Julius Caesar. Let any man of middle age, pondering this prospect consider what has happened within a single generation to the articles of faith his father regarded as eternal nay, to the very scepticisms and blasphemies of his youth (Bishop Colenso's criticism of the Pentateuch, for example!); and he will begin to realize how much of our barbarous Theology and Law the man of the future will do without. Bakoonin, the Dresden revolutionary leader with whom Wagner went out in 1849, put forward later on a program, often quoted with foolish horror, for the abolition of all institutions, religious, political, juridical, financial, legal, academic, and so on, so as to leave the will of man free to find its own way. All the loftiest spirits of that time were burning to raise Man up, to give him self-respect, to shake him out of his habit of grovelling before the ideals created by his own imagination, of attributing the good that sprang from the ceaseless energy of the life within himself to some superior power in the clouds, and of making a fetish of self-sacrifice to justify his own cowardice.

Farther on in The Ring we shall see the Hero arrive and make an end of dwarfs, giants, and gods. Meanwhile, let us not forget that godhood means to Wagner infirmity and compromise, and manhood strength and integrity. Above all, we must understand—for it is the key to much that we are to see—that the god, since his desire is toward a higher and fuller life, must long in his inmost soul for the advent of that greater power whose first work, though this he does not see as yet, must be his own undoing.

In the midst of all these far-reaching ideas, it is amusing to find Wagner still full of his ingrained theatrical professionalism, and introducing effects which now seem old-fashioned and stagey with as much energy and earnestness as if they were his loftiest inspirations. When Wotan wrests the ring from Alberic, the dwarf delivers a lurid and bloodcurdling stage curse, calling down on its every future possessor care, fear, and death. The musical phrase accompanying this outburst was a veritable harmonic and melodic bogey to mid-century ears, though time has now robbed it of its terrors. It sounds again when Fafnir slays Fasolt, and on every subsequent occasion when the ring brings death to its holder. This episode must justify itself purely as a piece of stage sensationalism. On deeper ground it is superfluous and confusing, as the ruin to which the pursuit of riches leads needs no curse to explain it; nor is there any sense in investing Alberic with providential powers in the matter.

THE VALKYRIES

Before the curtain rises on the Valkyries, let us see what has happened since it fell on The Rhine Gold. The persons of the drama will tell us presently; but as we probably do not understand German, that may not help us.

Wotan is still ruling the world in glory from his giant-built castle with his wife Fricka. But he has no security for the continuance of his reign, since Alberic may at any moment contrive to recover the ring, the full power of which he can wield because he has forsworn love. Such forswearing is not possible to Wotan: love, though not his highest need, is a higher than gold: otherwise he would be no god. Besides, as we have seen, his power has been established in the world by and as a system of laws enforced by penalties. These he must consent to be bound by himself; for a god who broke his own laws would betray the fact that legality and conformity are not the highest rule of conduct—a discovery fatal to his supremacy as Pontiff and Lawgiver. Hence he may not wrest the ring unlawfully from Fafnir, even if he could bring himself to forswear love.

In this insecurity he has hit on the idea of forming a heroic bodyguard. He has trained his love children as war-maidens (Valkyries) whose duty it is to sweep through battle-fields and bear away to Valhalla the souls of the bravest who fall there. Thus reinforced by a host of warriors, he has thoroughly indoctrinated them, Loki helping him as dialectician-in-chief, with the conventional system of law and duty, supernatural religion and self-sacrificing idealism, which they believe to be the essence of his godhood, but which is really only the machinery of the love of necessary power which is his mortal weakness. This process secures their fanatical devotion to his system of government, but he knows perfectly well that such systems, in spite of their moral pretensions, serve selfish and ambitious tyrants better than benevolent despots, and that, if once Alberic gets the ring back, he will easily out-Valhalla Valhalla, if not buy it over as a going concern. The only chance of permanent security, then, is the appearance in the world of a hero who, without any illicit prompting from Wotan, will destroy Alberic and wrest the ring from Fafnir. There will then, he believes, be no further cause for anxiety, since he does not yet conceive Heroism as a force hostile to Godhead. In his longing for a rescuer, it does not occur to him that when the Hero comes, his first exploit must be to sweep the gods and their ordinances from the path of the heroic will.

Indeed, he feels that in his own Godhead is the germ of such Heroism, and that from himself the Hero must spring. He takes to wandering, mostly in search of love, from Fricka and Valhalla. He seeks the First Mother; and through her womb, eternally fertile, the inner true thought that made him first a god is reborn as his daughter, uncorrupted by his ambition, unfettered by his machinery of power and his alliances with Fricka and Loki. This daughter, the Valkyrie Brynhild, is his true will, his real self, (as he thinks): to her he may say what he must not say to anyone, since in speaking to her he but speaks to himself. "Was Keinem in Worten unausgesprochen," he says to her, "bleib es ewig: mit mir nur rath' ich, red' ich zu dir."

But from Brynhild no hero can spring until there is a man of Wotan's race to breed with her. Wotan wanders further; and a mortal woman bears him twins: a son and a daughter. He separates them by letting the girl fall into the hands of a forest tribe which in due time gives her as a wife to a fierce chief, one Hunding. With the son he himself leads the life of a wolf, and teaches him the only power a god can teach, the power of doing without happiness. When he has given him this terrible training, he abandons him, and goes to the bridal feast of his daughter Sieglinda and Hunding. In the blue cloak of the wanderer, wearing the broad hat that flaps over the socket of his forfeited eye, he appears in Hunding's house, the middle pillar of which is a mighty tree. Into that tree, without a word, he strikes a sword up to the hilt, so that only the might of a hero can withdraw it. Then he goes out as silently as he came, blind to the truth that no weapon from the armory of Godhead can serve the turn of the true Human Hero. Neither Hunding nor any of his guests can move the sword; and there it stays awaiting the destined hand. That is the history of the generations between The Rhine Gold and The Valkyries.

The First Act

This time, as we sit looking expectantly at the curtain, we hear, not the deep booming of the Rhine, but the patter of a forest downpour, accompanied by the mutter of a storm which soon gathers into a roar and culminates in crashing thunderbolts. As it passes off, the curtain rises; and there is no mistaking whose forest habitation we are in; for the central pillar is a mighty tree, and the place fit for the dwelling of a fierce chief. The door opens: and an exhausted man reels in: an adept from the school of unhappiness. Sieglinda finds him lying on the hearth. He explains that he has been in a fight; that his weapons not being as strong as his arms, were broken; and that he had to fly. He desires some drink and a moment's rest; then he will go; for he is an unlucky person, and does not want to bring his ill-luck on the woman who is succoring him. But she, it appears, is also unhappy; and a strong sympathy springs up between them. When her husband arrives, he observes not only this sympathy, but a resemblance between them, a gleam of the snake in their eyes. They sit down to table; and the stranger tells them his unlucky story. He is the son of Wotan, who is known to him only as Wolfing, of the race of the Volsungs. The earliest thing he remembers is returning from a hunt with his father to find their home destroyed, his mother murdered, and his twin-sister carried off. This was the work of a tribe called the Neidings, upon whom he and Wolfing thenceforth waged implacable war until the day when his father disappeared, leaving no trace of himself but an empty wolfskin. The young Volsung was thus cast alone upon the world, finding most hands against him, and bringing no good luck even to his friends. His latest exploit has been the slaying of certain brothers who were forcing their sister to wed against her will. The result has been the slaughter of the woman by her brothers' clansmen, and his own narrow escape by flight.

His luck on this occasion is even worse than he supposes; for Hunding, by whose hearth he has taken refuge, is clansman to the slain brothers and is bound to avenge them. He tells the Volsung that in the morning, weapons or no weapons, he must fight for his life. Then he orders the woman to bed, and follows her himself, taking his spear with him.

The unlucky stranger, left brooding by the hearth, has nothing to console himself with but an old promise of his father's that he shall find a weapon to his hand when he most needs one. The last flicker of the dying fire strikes on the golden hilt of the sword that sticks in the tree; but he does not see it; and the embers sink into blackness. Then the woman returns. Hunding is safely asleep: she has drugged him. She tells the story of the one-eyed man who appeared at her forced marriage, and of the sword. She has always felt, she says, that her miseries will end in the arms of the hero who shall succeed in drawing it forth. The stranger, diffident as he is about his luck, has no misgivings as to his strength and destiny. He gives her his affection at once, and abandons himself to the charm of the night and the season; for it is the beginning of Spring. They soon learn from their confidences that she is his stolen twin-sister. He is transported to find that the heroic race of the Volsungs need neither perish nor be corrupted by a lower strain. Hailing the sword by the name of Nothung (or Needed), he plucks it from the tree as her bride-gift, and then, crying "Both bride and sister be of thy brother; and blossom the blood of the Volsungs!" clasps her as the mate the Spring has brought him.

The Second Act

So far, Wotan's plan seems prospering. In the mountains he calls his war-maiden Brynhild, the child borne to him by the First Mother, and bids her see to it that Hunding shall fall in the approaching combat. But he is reckoning without his consort, Fricka. What will she, the Law, say to the lawless pair who have heaped incest on adultery? A hero may have defied the law, and put his own will in its place; but can a god hold him guiltless, when the whole power of the gods can enforce itself only by law? Fricka, shuddering with horror, outraged in every instinct, comes clamoring for punishment. Wotan pleads the general necessity of encouraging heroism in order to keep up the Valhalla bodyguard; but his remonstrances only bring upon him torrents of reproaches for his own unfaithfulness to the law in roaming through the world and begetting war-maidens, "wolf cubs," and the like. He is hopelessly beaten in the argument. Fricka is absolutely right when she declares that the ending of the gods began when he brought this wolf-hero into the world; and now, to save their very existence, she pitilessly demands his destruction. Wotan has no power to refuse: it is Fricka's mechanical force, and not his thought, that really rules the world. He has to recall Brynhild; take back his former instructions; and ordain that Hunding shall slay the Volsung.

But now comes another difficulty. Brynhild is the inner thought and will of Godhead, the aspiration from the high life to the higher that is its divine element, and only becomes separated from it when its resort to kingship and priestcraft for the sake of temporal power has made it false to itself. Hitherto, Brynhild, as Valkyrie or hero chooser, has obeyed Wotan implicitly, taking her work as the holiest and bravest in his kingdom; and now he tells her what he could not tell Fricka—what indeed he could not tell to Brynhild, were she not, as she says, his own will—the whole story of Alberic and of that inspiration about the raising up of a hero. She thoroughly approves of the inspiration; but when the story ends in the assumption that she too must obey Fricka, and help Fricka's vassal,

Hunding, to undo the great work and strike the hero down, she for the first time hesitates to accept his command. In his fury and despair he overawes her by the most terrible threats of his anger; and she submits.

Then comes the Volsung Siegmund, following his sister bride, who has fled into the mountains in a revulsion of horror at having allowed herself to bring her hero to shame. Whilst she is lying exhausted and senseless in his arms, Brynhild appears to him and solemnly warns him that he must presently leave the earth with her. He asks whither he must follow her. To Valhalla, to take his place there among the heroes. He asks, shall he find his father there? Yes. Shall he find a wife there? Yes: he will be waited on by beautiful wishmaidens. Shall he meet his sister there? No. Then, says Siegmund, I will not come with you.

She tries to make him understand that he cannot help himself. Being a hero, he will not be so persuaded: he has his father's sword, and does not fear Hunding. But when she tells him that she comes from his father, and that the sword of a god will not avail in the hands of a hero, he accepts his fate, but will shape it with his own hand, both for himself and his sister, by slaying her, and then killing himself with the last stroke of the sword. And thereafter he will go to Hell, rather than to Valhalla.

How now can Brynhild, being what she is, choose her side freely in a conflict between this hero and the vassal of Fricka? By instinct she at once throws Wotan's command to the winds, and bids Siegmund nerve himself for the combat with Hunding, in which she pledges him the protection of her shield. The horn of Hunding is soon heard; and Siegmund's spirits rise to fighting pitch at once. The two meet; and the Valkyrie's shield is held before the hero. But when he delivers his sword-stroke at his foe, the weapon shivers on the spear of Wotan, who suddenly appears between them; and the first of the race of heroes falls with the weapon of the Law's vassal through his breast. Brynhild snatches the fragments of the broken sword, and flies, carrying off the woman with her on her war-horse; and Wotan, in terrible wrath, slays Hunding with a wave of his hand, and starts in pursuit of his disobedient daughter.

The Third Act

On a rocky peak, four of the Valkyries are waiting for the rest. The absent ones soon arrive, galloping through the air with slain heroes, gathered from the battle-field, hanging over their saddles. Only, Brynhild, who comes last, has for her spoil a live woman. When her eight sisters learn that she has defied Wotan, they dare not help her; and Brynhild has to rouse Sieglinda to make an effort to save herself, by reminding her that she bears in her the seed of a hero, and must face everything, endure anything, sooner than let that seed miscarry. Sieglinda, in a transport of exaltation, takes the fragments of the sword and flies into the forest. Then Wotan comes; the sisters fly in terror at his command; and he is left alone with Brynhild.

Here, then, we have the first of the inevitable moments which Wotan did not foresee. Godhead has now established its dominion over the world by a mighty Church, compelling obedience through its ally the Law, with its formidable State organization of force of arms and cunning of brain. It has submitted to this alliance to keep the Plutonic power in check—built it up primarily for the sake of that soul in itself which cares only to make the highest better and the best higher; and now here is that very soul separated from it and working for the destruction of its indispensable ally, the lawgiving State. How is the rebel to be disarmed? Slain it cannot be by Godhead, since it is still Godhead's own very dearest soul. But hidden, stifled, silenced it must be; or it will wreck the State and leave the Church defenseless. Not until it passes completely away from Godhead, and is reborn as the soul of the hero, can it work anything but the confusion and destruction of the existing order. How is the world to be protected against it in the meantime? Clearly Loki's help is needed here: it is the Lie that must, on the highest principles, hide the Truth. Let Loki surround this mountain top with the appearance of a consuming fire; and who will dare penetrate to Brynhild? It is true that if any man will walk boldly into that fire, he will discover it at once to be a lie, an illusion, a mirage through which he might carry a sack of gunpowder without being a penny the worse. Therefore let the fire seem so terrible that only the hero, when in the fulness of time he appears upon earth, will venture through it; and the problem is solved. Wotan, with a breaking heart, takes leave of Brynhild; throws her into a deep sleep; covers her with her long warshield; summons Loki, who comes in the shape of a wall of fire surrounding the mountain peak; and turns his back on Brynhild for ever.

The allegory here is happily not so glaringly obvious to the younger generations of our educated classes as it was forty years ago. In those days, any child who expressed a doubt as to the absolute truth of the Church's teaching, even to the extent of asking why Joshua told the sun to stand still instead of telling the earth to cease turning, or of pointing out that a whale's throat would hardly have been large enough to swallow Jonah, was unhesitatingly told that if it harboured such doubts it would spend all eternity after its death in horrible torments in a lake of burning brimstone. It is difficult to write or read this nowadays without laughing; yet no doubt millions of ignorant and credulous people are still teaching their children that. When Wagner himself was a little child, the fact that hell was a fiction devised for the intimidation and subjection of the masses, was a well-kept secret of the thinking and governing classes. At that time the fires of Loki were a very real terror to all except persons of exceptional force of character and intrepidity of thought. Even thirty years after Wagner had printed the verses of The Ring for private circulation, we find him excusing himself from perfectly explicit denial of current superstitions, by reminding his readers that it would expose him to prosecution. In England, so many of our respectable voters are still grovelling in a gloomy devil worship, of which the fires of Loki are the main bulwark, that no Government has yet had the conscience or the courage to repeal our monstrous laws against "blasphemy."

SIEGFRIED

Sieglinda, when she flies into the forest with the hero's son unborn in her womb, and the broken pieces of his sword in her hand, finds shelter in the smithy of a dwarf, where she brings forth her child and dies. This dwarf is no other than Mimmy, the brother of Alberic, the same who made for him the magic helmet. His aim in life is to gain possession of the helmet, the ring, and the treasure, and through them to obtain that Plutonic mastery of the world under the beginnings of which he himself writhed during Alberic's brief reign. Mimmy is a blinking, shambling, ancient creature, too weak and timid to dream of taking arms himself to despoil Fafnir, who still, transformed to a monstrous serpent, broods on the gold in a hole in the rocks. Mimmy needs the help of a hero for that; and he has craft enough to know that it is quite possible, and indeed much in the ordinary way of the world, for senile avarice and craft to set youth and bravery to work to win empire for it. He knows the pedigree of the child left on his hands, and nurses it to manhood with great care.

His pains are too well rewarded for his comfort. The boy Siegfried, having no god to instruct him in the art of unhappiness, inherits none of his father's ill luck, and all his father's hardihood. The fear against which Siegmund set his face like flint, and the woe which he wore down, are unknown to the son. The father was faithful and grateful: the son knows no law but his own humor; detests the ugly dwarf who has nursed him; chafes furiously under his claims for some return for his tender care; and is, in short, a totally unmoral person, a born anarchist, the ideal of Bakoonin, an anticipation of the "overman" of Nietzsche. He is enormously strong, full of life and fun, dangerous and destructive to what he dislikes, and affectionate to what he likes; so that it is fortunate that his likes and dislikes are sane and healthy. Altogether an inspiriting young forester, a son of the morning, in whom the heroic race has come out into the sunshine from the clouds of his grandfather's majestic entanglements with law, and the night of his father's tragic struggle with it.

The First Act

Mimmy's smithy is a cave, in which he hides from the light like the eyeless fish of the American caverns. Before the curtain rises the music already tells us that we are groping in darkness. When it does rise Mimmy is in difficulties. He is trying to make a sword for his nursling, who is now big enough to take the field against Fafnir. Mimmy can make mischievous swords; but it is not with dwarf made weapons that heroic man will hew the way of his own will through religions and governments and plutocracies and all the other devices of the kingdom of the fears of the unheroic. As fast as Mimmy makes swords, Siegfried Bakoonin smashes them, and then takes the poor old swordsmith by the scruff of the neck and chastises him wrathfully. The particular day on which the curtain rises begins with one of these trying domestic incidents. Mimmy has just done his best with a new sword of surpassing excellence. Siegfried returns home in rare spirits with a wild bear, to the extreme terror of the wretched dwarf. When the bear is dismissed, the new sword is produced. It is promptly smashed, as usual, with, also, the usual effects on the temper of Siegfried, who is quite boundless in his criticisms of the smith's boasted skill, and declares that he would smash the sword's maker too if he were not too disgusting to be handled.

Mimmy falls back on his stock defence: a string of maudlin reminders of the care with which he has nursed the little boy into manhood. Siegfried replies candidly that the strangest thing about all this care is that instead of making him grateful, it inspires him with a lively desire to wring the dwarf's neck. Only, he admits that he always comes back to his Mimmy, though he loathes him more than any living thing in the forest. On this admission the dwarf attempts to build a theory of filial instinct. He explains that he is Siegfried's father, and that this is why Siegfried cannot do without him. But Siegfried has learned from his forest companions, the birds and foxes and wolves, that mothers as well as fathers go to the making of children. Mimmy, on the desperate ground that man is neither bird nor fox, declares that he is Siegfried's father and mother both. He is promptly denounced as a filthy liar, because the birds and foxes are exactly like their parents, whereas Siegfried, having often watched his own image in the water, can testify that he is no more like Mimmy than a toad is like a trout. Then, to place the conversation on a plane of entire frankness, he throttles Mimmy until he is speechless. When the dwarf recovers, he is so daunted that he tells Siegfried the truth about his birth, and for testimony thereof produces the pieces of the sword that broke upon Wotan's spear. Siegfried instantly orders him to repair the sword on pain of an unmerciful thrashing, and rushes off into the forest, rejoicing in the discovery that he is no kin of Mimmy's, and need have no more to do with him when the sword is mended.

Poor Mimmy is now in a worse plight than ever; for he has long ago found that the sword utterly defies his skill: the steel will yield neither to his hammer nor to his furnace. Just then there walks into his cave a Wanderer, in a blue mantle, spear in hand, with one eye concealed by the brim of his wide hat. Mimmy, not by nature hospitable, tries to drive him away; but the Wanderer announces himself as a wise man, who can tell his host, in emergency, what it most concerns him to know. Mimmy, taking this offer in high dudgeon, because it implies that his visitor's wits are better than his own, offers to tell the wise one something that HE does not know: to wit, the way to the door. The imperturbable Wanderer's reply is to sit down and challenge the dwarf to a trial of wit. He wagers his head against Mimmy's that he will answer any three questions the dwarf can put to him.

Now here were Mimmy's opportunity, had he only the wit to ask what he wants to know, instead of pretending to know everything already. It is above all things needful to him at this moment to find out how that sword can be mended; and there has just dropped in upon him in his need the one person who can tell him. In such circumstances a wise man would hasten to show to his visitor his three deepest ignorances, and ask him to dispel them. The dwarf, being a crafty fool, desiring only to detect ignorance in his guest, asks him for information on the three points on which he is proudest of being thoroughly well instructed himself. His three questions are, Who dwell under the earth? Who dwell on the earth? and Who dwell in the cloudy heights above? The Wanderer, in reply, tells him of the dwarfs and of Alberic; of the earth, and the giants Fasolt and Fafnir; of the gods and of Wotan: himself, as Mimmy now recognizes with awe.

Next, it is Mimmy's turn to face three questions. What is that race, dearest to Wotan, against which Wotan has nevertheless done his worst? Mimmy can answer that: he knows the Volsungs, the race of heroes born of Wotan's infidelities to Fricka, and can tell the Wanderer the whole story of the twins and their son Siegfried. Wotan compliments him on his knowledge, and asks further with what sword Siegfried will slay Fafnir? Mimmy can answer that too: he has the whole history of the sword at his fingers' ends. Wotan hails him as the knowingest of the knowing, and then hurls at him the question he should himself have asked: Who will mend the sword? Mimmy, his head forfeited, confesses with loud lamentations that he cannot answer. The Wanderer reads him an appropriate little lecture on the folly of being too clever to ask what he wants to know, and informs him that a smith to whom fear is unknown will mend Nothung. To this smith he leaves the forfeited head of his host, and wanders off into the forest. Then Mimmy's nerves give way completely. He shakes like a man in delirium tremens, and has a horrible nightmare, in the supreme convulsion of which Siegfried, returning from the forest, presently finds him.

A curious and amusing conversation follows. Siegfried himself does not know fear, and is impatient to acquire it as an accomplishment. Mimmy is all fear: the world for him is a phantasmagoria of terrors. It is not that he is afraid of being eaten by bears in the forest, or of burning his fingers in the forge fire. A lively objection to being destroyed or maimed does not make a man a coward: on the contrary, it is the beginning of a brave man's wisdom. But in Mimmy, fear is not the effect of danger: it is natural quality of him which no security can allay. He is like many a poor newspaper editor, who dares not print the truth, however simple, even when it is obvious to himself and all his readers. Not that anything unpleasant would happen to him if he did—not, indeed that he could fail to become a distinguished and influential leader of opinion by fearlessly pursuing such a course, but solely because he lives in a world of imaginary terrors, rooted in a modest and gentlemanly mistrust of his own strength and worth, and consequently of the value of his opinion. Just so is Mimmy afraid of anything that can do him any good, especially of the light and the fresh air. He is also convinced that anybody who is not sufficiently steeped in fear to be constantly on his guard, must perish immediately on his first sally into the world. To preserve Siegfried for the enterprise to which he has destined him he makes a grotesque attempt to teach him fear. He appeals to his experience of the terrors of the forest, of its dark places, of its threatening noises its stealthy ambushes, its sinister flickering lights its heart-tightening ecstasies of dread.

All this has no other effect than to fill Siegfried with wonder and curiosity; for the forest is a place of delight for him. He is as eager to experience Mimmy's terrors as a schoolboy to feel what an electric shock is like. Then Mimmy has the happy idea of describing Fafnir to him as a likely person to give him an exemplary fright. Siegfried jumps at the idea, and, since Mimmy cannot mend the sword for him, proposes to set to work then and there to mend it for himself. Mimmy shakes his head, and bids him see now how his youthful laziness and frowardness have found him out—how he would not learn the smith's craft from Professor

Mimmy, and therefore does not know how even to begin mending the sword. Siegfried Bakoonin's retort is simple and crushing. He points out that the net result of Mimmy's academic skill is that he can neither make a decent sword himself nor even set one to rights when it is damaged. Reckless of the remonstrances of the scandalized professor, he seizes a file, and in a few moments utterly destroys the fragments of the sword by rasping them into a heap of steel filings. Then he puts the filings into a crucible; buries it in the coals; and sets to at the bellows with the shouting exultation of the anarchist who destroys only to clear the ground for creation. When the steel is melted he runs it into a mould; and lo! a sword-blade in the rough. Mimmy, amazed at the success of this violation of all the rules of his craft, hails Siegfried as the mightiest of smiths, professing himself barely worthy to be his cook and scullion; and forthwith proceeds to poison some soup for him so that he may murder him safely when Fafnir is slain. Meanwhile Siegfned forges and tempers and hammers and rivets, uproariously singing the while as nonsensically as the Rhine maidens themselves. Finally he assails the anvil on which Mimmy's swords have been shattered, and cleaves it with a mighty stroke of the newly forged Nothung.

The Second Act

In the darkest hour before the dawn of that night, we find ourselves before the cave of Fafnir, and there we find Alberic, who can find nothing better to do with himself than to watch the haunt of the dragon, and eat his heart out in vain longing for the gold and the ring. The wretched Fafnir, once an honest giant, can only make himself terrible enough to keep his gold by remaining a venomous reptile. Why he should not become an honest giant again and clear out of his cavern, leaving the gold and the ring and the rest of it for anyone fool enough to take them at such a price, is the first question that would occur to anyone except a civilized man, who would be too accustomed to that sort of mania to be at all surprised at it.

To Alberic in the night comes the Wanderer, whom the dwarf, recognizing his despoiler of old, abuses as a shameless thief, taunting him with the helpless way in which all his boasted power is tied up with the laws and bargains recorded on the heft of his spear, which, says Alberic truly, would crumble like chaff in his hands if he dared use it for his own real ends. Wotan, having already had to kill his own son with it, knows that very well; but it troubles him no more; for he is now at last rising to abhorrence of his own artificial power, and looking to the coming hero, not for its consolidation but its destruction. When Alberic breaks out again with his still unquenched hope of one day destroying the gods and ruling the world through the ring, Wotan is no longer shocked. He tells Alberic that Brother Mime approaches with a hero whom Godhead can neither help nor hinder. Alberic may try his luck against him without disturbance from Valhalla. Perhaps, he suggests, if Alberic warns Fafnir, and offers to deal with the hero for him, Fafnir, may give him the ring. They accordingly wake up the dragon, who condescends to enter into bellowing conversation, but is proof against their proposition, strong in the magic of property. "I have and hold," he says: "leave me to sleep." Wotan, with a wise laugh, turns to Alberic. "That shot missed," he says: "no use abusing me for it. And now let me tell you one thing. All things happen according to their nature; and you can't alter them." And so he leaves him Alberic, raging with the sense that his old enemy has been laughing at him, and yet prophetically convinced that the last word will not be with the god, hides himself as the day breaks, and his brother approaches with Siegfried.

Mimmy makes a final attempt to frighten Siegfried by discoursing of the dragon's terrible jaws, poisonous breath, corrosive spittle, and deadly, stinging tail. Siegfried is not interested in the tail: he wants to know whether the dragon has a heart, being confident of his ability to stick Nothung into it if it exists. Reassured on this point, he drives Mimmy away, and stretches himself under the trees, listening to the morning chatter of the birds. One of them has a great deal to say to him; but he cannot understand it; and after vainly trying to carry on the conversation with a reed which he cuts, he takes to entertaining the bird with tunes on his horn, asking it to send him a loving mate such as all the other creatures of the forest have. His tunes wake up the dragon; and Siegfried makes merry over the grim mate the bird has sent him. Fafnir is highly scandalized by the irreverence of the young Bakoonin. He loses his temper; fights; and is forthwith slain, to his own great astonishment.

In such conflicts one learns to interpret the messages of Nature a little. When Siegfried, stung by the dragon's vitriolic blood, pops his finger into his mouth and tastes it, he understands what the bird is saying to him, and, instructed by it concerning the treasures within his reach, goes into the cave to secure the gold, the ring and the wishing cap. Then Mimmy returns, and is confronted by Alberic. The two quarrel furiously over the sharing of the booty they have not yet secured, until Siegfried comes from the cave with the ring and the helmet, not much impressed by the heap of gold, and disappointed because he has not yet learned to fear.

He has, however, learnt to read the thoughts of such a creature as poor Mimmy, who, intending to overwhelm him with flattery and fondness, only succeeds in making such a self-revelation of murderous envy that Siegfried smites him with Nothung and slays him, to the keen satisfaction of the hidden Alberic. Caring nothing for the gold, which he leaves to the care of the slain; disappointed in his fancy for learning fear; and longing for a mate, he casts himself wearily down, and again appeals to his friend the bird, who tells him of a woman sleeping on a mountain peak within a fortress of fire that only the fearless can penetrate. Siegfried is up in a moment with all the tumult of spring in his veins, and follows the flight of the bird as it pilots him to the fiery mountain.

The Third Act

To the root of the mountain comes also the Wanderer, now nearing his doom. He calls up the First Mother from the depths of the earth, and begs counsel from her. She bids him confer with the Norns (the Fates). But they are of no use to him: what he seeks is some foreknowledge of the way of the Will in its perpetual strife with these helpless Fates who can only spin the net of circumstance and environment round the feet of men. Why not, says Erda then, go to the daughter I bore you, and take counsel with her? He has to explain how he has cut himself off from her, and set the fires of Loki between the world and her counsel. In that case the First Mother cannot help him: such a separation is part of the bewilderment that is ever the first outcome of her eternal work of thrusting the life energy of the world to higher and higher organization. She can show him no way of escape from the destruction he foresees. Then from the innermost of him breaks the confession that he rejoices in his doom, and now himself exults in passing away with all his ordinances and alliances, with the spear-sceptre which he has only wielded on condition of slaying his dearest children with it, with the kingdom, the power and the glory which will never again boast themselves as "world without end." And so he dismisses Erda to her sleep in the heart of the earth as the forest bird draws near, piloting the slain son's son to his goal.

Now it is an excellent thing to triumph in the victory of the new order and the passing away of the old; but if you happen to be part of the old order yourself, you must none the less fight for your life. It seems hardly possible that the British army at the battle of Waterloo did not include at least one Englishman intelligent enough to hope, for the sake of his country and humanity, that Napoleon might defeat the allied sovereigns; but such an Englishman would kill a French cuirassier rather than be killed by him just as energetically as the silliest soldier, ever encouraged by people who ought to know better, to call his ignorance, ferocity and folly, patriotism and duty. Outworn life may have become mere error;

but it still claims the right to die a natural death, and will raise its hand against the millennium itself in self-defence if it tries to come by the short cut of murder. Wotan finds this out when he comes face to face with Siegfried, who is brought to a standstill at the foot of the mountain by the disappearance of the bird. Meeting the Wanderer there, he asks him the way to the mountain where a woman sleeps surrounded by fire. The Wanderer questions him, and extracts his story from him, breaking into fatherly delight when Siegfried, describing the mending of the sword, remarks that all he knew about the business was that the broken bits of Nothung would be of no use to him unless he made a new sword out of them right over again from the beginning. But the Wanderer's interest is by no means reciprocated by Siegfried. His majesty and elderly dignity are thrown away on the young anarchist, who, unwilling to waste time talking, bluntly bids him either show him the way to the mountain, or else "shut his muzzle." Wotan is a little hurt. "Patience, my lad," he says: "if you were an old man I should treat you with respect." "That would be a precious notion," says Siegfried. "All my life long I was bothered and hampered by an old man until I swept him out of my way. I will sweep you in the same fashion if you don't let me pass. Why do you wear such a big hat; and what has happened to one of your eyes? Was it knocked out by somebody whose way you obstructed?" To which Wotan replies allegorically that the eye that is gone—the eye that his marriage with Fricka cost him—is now looking at him out of Siegfried's head. At this, Siegfried gives up the Wanderer as a lunatic, and renews his threats of personal violence. Then Wotan throws off the mask of the Wanderer; uplifts the world-governing spear; and puts forth all his divine awe and grandeur as the guardian of the mountain, round the crest of which the fires of Loki now break into a red background for the majesty of the god. But all this is lost on Siegfried Bakoonin. "Aha!" he cries, as the spear is levelled against his breast: "I have found my father's foe"; and the spear falls in two pieces under the stroke of Nothung. "Up then," says Wotan: "I cannot withhold you," and disappears forever from the eye of man. The fires roll down the mountain; but Siegfried goes at them as exultantly as he went at the forging of the sword or the heart of the dragon, and shoulders his way through them, joyously sounding his horn to the accompaniment of their crackling and seething. And never a hair of his head is singed. Those frightful flames which have scared mankind for centuries from the Truth, have not heat enough in them to make a child shut its eyes. They are mere phantasmagoria, highly creditable to Loki's imaginative stage-management; but nothing ever has perished or will perish eternally in them except the Churches which have been so poor and faithless as to trade for their power on the lies of a romancer.

BACK TO OPERA AGAIN

And now, O Nibelungen Spectator, pluck up; for all allegories come to an end somewhere; and the hour of your release from these explanations is at hand. The rest of what you are going to see is opera, and nothing but opera. Before many bars have been played, Siegfried and the wakened Brynhild, newly become tenor and soprano, will sing a concerted cadenza; plunge on from that to a magnificent love duet; and end with a precipitous allegro a capella, driven headlong to its end by the impetuous semiquaver triplets of the famous finales to the first act of Don Giovanni or the coda to the Leonore overture, with a specifically contrapuntal theme, points d'orgue, and a high C for the soprano all complete.

What is more, the work which follows, entitled Night Falls On The Gods, is a thorough grand opera. In it you shall see what you have so far missed, the opera chorus in full parade on the stage, not presuming to interfere with the prima donna as she sings her death song over the footlights. Nay, that chorus will have its own chance when it first appears, with a good roaring strain in C major, not, after all, so very different from, or at all less absurd than the choruses of courtiers in La Favorita or "Per te immenso giubilo" in Lucia. The harmony is no doubt a little developed, Wagner augmenting his fifths with a G sharp where Donizetti would have put his fingers in his ears and screamed for G natural. But it is an opera chorus all the same; and along with it we have theatrical grandiosities that recall Meyerbeer and Verdi: pezzi d'insieme for all the principals in a row, vengeful conjurations for trios of them, romantic death song for the tenor: in short, all manner of operatic conventions.

Now it is probable that some of us will have been so talked by the more superstitious Bayreuth pilgrims into regarding Die Gotterdammerung as the mighty climax to a mighty epic, more Wagnerian than all the other three sections put together, as not to dare notice this startling atavism, especially if we find the trio-conjurations more exhilarating than the metaphysical discourses of Wotan in the three true music dramas of The Ring. There is, however, no real atavism involved. Die Gotterdammerung, though the last of The Ring dramas in order of performance, was the first in order of conception and was indeed the root from which all the others sprang.

The history of the matter is as follows. All Wagner's works prior to The Ring are operas. The last of them, Lohengrin, is perhaps the best known of modern operas. As performed in its entirety at Bayreuth, it is even more operatic than it appears at Covent Garden, because it happens that its most old-fashioned features, notably some of the big set concerted pieces for principals and chorus (pezzi d'insieme as I have called them above), are harder to perform than the more modern and characteristically Wagnerian sections, and for that reason were cut out in preparing the abbreviated fashionable version. Thus Lohengrin came upon the ordinary operatic stage as a more advanced departure from current operatic models than its composer had made it. Still, it is unmistakably an opera, with chorus, concerted pieces, grand finales, and a heroine who, if she does not sing florid variations with flute obbligato, is none the less a very perceptible prima donna. In everything but musical technique the change from Lohengrin to The Rhine Gold is quite revolutionary.

The explanation is that Night Falls On The Gods came in between them, although its music was not finished until twenty years after that of The Rhine Gold, and thus belongs to a later and more masterful phase of Wagner's harmonic style. It first came into Wagner's head as an opera to be entitled Siegfied's Death, founded on the old Niblung Sagas, which offered to Wagner the same material for an effective theatrical tragedy as they did to Ibsen. Ibsen's Vikings in Helgeland is, in kind, what Siegfied's

Death was originally intended to be: that is, a heroic piece for the theatre, without the metaphysical or allegorical complications of The Ring. Indeed, the ultimate catastrophe of the Saga cannot by any perversion of ingenuity be adapted to the perfectly clear allegorical design of The Rhine Gold, The Valkyries, and Siegfried.

SIEGFRIED AS PROTESTANT

The philosophically fertile element in the original project of
Siegfried's Death was the conception of Siegfried himself as a type of
the healthy man raised to perfect confidence in his own impulses by an
intense and joyous vitality which is above fear, sickliness of conscience,
malice, and the makeshifts and moral crutches of law and order which
accompany them. Such a character appears extraordinarily fascinating
and exhilarating to our guilty and conscience-ridden generations, however
little they may understand him. The world has always delighted in the
man who is delivered from conscience. From Punch and Don Juan down
to Robert Macaire, Jeremy Diddler and the pantomime clown, he has
always drawn large audiences; but hitherto he has been decorously given
to the devil at the end. Indeed eternal punishment is sometimes deemed
too high a compliment to his nature. When the late Lord Lytton, in his
Strange Story, introduced a character personifying the joyousness of
intense vitality, he felt bound to deny him the immortal soul which was
at that time conceded even to the humblest characters in fiction, and to
accept mischievousness, cruelty, and utter incapacity for sympathy as the
inevitable consequence of his magnificent bodily and mental health.

In short, though men felt all the charm of abounding life and
abandonment to its impulses, they dared not, in their deep self-mistrust,
conceive it otherwise than as a force making for evil—one which must
lead to universal ruin unless checked and literally mortified by self-
renunciation in obedience to superhuman guidance, or at least to some
reasoned system of morals. When it became apparent to the cleverest of
them that no such superhuman guidance existed, and that their secularist

systems had all the fictitiousness of "revelation" without its poetry, there was no escaping the conclusion that all the good that man had done must be put down to his arbitrary will as well as all the evil he had done; and it was also obvious that if progress were a reality, his beneficent impulses must be gaining on his destructive ones. It was under the influence of these ideas that we began to hear about the joy of life where we had formerly heard about the grace of God or the Age of Reason, and that the boldest spirits began to raise the question whether churches and laws and the like were not doing a great deal more harm than good by their action in limiting the freedom of the human will. Four hundred years ago, when belief in God and in revelation was general throughout Europe, a similar wave of thought led the strongest-hearted peoples to affirm that every man's private judgment was a more trustworthy interpreter of God and revelation than the Church. This was called Protestantism; and though the Protestants were not strong enough for their creed, and soon set up a Church of their own, yet the movement, on the whole, has justified the direction it took. Nowadays the supernatural element in Protestantism has perished; and if every man's private judgment is still to be justified as the most trustworthy interpreter of the will of Humanity (which is not a more extreme proposition than the old one about the will of God) Protestantism must take a fresh step in advance, and become Anarchism. Which it has accordingly done, Anarchism being one of the notable new creeds of the eighteenth and nineteenth centuries.

The weak place which experience finds out in the Anarchist theory is its reliance on the progress already achieved by "Man." There is no such thing as Man in the world: what we have to deal with is a multitude of men, some of them great rascals, some of them great statesmen, others both, with a vast majority capable of managing their personal affairs, but not of comprehending social organization, or grappling with the problems created by their association in enormous numbers. If "Man" means this majority, then "Man" has made no progress: he has, on the contrary, resisted it. He will not even pay the cost of existing institutions:

71

the requisite money has to be filched from him by "indirect taxation." Such people, like Wagner's giants; must be governed by laws; and their assent to such government must be secured by deliberately filling them with prejudices and practicing on their imaginations by pageantry and artificial eminences and dignities. The government is of course established by the few who are capable of government, though its mechanism once complete, it may be, and generally is, carried on unintelligently by people who are incapable of it the capable people repairing it from time to time when it gets too far behind the continuous advance or decay of civilization. All these capable people are thus in the position of Wotan, forced to maintain as sacred, and themselves submit to, laws which they privately know to be obsolescent makeshifts, and to affect the deepest veneration for creeds and ideals which they ridicule among themselves with cynical scepticism. No individual Siegfried can rescue them from this bondage and hypocrisy; in fact, the individual Siegfried has come often enough, only to find himself confronted with the alternative of governing those who are not Siegfrieds or risking destruction at their hands. And this dilemma will persist until Wotan's inspiration comes to our governors, and they see that their business is not the devising of laws and institutions to prop up the weaknesses of mobs and secure the survival of the unfittest, but the breeding of men whose wills and intelligences may be depended on to produce spontaneously the social well-being our clumsy laws now aim at and miss. The majority of men at present in Europe have no business to be alive; and no serious progress will be made until we address ourselves earnestly and scientifically to the task of producing trustworthy human material for society. In short, it is necessary to breed a race of men in whom the life-giving impulses predominate, before the New Protestantism becomes politically practicable.*

* The necessity for breeding the governing class from a selected stock has always been recognized by Aristocrats, however erroneous their methods of selection. We have changed our system from Aristocracy to Democracy without

considering that we were at the same time changing, as regards our governing class, from Selection to Promiscuity. Those who have taken a practical part in modern politics best know how farcical the result is.

The most inevitable dramatic conception, then, of the nineteenth century, is that of a perfectly naive hero upsetting religion, law and order in all directions, and establishing in their place the unfettered action of Humanity doing exactly what it likes, and producing order instead of confusion thereby because it likes to do what is necessary for the good of the race. This conception, already incipient in Adam Smith's Wealth of Nations, was certain at last to reach some great artist, and be embodied by him in a masterpiece. It was also certain that if that master happened to be a German, he should take delight in describing his hero as the Freewiller of Necessity, thereby beyond measure exasperating Englishmen with a congenital incapacity for metaphysics.

PANACEA QUACKERY,
OTHERWISE IDEALISM

Unfortunately, human enlightenment does not progress by nicer and nicer adjustments, but by violent corrective reactions which invariably send us clean over our saddle and would bring us to the ground on the other side if the next reaction did not send us back again with equally excessive zeal. Ecclesiasticism and Constitutionalism send us one way, Protestantism and Anarchism the other; Order rescues us from confusion and lands us in Tyranny; Liberty then saves the situation and is presently found to be as great a nuisance as Despotism. A scientifically balanced application of these forces, theoretically possible, is practically incompatible with human passion. Besides, we have the same weakness in morals as in medicine: we cannot be cured of running after panaceas, or, as they are called in the sphere of morals, ideals. One generation sets up duty, renunciation, self-sacrifice as a panacea. The next generation, especially the women, wake up at the age of forty or thereabouts to the fact that their lives have been wasted in the worship of this ideal, and, what is still more aggravating, that the elders who imposed it on them did so in a fit of satiety with their own experiments in the other direction. Then that defrauded generation foams at the mouth at the very mention of duty, and sets up the alternative panacea of love, their deprivation of which seems to them to have been the most cruel and mischievous feature of their slavery to duty. It is useless to warn them that this reaction, if prescribed as a panacea, will prove as great a failure as all the other reactions have done; for they do not recognize its identity with any reaction that ever occurred before. Take for instance the hackneyed historic example of the austerity of the Commonwealth being followed by the licence of the Restoration. You cannot persuade any moral enthusiast to accept this as a pure oscillation from action to reaction. If he is a Puritan he looks upon the Restoration as a national disaster: if he is an artist he regards it as the salvation of the country from gloom, devil worship and starvation of the affections. The Puritan is ready to try the Commonwealth again with a few modern improvements: the Amateur is equally ready to try the Restoration with modern enlightenments. And so for the present we must be content to proceed by reactions, hoping that each will establish some permanently practical and beneficial reform or moral habit that will survive the correction of its excesses by the next reaction.

DRAMATIC ORIGIN OF WOTAN

We can now see how a single drama in which Wotan does not appear, and of which Siegfried is the hero, expanded itself into a great fourfold drama of which Wotan is the hero. You cannot dramatize a reaction by personifying the reacting force only, any more than Archimedes could lift the world without a fulcrum for his lever. You must also personify the established power against which the new force is reacting; and in the conflict between them you get your drama, conflict being the essential ingredient in all drama. Siegfried, as the hero of Die Gotterdammerung, is only the primo tenore robusto of an opera book, deferring his death, after he has been stabbed in the last act, to sing rapturous love strains to the heroine exactly like Edgardo in Donizetti's Lucia. In order to make him intelligible in the wider significance which his joyous, fearless, conscienceless heroism soon assumed in Wagner's imagination, it was necessary to provide him with a much vaster dramatic antagonist than the operatic villain Hagen. Hence Wagner had to create Wotan as the anvil for Siegfried's hammer; and since there was no room for Wotan in the original opera book, Wagner had to work back to a preliminary drama reaching primarily to the very beginnings of human society. And since, on this world-embracing scale, it was clear that Siegfried must come into conflict with many baser and stupider forces than those lofty ones of supernatural religion and political constitutionalism typified by Wotan and his wife Fricka, these minor antagonists had to be dramatized also in the persons of Alberic, Mime, Fafnir, Loki, and the rest. None of these appear in Night Falls On The Gods save Alberic, whose weird dream-colloquy with Hagen, effective as it is, is as purely theatrical as the scene of the Ghost in Hamlet, or the statue in Don Giovanni. Cut the conference of the Norns and the visit of Valtrauta to Brynhild out of Night Falls On The Gods, and the drama remains coherent and complete without them. Retain them, and the play becomes connected by conversational references with the three music dramas; but the connection establishes no philosophic coherence, no real identity between the operatic Brynhild of the Gibichung episode (presently to be related) and the daughter of Wotan and the First Mother.

THE LOVE PANACEA

We shall now find that at the point where The Ring changes from music drama into opera, it also ceases to be philosophic, and becomes didactic. The philosophic part is a dramatic symbol of the world as Wagner observed it. In the didactic part the philosophy degenerates into the prescription of a romantic nostrum for all human ills. Wagner, only mortal after all, succumbed to the panacea mania when his philosophy was exhausted, like any of the rest of us.

The panacea is by no means an original one. Wagner was anticipated in the year 1819 by a young country gentleman from Sussex named Shelley, in a work of extraordinary artistic power and splendor. Prometheus Unbound is an English attempt at a Ring; and when it is taken into account that the author was only 27 whereas Wagner was 40 when he completed the poem of The Ring, our vulgar patriotism may find an envious satisfaction in insisting upon the comparison. Both works set forth the same conflict between humanity and its gods and governments, issuing in the redemption of man from their tyranny by the growth of his will into perfect strength and self-confidence; and both finish by a lapse into panacea-mongering didacticism by the holding up of Love as the remedy for all evils and the solvent of all social difficulties.

The differences between Prometheus Unbound and The Ring are as interesting as the likenesses. Shelley, caught in the pugnacity of his youth and the first impetuosity of his prodigious artistic power by the first fierce attack of the New Reformation, gave no quarter to the antagonist of his hero. His Wotan, whom he calls Jupiter, is the almighty fiend into whom the Englishman's God had degenerated during two centuries of ignorant

Bible worship and shameless commercialism. He is Alberic, Fafnir Loki and the ambitious side of Wotan all rolled into one melodramatic demon who is finally torn from his throne and hurled shrieking into the abyss by a spirit representing that conception of Eternal Law which has been replaced since by the conception of Evolution. Wagner, an older, more experienced man than the Shelley of 1819, understood Wotan and pardoned him, separating him tenderly from all the compromising alliances to which Shelley fiercely held him; making the truth and heroism which overthrow him the children of his inmost heart; and representing him as finally acquiescing in and working for his own supersession and annihilation. Shelley, in his later works, is seen progressing towards the same tolerance, justice, and humility of spirit, as he advanced towards the middle age he never reached. But there is no progress from Shelley to Wagner as regards the panacea, except that in Wagner there is a certain shadow of night and death come on it: nay, even a clear opinion that the supreme good of love is that it so completely satisfies the desire for life, that after it the Will to Live ceases to trouble us, and we are at last content to achieve the highest happiness of death.

This reduction of the panacea to absurdity was not forced upon Shelley, because the love which acts as a universal solvent in his Prometheus Unbound is a sentiment of affectionate benevolence which has nothing to do with sexual passion. It might, and in fact does exist in the absence of any sexual interest whatever. The words mercy and kindness connote it less ambiguously than the word love. But Wagner sought always for some point of contact between his ideas and the physical senses, so that people might not only think or imagine them in the eighteenth century fashion, but see them on the stage, hear them from the orchestra, and feel them through the infection of passionate emotion. Dr. Johnson kicking the stone to confute Berkeley is not more bent on common-sense concreteness than Wagner: on all occasions he insists on the need for sensuous apprehension to give reality to abstract comprehension, maintaining, in fact, that reality has no other meaning. Now he could apply this process to poetic love only by following it back to its alleged origin in sexual passion, the emotional phenomena of which he has expressed in music with a frankness and forcible naturalism which would possibly have scandalized Shelley. The love duet in the first act of The Valkyries is brought to a point at which the conventions of our society demand the precipitate fall of the curtain; whilst the prelude to Tristan and Isolde is such an astonishingly intense and faithful translation into music of the emotions which accompany the union of a pair of lovers, that it is questionable whether the great popularity of this piece at our orchestral concerts really means that our audiences are entirely catholic in their respect for life in all its beneficently creative functions, or whether they simply enjoy the music without understanding it.

But however offensive and inhuman may be the superstition which brands such exaltations of natural passion as shameful and indecorous, there is at least as much common sense in disparaging love as in setting it up as a panacea. Even the mercy and lovingkindness of Shelley do not hold good as a universal law of conduct: Shelley himself makes extremely short work of Jupiter, just as Siegfried does of Fafnir, Mime, and Wotan; and the fact that Prometheus is saved from doing the destructive part of his work by the intervention of that very nebulous personification of Eternity called Demogorgon, does not in the least save the situation, because, flatly, there is no such person as Demogorgon, and if Prometheus does not pull down Jupiter himself, no one else will. It would be exasperating, if it were not so funny, to see these poets leading their heroes through blood and destruction to the conclusion that, as Browning's David puts it (David of all people!), "All's Love; yet all's Law."

Certainly it is clear enough that such love as that implied by Siegfried's first taste of fear as he cuts through the mailed coat of the sleeping figure on the mountain, and discovers that it is a woman; by her fierce revolt against being touched by him when his terror gives way to ardor; by his manly transports of victory; and by the womanly mixture of rapture and horror with which she abandons herself to the passion which has seized on them both, is an experience which it is much better, like the vast majority of us, never to have passed through, than to allow it to play more than a recreative holiday part in our lives. It did not play a very large part in Wagner's own laborious life, and does not occupy more than two scenes of The Ring. Tristan and Isolde, wholly devoted to it, is a poem of destruction and death. The Mastersingers, a work full of health, fun and happiness, contains not a single bar of love music that can be described as passionate: the hero of it is a widower who cobbles shoes, writes verses, and contents himself with looking on at the sweethearting of his customers. Parsifal makes an end of it altogether. The truth is that the love panacea in Night Falls On The Gods and in the last act of Siegfried is a survival of the first crude operatic conception of the story, modified by an anticipation of Wagner's later, though not latest, conception of love as the fulfiller of our Will to Live and consequently our reconciler to night and death.

NOT LOVE, BUT LIFE

The only faith which any reasonable disciple can gain from The Ring is not in love, but in life itself as a tireless power which is continually driving onward and upward—not, please observe, being beckoned or drawn by Das Ewig Weibliche or any other external sentimentality, but growing from within, by its own inexplicable energy, into ever higher and higher forms of organization, the strengths and the needs of which are continually superseding the institutions which were made to fit our former requirements. When your Bakoonins call out for the demolition of all these venerable institutions, there is no need to fly into a panic and lock them up in prison whilst your parliament is bit by bit doing exactly what they advised you to do. When your Siegfrieds melt down the old weapons into new ones, and with disrespectful words chop in twain the antiquated constable's staves in the hands of their elders, the end of the world is no nearer than it was before. If human nature, which is the highest organization of life reached on this planet, is really degenerating, then human society will decay; and no panic-begotten penal measures can possibly save it: we must, like Prometheus, set to work to make new men instead of vainly torturing old ones. On the other hand, if the energy of life is still carrying human nature to higher and higher levels, then the more young people shock their elders and deride and discard their pet institutions the better for the hopes of the world, since the apparent growth of anarchy is only the measure of the rate of improvement. History, as far as we are capable of history (which is not saying much as yet), shows that all changes from crudity of social organization to complexity, and from mechanical agencies in government to living ones, seem anarchic at first sight. No doubt it is natural to a snail to think that any evolution which threatens to do away with shells will result in general death from exposure. Nevertheless, the most elaborately housed beings today are born not only without houses on their backs but without even fur or feathers to clothe them.

ANARCHISM NO PANACEA

One word of warning to those who may find themselves attracted by Siegfried's Anarchism, or, if they prefer a term with more respectable associations, his neo-Protestantism. Anarchism, as a panacea, is just as hopeless as any other panacea, and will still be so even if we breed a race of perfectly benevolent men. It is true that in the sphere of thought, Anarchism is an inevitable condition of progressive evolution. A nation without Freethinkers—that is, without intellectual Anarchists—will share the fate of China. It is also true that our criminal law, based on a conception of crime and punishment which is nothing but our vindictiveness and cruelty in a virtuous disguise, is an unmitigated and abominable nuisance, bound to be beaten out of us finally by the mere weight of our experience of its evil and uselessness. But it will not be replaced by anarchy. Applied to the industrial or political machinery of modern society, anarchy must always reduce itself speedily to absurdity. Even the modified form of anarchy on which modern civilization is based: that is, the abandonment of industry, in the name of individual liberty, to the upshot of competition for personal gain between private capitalists, is a disastrous failure, and is, by the mere necessities of the case, giving way to ordered Socialism. For the economic rationale of this, I must refer disciples of Siegfried to a tract from my hand published by the Fabian Society and entitled The Impossibilities of Anarchism, which explains why, owing to the physical constitution of our globe, society cannot effectively organize the production of its food, clothes and housing, nor distribute them fairly and economically on any anarchic plan: nay, that without concerting our social action to a much higher degree than we do at present we can never get rid of the wasteful and iniquitous welter of a little riches and a deal of poverty which current political humbug calls our prosperity and civilization. Liberty is an excellent thing; but it cannot begin until society has paid its daily debt to Nature by first earning its living. There is no liberty before that except the liberty to live at somebody else's expense, a liberty much sought after nowadays, since it is the criterion of gentility, but not wholesome from the point of view of the common weal.

SIEGFRIED CONCLUDED

In returning now to the adventures of Siegfried there is little more to be described except the finale of an opera. Siegfried, having passed unharmed through the fire, wakes Brynhild and goes through all the fancies and ecstasies of love at first sight in a duet which ends with an apostrophe to "leuchtende Liebe, lachender Tod!", which has been romantically translated into "Love that illumines, laughing at Death," whereas it really identifies enlightening love and laughing death as involving each other so closely as to be usually one and the same thing.

NIGHT FALLS ON THE GODS

PROLOGUE

Die Gottrerdammerung begins with an elaborate prologue. The three Norns sit in the night on Brynhild's mountain top spinning their thread of destiny, and telling the story of Wotan's sacrifice of his eye, and of his breaking off a bough from the World Ash to make a heft for his spear, also how the tree withered after suffering that violence. They have also some fresher news to discuss. Wotan, on the breaking of his spear by Siegfried, has called all his heroes to cut down the withered World Ash and stack its faggots in a mighty pyre about Valhalla. Then, with his broken spear in his hand, he has seated himself in state in the great hall, with the Gods and Heroes assembled about him as if in council, solemnly waiting for the end. All this belongs to the old legendary materials with which Wagner began The Ring.

The tale is broken by the thread snapping in the hands of the third Norn; for the hour has arrived when man has taken his destiny in his own hands to shape it for himself, and no longer bows to circumstance, environment, necessity (which he now freely wills), and all the rest of the inevitables. So the Norns recognize that the world has no further use for them, and sink into the earth to return to the First Mother. Then the day dawns; and Siegfried and Brynhild come, and have another duet. He gives her his ring; and she gives him her horse. Away then he goes in search of more adventures; and she watches him from her crag until he disappears. The curtain falls; but we can still hear the trolling of his horn, and the merry clatter of his horse's shoes trotting gaily down the valley. The sound is lost in the grander rhythm of the Rhine as he reaches its banks. We hear again an echo of the lament of the Rhine maidens for the ravished gold; and then, finally, a new strain, which does not surge like the mighty flood of the river, but has an unmistakable tramp of hardy men and a strong land flavor about it. And on this the opera curtain at last goes up—for please remember that all that has gone before is only the overture.

The First Act

We now understand the new tramping strain. We are in the Rhineside hall of the Gibichungs, in the resence of King Gunther, his sister Gutrune, and Gunther's grim half brother Hagen, the villain of the piece. Gunther is a fool, and has for Hagen's intelligence the respect a fool always has for the brains of a scoundrel. Feebly fishing for compliments, he appeals to Hagen to pronounce him a fine fellow and a glory to the race of Gibich. Hagen declares that it is impossible to contemplate him without envy, but thinks it a pity that he has not yet found a wife glorious enough for him. Gunther doubts whether so extraordinary a person can possibly exist. Hagen then tells him of Brynhild and her rampart of fire; also of Siegfried. Gunther takes this rather in bad part, since not only is he afraid of the fire, but Siegfried, according to Hagen, is not, and will therefore achieve this desirable match himself. But Hagen points out that since Siegfried is riding about in quest of adventures, he will certainly pay an early visit to the renowned chief of the Gibichungs. They can then give him a philtre which will make him fall in love with Gutrune and forget every other woman he has yet seen.

Gunther is transported with admiration of Hagen's cunning when he takes in this plan; and he has hardly assented to it when Siegfried, with operatic opportuneness, drops in just as Hagen expected, and is duly drugged into the heartiest love for Gutrune and total oblivion of

Brynhild and his own past. When Gunther declares his longing for the bride who lies inaccessible within a palisade of flame, Siegfried at once offers to undertake the adventure for him. Hagen then explains to both of them that Siegfried can, after braving the fire, appear to Brynhild in the semblance of Gunther through the magic of the wishing cap (or Tarnhelm, as it is called throughout The Ring), the use of which Siegfried now learns for the first time. It is of course part of the bargain that Gunther shall give his sister to Siegfried in marriage. On that they swear blood-brotherhood; and at this opportunity the old operatic leaven breaks out amusingly in Wagner. With tremendous exordium of brass, the tenor and baritone go at it with a will, showing off the power of their voices, following each other in canonic imitation, singing together in thirds and sixths, and finishing with a lurid unison, quite in the manner of Ruy Gomez and Ernani, or Othello and Iago. Then without further ado Siegfried departs on his expedition, taking Gunther with him to the foot of the mountain, and leaving Hagen to guard the hall and sing a very fine solo which has often figured in the programs of the Richter concerts, explaining that his interest in the affair is that Siegfried will bring back the Ring, and that he, Hagen, will presently contrive to possess himself of that Ring and become Plutonic master of the world.

And now it will be asked how does Hagen know all about the Plutonic empire; and why was he able to tell Gunther about Brynhild and Siegfried, and to explain to Siegfried the trick of the Tarnhelm. The explanation is that though Hagen's mother was the mother of Gunther, his father was not the illustrious Gibich, but no less a person than our old friend Alberic, who, like Wotan, has begotten a son to do for him what he cannot do for himself.

In the above incidents, those gentle moralizers who find the serious philosophy of the music dramas too terrifying for them, may allegorize pleasingly on the philtre as the maddening chalice of passion which, once tasted, causes the respectable man to forget his lawfully wedded wife and plunge into adventures which eventually lead him headlong to destruction.

We now come upon a last relic of the tragedy of Wotan. Returning to Brynhild's mountain, we find her visited by her sister Valkyrie Valtrauta, who has witnessed Wotan's solemn preparations with terror. She repeats to Brynhild the account already given by the Norns. Clinging in anguish to Wotan's knees, she has heard him mutter that were the ring returned to the daughters of the deep Rhine, both Gods and world would be redeemed from that stage curse off Alberic's in The Rhine Gold. On this she has rushed on her warhorse through the air to beg Brynhild to give the Rhine back its ring. But this is asking Woman to give up love for the sake of Church and State. She declares that she will see them both perish first; and Valtrauta returns to Valhalla in despair. Whilst Brynhild is watching the course of the black thundercloud that marks her sister's flight, the fires of Loki again flame high round the mountain; and the horn of Siegfried is heard as he makes his way through them. But the man who now appears wears the Tarnhelm: his voice is a strange voice: his figure is the unknown one of the king of the Gibichungs. He tears the ring from her finger, and, claiming her as his wife, drives her into the cave without pity for her agony of horror, and sets Nothung between them in token of his loyalty to the friend he is impersonating. No explanation of this highway robbery of the ring is offered. Clearly, this Siegfried is not the Siegfried of the previous drama.

The Second Act

In the second act we return to the hall of Gibich, where Hagen, in the last hours of that night, still sits, his spear in his hand, and his shield beside him. At his knees crouches a dwarfish spectre, his father Alberic, still full of his old grievances against Wotan, and urging his son in his dreams to win back the ring for him. This Hagen swears to do; and as the apparition of his father vanishes, the sun rises and Siegfried suddenly comes from the river bank tucking into his belt the Tarnhelm, which has transported hi from the mountain like the enchanted carpet of the Arabian tales. He describes his adventures to Gutrune until Gunther's boat is seen approaching, when Hagen seizes a cowhorn and calls the tribesmen to welcome their chief and his bride. It is most exhilarating, this colloquy with the startled and hastily armed clan, ending with a thundering chorus, the drums marking the time with mighty pulses from dominant to tonic, much as Rossini would have made them do if he had been a pupil of Beethoven's.

A terrible scene follows. Gunther leads his captive bride straight into the presence of Siegfried, whom she claims as her husband by the ring, which she is astonished to see on his finger: Gunther, as she supposes, having torn it from her the night before. Turning on Gunther, she says "Since you took that ring from me, and married me with it, tell him of your right to it; and make him give it back to you." Gunther stammers, "The ring! I gave him no ring—er—do you know him?" The rejoinder is obvious. "Then where are you hiding the ring that you had from me?" Gunther's confusion enlightens her; and she calls Siegfried trickster and thief to his face. In vain he declares that he got the ring from no woman, but from a dragon whom he slew; for he is manifestly puzzled; and she, seizing her opportunity, accuses him before the clan of having played Gunther false with her.

Hereupon we have another grandiose operatic oath, Siegfried attesting his innocence on Hagen's spear, and Brynhild rushing to the footlights and thrusting him aside to attest his guilt, whilst the clansmen call upon their gods to send down lightnings and silence the perjured. The gods do not respond; and Siegfried, after whispering to Gunther that the Tarnhelm seems to have been only half effectual after all, laughs his way out of the general embarrassment and goes off merrily to prepare for his wedding, with his arm round Gutrune's waist, followed by the clan. Gunther, Hagen and Brynhild are left together to plot operatic vengeance. Brynhild, it appears, has enchanted Siegfried in such a fashion that no weapon can hurt him. She has, however, omitted to protect his back, since it is impossible that he should ever turn that to a foe. They agree accordingly that on the morrow a great hunt shall take place, at which Hagen shall thrust his spear into the hero's vulnerable back. The blame is to be laid on the tusk of a wild boar. Gunther, being a fool, is remorseful about his oath of blood-brotherhood and about his sister's bereavement, without having the strength of mind to prevent the murder. The three burst into a herculean trio, similar in conception to that of the three conspirators in Un Ballo in Maschera; and the act concludes with a joyous strain heralding the appearance of Siegfried's wedding procession, with strewing of flowers, sacrificing to the gods, and carrying bride and bridegroom in triumph.

It will be seen that in this act we have lost all connection with the earlier drama. Brynhild is not only not the Brynhild of The Valkyries, she is the Hiordis of Ibsen, a majestically savage woman, in whom jealousy and revenge are intensified to heroic proportions. That is the inevitable theatrical treatment of the murderous heroine of the Saga. Ibsen's aim in The Vikings was purely theatrical, and not, as in his later dramas, also philosophically symbolic. Wagner's aim in Siegfried's Death was equally theatrical, and not, as it afterwards became in the dramas of which Siegfried's antagonist Wotan is the hero, likewise philosophically symbolic. The two master-dramatists therefore produce practically the same version of Brynhild. Thus on the second evening of The Ring we see Brynhild in the character of the truth-divining instinct in religion, cast into an enchanted slumber and surrounded by the fires of hell lest she should overthrow a Church corrupted by its alliance with government. On the fourth evening, we find her swearing a malicious lie to gratify her personal jealousy, and then plotting a treacherous murder with a fool and a scoundrel. In the original draft of Siegfried's Death, the incongruity is carried still further by the conclusion, at which the dead Brynhild, restored to her godhead by Wotan, and again a Valkyrie, carries the slain Siegfried to Valhalla to live there happily ever after with its pious heroes.

As to Siegfried himself, he talks of women, both in this second act and the next, with the air of a man of the world. "Their tantrums," he says, "are soon over." Such speeches do not belong to the novice of the preceding drama, but to the original Siegfried's Tod, with its leading characters sketched on the ordinary romantic lines from the old Sagas, and not yet reminted as the original creations of Wagner's genius whose acquaintance we have made on the two previous evenings. The very title "Siegfried's Death" survives as a strong theatrical point in the following passage. Gunther, in his rage and despair, cries, "Save me, Hagen: save my honor and thy mother's who bore us both." "Nothing can save thee," replies Hagen: "neither brain nor hand, but SIEGFRIED'S DEATH." And Gunther echoes with a shudder, "SIEGFRIED'S DEATH!"

A WAGNERIAN
NEWSPAPER CONTROVERSY

The devotion which Wagner's work inspires has been illustrated lately in a public correspondence on this very point. A writer in The Daily Telegraph having commented on the falsehood uttered by Brynhild in accusing Siegfried of having betrayed Gunther with her, a correspondence in defence of the beloved heroine was opened in The Daily Chronicle. The imputation of falsehood to Brynhild was strongly resented and combated, in spite of the unanswerable evidence of the text. It was contended that Brynhild's statement must be taken as establishing the fact that she actually was ravished by somebody whom she believed to be Siegfried, and that since this somebody cannot have been Siegfried, he being as incapable of treachery to Gunther as she of falsehood, it must have been Gunther himself after a second exchange of personalities not mentioned in the text. The reply to this—if so obviously desperate a hypothesis needs a reply—is that the text is perfectly explicit as to Siegfried, disguised as Gunther, passing the night with Brynhild with Nothung dividing them, and in the morning bringing her down the mountain THROUGH THE FIRE (an impassable obstacle to Gunther) and there transporting himself in a single breath, by the Tarnhelm's magic, back to the hall of the Gibichungs, leaving the real Gunther to bring Brynhild down the river after him. One controversialist actually pleaded for the expedition occupying two nights, on the second of which the alleged outrage might have taken place. But the time is accounted for to the last minute: it all takes place during the single night watch of Hagen. There is no possible way out of the plain fact that Brynhild's accusation is to her own knowledge false; and the impossible ways just cited are only interesting as examples of the fanatical worship which Wagner and his creations have been able to inspire in minds of exceptional power and culture.

More plausible was the line taken by those who admitted the falsehood. Their contention was that when Wotan deprived Brynhild of her Godhead, he also deprived her of her former high moral attributes; so that Siegfried's kiss awakened an ordinary mortal jealous woman. But a goddess can become mortal and jealous without plunging at once into perjury and murder. Besides, this explanation involves the sacrifice of the whole significance of the allegory, and the reduction of The Ring to the plane of a child's conception of The Sleeping Beauty. Whoever does not understand that, in terms of The Ring philosophy, a change from godhead to humanity is a step higher and not a degradation, misses the whole point of The Ring. It is precisely because the truthfulness of Brynhild is proof against Wotan's spells that he has to contrive the fire palisade with Loki, to protect the fictions and conventions of Valhalla against her.

The only tolerable view is the one supported by the known history of The Ring, and also, for musicians of sufficiently fine judgment, by the evidence of the scores; of which more anon. As a matter of fact Wagner began, as I have said, with Siegfried's Death. Then, wanting to develop the idea of Siegfried as neo-Protestant, he went on to The Young Siegfried. As a Protestant cannot be dramatically projected without a pontifical antagonist. The Young Siegfried led to The Valkyries, and that again to its preface The Rhine Gold (the preface is always written after the book is finished). Finally, of course, the whole was revised. The revision, if carried out strictly, would have involved the cutting out of Siegfried's Death, now become inconsistent and superfluous; and that would have involved, in turn, the facing of the fact that The Ring was no longer a Niblung epic, and really demanded modern costumes, tall hats for Tarnhelms, factories for Nibelheims, villas for Valhallas, and so on—in short, a complete confession of the extent to which the old Niblung epic had become the merest pretext and name directory in the course of Wagner's travail. But, as Wagner's most eminent English interpreter once put it to me at Bayreuth between the acts of Night Falls On The Gods, the master wanted to "Lohengrinize" again after his long abstention from opera; and Siegfried's Death (first sketched in 1848, the year before the rising in Dresden and the subsequent events which so deepened Wagner's sense of life and the seriousness of art) gave him exactly the libretto he required for that outbreak of the old operatic Adam in him. So he changed it into Die Gotterdammerung, retaining the traditional plot of murder and jealousy, and with it, necessarily, his original second act, in spite of the incongruity of its Siegfried and Brynhild with the Siegfried and Brynhild of the allegory. As to the legendary matter about the world-ash and the destruction of Valhalla by Loki, it fitted in well enough; for though, allegorically, the blow by which Siegfried breaks the god's spear is the end of Wotan and of Valhalla, those who do not see the allegory, and take the story literally, like children, are sure to ask what becomes of Wotan after Siegfried gets past him up the mountain; and to this question the old tale told in Night Falls On The Gods is as good an answer as another. The very senselessness of the scenes of the Norns and of Valtrauta in relation to the three foregoing dramas, gives them a highly effective air of mystery; and no one ventures to challenge their consequentiality, because we are all more apt to pretend to understand great works of art than to confess that the meaning (if any) has escaped us. Valtrauta, however, betrays her irrelevance by explaining that the gods can be saved by the restoration of the ring to the Rhine maidens. This, considered as part of the previous allegory, is nonsense; so that even this scene, which has a more plausible air of organic connection with The Valkyries than any other in Night Falls On The Gods, is as clearly part of a different and earlier conception as the episode which concludes it, in which Siegfried actually robs Brynhild of her ring, though he has no recollection of having given it to her. Night Falls On The Gods, in fact, was not even revised into any real coherence with the world-poem which sprang from it; and that is the authentic solution of all the controversies which have arisen over it.

The Third Act

The hunting party comes off duly. Siegfried strays from it and meets the Rhine maidens, who almost succeed in coaxing the ring from him. He pretends to be afraid of his wife; and they chaff him as to her beating him and so forth; but when they add that the ring is accursed and will bring death upon him, he discloses to them, as unconsciously as Julius Caesar disclosed it long ago, that secret of heroism, never to let your life be shaped by fear of its end.* So he keeps the ring; and they leave him to his fate. The hunting party now finds him; and they all sit down together to make a meal by the river side, Siegfried telling them meanwhile the story of his adventures. When he approaches the subject of Brynhild, as to whom his memory is a blank, Hagen pours an antidote to the love philtre into his drinking horn, whereupon, his memory returning, he proceeds to narrate the incident of the fiery mountain, to Gunther's intense mortification. Hagen then plunges his spear into the back of Siegfried, who falls dead on his shield, but gets up again, after the old operatic custom, to sing about thirty bars to his love before allowing himself to be finally carried off to the strains of the famous Trauermarsch.

* "We must learn to die, and to die in the fullest sense of the word. The fear of the end is the source of all lovelessness; and this fear is generated only when love begins to wane. How came it that this loves the highest blessedness to all things living, was so far lost sight of by the human race that at last it came to this: all that mankind did, ordered, and established, was conceived only in fear of the end? My poem sets this forth."—Wagner to Roeckel, 25th Jan. 1854.

The scene then changes to the hall of the Gibichungs by the Rhine. It is night; and Gutrune, unable to sleep, and haunted by all sorts of vague terrors, is waiting for the return of her husband, and wondering whether a ghostly figure she has seen gliding down to the river bank is Brynhild, whose room is empty. Then comes the cry of Hagen, returning with the hunting party to announce the death of Siegfried by the tusk of a wild boar. But Gutrune divines the truth; and Hagen does not deny it. Siegfried's body is brought in; Gunther claims the ring; Hagen will not suffer him to take it; they fight; and Gunther is slain. Hagen then attempts to take it; but the dead man's hand closes on it and raises itself threateningly. Then Brynhild comes; and a funeral pyre is raised whilst she declaims a prolonged scene, extremely moving and imposing, but yielding nothing to resolute intellectual criticism except a very powerful and elevated exploitation of theatrical pathos, psychologically identical with the scene of Cleopatra and the dead Antony in Shakespeare's tragedy. Finally she flings a torch into the pyre, and rides her war-horse into the flames. The hall of the Gibichungs catches fire, as most halls would were a cremation attempted in the middle of the floor (I permit myself this gibe purposely to emphasize the excessive artificiality of the scene); but the Rhine overflows its banks to allow the three Rhine maidens to take the ring from Siegfried's finger, incidentally extinguishing the conflagration as it does so. Hagen attempts to snatch the ring from the maidens, who promptly drown him; and in the distant heavens the Gods and their castle are seen perishing in the fires of Loki as the curtain falls.

FORGOTTEN ERE FINISHED

In all this, it will be observed, there is nothing new. The musical fabric is enormously elaborate and gorgeous; but you cannot say, as you must in witnessing The Rhine Gold, The Valkyries, and the first two acts of Siegfried, that you have never seen anything like it before, and that the inspiration is entirely original. Not only the action, but most of the poetry, might conceivably belong to an Elizabethan drama. The situation of Cleopatra and Antony is unconsciously reproduced without being bettered, or even equalled in point of majesty and musical expression. The loss of all simplicity and dignity, the impossibility of any credible scenic presentation of the incidents, and the extreme staginess of the conventions by which these impossibilities are got over, are no doubt covered from the popular eye by the overwhelming prestige of Die Gotterdammerung as part of so great a work as The Ring, and by the extraordinary storm of emotion and excitement which the music keeps up. But the very qualities that intoxicate the novice in music enlighten the adept. In spite of the fulness of the composer's technical accomplishment, the finished style and effortless mastery of harmony and instrumentation displayed, there is not a bar in the work which moves us as the same themes moved us in The Valkyries, nor is anything but external splendor added to the life and humor of Siegfried.

In the original poem, Brynhild delays her self-immolation on the pyre of Siegfried to read the assembled choristers a homily on the efficacy of the Love panacea. "My holiest wisdom's hoard," she says, "now I make known to the world. I believe not in property, nor money, nor godliness, nor hearth and high place, nor pomp and peerage, nor contract and custom, but in Love. Let that only prevail; and ye shall be blest in weal or woe." Here the repudiations still smack of Bakoonin; but the saviour is no longer the volition of the full-grown spirit of Man, the Free Willer of Necessity, sword in hand, but simply Love, and not even Shelleyan love, but vehement sexual passion. It is highly significant of the extent to which this uxorious commonplace lost its hold of Wagner (after disturbing his conscience, as he confesses to Roeckel, for years) that it disappears in the full score of Night Falls On The Gods, which was not completed until he was on the verge of producing Parsifal, twenty years after the publication of the poem. He cut the homily out, and composed the music of the final scene with a flagrant recklessness of the old intention. The rigorous logic with which representative musical themes are employed in the earlier dramas is here abandoned without scruple; and for the main theme at the conclusion he selects a rapturous passage sung by Sieglinda in the third act of The Valkyries when Brynhild inspires her with a sense of her high destiny as the mother of the unborn hero. There is no dramatic logic whatever in the recurrence of this theme to express the transport in which Brynhild immolates herself. There is of course an excuse for it, inasmuch as both women have an impulse of self-sacrifice for the sake of Siegfried; but this is really hardly more than an excuse; since the Valhalla theme might be attached to Alberic on the no worse ground that both he and Wotan are inspired by ambition, and that the ambition has the same object, the possession of the ring. The common sense of the matter is that the only themes which had fully retained their significance in Wagner's memory at the period of the composition of Night Falls On The Gods are those which are mere labels of external features, such as the Dragon, the Fire, the Water and so on. This particular theme of Sieglinda's is, in truth, of no great musical merit: it might easily be the pet climax of a popular sentimental ballad: in fact, the gushing effect which is its sole valuable quality is so cheaply attained that it is hardly going too far to call it the most trumpery phrase in the entire tetralogy. Yet, since it undoubtedly does gush very emphatically, Wagner chose, for convenience' sake, to work up this final scene with it rather than with the more distinguished, elaborate and beautiful themes connected with the love of Brynhild and Siegfried.

He would certainly not have thought this a matter of no consequence had he finished the whole work ten years earlier. It must always be borne in mind that the poem of The Ring was complete and printed in 1853, and represents the sociological ideas which, after germinating in the European atmosphere for many years, had been brought home to Wagner, who was intensely susceptible to such ideas, by the crash of 1849 at Dresden. Now no man whose mind is alive and active, as Wagner's was to the day of his death, can keep his political and spiritual opinions, much less his philosophic consciousness, at a standstill for quarter of a century until he finishes an orchestral score. When Wagner first sketched Night Falls On The Gods he was 35. When he finished the score for the first Bayreuth festival in 1876 he had turned 60. No wonder he had lost his old grip of it and left it behind him. He even tampered with The Rhine Gold for the sake of theatrical effect when stage-managing it, making Wotan pick up and brandish a sword to give visible point to his sudden inspiration as to the raising up of a hero. The sword had first to be discovered by Fafnir among the Niblung treasures and thrown away by him as useless. There is no sense in this device; and its adoption shows the same recklessness as to the original intention which we find in the music of the last act of The Dusk of the Gods.*

* Die Gotterdammerung means literally Godsgloaming. The English versions of the opera are usually called The Dusk of the Gods, or The Twilight of the Gods. I have purposely introduced the ordinary title in the sentence above for the reader's information.

WHY HE CHANGED HIS MIND

Wagner, however, was not the man to allow his grip of a great philosophic theme to slacken even in twenty-five years if the theme still held good as a theory of actual life. If the history of Germany from 1849 to 1876 had been the history of Siegfried and Wotan transposed into the key of actual life Night Falls On The Gods would have been the logical consummation of Das Rheingold and The Valkyrie instead of the operatic anachronism it actually is.

But, as a matter of fact, Siegfried did not succeed and Bismarck did. Roeckel was a prisoner whose imprisonment made no difference; Bakoonin broke up, not Walhall, but the International, which ended in an undignified quarrel between him and Karl Marx. The Siegfrieds of 1848 were hopeless political failures, whereas the Wotans and Alberics and Lows were conspicuous political successes. Even the Mimes held their own as against Siegfried. With the single exception of Ferdinand Lassalle, there was no revolutionary leader who was not an obvious impossibilist in practical politics; and Lassalle got himself killed in a romantic and quite indefensible duel after wrecking his health in a titanic oratorical campaign which convinced him that the great majority of the working classes were not ready to join him, and that the minority who were ready did not understand him. The International, founded in 1861 by Karl Marx in London, and mistaken for several years by nervous newspapers for a red spectre, was really only a turnip ghost. It achieved some beginnings of International Trade Unionism by inducing English workmen to send money to support strikes on the continent, and recalling English workers who had been taken across the North Sea to defeat such strikes; but on its revolutionary socialistic side it was a romantic figment. The suppression of the Paris Commune, one of the most tragic examples in history of the pitilessness with which capable practical administrators and soldiers are forced by the pressure of facts to destroy romantic amateurs and theatrical dreamers, made an end of melodramatic Socialism. It was as easy for Marx to hold up Thiers as the most execrable of living scoundrels and to put upon Gallifet the brand that still makes him impossible in French politics as it was for Victor Hugo to bombard Napoleon III from his paper battery in Jersey. It was also easy to hold up Felix Pyat and Delescluze as men of much loftier ideals than Thiers and Gallifet; but the one fact that could not be denied was that when it came to actual shooting, it was Gallifet who got Delescluze shot and not Delescluze who got Gallifet shot, and that when it came to administering the affairs of France, Thiers could in one way or another get it done, whilst Pyat could neither do it nor stop talking and allow somebody else to do it. True, the penalty of following Thiers was to be exploited by the landlord and capitalist; but then the penalty of following Pyat was to get shot like a mad dog, or at best get sent to New Caledonia, quite unnecessarily and uselessly.

To put it in terms of Wagner's allegory, Alberic had got the ring back again and was marrying into the best Walhall families with it. He had thought better of his old threat to dethrone Wotan and Loki. He had found that Nibelheim was a very gloomy place and that if he wanted to live handsomely and safely, he must not only allow Wotan and Loki to organize society for him, but pay them very handsomely for doing it. He wanted splendor, military glory, loyalty, enthusiasm, and patriotism; and his greed and gluttony were wholly unable to create them, whereas Wotan and Loki carried them all to a triumphant climax in Germany in 1871, when Wagner himself celebrated the event with his Kaisermarsch, which sounded much more convincing than the Marseillaise or the Carmagnole.

How, after the Kaisermarsch, could Wagner go back to his idealization of Siegfried in 1853? How could he believe seriously in Siegfried slaying the dragon and charging through the mountain fire, when the immediate foreground was occupied by the Hotel de Ville with Felix Pyat endlessly discussing the principles of Socialism whilst the shells of Thiers were already battering the Arc de Triomphe, and ripping up the pavement of the Champs Elysees? Is it not clear that things had taken an altogether unexpected turn—that although the Ring may, like the famous Communist Manifesto of Marx and Engels, be an inspired guest at the historic laws and predestined end of our capitalistic-theocratic epoch, yet Wagner, like Marx, was too inexperienced in technical government and administration and too melodramatic in his hero-contra-villain conception of the class struggle, to foresee the actual process by which his generalization would work out, or the part to be played in it by the classes involved?

Let us go back for a moment to the point at which the Niblung legend first becomes irreconcilable with Wagner's allegory. Fafnir in the allegory becomes a capitalist; but Fafnir in the legend is a mere hoarder. His gold does not bring him in any revenue. It does not even support him: he has to go out and forage for food and drink. In fact, he is on the way to his drinking-pool when Siegfried kills him. And Siegfried himself has no more use for gold than Fafnir: the only difference between them in this respect is that Siegfried does not waste his time in watching a barren treasure that is no use to him, whereas Fafnir sacrifices his humanity and his life merely to prevent anybody else getting it. This contrast is true to human nature; but it shunts The Ring drama off the economic lines of the allegory. In real life, Fafnir is not a miser: he seeks dividends, comfortable life, and admission to the circles of Wotan and Loki. His only means of procuring these is to restore the gold to Alberic in exchange for scrip in Alberic's enterprises. Thus fortified with capital, Alberic exploits his fellow dwarfs as before, and also exploits Fafair's fellow giants who have no capital. What is more, the toil, forethought and self-control which the exploitation involves, and the self-respect and social esteem which its success wins, effect an improvement in Alberic's own character which neither Marx nor Wagner appear to have foreseen. He discovers that to be a dull, greedy, narrow-minded money-grubber is not the way to make money on a large scale; for though greed may suffice to turn tens into hundreds and even hundreds into thousands, to turn thousands into hundreds of thousands requires magnanimity and a will to power rather than to pelf. And to turn thousands into millions, Alberic must make himself an earthly providence for masses of workmen: he must create towns and govern markets. In the meantime, Fafair, wallowing in dividends which he has done nothing to earn, may rot, intellectually and morally, from mere disuse of his energies and lack of incentive to excel; but the more imbecile he becomes, the more dependent he is upon Alberic, and the more the responsibility of keeping the world-machine in working order falls upon Alberic. Consequently, though Alberic in Also may have been merely the vulgar Manchester Factory-owner portrayed by Engels, in 1876 he was well on the way towards becoming Krupp of Essen or Carnegie of Homestead.

Now, without exaggerating the virtues of these gentlemen, it will be conceded by everybody except perhaps those veteran German Social-Democrats who have made a cult of obsolescence under the name of Marxism, that the modern entrepreneur is not to be displaced and dismissed so lightly as Alberic is dismissed in The Ring. They are really the masters of the whole situation. Wotan is hardly less dependent on them than Fafnir; the War-Lord visits their work, acclaims them in stirring speeches, and casts down their enemies; whilst Loki makes commercial treaties for them and subjects all his diplomacy to their approval.

The end cannot come until Siegfried learns Alberic's trade and shoulders Alberic's burden. Not having as yet done so, he is still completely mastered by Alberic. He does not even rebel against him except when he is too stupid and ignorant, or too romantically impracticable, to see that Alberic's work, like Wotan's work and Loki's work, is necessary work, and that therefore Alberic can never be superseded by a warrior, but only by a capable man of business who is prepared to continue his work without a day's intermission. Even though the proletarians of all lands were to become "class conscious," and obey the call of Marx by uniting to carry the Class struggle to a proletarian victory in which all capital should become common property, and all Monarchs, Millionaires, Landlords and Capitalists become common citizens, the triumphant proletarians would have either to starve in Anarchy the next day or else do the political and industrial work which is now being done tant bien que mal by our Romanoffs, our Hohenzollerns, our Krupps, Carnegies, Levers, Pierpont Morgans, and their political retinues. And in the meantime these magnates must defend their power and property with all their might against the revolutionary forces until these forces become positive, executive, administrative forces, instead of the conspiracies of protesting, moralizing, virtuously indignant amateurs who mistook Marx for a man of affairs and Thiers for a stage villain. But all this represents a development of which one gathers no forecast from Wagner or Marx. Both of them prophesied the end of our epoch, and, so far as one can guess, prophesied it rightly. They also brought its industrial history up to the year 1848 far more penetratingly than the academic historians of their time. But they broke off there and left a void between 1848 and the end, in which we, who have to live in that period, get no guidance from them. The Marxists wandered for years in this void, striving, with fanatical superstition, to suppress the Revisionists who, facing the fact that the Social-Democratic party was lost, were trying to find the path by the light of contemporary history instead of vainly consulting the oracle in the pages of Das Kapital. Marx himself was too simpleminded a recluse and too full of the validity of his remoter generalizations, and the way in which the rapid integration of capital in Trusts and Kartels was confirming them, to be conscious of the void himself.

Wagner, on the other hand, was comparatively a practical man. It is possible to learn more of the world by producing a single opera, or even conducting a single orchestral rehearsal, than by ten years reading in the

Library of the British Museum. Wagner must have learnt between Das Rheingold and the Kaisermarsch that there are yet several dramas to be interpolated in The Ring after The Valkyries before the allegory can tell the whole story, and that the first of these interpolated dramas will be much more like a revised Rienzi than like Siegfried. If anyone doubts the extent to which Wagner's eyes had been opened to the administrative-childishness and romantic conceit of the heroes of the revolutionary generation that served its apprenticeship on the barricades of 1848-9, and perished on those of 1870 under Thiers' mitrailleuses, let him read Eine Kapitulation, that scandalous burlesque in which the poet and composer of Siegfried, with the levity of a schoolboy, mocked the French republicans who were doing in 1871 what he himself was exiled for doing in 1849. He had set the enthusiasm of the Dresden Revolution to his own greatest music; but he set the enthusiasm of twenty years later in derision to the music of Rossini. There is no mistaking the tune he meant to suggest by his doggerel of Republik, Republik, Republik-lik-lik. The Overture to William Tell is there as plainly as if it were noted down in full score.

In the case of such a man as Wagner, you cannot explain this volte-face as mere jingoism produced by Germany's overwhelming victory in the Franco-Prussian War, nor as personal spite against the Parisians for the Tannhauser fiasco. Wagner had more cause for personal spite against his own countrymen than he ever had against the French. No doubt his outburst gratified the pettier feelings which great men have in common with small ones; but he was not a man to indulge in such gratifications, or indeed to feel them as gratifications, if he had not arrived at a profound philosophical contempt for the inadequacy of the men who were trying to wield Nothung, and who had done less work for Wagner's own art than a single German King and he, too, only a mad one. Wagner had by that time done too much himself not to know that the world is ruled by deeds, not by good intentions, and that one efficient sinner is worth ten futile saints and martyrs.

I need not elaborate the point further in these pages. Like all men of genius, Wagner had exceptional sincerity, exceptional respect for facts, exceptional freedom from the hypnotic influence of sensational popular movements, exceptional sense of the realities of political power as distinguished from the presences and idolatries behind which the real masters of modern States pull their wires and train their guns. When he scored Night Falls On The Gods, he had accepted the failure of Siegfried and the triumph of the Wotan-Loki-Alberic-trinity as a fact. He had given up dreaming of heroes, heroines, and final solutions, and had conceived a new protagonist in Parsifal, whom he announced, not as a hero, but as a fool; who was armed, not with a sword which cut irresistibly, but with a spear which he held only on condition that he did not use it; and who instead of exulting in the slaughter of a dragon was frightfully ashamed of having shot a swan. The change in the conception of the Deliverer could hardly be more complete. It reflects the change which took place in Wagner's mind between the composition of The Rhine Gold and Night Falls On The Gods; and it explains why he dropped The Ring allegory and fell back on the status quo ante by Lohengrinizing.

If you ask why he did not throw Siegfried into the waste paper basket and rewrite The Ring from The Valkyries onwards, one must reply that the time had not come for such a feat. Neither Wagner nor anyone else then living knew enough to achieve it. Besides, what he had already done had reached the omit of even his immense energy and perseverance and so he did the best he could with the unfinished and for ever unfinishable work, rounding it off with an opera much as Rossini rounded off some of his religious compositions with a galop. Only, Rossini on such occasions wrote in his score "Excusez du pen," but Wagner left us to find out the change for ourselves, perhaps to test how far we had really followed his meaning.

WAGNER'S OWN EXPLANATION

And now, having given my explanation of The Ring, can I give Wagner's explanation of it? If I could (and I can) I should not by any means accept it as conclusive. Nearly half a century has passed since the tetralogy was written; and in that time the purposes of many half instinctive acts of genius have become clearer to the common man than they were to the doers. Some years ago, in the course of an explanation of Ibsen's plays, I pointed out that it was by no means certain or even likely that Ibsen was as definitely conscious of his thesis as I. All the stupid people, and some critics who, though not stupid, had not themselves written what the Germans call "tendency" works, saw nothing in this but a fantastic affectation of the extravagant self-conceit of knowing more about Ibsen than Ibsen himself. Fortunately, in taking exactly the same position now with regard to Wagner, I can claim his own authority to support me. "How," he wrote to Roeckel on the 23rd. August 1856, "can an artist expect that what he has felt intuitively should be perfectly realized by others, seeing that he himself feels in the presence of his work, if it is true Art, that he is confronted by a riddle, about which he, too, might have illusions, just as another might?"

The truth is, we are apt to deify men of genius, exactly as we deify the creative force of the universe, by attributing to logical design what is the result of blind instinct. What Wagner meant by "true Art" is the operation of the artist's instinct, which is just as blind as any other instinct. Mozart, asked for an explanation of his works, said frankly "How do I know?" Wagner, being a philosopher and critic as well as a composer, was always looking for moral explanations of what he had created and he hit on several very striking ones, all different. In the same way one can conceive Henry the Eighth speculating very brilliantly about the circulation of his own blood without getting as near the truth as Harvey did long after his death.

None the less, Wagner's own explanations are of exceptional interest. To begin with, there is a considerable portion of The Ring, especially the portraiture of our capitalistic industrial system from the socialist's point of new in the slavery of the Niblungs and the tyranny of Alberic, which is unmistakable, as it dramatizes that portion of human activity which lies well within the territory covered by our intellectual consciousness. All this is concrete Home Office business, so to speak: its meaning was as clear to Wagner as it is to us. Not so that part of the work which deals with the destiny of Wotan. And here, as it happened, Wagner's recollection of what he had been driving at was completely upset by his discovery, soon after the completion of The Ring poem, of Schopenhaur's famous treatise "The World as Will and Representation." So obsessed did he become with this masterpiece of philosophic art that he declared that it contained the intellectual demonstration of the conflict of human forces which he himself had demonstrated artistically in his great poem. "I must confess," he writes to Roeckel, "to having arrived at a clear understanding of my own works of art through the help of another, who has provided me with the reasoned conceptions corresponding to my intuitive principles."

Schopenhaur, however, had done nothing of the sort. Wagner's determination to prove that he had been a Schopenhaurite all along without knowing it only shows how completely the fascination of the great treatise on The Will had run away with his memory. It is easy to see how this happened. Wagner says of himself that "seldom has there taken place in the soul of one and the same man so profound a division and estrangement between the intuitive or impulsive part of his nature and his consciously or reasonably formed ideas." And since Schopenhaur's great contribution to modern thought was to educate us into clear consciousness of this distinction—a distinction familiar, in a fanciful way, to the Ages of Faith and Art before the Renascence, but afterwards swamped in the Rationalism of that movement—it was inevitable that Wagner should jump at Schopenhaur's metaphysiology (I use a word less likely to be mistaken than metaphysics) as the very thing for him. But metaphysiology is one thing, political philosophy another. The political philosophy of Siegfried is exactly contrary to the political philosphy of Schopenhaur, although the same clear metaphysiological distinction between the instinctive part of man (his Will) and his reasoning faculty (dramatized in The Ring as Loki) is insisted on in both. The difference is that to Schopenhaur the Will is the universal tormentor of man, the author of that great evil, Life; whilst reason is the divine gift that is finally to overcome this life-creating will and lead, through its aboegation, to cessation and peace, annihilation and Nirvana. This is the doctrine of Pessimism. Now Wagner was, when he wrote The Ring, a most sanguine revolutionary Meliorist, contemptuous of the reasoning faculty, which he typified in the shifty, unreal, delusive Loki, and full of faith in the life-giving Will, which he typified in the glorious Siegfried. Not until he read Schopenhaur did he become bent on proving that he had always been a Pessimist at heart, and that Loki was the most sensible and worthy adviser of Wotan in The Rhine Gold.

Sometimes he faces the change in his opinions frankly enough. "My Niblung drama," he writes to Roeckel, "had taken form at a time when I had built up with my reason an optimistic world on Hellenic principles, believing that nothing was necessary for the realization of such a world but that men should wish it. I ingeniously set aside-the problem why they did not wish it. I remember that it was with this definite creative purpose that I conceived the personality of Siegfried, with the intention of representing an existence free from pain." But he appeals to his earlier works to show that behind all these artificial optimistic ideas there was always with him an intuition of "the sublime tragedy of renunciation, the negation of the will." In trying to explain this, he s full of ideas philosophically, and full of the most amusing contradictions personally. Optimism, as an accidental excursion into the barren paths of reason on his own part, he calls "Hellenic." In others he denounces it as rank Judaism, the Jew having at that time become for him the whipping boy for all modern humamty. In a letter from London he expounds Schopenhaur to Roeckel with enthusiasm, preaching the renunciation of the Will to Live as the redemption from all error and vain pursuits: in the next letter he resumes the subject with unabated interest, and finishes by mentioning that on leaving London he went to Geneva and underwent "a most beneficial course of hydropathy." Seven months before this he had written as follows: "Believe me, I too was once possessed by the idea of a country life. In order to become a radically healthy human being, I went two years ago to a Hydropathic Establishment, prepared to give up Art and everything if I could once more become a child of Nature. But, my good friend, I was obliged to laugh at my own naivete when I found myself almost going mad. None of us will reach the promised land: we shall all die in the wilderness. Intellect is, as some one has said, a sort of disease: it is incurable."

Roeckel knew his man of old, and evidently pressed him for explanations of the inconsistencies of The Ring with Night Falls On The Gods. Wagner defended himself with unfailing cleverness and occasional petulances, ranging from such pleas as "I believe a true instinct has kept me from a too great definiteness; for it has been borne in on me that an absolute disclosure of the intention disturbs true insight," to a volley of explanations and commentaries on the explanations. He gets excited and annoyed because Roeckel will not admire the Brynhild of Night Falls On The Gods; re-invents the Tarnhelm scene; and finally, the case being desperate, exclaims, "It is wrong of you to challenge me to explain it in words: you must feel that something is being enacted that is not to be expressed in mere words."

THE PESSIMIST AS AMORIST

Sometimes he gets very far away from Pessimism indeed, and recommends Roeckel to solace his captivity, not by conquering the will to live at liberty, but by "the inspiring influences of the Beautiful." The next moment he throws over even Art for Life. "Where life ends," he says, very wittily, "Art begins. In youth we turn to Art, we know not why; and only when we have gone through with Art and come out on the other side, we learn to our cost that we have missed Life itself." His only comfort is that he is beloved. And on the subject of love he lets himself loose in a manner that would have roused the bitterest scorn in Schopenhaur, though, as we have seen (Love Panacea), it is highly characteristic of Wagner. "Love in its most perfect reality," he says, "is only possible between the sexes: it is only as man and woman that human beings can truly love. Every other manifestation of love can be traced back to that one absorbingly real feeling, of which all other affections are but an emanation, a connection, or an imitation. It is an error to look on this as only one of the forms in which love is revealed, as if there were other forms coequal with it, or even superior to it. He who after the manner of metaphysicians prefers UNREALITY to REALITY, and derives the concrete from the abstract—in short, puts the word before the fact—may be right in esteeming the idea of love as higher than the expression of love, and may affirm that actual love made manifest in feeling is nothing but the outward and visible sign of a pre-existent, non-sensuous, abstract love; and he will do well to despise that sensuous function in general. In any case it were safe to bet that such a man had never loved or been loved as human beings can love, or he would have understood that in despising this feeling, what he condemned was its sensual expression, the outcome of man's animal nature, and not true human love. The highest satisfaction and expression of the individual is only to be found in his complete absorption, and that is only possible through love. Now a human being is both MAN and WOMAN: it is only when these two are united that the real human being exists; and thus it is only by love that man and woman attain to the full measure of humanity. But when nowadays we talk of a human being, such heartless blockheads are we that quite involuntarily we only think of man. It is only in the union of man and woman by love (sensuous and supersensuous) that the human being exists; and as the human being cannot rise to the conception of anything higher than his own existence—his own being—so the transcendent act of his life is this consummation of his humanity through love."

It is clear after this utterance from the would-be Schopenhaurian, that Wagner's explanations of his works for the most part explain nothing but the mood in which he happened to be on the day he advanced them, or the train of thought suggested to his very susceptible imagination and active mind by the points raised by his questioner. Especially in his private letters, where his outpourings are modified by his dramatic consciousness of the personality of his correspondent, do we find him taking all manner of positions, and putting forward all sorts of cases which must be taken as clever and suggestive special pleadings, and not as serious and permanent expositions of his works. These works must speak for themselves: if The Ring says one thing, and a letter written afterwards says that it said something else, The Ring must be taken to confute the letter just as conclusively as if the two had been written by different hands. However, nobody fairly well acquainted with Wagner's utterances as a whole will find any unaccountable contradictions in them. As in all men of his type, our manifold nature was so marked in him that he was like several different men rolled into one. When he had exhausted himself in the character of the most pugnacious, aggressive, and sanguine of reformers, he rested himself as a Pessimist and Ninanist. In The Ring the quietism of Brynhild's "Rest, rest, thou God" is sublime in its deep conviction; but you have only to turn back the pages to find the irrepressible bustle of Siegfried and the revelry of the clansmen expressed with equal zest. Wagner was not a Schopenhaurite every day in the week, nor even a Wagnerite. His mind changes as often as his mood. On Monday nothing will ever induce him to return to quilldriving: on Tuesday he begins a new pamphlet. On Wednesday he is impatient of the misapprehensions of people who cannot see how impossible it is for him to preside as a conductor over platform performances of fragments of his works, which can only be understood when presented strictly according to his intention on the stage: on Thursday he gets up a concert of Wagnerian selections, and when it is over writes to his friends describing how profoundly both bandsmen and audience were impressed. On Friday he exults in the self-assertion of Siegfried's will against all moral ordinances, and is full of a revolutionary sense of "the universal law of change and renewal": on Saturday he has an attack of holiness, and asks, "Can you conceive a moral action of which the root idea is not renunciation?" In short, Wagner can be quoted against himself almost without limit, much as Beethoven's adagios could be quoted against his scherzos if a dispute arose between two fools as to whether he was a melancholy man or a merry one.

THE MUSIC OF THE RING

THE REPRESENTATIVE THEMES

To be able to follow the music of The Ring, all that is necessary is to become familiar enough with the brief musical phrases out of which it is built to recognize them and attach a certain definite significance to them, exactly as any ordinary Englishman recognizes and attaches a definite significance to the opening bars of God Save the King. There is no difficulty here: every soldier is expected to learn and distinguish between different bugle calls and trumpet calls; and anyone who can do this can learn and distinguish between the representative themes or "leading motives" (Leitmotifs) of The Ring. They are the easier to learn because they are repeated again and again; and the main ones are so emphatically impressed on the ear whilst the spectator is looking for the first time at the objects, or witnessing the first strong dramatic expression of the ideas they denote, that the requisite association is formed unconsciously. The themes are neither long, nor complicated, nor difficult. Whoever can pick up the flourish of a coach-horn, the note of a bird, the rhythm of the postman's knock or of a horse's gallop, will be at no loss in picking up the themes of The Ring. No doubt, when it comes to forming the necessary mental association with the theme, it may happen that the spectator may find his ear conquering the tune more easily than his mind conquers the thought. But for the most part the themes do not denote thoughts at all, but either emotions of a quite simple universal kind, or the sights, sounds and fancies common enough to be familiar to children. Indeed some of them are as frankly childish as any of the funny little orchestral interludes which, in Haydn's Creation, introduce the horse, the deer, or the worm. We have both the horse and the worm in The Ring, treated exactly in Haydn's manner, and with an effect not a whit less ridiculous to superior people who decline to take it good-humoredly. Even the complaisance of good Wagnerites is occasionally rather overstrained by the way in which Brynhild's allusions to her charger Grani elicit from the band a little rum-ti-tum triplet which by itself is in no way suggestive of a horse, although a continuous rush of such triplets makes a very exciting musical gallop.

Other themes denote objects which cannot be imitatively suggested by music: for instance, music cannot suggest a ring, and cannot suggest gold; yet each of these has a representative theme which pervades the score in all directions. In the case of the gold the association is established by the very salient way in which the orchestra breaks into the pretty theme in the first act of The Rhine Gold at the moment when the sunrays strike down through the water and light up the glittering treasure, hitherto invisible. The reference of the strange little theme of the wishing cap is equally manifest from the first, since the spectator's attention is wholly taken up with the Tarnhelm and its magic when the theme is first pointedly uttered by the orchestra. The sword theme is introduced at the end of The Rhine Gold to express Wotan's hero inspiration; and I have already mentioned that Wagner, unable, when it came to practical stage management, to forego the appeal to the eye as well as to the thought, here made Wotan pick up a sword and brandish it, though no such instruction appears in the printed score. When this sacrifice to Wagner's scepticism as to the reality of any appeal to an audience that is not made through their bodily sense is omitted, the association of the theme with the sword is not formed until that point in the first act of The Valkyries at which Siegmund is left alone by Hunding's hearth, weaponless, with the assurance that he will have to fight for his life at dawn with his host. He recalls then how his father promised him a sword for his hour of need; and as he does so, a flicker from the dying fire is caught by the golden hilt of the sword in the tree, when the theme immediately begins to gleam through the quiver of sound from the orchestra, and only dies out as the fire sinks and the sword is once more hidden by the darkness. Later on, this theme, which is never silent whilst Sieglinda is dwelling on the story of the sword, leaps out into the most dazzling splendor the band can give it when Siegmund triumphantly draws the weapon from the tree. As it consists of seven notes only, with a very marked measure, and a melody like a simple flourish on a trumpet or post horn, nobody capable of catching a tune can easily miss it.

The Valhalla theme, sounded with solemn grandeur as the home of the gods first appears to us and to Wotan at the beginning of the second scene of The Rhine Gold, also cannot be mistaken. It, too, has a memorable rhythm; and its majestic harmonies, far from presenting those novel or curious problems in polyphony of which Wagner still stands suspected by superstitious people, are just those three simple chords which festive students who vamp accompaniments to comic songs "by ear" soon find sufficient for nearly all the popular tunes in the world.

On the other hand, the ring theme, when it begins to hurtle through the third scene of The Rhine Gold, cannot possibly be referred to any special feature in the general gloom and turmoil of the den of the dwarfs. It is not a melody, but merely the displaced metric accent which musicians call syncopation, rung on the notes of the familiar chord formed by piling three minor thirds on top of one another (technically, the chord of the minor ninth, ci-devant diminished seventh). One soon picks it up and identifies it; but it does not get introduced in the unequivocally clear fashion of the themes described above, or of that malignant monstrosity, the theme which denotes the curse on the gold. Consequently it cannot be said that the musical design of the work is perfectly clear at the first hearing as regards all the themes; but it is so as regards most of them, the main lines being laid down as emphatically and intelligibly as the dramatic motives in a Shakespearean play. As to the coyer subtleties of the score, their discovery provides fresh interest for repeated hearings, giving The Ring a Beethovenian inexhaustibility and toughness of wear.

The themes associated with the individual characters get stamped on the memory easily by the simple association of the sound of the theme with the appearance of the person indicated. Its appropriateness is generally pretty obvious. Thus, the entry of the giants is made to a vigorous stumping, tramping measure. Mimmy, being a quaint, weird old creature, has a quaint, weird theme of two thin chords that creep down eerily one to the other. Gutrune's theme is pretty and caressing: Gunther's bold, rough, and commonplace. It is a favorite trick of Wagner's, when one of his characters is killed on the stage, to make the theme attached to that character weaken, fail, and fade away with a broken echo into silence.

THE CHARACTERIZATION

All this, however, is the mere child's play of theme work. The more complex characters, instead of having a simple musical label attached to them, have their characteristic ideas and aspirations identified with special representative themes as they come into play in the drama; and the chief merit of the thematic structure of The Ring is the mastery with which the dramatic play of the ideas is reflected in the contrapuntal play of the themes. We do not find Wotan, like the dragon or the horse, or, for the matter of that, like the stage demon in Weber's Freischutz or Meyerbeer's Robert the Devil, with one fixed theme attached to him like a name plate to an umbrella, blaring unaltered from the orchestra whenever he steps on the stage. Sometimes we have the Valhalla theme used to express the greatness of the gods as an idea of Wotan's. Again, we have his spear, the symbol of his power, identified with another theme, on which Wagner finally exercises his favorite device by making it break and fail, cut through, as it were, by the tearing sound of the theme identified with the sword, when Siegfried shivers the spear with the stroke of Nothung. Yet another theme connected with Wotan is the Wanderer music which breaks with such a majestic reassurance on the nightmare terror of Mimmy when Wotan appears at the mouth of his cave in the scene of the three riddles. Thus not only are there several Wotan themes, but each varies in its inflexions and shades of tone color according to its dramatic circumstances. So, too, the merry ham tune of the young Siegfried changes its measure, loads itself with massive harmonies, and becomes an exordium of the most imposing splendor when it heralds his entry as full-fledged hero in the prologue to Night

Falls On The Gods. Even Mimmy has his two or three themes: the weird one already described; the little one in triple measure imitating the tap of his hammer, and fiercely mocked in the savage laugh of Alberic at his death; and finally the crooning tune in which he details all his motherly kindnesses to the little foundling Siegfried. Besides this there are all manner of little musical blinkings and shamblings and whinings, the least hint of which from the orchestra at any moment instantly brings Mimmy to mind, whether he is on the stage at the time or not.

In truth, dramatic characterization in music cannot be carried very far by the use of representative themes. Mozart, the greatest of all masters of this art, never dreamt of employing them; and, extensively as they are used in The Ring, they do not enable Wagner to dispense with the Mozartian method. Apart from the themes, Siegfried and Mimmy are still as sharply distinguished from one another by the character of their music as Don Giovanni from Leporello, Wotan from Gutrune as Sarastro from Papagena. It is true that the themes attached to the characters have the same musical appropriateness as the rest of the music: for example, neither the Valhalla nor the spear themes could, without the most ludicrous incongruity, be used for the forest bird or the unstable, delusive Loki; but for all that the musical characterization must be regarded as independent of the specific themes, since the entire elimination of the thematic system from the score would leave the characters as well distinguished musically as they are at present.

One more illustration of the way in which the thematic system is worked. There are two themes connected with Loki. One is a rapid, sinuous, twisting, shifty semiquaver figure suggested by the unsubstantial, elusive logic-spinning of the clever one's braincraft. The other is the fire theme. In the first act of Siegfried, Mimmy makes his unavailing attempt to explain fear to Siegfried. With the horror fresh upon him of the sort of nightmare into which he has fallen after the departure of the Wanderer, and which has taken the form, at once fanciful and symbolic, of a delirious dread of light, he asks Siegfried whether he has never, whilst wandering in the forest, had his heart set hammering in frantic dread by the mysterious lights of the gloaming. To this, Siegfried, greatly astonished, replies that on such occasions his heart is altogether healthy and his sensations perfectly normal. Here Mimmy's question is accompanied by the tremulous sounding of the fire theme with its harmonies most oppressively disturbed and troubled; whereas with Siegfried's reply they become quite clear and straightforward, making the theme sound bold, brilliant, and serene. This is a typical instance of the way in which the themes are used.

The thematic system gives symphonic interest, reasonableness, and unity to the music, enabling the composer to exhaust every aspect and quality of his melodic material, and, in Beethoven's manner, to work miracles of beauty, expression and significance with the briefest phrases. As a set-off against this, it has led Wagner to indulge in repetitions that would be intolerable in a purely dramatic work. Almost the first thing that a dramatist has to learn in constructing a play is that the persons must not come on the stage in the second act and tell one another at great length what the audience has already seen pass before its eyes in the first act. The extent to which Wagner has been seduced into violating this rule by his affection for his themes is startling to a practiced playwright. Siegfried inherits from Wotan a mania for autobiography which leads him to inflict on every one he meets the story of Mimmy and the dragon, although the audience have spent a whole evening witnessing the events he is narrating. Hagen tells the story to Gunther; and that same night Alberic's ghost tells it over again to Hagen, who knows it already as well as the audience. Siegfried tells the Rhine maidens as much of it as they will listen to, and then keeps telling it to his hunting companions until they kill him. Wotan's autobiography on the second evening becomes his biography in the mouths of the Norns on the fourth. The little that the Norns add to it is repeated an hour later by Valtrauta. How far all this repetition is tolerable is a matter of individual taste. A good story will bear repetition; and if it has woven into it such pretty tunes as the

Rhine maidens' yodel, Mimmy's tinkling anvil beat, the note of the forest bird, the call of Siegfried's horn, and so on, it will bear a good deal of rehearing. Those who have but newly learnt their way through The Ring will not readily admit that there is a bar too much repetition.

But how if you find some anti-Wagnerite raising the question whether the thematic system does not enable the composer to produce a music drama with much less musical fertility than was required from his predecessors for the composition of operas under the old system!

Such discussions are not within the scope of this little book. But as the book is now finished (for really nothing more need be said about The Ring), I am quite willing to add a few pages of ordinary musical criticism, partly to please the amateurs who enjoy that sort of reading, and partly for the guidance of those who wish to obtain some hints to help them through such critical small talk about Wagner and Bayreuth as may be forced upon them at the dinner table or between the acts.

THE OLD AND THE NEW MUSIC

In the old-fashioned opera every separate number involved the composition of a fresh melody; but it is quite a mistake to suppose that this creative-effort extended continuously throughout the number from the first to the last bar. When a musician composes according to a set metrical pattern, the selection of the pattern and the composition of the first stave (a stave in music corresponds to a line in verse) generally completes the creative effort. All the rest follows more or less mechanically to fill up the pattern, an air being very like a wall-paper design in this respect. Thus the second stave is usually a perfectly obvious consequence of the first; and the third and fourth an exact or very slightly varied repetition of the first and second. For example, given the first line of Pop Goes the Weasel or Yankee Doodle, any musical cobbler could supply the remaining three. There is very little tune turning of this kind in The Ring; and it is noteworthy that where it does occur, as in Siegmund's spring song and Mimmy's croon, "Ein zullendes Kind," the effect of the symmetrical staves, recurring as a mere matter of form, is perceptibly poor and platitudinous compared with the free flow of melody which prevails elsewhere.

The other and harder way of composing is to take a strain of free melody, and ring every variety of change of mood upon it as if it were a thought that sometimes brought hope, sometimes melancholy, sometimes exultation, sometimes raging despair and so on. To take several themes of this kind, and weave them together into a rich musical fabric passing panoramically before the ear with a continually varying flow of sentiment, is the highest feat of the musician: it is in this way that we get the fugue of Bach and the symphony of Beethoven. The admittedly inferior musician is the one who, like Auber and Offenbach, not to mention our purveyors of drawing-room ballads, can produce an unlimited quantity of symmetrical tunes, but cannot weave themes symphonically.

When this is taken into account, it will be seen that the fact that there is a great deal of repetition in The Ring does not distinguish it from the old-fashioned operas. The real difference is that in them the repetition was used for the mechanical completion of conventional metric patterns, whereas in The Ring the recurrence of the theme is an intelligent and interesting consequence of the recurrence of the dramatic phenomenon which it denotes. It should be remembered also that the substitution of symphonically treated themes for tunes with symmetrical eight-bar staves and the like, has always been the rule in the highest forms of music. To describe it, or be affected by it, as an abandonment of melody, is to confess oneself an ignoramus conversant only with dance tunes and ballads.

The sort of stuff a purely dramatic musician produces when he hampers himself with metric patterns in composition is not unlike what might have resulted in literature if Carlyle (for example) had been compelled by convention to write his historical stories in rhymed stanzas. That is to say, it limits his fertility to an occasional phrase, and three quarters of the time exercises only his barren ingenuity in fitting rhymes and measures to it. In literature the great masters of the art have long emancipated themselves from metric patterns. Nobody claims that the hierarchy of modern impassioned prose writers, from Bunyan to Ruskin, should be placed below the writers of pretty lyrics, from Herrick to Mr. Austin Dobson. Only in dramatic literature do we find the devastating tradition of blank verse still lingering, giving factitious prestige to the platitudes of dullards, and robbing the dramatic style of the genuine poet of its full natural endowment of variety, force and simplicity.

This state of things, as we have seen, finds its parallel in musical art, since music can be written in prose themes or in versified tunes; only here nobody dreams of disputing the greater difficulty of the prose forms, and the comparative triviality of versification. Yet in dramatic music, as in dramatic literature, the tradition of versification clings with the same pernicious results; and the opera, like the tragedy, is conventionally made like a wall paper. The theatre seems doomed to be in all things the last refuge of the hankering after cheap prettiness in art.

Unfortunately this confusion of the decorative with the dramatic element in both literature and music is maintained by the example of great masters in both arts. Very touching dramatic expression can be combined with decorative symmetry of versification when the artist happens to possess both the decorative and dramatic gifts, and to have cultivated both hand in hand. Shakespeare and Shelley, for instance, far from being hampered by the conventional obligation to write their dramas in verse, found it much the easiest and cheapest way of producing them. But if Shakespeare had been compelled by custom to write entirely in prose, all his ordinary dialogue might have been as good as the first scene of As You Like It; and all his lofty passages as fine as "What a piece of work is Man!", thus sparing us a great deal of blank verse in which the thought is commonplace, and the expression, though catchingly turned, absurdly pompous. The Cent might either have been a serious drama or might never have been written at all if Shelley had not been allowed to carry off its unreality by Elizabethan versification. Still, both poets have achieved many passages in which the decorative and dramatic qualities are not only reconciled, but seem to enhance one another to a pitch otherwise unattainable.

Just so in music. When we find, as in the case of Mozart, a prodigiously gifted and arduously trained musician who is also, by a happy accident, a dramatist comparable to Moliere, the obligation to compose operas in versified numbers not only does not embarrass him, but actually saves him trouble and thought. No matter what his dramatic mood may be, he expresses it in exquisite musical verses more easily than a dramatist of ordinary singleness of talent can express it in prose. Accordingly, he too, like Shakespeare and Shelley, leaves versified airs, like Dalla sua pace, or Gluck's Che fare senza Euridice, or Weber's Leise, leise, which are as dramatic from the first note to the last as the untrammelled themes of The Ring. In consequence, it used to be professorially demanded that all dramatic music should present the same double aspect. The demand was unreasonable, since symmetrical versification is no merit in dramatic music: one might as well stipulate that a dinner fork should be constructed so as to serve also as a tablecloth. It was an ignorant demand too, because it is not true that the composers of these exceptional examples were always, or even often, able to combine dramatic expression with symmetrical versification. Side by side with Dalla sua pace we have Il mio tesoro and Non mi dir, in which exquisitely expressive opening phrases lead to decorative passages which are as grotesque from the dramatic point of view as the music which Alberic sings when he is slipping and sneezing in the Rhine mud is from the decorative point of view. Further, there is to be considered the mass of shapeless "dry recitative" which separates these symmetrical numbers, and which might have been raised to considerable dramatic and musical importance had it been incorporated into a continuous musical fabric by thematic treatment. Finally, Mozart's most dramatic finales and concerted numbers are more or less in sonata form, like symphonic movements, and must therefore be classed as musical prose. And sonata form dictates repetitions and recapitulations from which the perfectly unconventional form adopted by Wagner is free. On the whole, there is more scope for both repetition and convention in the old form than in the new; and the poorer a composer's musical gift is, the surer he is to resort to the eighteenth century patterns to eke out his invention.

THE NINETEENTH CENTURY

When Wagner was born in 1813, music had newly become the most astonishing, the most fascinating, the most miraculous art in the world. Mozart's Don Giovanni had made all musical Europe conscious of the enchantments of the modern orchestra and of the perfect adaptability of music to the subtlest needs of the dramatist. Beethoven had shown how those inarticulate mood-poems which surge through men who have, like himself, no exceptional command of words, can be written down in music as symphonies. Not that Mozart and Beethoven invented these applications of their art; but they were the first whose works made it clear that the dramatic and subjective powers of sound were enthralling enough to stand by themselves quite apart from the decorative musical structures of which they had hitherto been a mere feature. After the finales in Figaro and Don Giovanni, the possibility of the modern music drama lay bare. After the symphonies of Beethoven it was certain that the poetry that lies too deep for words does not lie too deep for music, and that the vicissitudes of the soul, from the roughest fun to the loftiest aspiration, can make symphonies without the aid of dance tunes. As much, perhaps, will be claimed for the preludes and fugues of Bach; but Bach's method was unattainable: his compositions were wonderful webs of exquisitely beautiful Gothic traceries in sound, quite beyond all ordinary human talent. Beethoven's far blunter craft was thoroughly popular and practicable: not to save his soul could he have drawn one long Gothic line in sound as Bach could, much less have woven several of them together with so apt a harmony that even when the composer is unmoved its progressions saturate themselves with the emotion which (as modern critics are a little apt to forget) springs as warmly from our delicately touched admiration as from our sympathies, and sometimes makes us give a composer credit for pathetic intentions which he does not entertain, just as a boy imagines a treasure of tenderness and noble wisdom in the beauty of a woman. Besides, Bach set comic dialogue to music exactly as he set the recitatives of the Passion, there being for him, apparently, only one recitative possible, and that the musically best. He reserved the expression of his merry mood for the regular set numbers in which he could make one of his wonderful contrapuntal traceries of pure ornament with the requisite gaiety of line and movement. Beethoven bowed to no ideal of beauty: he only sought the expression for his feeling. To him a joke was a joke; and if it sounded funny in music he was satisfied. Until the old habit of judging all music by its decorative symmetry had worn out, musicians were shocked by his symphonies, and, misunderstanding his integrity, openly questioned his sanity. But to those who were not looking for pretty new sound patterns, but were longing for the expression of their moods in music, he achieved revelation, because, being single in his aim to express his own moods, he anticipated with revolutionary courage and frankness all the moods of the rising generations of the nineteenth century.

The result was inevitable. In the nineteenth century it was no longer necessary to be a born pattern designer in sound to be a composer. One had but to be a dramatist or a poet completely susceptible to the dramatic and descriptive powers of sound. A race of literary and theatrical musicians appeared; and Meyerbeer, the first of them, made an extraordinary impression. The frankly delirious description of his Robert the Devil in Balzac's short story entitled Gambra, and Goethe's astonishingly mistaken notion that he could have composed music for Faust, show how completely the enchantments of the new dramatic music upset the judgment of artists of eminent discernment. Meyerbeer was, people said (old gentlemen still say so in Paris), the successor of Beethoven: he was, if a less perfect musician than Mozart, a profounder genius. Above all, he was original and daring. Wagner himself raved about the duet in the fourth act of Les Huguenots as wildly as anyone.

Yet all this effect of originality and profundity was produced by a quite limited talent for turning striking phrases, exploiting certain curious and rather catching rhythms and modulations, and devising suggestive or eccentric instrumentation. On its decorative side, it was the same phenomenon in music as the Baroque school in architecture: an energetic struggle to enliven organic decay by mechanical oddities and novelties. Meyerbeer was no symphonist. He could not apply the thematic system to his striking phrases, and so had to cobble them into metric patterns in the old style; and as he was no "absolute musician" either, he hardly got his metric patterns beyond mere quadrille tunes, which were either wholly undistinguished, or else made remarkable by certain brusqueries which, in the true rococo manner, owed their singularity to their senselessness. He could produce neither a thorough music drama nor a charming opera. But with all this, and worse, Meyerbeer had some genuine dramatic energy, and even passion; and sometimes rose to the occasion in a manner which, whilst the imagination of his contemporaries remained on fire with the novelties of dramatic music, led them to overrate him with an extravagance which provoked Wagner to conduct a long critical campaign against his leadership. Thirty years ago this campaign was mentably ascribed to the professional jealousy of a disappointed rival. Nowadays young people cannot understand how anyone could ever have taken Meyerbeer's influence seriously. Those who remember how his reputation stood half a century ago, and who realize what a nothoroughfare the path he opened proved to be, even to himself, know how inevitable and how impersonal Wagner's attack was.

Wagner was the literary musician par excellence. He could not, like Mozart and Beethoven, produce decorative tone structures independently of any dramatic or poetic subject matter, because, that craft being no longer necessary for his purpose, he did not cultivate it. As Shakespeare, compared with Tennyson, appears to have an exclusively dramatic talent, so exactly does Wagner compared with Mendelssohn. On the other hand, he had not to go to third rate literary hacks for "librettos" to set to music: he produced his own dramatic poems, thus giving dramatic integrity to opera, and making symphony articulate. A Beethoven symphony (except the articulate part of the ninth) expresses noble feeling, but not thought: it has moods, but no ideas. Wagner added thought and produced the music drama. Mozart's loftiest opera, his Ring, so to speak, The Magic Flute, has a libretto which, though none the worse for seeming, like The Rhine Gold, the merest Christmas tomfoolery to shallow spectators, is the product of a talent immeasurably inferior to Mozart's own. The libretto of Don Giovanni is coarse and trivial: its transfiguration by Mozart's music may be a marvel; but nobody will venture to contend that such transfigurations, however seductive, can be as satisfactory as tone poetry or drama in which the musician and the poet are at the same level. Here, then, we have the simple secret of Wagner's preeminence as a dramatic musician. He wrote the poems as well as composed the music of his "stage festival plays," as he called them.

Up to a certain point in his career Wagner paid the penalty of undertaking two arts instead of one. Mozart had his trade as a musician at his fingers' ends when he was twenty, because he had served an arduous apprenticeship to that trade and no other. Wagner was very far from having attained equal mastery at thirty-five: indeed he himself has told us that not until he had passed the age at which Mozart died did he compose with that complete spontaneity of musical expression which can only be attained by winning entire freedom from all preoccupation with the difficulties of technical processes. But when that time came, he was not only a consummate musician, like Mozart, but a dramatic poet and a critical and philosophical essayist, exercising a considerable influence on his century. The sign of this consummation was his ability at last to play with his art, and thus to add to his already famous achievements in sentimental drama that lighthearted art of comedy of which the greatest masters, like Moliere and Mozart, are so much rarer than the tragedians and sentimentalists. It was then that he composed the first two acts of Siegfried, and later on The Mastersingers, a professedly comedic work, and a quite Mozartian garden of melody, hardly credible as the work of the straining artifices of Tanehauser. Only, as no man ever learns to do one thing by doing something else, however closely allied the two things may be, Wagner still produced no music independently of his poems. The overture to The Mastersingers is delightful when you know what it is all about; but only those to whom it came as a concert piece without any such clue, and who judged its reckless counterpoint by the standard of Bach and of Mozart's Magic Flute overture, can realize how atrocious it used to sound to musicians of the old school. When I first heard it, with the clear march of the polyphony in Bach's B minor Mass fresh in my memory, I confess I thought that the parts had got dislocated, and that some of the band were half a bar behind the others. Perhaps they were; but now that I am familiar with the work, and with Wagner's harmony, I can still quite understand certain passages producing that effect organ admirer of Bach even when performed with perfect accuracy.

THE MUSIC OF THE FUTURE

The success of Wagner has been so prodigious that to his dazzled disciples it seems that the age of what he called "absolute" music must be at an end, and the musical future destined to be an exclusively Wagnerian one inaugurated at Bayreuth. All great geniuses produce this illusion. Wagner did not begin a movement: he consummated it. He was the summit of the nineteenth century school of dramatic music in the same sense as Mozart was the summit (the word is Gounod's) of the eighteenth century school. And those who attempt to carry on his Bayreuth tradition will assuredly share the fate of the forgotten purveyors of second-hand Mozart a hundred years ago. As to the expected supersession of absolute music, it is sufficient to point to the fact that Germany produced two absolute musicians of the first class during Wagner's lifetime: one, the greatly gifted Goetz, who died young; the other, Brahms, whose absolute musical endowment was as extraordinary as his thought was commonplace. Wagner had for him the contempt of the original thinker for the man of second-hand ideas, and of the strenuously dramatic musician for mere brute musical faculty; but though his contempt was perhaps deserved by the Triumphlieds, and Schicksalslieds, and Elegies and Requiems in which Brahms took his brains so seriously, nobody can listen to Brahms' natural utterance of the richest absolute music, especially in his chamber compositions, without rejoicing in his amazing gift. A reaction to absolute music, starting partly from Brahms, and partly from such revivals of medieval music as those of De Lange in Holland and Mr. Arnold Dolmetsch in England, is both likely and promising; whereas there is no more hope in attempts to out-Wagner Wagner in music drama than there was in the old attempts—or for the matter of that, the new ones—to make Handel the starting point of a great school of oratorio.

BAYREUTH

When the Bayreuth Festival Playhouse was at last completed, and opened in 1876 with the first performance of The Ring, European society was compelled to admit that Wagner was "a success." Royal personages, detesting his music, sat out the performances in the row of boxes set apart for princes. They all complimented him on the astonishing "push" with which, in the teeth of all obstacles, he had turned a fabulous and visionary project into a concrete commercial reality, patronized by the public at a pound a head. It is as well to know that these congratulations had no other effect upon Wagner than to open his eyes to the fact that the Bayreuth experiment, as an attempt to evade the ordinary social and commercial conditions of theatrical enterprise, was a failure. His own account of it contrasts the reality with his intentions in a vein which would be bitter if it were not so humorous. The precautions taken to keep the seats out of the hands of the frivolous public and in the hands of earnest disciples, banded together in little Wagner Societies throughout Europe, had ended in their forestalling by ticket speculators and their sale to just the sort of idle globe-trotting tourists against whom the temple was to have been strictly closed. The money, supposed to be contributed by the faithful, was begged by energetic subscription-hunting ladies from people who must have had the most grotesque misconceptions of the composer's aims—among others, the Khedive of Egypt and the Sultan of Turkey!

The only change that has occurred since then is that subscriptions are no longer needed; for the Festival Playhouse apparently pays its own way now, and is commercially on the same footing as any other theatre.

The only qualification required from the visitor is money. A Londoner spends twenty pounds on a visit: a native Bayreuther spends one pound. In either case "the Folk," on whose behalf Wagner turned out in 1849, are effectually excluded; and the Festival Playhouse must therefore be classed as infinitely less Wagnerian in its character than Hampton Court Palace. Nobody knew this better than Wagner; and nothing can be further off the mark than to chatter about Bayreuth as if it had succeeded in escaping from the conditions of our modern civilization any more than the Grand Opera in Paris or London.

Within these conditions, however, it effected a new departure in that excellent German institution, the summer theatre. Unlike our opera houses, which are constructed so that the audience may present a splendid pageant to the delighted manager, it is designed to secure an uninterrupted view of the stage, and an undisturbed hearing of the music, to the audience. The dramatic purpose of the performances is taken with entire and elaborate seriousness as the sole purpose of them; and the management is jealous for the reputation of Wagner. The commercial success which has followed this policy shows that the public wants summer theatres of the highest class. There is no reason why the experiment should not be tried in England. If our enthusiasm for Handel can support Handel Festivals, laughably dull, stupid and anti-Handelian as these choral monstrosities are, as well as annual provincial festivals on the same model, there is no likelihood of a Wagner Festival failing. Suppose, for instance, a Wagner theatre were built at Hampton Court or on Richmond Hill, not to say Margate pier, so that we could have a delightful summer evening holiday, Bayreuth fashion, passing the hours between the acts in the park or on the river before sunset, is it seriously contended that there would be any lack of visitors? If a little of the money that is wasted on grand stands, Eiffel towers, and dismal Halls by the Sea, all as much tied to brief annual seasons as Bayreuth, were applied in this way, the profit would be far more certain and the social utility prodigiously greater. Any English enthusiasm for Bayreuth that does not take the form of clamor for a Festival Playhouse in England may be set aside as mere pilgrimage mania.

Those who go to Bayreuth never repent it, although the performances there are often far from delectable. The singing is sometimes tolerable, and sometimes abominable. Some of the singers are mere animated beer casks, too lazy and conceited to practise the self-control and physical training that is expected as a matter of course from an acrobat, a jockey or a pugilist. The women's dresses are prudish and absurd. It is true that Kundry no longer wears an early Victorian ball dress with "ruchings," and that Fresh has been provided with a quaintly modish copy of the flowered gown of Spring in Botticelli's famous picture; but the mailclad Brynhild still climbs the mountains with her legs carefully hidden in a long white skirt, and looks so exactly like Mrs. Leo Hunter as Minerva that it is quite impossible to feel a ray of illusion whilst looking at her. The ideal of womanly beauty aimed at reminds Englishmen of the barmaids of the seventies, when the craze for golden hair was at its worst. Further, whilst Wagner's stage directions are sometimes disregarded as unintelligently as at Covent Garden, an intolerably old-fashioned tradition of half rhetorical, half historical-pictorial attitude and gesture prevails. The most striking moments of the drama are conceived as tableaux vivants with posed models, instead of as passages of action, motion and life.

I need hardly add that the supernatural powers of control attributed by credulous pilgrims to Madame Wagner do not exist. Prima donnas and tenors are as unmanageable at Bayreuth as anywhere else. Casts are capriciously changed; stage business is insufficiently rehearsed; the public are compelled to listen to a Brynhild or Siegfried of fifty when they have carefully arranged to see one of twenty-five, much as in any ordinary opera house. Even the conductors upset the arrangements occasionally. On the other hand, if we leave the vagaries of the stars out of account, we may safely expect always that in thoroughness of preparation of the chief work of the season, in strenuous artistic pretentiousness, in pious conviction that the work is of such enormous importance as to be worth doing well at all costs, the Bayreuth performances will deserve their reputation. The band is placed out of sight of the audience, with the more formidable instruments beneath the stage, so that the singers have not to sing THROUGH the brass. The effect is quite perfect.

BAYREUTH IN ENGLAND

I purposely dwell on the faults of Bayreuth in order to show that there is no reason in the world why as good and better performances of The Ring should not be given in England. Wagner's scores are now before the world; and neither his widow nor his son can pretend to handle them with greater authority than any artist who feels the impulse to interpret them. Nobody will ever know what Wagner himself thought of the artists who established the Bayreuth tradition: he was obviously not in a position to criticize them. For instance, had Rubini survived to create Siegmund, it is quite certain that we should not have had from Wagner's pen so amusing and vivid a description as we have of his Ottavio in the old Paris days. Wagner was under great obligations to the heroes and heroines of 1876; and he naturally said nothing to disparage their triumphs; but there is no reason to believe that all or indeed any of them satisfied him as Schnorr of Carolsfeld satisfied him as Tristan, or Schroder Devrient as Fidelio. It is just as likely as not that the next Schnorr or Schroder may arise in England. If that should actually happen, neither of them will need any further authority than their own genius and Wagner's scores for their guidance. Certainly the less their spontaneous impulses are sophisticated by the very stagey traditions which Bayreuth is handing down from the age of Crummles, the better.

WAGNERIAN SINGERS

No nation need have much difficulty in producing a race of Wagnerian singers. With the single exception of Handel, no composer has written music so well calculated to make its singers vocal athletes as Wagner. Abominably as the Germans sing, it is astonishing how they thrive physically on his leading parts. His secret is the Handelian secret. Instead of specializing his vocal parts after the manner of Verdi and Gounod for high sopranos, screaming tenors, and high baritones with an effective compass of about a fifth at the extreme tiptop of their ranges, and for contraltos with chest registers forced all over their compass in the manner of music hall singers, he employs the entire range of the human voice freely, demanding from everybody very nearly two effective octaves, so that the voice is well exercised all over, and one part of it relieves the other healthily and continually. He uses extremely high notes very sparingly, and is especially considerate in the matter of instrumental accompaniment. Even when the singer appears to have all the thunders of the full orchestra raging against him, a glance at the score will show that he is well heard, not because of any exceptionally stentorian power in his voice, but because Wagner meant him to be heard and took the greatest care not to overwhelm him. Such brutal opacities of accompaniment as we find in Rossini's Stabat or Verdi's Trovatore, where the strings play a rum-tum accompaniment whilst the entire wind band blares away, fortissimo, in unison with the unfortunate singer, are never to be found in Wagner's work. Even in an ordinary opera house, with the orchestra ranged directly between the singers and the audience, his instrumentation is more transparent to the human voice than that of any other composer since Mozart. At the Bayreuth Buhnenfestspielhaus, with the brass under the stage, it is perfectly so.

On every point, then, a Wagner theatre and Wagner festivals are much more generally practicable than the older and more artificial forms of dramatic music. A presentable performance of The Ring is a big undertaking only in the sense in which the construction of a railway is a big undertaking: that is, it requires plenty of work and plenty of professional skill; but it does not, like the old operas and oratorios, require those extraordinary vocal gifts which only a few individuals scattered here and there throughout Europe are born with. Singers who could never execute the roulades of Semiramis, Assur, and Arsaces in Rossini's Semiramide, could sing the parts of Brynhild, Wotan and Erda without missing a note. Any Englishman can understand this if he considers for a moment the difference between a Cathedral service and an Italian opera at Covent Garden. The service is a much more serious matter than the opera. Yet provincial talent is sufficient for it, if the requisite industry and devotion are forthcoming. Let us admit that geniuses of European celebrity are indispensable at the Opera (though I know better, having seen lusty troopers and porters, without art or manners, accepted by fashion as principal tenors at that institution during the long interval between Mario and Jean de Reszke); but let us remember that Bayreuth has recruited its Parsifals from the peasantry, and that the artisans of a village in the Bavarian Alps are capable of a famous and elaborate Passion Play, and then consider whether England is so poor in talent that its amateurs must journey to the centre of Europe to witness a Wagner Festival.

The truth is, there is nothing wrong with England except the wealth which attracts teachers of singing to her shores in sufficient numbers to extinguish the voices of all natives who have any talent as singers. Our salvation must come from the class that is too poor to have lessons.

THE DARK LADY OF THE SONNETS

PREFACE TO THE
DARK LADY OF THE SONNETS

How the Play came to be Written

I had better explain why, in this little *piece d'occasion*, written for a performance in aid of the funds of the project for establishing a National Theatre as a memorial to Shakespear, I have identified the Dark Lady with Mistress Mary Fitton. First, let me say that I do not contend that the Dark Lady was Mary Fitton, because when the case in Mary's favor (or against her, if you please to consider that the Dark Lady was no better than she ought to have been) was complete, a portrait of Mary came to light and turned out to be that of a fair lady, not of a dark one. That settles the question, if the portrait is authentic, which I see no reason to doubt, and the lady's hair undyed, which is perhaps less certain. Shakespear rubbed in the lady's complexion in his sonnets mercilessly; for in his day black hair was as unpopular as red hair was in the early days of Queen Victoria. Any tinge lighter than raven black must be held fatal to the strongest claim to be the Dark Lady. And so, unless it can be shewn that Shakespear's sonnets exasperated Mary Fitton into dyeing her hair and getting painted in false colors, I must give up all pretence that my play is historical. The later suggestion of Mr Acheson that the Dark Lady, far from being a maid of honor, kept a tavern in Oxford and was the mother of Davenant the poet, is the one I should have adopted had I wished to be up to date. Why, then, did I introduce the Dark Lady as Mistress Fitton?

Well, I had two reasons. The play was not to have been written by me at all, but by Mrs Alfred Lyttelton; and it was she who suggested a scene of jealousy between Queen Elizabeth and the Dark Lady at the expense of the unfortunate Bard. Now this, if the Dark Lady was a maid of honor, was quite easy. If she were a tavern landlady, it would have strained all probability. So I stuck to Mary Fitton. But I had another and more personal reason. I was, in a manner, present at the birth of the Fitton theory. Its parent and I had become acquainted; and he used to consult me on obscure passages in the sonnets, on which, as far as I can remember, I never succeeded in throwing the faintest light, at a time when nobody else thought my opinion, on that or any other subject, of the slightest importance. I thought it would be friendly to immortalize him, as the silly literary saying is, much as Shakespear immortalized Mr W. H., as he said he would, simply by writing about him.

Let me tell the story formally.

THOMAS TYLER

Throughout the eighties at least, and probably for some years before, the British Museum reading room was used daily by a gentleman of such astonishing and crushing ugliness that no one who had once seen him could ever thereafter forget him. He was of fair complexion, rather golden red than sandy; aged between forty-five and sixty; and dressed in frock coat and tall hat of presentable but never new appearance. His figure was rectangular, waistless, neckless, ankleless, of middle height, looking shortish because, though he was not particularly stout, there was nothing slender about him. His ugliness was not unamiable; it was accidental, external, excrescential. Attached to his face from the left ear to the point of his chin was a monstrous goitre, which hung down to his collar bone, and was very inadequately balanced by a smaller one on his right eyelid. Nature's malice was so overdone in his case that it somehow failed to produce the effect of repulsion it seemed to have aimed at. When you first met Thomas Tyler you could think of nothing else but whether surgery could really do nothing for him. But after a very brief acquaintance you never thought of his disfigurements at all, and talked to him as you might to Romeo or Lovelace; only, so many people, especially women, would not risk the preliminary ordeal, that he remained a man apart and a bachelor all his days. I am not to be frightened or prejudiced by a tumor; and I struck up a cordial acquaintance with him, in the course of which he kept me pretty closely on the track of his work at the Museum, in which I was then, like himself, a daily reader.

He was by profession a man of letters of an uncommercial kind. He was a specialist in pessimism; had made a translation of Ecclesiastes of which eight copies a year were sold; and followed up the pessimism of Shakespear and Swift with keen interest. He delighted in a hideous conception which he called the theory of the cycles, according to which the history of mankind and the universe keeps eternally repeating itself without the slightest variation throughout all eternity; so that he had lived and died and had his goitre before and would live and die and have it again and again and again. He liked to believe that nothing that happened to him was completely novel: he was persuaded that he often had some recollection of its previous occurrence in the last cycle. He hunted out allusions to this favorite theory in his three favorite pessimists. He tried his hand occasionally at deciphering ancient inscriptions, reading them as people seem to read the stars, by discovering bears and bulls and swords and goats where, as it seems to me, no sane human being can see anything but stars higgledy-piggledy. Next to the translation of Ecclesiastes, his *magnum opus* was his work on Shakespear's Sonnets, in which he accepted a previous identification of Mr W. H., the "onlie begetter" of the sonnets, with the Earl of Pembroke (William Herbert), and promulgated his own identification of Mistress Mary Fitton with the Dark Lady. Whether he was right or wrong about the Dark Lady did not matter urgently to me: she might have been Maria Tompkins for all I cared. But Tyler would have it that she was Mary Fitton; and he tracked Mary down from the first of her marriages in her teens to her tomb in Cheshire, whither he made a pilgrimage and whence returned in triumph with a picture of her statue, and the news that he was convinced she was a dark lady by traces of paint still discernible.

In due course he published his edition of the Sonnets, with the evidence he had collected. He lent me a copy of the book, which I never returned. But I reviewed it in the Pall Mall Gazette on the 7th of January 1886, and thereby let loose the Fitton theory in a wider circle of readers than the book could reach. Then Tyler died, sinking unnoted like a stone in the sea. I observed that Mr Acheson, Mrs Davenant's champion, calls him Reverend. It may very well be that he got his knowledge of

Hebrew in reading for the Church; and there was always something of the clergyman or the schoolmaster in his dress and air. Possibly he may actually have been ordained. But he never told me that or anything else about his affairs; and his black pessimism would have shot him violently out of any church at present established in the West. We never talked about affairs: we talked about Shakespear, and the Dark Lady, and Swift, and Koheleth, and the cycles, and the mysterious moments when a feeling came over us that this had happened to us before, and about the forgeries of the Pentateuch which were offered for sale to the British Museum, and about literature and things of the spirit generally. He always came to my desk at the Museum and spoke to me about something or other, no doubt finding that people who were keen on this sort of conversation were rather scarce. He remains a vivid spot of memory in the void of my forgetfulness, a quite considerable and dignified soul in a grotesquely disfigured body.

FRANK HARRIS

To the review in the Pall Mall Gazette I attribute, rightly or wrongly, the introduction of Mary Fitton to Mr Frank Harris. My reason for this is that Mr Harris wrote a play about Shakespear and Mary Fitton; and when I, as a pious duty to Tyler's ghost, reminded the world that it was to Tyler we owed the Fitton theory, Frank Harris, who clearly had not a notion of what had first put Mary into his head, believed, I think, that I had invented Tyler expressly for his discomfiture; for the stress I laid on Tyler's claims must have seemed unaccountable and perhaps malicious on the assumption that he was to me a mere name among the thousands of names in the British Museum catalogue. Therefore I make it clear that I had and have personal reasons for remembering Tyler, and for regarding myself as in some sort charged with the duty of reminding the world of his work. I am sorry for his sake that Mary's portrait is fair, and that Mr W. H. has veered round again from Pembroke to Southampton; but even so his work was not wasted: it is by exhausting all the hypotheses that we reach the verifiable one; and after all, the wrong road always leads somewhere.

Frank Harris's play was written long before mine. I read it in manuscript before the Shakespear Memorial National Theatre was mooted; and if there is anything except the Fitton theory (which is Tyler's property) in my play which is also in Mr Harris's it was I who annexed it from him and not he from me. It does not matter anyhow, because this play of mine is a brief trifle, and full of manifest impossibilities at that; whilst Mr Harris's play is serious both in size, intention, and quality. But there could not in the nature of things be much resemblance, because Frank conceives

Shakespear to have been a broken-hearted, melancholy, enormously sentimental person, whereas I am convinced that he was very like myself: in fact, if I had been born in 1556 instead of in 1856, I should have taken to blank verse and given Shakespear a harder run for his money than all the other Elizabethans put together. Yet the success of Frank Harris's book on Shakespear gave me great delight.

To those who know the literary world of London there was a sharp stroke of ironic comedy in the irresistible verdict in its favor. In critical literature there is one prize that is always open to competition, one blue ribbon that always carries the highest critical rank with it. To win, you must write the best book of your generation on Shakespear. It is felt on all sides that to do this a certain fastidious refinement, a delicacy of taste, a correctness of manner and tone, and high academic distinction in addition to the indispensable scholarship and literary reputation, are needed; and men who pretend to these qualifications are constantly looked to with a gentle expectation that presently they will achieve the great feat. Now if there is a man on earth who is the utter contrary of everything that this description implies; whose very existence is an insult to the ideal it realizes; whose eye disparages, whose resonant voice denounces, whose cold shoulder jostles every decency, every delicacy, every amenity, every dignity, every sweet usage of that quiet life of mutual admiration in which perfect Shakespearian appreciation is expected to arise, that man is Frank Harris. Here is one who is extraordinarily qualified, by a range of sympathy and understanding that extends from the ribaldry of a buccaneer to the shyest tendernesses of the most sensitive poetry, to be all things to all men, yet whose proud humor it is to be to every man, provided the man is eminent and pretentious, the champion of his enemies. To the Archbishop he is an atheist, to the atheist a Catholic mystic, to the Bismarckian Imperialist an Anacharsis Klootz, to Anacharsis Klootz a Washington, to Mrs Proudie a Don Juan, to Aspasia a John Knox: in short, to everyone his complement rather than his counterpart, his antagonist rather than his fellow-creature. Always provided, however, that the persons thus confronted are respectable persons. Sophie Perovskaia, who perished on the scaffold for blowing Alexander II to fragments, may perhaps have echoed Hamlet's

> Oh God, Horatio, what a wounded name—
> Things standing thus unknown—I leave behind!

but Frank Harris, in his Sonia, has rescued her from that injustice, and enshrined her among the saints. He has lifted the Chicago anarchists out of their infamy, and shewn that, compared with the Capitalism that killed them, they were heroes and martyrs. He has done this with the most unusual power of conviction. The story, as he tells it, inevitably and irresistibly displaces all the vulgar, mean, purblind, spiteful versions. There is a precise realism and an unsmiling, measured, determined sincerity which gives a strange dignity to the work of one whose fixed practice and ungovernable impulse it is to kick conventional dignity whenever he sees it.

HARRIS "DURCH MITLEID WISSEND"

Frank Harris is everything except a humorist, not, apparently, from stupidity, but because scorn overcomes humor in him. Nobody ever dreamt of reproaching Milton's Lucifer for not seeing the comic side of his fall; and nobody who has read Mr Harris's stories desires to have them lightened by chapters from the hand of Artemus Ward. Yet he knows the taste and the value of humor. He was one of the few men of letters who really appreciated Oscar Wilde, though he did not rally fiercely to Wilde's side until the world deserted Oscar in his ruin. I myself was present at a curious meeting between the two, when Harris, on the eve of the Queensberry trial, prophesied to Wilde with miraculous precision exactly what immediately afterwards happened to him, and warned him to leave the country. It was the first time within my knowledge that such a forecast proved true. Wilde, though under no illusion as to the folly of the quite unselfish suit-at-law he had been persuaded to begin, nevertheless so miscalculated the force of the social vengeance he was unloosing on himself that he fancied it could be stayed by putting up the editor of The Saturday Review (as Mr Harris then was) to declare that he considered Dorian Grey a highly moral book, which it certainly is. When Harris foretold him the truth, Wilde denounced him as a fainthearted friend who was failing him in his hour of need, and left the room in anger. Harris's idiosyncratic power of pity saved him from feeling or shewing the smallest resentment; and events presently proved to Wilde how insanely he had been advised in taking the action, and how accurately Harris had gauged the situation.

The same capacity for pity governs Harris's study of Shakespear, whom, as I have said, he pities too much; but that he is not insensible to humor is shewn not only by his appreciation of Wilde, but by the fact that the group of contributors who made his editorship of The Saturday Review so remarkable, and of whom I speak none the less highly because I happened to be one of them myself, were all, in their various ways, humorists.

"SIDNEY'S SISTER: PEMBROKE'S MOTHER"

And now to return to Shakespear. Though Mr Harris followed Tyler in identifying Mary Fitton as the Dark Lady, and the Earl of Pembroke as the addressee of the other sonnets and the man who made love successfully to Shakespear's mistress, he very characteristically refuses to follow Tyler on one point, though for the life of me I cannot remember whether it was one of the surmises which Tyler published, or only one which he submitted to me to see what I would say about it, just as he used to submit difficult lines from the sonnets.

This surmise was that "Sidney's sister: Pembroke's mother" set Shakespear on to persuade Pembroke to marry, and that this was the explanation of those earlier sonnets which so persistently and unnaturally urged matrimony on Mr W. H. I take this to be one of the brightest of Tyler's ideas, because the persuasions in the sonnets are unaccountable and out of character unless they were offered to please somebody whom Shakespear desired to please, and who took a motherly interest in Pembroke. There is a further temptation in the theory for me. The most charming of all Shakespear's old women, indeed the most charming of all his women, young or old, is the Countess of Rousillon in All's Well That Ends Well. It has a certain individuality among them which suggests a portrait. Mr Harris will have it that all Shakespear's nice old women are drawn from his beloved mother; but I see no evidence whatever that Shakespear's mother was a particularly nice woman or that he was particularly fond of her. That she was a simple incarnation of extravagant maternal pride like the mother of Coriolanus in Plutarch, as Mr Harris

155

asserts, I cannot believe: she is quite as likely to have borne her son a grudge for becoming "one of these harlotry players" and disgracing the Ardens. Anyhow, as a conjectural model for the Countess of Rousillon, I prefer that one of whom Jonson wrote

> Sidney's sister: Pembroke's mother:
> Death: ere thou has slain another,
> Learnd and fair and good as she,
> Time shall throw a dart at thee.

But Frank will not have her at any price, because his ideal Shakespear is rather like a sailor in a melodrama; and a sailor in a melodrama must adore his mother. I do not at all belittle such sailors. They are the emblems of human generosity; but Shakespear was not an emblem: he was a man and the author of Hamlet, who had no illusions about his mother. In weak moments one almost wishes he had.

SHAKESPEAR'S SOCIAL STANDING

On the vexed question of Shakespear's social standing Mr Harris says that Shakespear "had not had the advantage of a middle-class training." I suggest that Shakespear missed this questionable advantage, not because he was socially too low to have attained to it, but because he conceived himself as belonging to the upper class from which our public school boys are now drawn. Let Mr Harris survey for a moment the field of contemporary journalism. He will see there some men who have the very characteristics from which he infers that Shakespear was at a social disadvantage through his lack of middle-class training. They are rowdy, ill-mannered, abusive, mischievous, fond of quoting obscene schoolboy anecdotes, adepts in that sort of blackmail which consists in mercilessly libelling and insulting every writer whose opinions are sufficiently heterodox to make it almost impossible for him to risk perhaps five years of a slender income by an appeal to a prejudiced orthodox jury; and they see nothing in all this cruel blackguardism but an uproariously jolly rag, although they are by no means without genuine literary ability, a love of letters, and even some artistic conscience. But he will find not one of the models of his type (I say nothing of mere imitators of it) below the rank that looks at the middle class, not humbly and enviously from below, but insolently from above. Mr Harris himself notes Shakespear's contempt for the tradesman and mechanic, and his incorrigible addiction to smutty jokes. He does us the public service of sweeping away the familiar plea of the Bardolatrous ignoramus, that Shakespear's coarseness was part of the manners of his time, putting his pen with precision on the one name, Spenser, that is necessary to expose such a libel on Elizabethan decency.

There was nothing whatever to prevent Shakespear from being as decent as More was before him, or Bunyan after him, and as self-respecting as Raleigh or Sidney, except the tradition of his class, in which education or statesmanship may no doubt be acquired by those who have a turn for them, but in which insolence, derision, profligacy, obscene jesting, debt contracting, and rowdy mischievousness, give continual scandal to the pious, serious, industrious, solvent bourgeois. No other class is infatuated enough to believe that gentlemen are born and not made by a very elaborate process of culture. Even kings are taught and coached and drilled from their earliest boyhood to play their part. But the man of family (I am convinced that Shakespear took that view of himself) will plunge into society without a lesson in table manners, into politics without a lesson in history, into the city without a lesson in business, and into the army without a lesson in honor.

It has been said, with the object of proving Shakespear a laborer, that he could hardly write his name. Why? Because he "had not the advantage of a middle-class training." Shakespear himself tells us, through Hamlet, that gentlemen purposely wrote badly lest they should be mistaken for scriveners; but most of them, then as now, wrote badly because they could not write any better. In short, the whole range of Shakespear's foibles: the snobbishness, the naughtiness, the contempt for tradesmen and mechanics, the assumption that witty conversation can only mean smutty conversation, the flunkeyism towards social superiors and insolence towards social inferiors, the easy ways with servants which is seen not only between The Two Gentlemen of Verona and their valets, but in the affection and respect inspired by a great servant like Adam: all these are the characteristics of Eton and Harrow, not of the public elementary or private adventure school. They prove, as everything we know about Shakespear suggests, that he thought of the Shakespears and Ardens as families of consequence, and regarded himself as a gentleman under a cloud through his father's ill luck in business, and never for a moment as a man of the people. This is at once the explanation of and excuse for his snobbery. He was not a parvenu trying to cover his humble origin with a purchased coat of arms: he was a gentleman resuming what he conceived to be his natural position as soon as he gained the means to keep it up.

THIS SIDE IDOLATRY

There is another matter which I think Mr Harris should ponder. He says that Shakespear was but "little esteemed by his own generation." He even describes Jonson's description of his "little Latin and less Greek" as a sneer, whereas it occurs in an unmistakably sincere eulogy of Shakespear, written after his death, and is clearly meant to heighten the impression of Shakespear's prodigious natural endowments by pointing out that they were not due to scholastic acquirements. Now there is a sense in which it is true enough that Shakespear was too little esteemed by his own generation, or, for the matter of that, by any subsequent generation. The bargees on the Regent's Canal do not chant Shakespear's verses as the gondoliers in Venice are said to chant the verses of Tasso (a practice which was suspended for some reason during my stay in Venice: at least no gondolier ever did it in my hearing). Shakespear is no more a popular author than Rodin is a popular sculptor or Richard Strauss a popular composer. But Shakespear was certainly not such a fool as to expect the Toms, Dicks, and Harrys of his time to be any more interested in dramatic poetry than Newton, later on, expected them to be interested in fluxions. And when we come to the question whether Shakespear missed that assurance which all great men have had from the more capable and susceptible members of their generation that they were great men, Ben Jonson's evidence disposes of so improbable a notion at once and for ever. "I loved the man," says Ben, "this side idolatry, as well as any." Now why in the name of common sense should he have made that qualification unless there had been, not only idolatry, but idolatry fulsome enough to irritate Jonson into an express disavowal of it? Jonson, the bricklayer, must have felt sore sometimes when Shakespear spoke and wrote of bricklayers as his inferiors. He must have felt it a little hard that being a better scholar, and perhaps a braver and tougher man physically than Shakespear, he was not so successful or so well liked. But in spite of this he praised Shakespear to the utmost stretch of his powers of eulogy: in fact, notwithstanding his disclaimer, he did not stop "this side idolatry." If, therefore, even Jonson felt himself forced to clear himself of extravagance and absurdity in his appreciation of Shakespear, there must have been many people about who idolized Shakespear as American ladies idolize Paderewski, and who carried Bardolatry, even in the Bard's own time, to an extent that threatened to make his reasonable admirers ridiculous.

SHAKESPEAR'S PESSIMISM

I submit to Mr Harris that by ruling out this idolatry, and its possible effect in making Shakespear think that his public would stand anything from him, he has ruled out a far more plausible explanation of the faults of such a play as Timon of Athens than his theory that Shakespear's passion for the Dark Lady "cankered and took on proud flesh in him, and tortured him to nervous breakdown and madness." In Timon the intellectual bankruptcy is obvious enough: Shakespear tried once too often to make a play out of the cheap pessimism which is thrown into despair by a comparison of actual human nature with theoretical morality, actual law and administration with abstract justice, and so forth. But Shakespear's perception of the fact that all men, judged by the moral standard which they apply to others and by which they justify their punishment of others, are fools and scoundrels, does not date from the Dark Lady complication: he seems to have been born with it. If in The Comedy of Errors and A Midsummer Night's Dream the persons of the drama are not quite so ready for treachery and murder as Laertes and even Hamlet himself (not to mention the procession of ruffians who pass through the latest plays) it is certainly not because they have any more regard for law or religion. There is only one place in Shakespear's plays where the sense of shame is used as a human attribute; and that is where Hamlet is ashamed, not of anything he himself has done, but of his mother's relations with his uncle. This scene is an unnatural one: the son's reproaches to his mother, even the fact of his being able to discuss the subject with her, is more repulsive than her relations with her deceased husband's brother.

Here, too, Shakespear betrays for once his religious sense by making Hamlet, in his agony of shame, declare that his mother's conduct makes "sweet religion a rhapsody of words." But for that passage we might almost suppose that the feeling of Sunday morning in the country which Orlando describes so perfectly in As You Like It was the beginning and end of Shakespear's notion of religion. I say almost, because Isabella in Measure for Measure has religious charm, in spite of the conventional theatrical assumption that female religion means an inhumanly ferocious chastity. But for the most part Shakespear differentiates his heroes from his villains much more by what they do than by what they are. Don John in Much Ado is a true villain: a man with a malicious will; but he is too dull a duffer to be of any use in a leading part; and when we come to the great villains like Macbeth, we find, as Mr Harris points out, that they are precisely identical with the heroes: Macbeth is only Hamlet incongruously committing murders and engaging in hand-to-hand combats. And Hamlet, who does not dream of apologizing for the three murders he commits, is always apologizing because he has not yet committed a fourth, and finds, to his great bewilderment, that he does not want to commit it. "It cannot be," he says, "but I am pigeon-livered, and lack gall to make oppression bitter; else, ere this, I should have fatted all the region kites with this slave's offal." Really one is tempted to suspect that when Shylock asks "Hates any man the thing he would not kill?" he is expressing the natural and proper sentiments of the human race as Shakespear understood them, and not the vindictiveness of a stage Jew.

GAIETY OF GENIUS

In view of these facts, it is dangerous to cite Shakespear's pessimism as evidence of the despair of a heart broken by the Dark Lady. There is an irrepressible gaiety of genius which enables it to bear the whole weight of the world's misery without blenching. There is a laugh always ready to avenge its tears of discouragement. In the lines which Mr Harris quotes only to declare that he can make nothing of them, and to condemn them as out of character, Richard III, immediately after pitying himself because

> There is no creature loves me
> And if I die no soul will pity me,

adds, with a grin,

> Nay, wherefore should they, since that I myself
> Find in myself no pity for myself?

Let me again remind Mr Harris of Oscar Wilde. We all dreaded to read De Profundis: our instinct was to stop our ears, or run away from the wail of a broken, though by no means contrite, heart. But we were throwing away our pity. De Profundis was de profundis indeed: Wilde was too good a dramatist to throw away so powerful an effect; but none the less it was de profundis in excelsis. There was more laughter between the lines of that book than in a thousand farces by men of no genius. Wilde, like Richard and Shakespear, found in himself no pity for himself. There is nothing that marks the born dramatist more unmistakably than this discovery of comedy in his own misfortunes almost in proportion to the pathos with which the ordinary man announces their tragedy. I cannot for the life of me see the broken heart in Shakespear's latest works. "Hark, hark! the lark at heaven's gate sings" is not the lyric of a broken man; nor is Cloten's comment that if Imogen does not appreciate it, "it is a vice in her ears which horse hairs, and cats' guts, and the voice of unpaved eunuch to boot, can never amend," the sally of a saddened one. Is it not clear that to the last there was in Shakespear an incorrigible divine levity, an inexhaustible joy that derided sorrow? Think of the poor Dark Lady having to stand up to this unbearable power of extracting a grim fun from everything. Mr Harris writes as if Shakespear did all the suffering and the Dark Lady all the cruelty. But why does he not put himself in the Dark Lady's place for a moment as he has put himself so successfully in Shakespear's? Imagine her reading the hundred and thirtieth sonnet!

> My mistress' eyes are nothing like the sun;
> Coral is far more red than her lips' red;
> If snow be white, why then her breasts are dun;
> If hairs be wire, black wires grow on her head;
> I have seen roses damasked, red and white,
> But no such roses see I in her cheeks;
> And in some perfumes is there more delight
> Than in the breath that from my mistress reeks.
> I love to hear her speak; yet well I know
> That music hath a far more pleasing sound.
> I grant I never saw a goddess go:
> My mistress, when she walks, treads on the ground.
>> And yet, by heaven, I think my love as rare
>> As any she belied with false compare.

Take this as a sample of the sort of compliment from which she was never for a moment safe with Shakespear. Bear in mind that she was not a comedian; that the Elizabethan fashion of treating brunettes as ugly woman must have made her rather sore on the subject of her complexion; that no human being, male or female, can conceivably enjoy being chaffed on that point in the fourth couplet about the perfumes; that Shakespear's revulsions, as the sonnet immediately preceding shews, were as violent as his ardors, and were expressed with the realistic power and horror that makes Hamlet say that the heavens got sick when they saw the queen's conduct; and then ask Mr Harris whether any woman could have stood it for long, or have thought the "sugred" compliment worth the cruel wounds, the cleaving of the heart in twain, that seemed to Shakespear as natural and amusing a reaction as the burlesquing of his heroics by Pistol, his sermons by Falstaff, and his poems by Cloten and Touchstone.

JUPITER AND SEMELE

This does not mean that Shakespear was cruel: evidently he was not; but it was not cruelty that made Jupiter reduce Semele to ashes: it was the fact that he could not help being a god nor she help being a mortal. The one thing Shakespear's passion for the Dark Lady was not, was what Mr Harris in one passage calls it: idolatrous. If it had been, she might have been able to stand it. The man who "dotes yet doubts, suspects, yet strongly loves," is tolerable even by a spoilt and tyrannical mistress; but what woman could possibly endure a man who dotes without doubting; who *knows*, and who is hugely amused at the absurdity of his infatuation for a woman of whose mortal imperfections not one escapes him: a man always exchanging grins with Yorick's skull, and inviting "my lady" to laugh at the sepulchral humor of the fact that though she paint an inch thick (which the Dark Lady may have done), to Yorick's favor she must come at last. To the Dark Lady he must sometimes have seemed cruel beyond description: an intellectual Caliban. True, a Caliban who could say

Be not afeard: the isle is full of noises
Sounds and sweet airs that give delight and hurt not.
Sometimes a thousand twangling instruments
Will hum about mine ears; and sometimes voices,
That, if I then had waked after long sleep
Will make me sleep again; and then, in dreaming,
The clouds, methought, would open and shew riches
Ready to drop on me: that when I wak'd
I cried to dream again.

which is very lovely; but the Dark Lady may have had that vice in her ears which Cloten dreaded: she may not have seen the beauty of it, whereas there can be no doubt at all that of "My mistress' eyes are nothing like the sun," &c., not a word was lost on her.

And is it to be supposed that Shakespear was too stupid or too modest not to see at last that it was a case of Jupiter and Semele? Shakespear was most certainly not modest in that sense. The timid cough of the minor poet was never heard from him.

> Not marble, nor the gilded monuments
> Of princes, shall outlive this powerful rhyme

is only one out of a dozen passages in which he (possibly with a keen sense of the fun of scandalizing the modest coughers) proclaimed his place and his power in "the wide world dreaming of things to come." The Dark Lady most likely thought this side of him insufferably conceited; for there is no reason to suppose that she liked his plays any better than Minna Wagner liked Richard's music dramas: as likely as not, she thought The Spanish Tragedy worth six Hamlets. He was not stupid either: if his class limitations and a profession that cut him off from actual participation in great affairs of State had not confined his opportunities of intellectual and political training to private conversation and to the Mermaid Tavern, he would probably have become one of the ablest men of his time instead of being merely its ablest playwright. One might surmise that Shakespear found out that the Dark Lady's brains could no more keep pace with his than Anne Hathaway's, if there were any evidence that their friendship ceased when he stopped writing sonnets to her. As a matter of fact the consolidation of a passion into an enduring intimacy generally puts an end to sonnets.

That the Dark Lady broke Shakespear's heart, as Mr Harris will have it she did, is an extremely unShakespearian hypothesis. "Men have died from time to time, and worms have eaten them; but not for love," says

Rosalind. Richard of Gloster, into whom Shakespear put all his own impish superiority to vulgar sentiment, exclaims

> And this word "love," which greybeards call divine,
> Be resident in men like one another
> And not in me: I am myself alone.

Hamlet has not a tear for Ophelia: her death moves him to fierce disgust for the sentimentality of Laertes by her grave; and when he discusses the scene with Horatio immediately after, he utterly forgets her, though he is sorry he forgot himself, and jumps at the proposal of a fencing match to finish the day with. As against this view Mr Harris pleads Romeo, Orsino, and even Antonio; and he does it so penetratingly that he convinces you that Shakespear did betray himself again and again in these characters; but self-betrayal is one thing; and self-portrayal, as in Hamlet and Mercutio, is another. Shakespear never "saw himself," as actors say, in Romeo or Orsino or Antonio. In Mr Harris's own play Shakespear is presented with the most pathetic tenderness. He is tragic, bitter, pitiable, wretched and broken among a robust crowd of Jonsons and Elizabeths; but to me he is not Shakespear because I miss the Shakespearian irony and the Shakespearian gaiety. Take these away and Shakespear is no longer Shakespear: all the bite, the impetus, the strength, the grim delight in his own power of looking terrible facts in the face with a chuckle, is gone; and you have nothing left but that most depressing of all things: a victim. Now who can think of Shakespear as a man with a grievance? Even in that most thoroughgoing and inspired of all Shakespear's loves: his love of music (which Mr Harris has been the first to appreciate at anything like its value), there is a dash of mockery. "Spit in the hole, man; and tune again." "Divine air! Now is his soul ravished. Is it not strange that sheep's guts should hale the souls out of men's bodies?" "An he had been a dog that should have howled thus, they would have hanged him." There is just as much Shakespear here as in the inevitable quotation about the sweet south and the bank of violets.

I lay stress on this irony of Shakespear's, this impish rejoicing in pessimism, this exultation in what breaks the hearts of common men, not only because it is diagnostic of that immense energy of life which we call genius, but because its omission is the one glaring defect in Mr Harris's otherwise extraordinarily penetrating book. Fortunately, it is an omission that does not disable the book as (in my judgment) it disabled the hero of the play, because Mr Harris left himself out of his play, whereas he pervades his book, mordant, deep-voiced, and with an unconquerable style which is the man.

THE IDOL OF THE BARDOLATERS

There is even an advantage in having a book on Shakespear with the Shakespearian irony left out of account. I do not say that the missing chapter should not be added in the next edition: the hiatus is too great: it leaves the reader too uneasy before this touching picture of a writhing worm substituted for the invulnerable giant. But it is none the less probable that in no other way could Mr Harris have got at his man as he has. For, after all, what is the secret of the hopeless failure of the academic Bardolaters to give us a credible or even interesting Shakespear, and the easy triumph of Mr Harris in giving us both? Simply that Mr Harris has assumed that he was dealing with a man, whilst the others have assumed that they were writing about a god, and have therefore rejected every consideration of fact, tradition, or interpretation, that pointed to any human imperfection in their hero. They thus leave themselves with so little material that they are forced to begin by saying that we know very little about Shakespear. As a matter of fact, with the plays and sonnets in our hands, we know much more about Shakespear than we know about Dickens or Thackeray: the only difficulty is that we deliberately suppress it because it proves that Shakespear was not only very unlike the conception of a god current in Clapham, but was not, according to the same reckoning, even a respectable man. The academic view starts with a Shakespear who was not scurrilous; therefore the verses about "lousy Lucy" cannot have been written by him, and the cognate passages in the plays are either strokes of character-drawing or gags interpolated by the actors. This ideal Shakespear was too well behaved to get drunk; therefore the tradition that his death was hastened by a drinking bout with Jonson and Drayton must be rejected, and the remorse of Cassio treated as a thing observed, not experienced: nay, the disgust of Hamlet at the drinking customs of Denmark is taken to establish Shakespear as the superior of Alexander in self-control, and the greatest of teetotallers.

Now this system of inventing your great man to start with, and then rejecting all the materials that do not fit him, with the ridiculous result that you have to declare that there are no materials at all (with your waste-paper basket full of them), ends in leaving Shakespear with a much worse character than he deserves. For though it does not greatly matter whether he wrote the lousy Lucy lines or not, and does not really matter at all whether he got drunk when he made a night of it with Jonson and Drayton, the sonnets raise an unpleasant question which does matter a good deal; and the refusal of the academic Bardolaters to discuss or even mention this question has had the effect of producing a silent verdict against Shakespear. Mr Harris tackles the question openly, and has no difficulty whatever in convincing us that Shakespear was a man of normal constitution sexually, and was not the victim of that most cruel and pitiable of all the freaks of nature: the freak which transposes the normal aim of the affections. Silence on this point means condemnation; and the condemnation has been general throughout the present generation, though it only needed Mr Harris's fearless handling of the matter to sweep away what is nothing but a morbid and very disagreeable modern fashion. There is always some stock accusation brought against eminent persons. When I was a boy every well-known man was accused of beating his wife. Later on, for some unexplained reason, he was accused of psychopathic derangement. And this fashion is retrospective. The cases of Shakespear and Michel Angelo are cited as proving that every genius of the first magnitude was a sufferer; and both here and in Germany there are circles in which such derangement is grotesquely reverenced as part of the stigmata of heroic powers. All of which is gross nonsense. Unfortunately, in Shakespear's case, prudery, which cannot prevent the accusation from being whispered, does prevent the refutation from being shouted. Mr Harris, the deep-voiced, refuses to be silenced. He dismisses with proper contempt the stupidity which places an outrageous construction on Shakespear's apologies in the sonnets for neglecting that "perfect ceremony" of love which consists in returning calls and making protestations and giving presents and paying the trumpery attentions which men of genius always refuse to bother about, and to which touchy people who have no genius attach so much importance. No leader who had not been tampered with by the psychopathic monomaniacs could ever put any construction but the obvious and innocent one on these passages. But the general vocabulary of the sonnets to Pembroke (or whoever "Mr W. H." really was) is so overcharged according to modern ideas that a reply on the general case is necessary.

SHAKESPEAR'S ALLEGED
SYCOPHANCY AND PERVERSION

That reply, which Mr Harris does not hesitate to give, is twofold: first, that Shakespear was, in his attitude towards earls, a sycophant; and, second, that the normality of Shakespear's sexual constitution is only too well attested by the excessive susceptibility to the normal impulse shewn in the whole mass of his writings. This latter is the really conclusive reply. In the case of Michel Angelo, for instance, one must admit that if his works are set beside those of Titian or Paul Veronese, it is impossible not to be struck by the absence in the Florentine of that susceptibility to feminine charm which pervades the pictures of the Venetians. But, as Mr Harris points out (though he does not use this particular illustration) Paul Veronese is an anchorite compared to Shakespear. The language of the sonnets addressed to Pembroke, extravagant as it now seems, is the language of compliment and fashion, transfigured no doubt by Shakespear's verbal magic, and hyperbolical, as Shakespear always seems to people who cannot conceive so vividly as he, but still unmistakable for anything else than the expression of a friendship delicate enough to be wounded, and a manly loyalty deep enough to be outraged. But the language of the sonnets to the Dark Lady is the language of passion: their cruelty shews it. There is no evidence that Shakespear was capable of being unkind in cold blood. But in his revulsions from love, he was bitter, wounding, even ferocious; sparing neither himself nor the unfortunate woman whose only offence was that she had reduced the great man to the common human denominator.

In seizing on these two points Mr Harris has made so sure a stroke, and placed his evidence so featly that there is nothing left for me to do but to plead that the second is sounder than the first, which is, I think, marked by the prevalent mistake as to Shakespear's social position, or, if you prefer it, the confusion between his actual social position as a penniless tradesman's son taking to the theatre for a livelihood, and his own conception of himself as a gentleman of good family. I am prepared to contend that though Shakespear was undoubtedly sentimental in his expressions of devotion to Mr W. H. even to a point which nowadays makes both ridiculous, he was not sycophantic if Mr W. H. was really attractive and promising, and Shakespear deeply attached to him. A sycophant does not tell his patron that his fame will survive, not in the renown of his own actions, but in the sonnets of his sycophant. A sycophant, when his patron cuts him out in a love affair, does not tell his patron exactly what he thinks of him. Above all, a sycophant does not write to his patron precisely as he feels on all occasions; and this rare kind of sincerity is all over the sonnets. Shakespear, we are told, was "a very civil gentleman." This must mean that his desire to please people and be liked by them, and his reluctance to hurt their feelings, led him into amiable flattery even when his feelings were not strongly stirred. If this be taken into account along with the fact that Shakespear conceived and expressed all his emotions with a vehemence that sometimes carried him into ludicrous extravagance, making Richard offer his kingdom for a horse and Othello declare of Cassio that

> Had all his hairs been lives, my great revenge
> Had stomach for them all,

we shall see more civility and hyperbole than sycophancy even in the earlier and more coldblooded sonnets.

SHAKESPEAR AND DEMOCRACY

Now take the general case pled against Shakespear as an enemy of democracy by Tolstoy, the late Ernest Crosbie and others, and endorsed by Mr Harris. Will it really stand fire? Mr Harris emphasizes the passages in which Shakespear spoke of mechanics and even of small master tradesmen as base persons whose clothes were greasy, whose breath was rank, and whose political imbecility and caprice moved Coriolanus to say to the Roman Radical who demanded at least "good words" from him

> He that will give good words to thee will flatter
> Beneath abhorring.

But let us be honest. As political sentiments these lines are an abomination to every democrat. But suppose they are not political sentiments! Suppose they are merely a record of observed fact. John Stuart Mill told our British workmen that they were mostly liars. Carlyle told us all that we are mostly fools. Matthew Arnold and Ruskin were more circumstantial and more abusive. Everybody, including the workers themselves, know that they are dirty, drunken, foul-mouthed, ignorant, gluttonous, prejudiced: in short, heirs to the peculiar ills of poverty and slavery, as well as co-heirs with the plutocracy to all the failings of human nature. Even Shelley admitted, 200 years after Shakespear wrote Coriolanus, that universal suffrage was out of the question. Surely the real test, not of Democracy, which was not a live political issue in Shakespear's time, but of impartiality in judging classes, which is what one demands from a great human poet, is not that he should flatter the poor and denounce the rich, but that he should weigh them both in the same balance. Now whoever will read Lear and Measure for Measure will find stamped on his mind such an appalled sense of the danger of dressing man in a little brief authority, such a merciless stripping of the purple from the "poor, bare, forked animal" that calls itself a king and fancies itself a god, that one wonders what was the real nature of the mysterious restraint that kept "Eliza and our James" from teaching Shakespear to be civil to crowned heads, just as one wonders why Tolstoy was allowed to go free when so many less terrible levellers went to the galleys or Siberia. From the mature Shakespear we get no such scenes of village snobbery as that between the stage country gentleman Alexander Iden and the stage Radical Jack Cade. We get the shepherd in As You Like It, and many honest, brave, human, and loyal servants, beside the inevitable comic ones. Even in the Jingo play, Henry V, we get Bates and Williams drawn with all respect and honor as normal rank and file men. In Julius Caesar, Shakespear went to work with a will when he took his cue from Plutarch in glorifying regicide and transfiguring the republicans. Indeed hero-worshippers have never forgiven him for belittling Caesar and failing to see that side of his assassination which made Goethe denounce it as the most senseless of crimes. Put the play beside the Charles I of Wills, in which Cromwell is written down to a point at which the Jack Cade of Henry VI becomes a hero in comparison; and then believe, if you can, that Shakespear was one of them that "crook the pregnant hinges of the knee where thrift may follow fawning." Think of Rosencrantz, Guildenstern, Osric, the fop who annoyed Hotspur, and a dozen passages concerning such people! If such evidence can prove anything (and Mr Harris relies throughout on such evidence) Shakespear loathed courtiers.

If, on the other hand, Shakespear's characters are mostly members of the leisured classes, the same thing is true of Mr Harris's own plays and mine. Industrial slavery is not compatible with that freedom of adventure, that personal refinement and intellectual culture, that scope of action, which the higher and subtler drama demands.

Even Cervantes had finally to drop Don Quixote's troubles with innkeepers demanding to be paid for his food and lodging, and make him as free of economic difficulties as Amadis de Gaul. Hamlet's experiences simply could not have happened to a plumber. A poor man is useful on the stage only as a blind man is: to excite sympathy. The poverty of the apothecary in Romeo and Juliet produces a great effect, and even points the sound moral that a poor man cannot afford to have a conscience; but if all the characters of the play had been as poor as he, it would have been nothing but a melodrama of the sort that the Sicilian players gave us here; and that was not the best that lay in Shakespear's power. When poverty is abolished, and leisure and grace of life become general, the only plays surviving from our epoch which will have any relation to life as it will be lived then will be those in which none of the persons represented are troubled with want of money or wretched drudgery. Our plays of poverty and squalor, now the only ones that are true to the life of the majority of living men, will then be classed with the records of misers and monsters, and read only by historical students of social pathology.

Then consider Shakespear's kings and lords and gentlemen! Would even John Ball or Jeremiah complain that they are flattered? Surely a more mercilessly exposed string of scoundrels never crossed the stage. The very monarch who paralyzes a rebel by appealing to the divinity that hedges a king, is a drunken and sensual assassin, and is presently killed contemptuously before our eyes in spite of his hedge of divinity. I could write as convincing a chapter on Shakespear's Dickensian prejudice against the throne and the nobility and gentry in general as Mr Harris or Ernest Crosbie on the other side. I could even go so far as to contend that one of Shakespear's defects is his lack of an intelligent comprehension of feudalism. He had of course no prevision of democratic Collectivism. He was, except in the commonplaces of war and patriotism, a privateer through and through. Nobody in his plays, whether king or citizen, has any civil public business or conception of such a thing, except in the method of appointing constables, to the abuses in which he called attention quite in the vein of the Fabian Society. He was concerned about drunkenness and about the idolatry and hypocrisy of our judicial system; but his implied remedy was personal sobriety and freedom from idolatrous illusion in so far as he had any remedy at all, and did not merely despair of human nature. His first and last word on parliament was "Get thee glass eyes, and, like a scurvy politician, seem to see the thing thou dost not." He had no notion of the feeling with which the land nationalizers of today regard the fact that he was a party to the enclosure of common lands at Wellcome. The explanation is, not a general deficiency in his mind, but the simple fact that in his day what English land needed was individual appropriation and cultivation, and what the English Constitution needed was the incorporation of Whig principles of individual liberty.

SHAKESPEAR AND THE BRITISH PUBLIC

I have rejected Mr Harris's view that Shakespear died broken-hearted of "the pangs of love despised." I have given my reasons for believing that Shakespear died game, and indeed in a state of levity which would have been considered unbecoming in a bishop. But Mr Harris's evidence does prove that Shakespear had a grievance and a very serious one. He might have been jilted by ten dark ladies and been none the worse for it; but his treatment by the British Public was another matter. The idolatry which exasperated Ben Jonson was by no means a popular movement; and, like all such idolatries, it was excited by the magic of Shakespear's art rather than by his views.

He was launched on his career as a successful playwright by the Henry VI trilogy, a work of no originality, depth, or subtlety except the originality, depth, and subtlety of the feelings and fancies of the common people. But Shakespear was not satisfied with this. What is the use of being Shakespear if you are not allowed to express any notions but those of Autolycus? Shakespear did not see the world as Autolycus did: he saw it, if not exactly as Ibsen did (for it was not quite the same world), at least with much of Ibsen's power of penetrating its illusions and idolatries, and with all Swift's horror of its cruelty and uncleanliness.

Now it happens to some men with these powers that they are forced to impose their fullest exercise on the world because they cannot produce popular work. Take Wagner and Ibsen for instance! Their earlier works are no doubt much cheaper than their later ones; still, they were not popular when they were written. The alternative of doing popular work was never really open to them: had they stooped they would have picked up less than they snatched from above the people's heads. But Handel and Shakespear were not held to their best in this way. They could turn out anything they were asked for, and even heap up the measure. They reviled the British Public, and never forgave it for ignoring their best work and admiring their splendid commonplaces; but they produced the commonplaces all the same, and made them sound magnificent by mere brute faculty for their art. When Shakespear was forced to write popular plays to save his theatre from ruin, he did it mutinously, calling the plays "As *You* Like It," and "Much Ado About Nothing." All the same, he did it so well that to this day these two genial vulgarities are the main Shakespearian stock-in-trade of our theatres. Later on Burbage's power and popularity as an actor enabled Shakespear to free himself from the tyranny of the box office, and to express himself more freely in plays consisting largely of monologue to be spoken by a great actor from whom the public would stand a good deal. The history of Shakespear's tragedies has thus been the history of a long line of famous actors, from Burbage and Betterton to Forbes Robertson; and the man of whom we are told that "when he would have said that Richard died, and cried A horse! A horse! he Burbage cried" was the father of nine generations of Shakespearian playgoers, all speaking of Garrick's Richard, and Kean's Othello, and Irving's Shylock, and Forbes Robertson's Hamlet without knowing or caring how much these had to do with Shakespear's Richard and Othello and so forth. And the plays which were written without great and predominant parts, such as Troilus and Cressida, All's Well That Ends Well, and Measure for Measure, have dropped on our stage as dead as the second part of Goethe's Faust or Ibsen's Emperor or Galilean.

Here, then, Shakespear had a real grievance; and though it is a sentimental exaggeration to describe him as a broken-hearted man in the face of the passages of reckless jollity and serenely happy poetry in his latest plays, yet the discovery that his most serious work could reach success only when carried on the back of a very fascinating actor who was enormously overcharging his part, and that the serious plays which did not contain parts big enough to hold the overcharge were left on the shelf, amply accounts for the evident fact that Shakespear did not end his life in a glow of enthusiastic satisfaction with mankind and with the theatre, which is all that Mr Harris can allege in support of his broken-heart theory. But even if Shakespear had had no failures, it was not possible for a man of his powers to observe the political and moral conduct of his contemporaries without perceiving that they were incapable of dealing with the problems raised by their own civilization, and that their attempts to carry out the codes of law and to practise the religions offered to them by great prophets and law-givers were and still are so foolish that we now call for The Superman, virtually a new species, to rescue the world from mismanagement. This is the real sorrow of great men; and in the face of it the notion that when a great man speaks bitterly or looks melancholy he must be troubled by a disappointment in love seems to me sentimental trifling.

If I have carried the reader with me thus far, he will find that trivial as this little play of mine is, its sketch of Shakespear is more complete than its levity suggests. Alas! its appeal for a National Theatre as a monument to Shakespear failed to touch the very stupid people who cannot see that a National Theatre is worth having for the sake of the National Soul. I had unfortunately represented Shakespear as treasuring and using (as I do myself) the jewels of unconsciously musical speech which common people utter and throw away every day; and this was taken as a disparagement of Shakespear's "originality." Why was I born with such contemporaries? Why is Shakespear made ridiculous by such a posterity?

The Dark Lady of The Sonnets was first performed at the Haymarket Theatre, on the afternoon of Thursday, the 24th November 1910, by Mona Limerick as the Dark Lady, Suzanne Sheldon as Queen Elizabeth, Granville Barker as Shakespear, and Hugh Tabberer as the Warder.

THE DARK LADY OF THE SONNETS

Fin de siecle 15-1600. Midsummer night on the terrace of the Palace at Whitehall,
overlooking the Thames. The Palace clock chimes four quarters and strikes eleven.
A Beefeater on guard. A Cloaked Man approaches.

THE BEEFEATER. Stand. Who goes there? Give the word.

THE MAN. Marry! I cannot. I have clean forgotten it.

THE BEEFEATER. Then cannot you pass here. What is your business?
Who are you? Are you a true man?

THE MAN. Far from it, Master Warder. I am not the same man two
days together: sometimes Adam, sometimes Benvolio, and anon the
Ghost.

THE BEEFEATER. *[recoiling]* A ghost! Angels and ministers of grace
defend us!

THE MAN. Well said, Master Warder. With your leave I will set that
down in writing; for I have a very poor and unhappy brain for
remembrance. *[He takes out his tablets and writes]*. Methinks this is a
good scene, with you on your lonely watch, and I approaching like
a ghost in the moonlight. Stare not so amazedly at me; but mark
what I say. I keep tryst here to-night with a dark lady. She promised
to bribe the warder. I gave her the wherewithal: four tickets for the
Globe Theatre.

THE BEEFEATER. Plague on her! She gave me two only.

THE MAN. *[detaching a tablet]* My friend: present this tablet, and you will
be welcomed at any time when the plays of Will Shakespear are in

183

hand. Bring your wife. Bring your friends. Bring the whole garrison. There is ever plenty of room.

THE BEEFEATER. I care not for these new-fangled plays. No man can understand a word of them. They are all talk. Will you not give me a pass for The Spanish Tragedy?

THE MAN. To see The Spanish Tragedy one pays, my friend. Here are the means. *[He gives him a piece of gold]*.

THE BEEFEATER. *[overwhelmed]* Gold! Oh, sir, you are a better paymaster than your dark lady.

THE MAN. Women are thrifty, my friend.

THE BEEFEATER. Tis so, sir. And you have to consider that the most open handed of us must een cheapen that which we buy every day. This lady has to make a present to a warder nigh every night of her life.

THE MAN. *[turning pale]* I'll not believe it.

THE BEEFEATER. Now you, sir, I dare be sworn, do not have an adventure like this twice in the year.

THE MAN. Villain: wouldst tell me that my dark lady hath ever done thus before? that she maketh occasions to meet other men?

THE BEEFEATER. Now the Lord bless your innocence, sir, do you think you are the only pretty man in the world? A merry lady, sir: a warm bit of stuff. Go to: I'll not see her pass a deceit on a gentleman that hath given me the first piece of gold I ever handled.

THE MAN. Master Warder: is it not a strange thing that we, knowing that all women are false, should be amazed to find our own particular drab no better than the rest?

THE BEEFEATER. Not all, sir. Decent bodies, many of them.

THE MAN. *[intolerantly]* No. All false. All. If thou deny it, thou liest.

THE BEEFEATER. You judge too much by the Court, sir. There, indeed, you may say of frailty that its name is woman.

THE MAN. *[pulling out his tablets again]* Prithee say that again: that about frailty: the strain of music.

THE BEEFEATER. What strain of music, sir? I'm no musician, God knows.

THE MAN. There is music in your soul: many of your degree have it very notably. *[Writing]* "Frailty: thy name is woman!" *[Repeating it affectionately]* "Thy name is woman."

THE BEEFEATER. Well, sir, it is but four words. Are you a snapper-up of such unconsidered trifles?

THE MAN. *[eagerly]* Snapper-up of—*[he gasps]* Oh! Immortal phrase! *[He writes it down]*. This man is a greater than I.

THE BEEFEATER. You have my lord Pembroke's trick, sir.

THE MAN. Like enough: he is my near friend. But what call you his trick?

THE BEEFEATER. Making sonnets by moonlight. And to the same lady too.

THE MAN. No!

THE BEEFEATER. Last night he stood here on your errand, and in your shoes.

THE MAN. Thou, too, Brutus! And I called him friend!

THE BEEFEATER. Tis ever so, sir.

THE MAN. Tis ever so. Twas ever so. *[He turns away, overcome]*. Two Gentlemen of Verona! Judas! Judas!!

THE BEEFEATER. Is he so bad as that, sir?

THE MAN. *[recovering his charity and self-possession]* Bad? Oh no. Human, Master Warder, human. We call one another names when we are offended, as children do. That is all.

THE BEEFEATER. Ay, sir: words, words, words. Mere wind, sir. We fill our bellies with the east wind, sir, as the Scripture hath it. You cannot feed capons so.

THE MAN. A good cadence. By your leave *[He makes a note of it]*.

THE BEEFEATER. What manner of thing is a cadence, sir? I have not heard of it.

THE MAN. A thing to rule the world with, friend.

THE BEEFEATER. You speak strangely, sir: no offence. But, an't like you, you are a very civil gentleman; and a poor man feels drawn to you, you being, as twere, willing to share your thought with him.

THE MAN. Tis my trade. But alas! the world for the most part will none of my thoughts.

Lamplight streams from the palace door as it opens from within.

THE BEEFEATER. Here comes your lady, sir. I'll to t'other end of my ward. You may een take your time about your business: I shall not return too suddenly unless my sergeant comes prowling round. Tis a fell sergeant, sir: strict in his arrest. Go'd'en, sir; and good luck! *[He goes].*

THE MAN. "Strict in his arrest"! "Fell sergeant"! *[As if tasting a ripe plum]* O-o-o-h! *[He makes a note of them].*

A Cloaked Lady gropes her way from the palace and wanders along the terrace, walking in her sleep.

THE LADY. *[rubbing her hands as if washing them]* Out, damned spot. You will mar all with these cosmetics. God made you one face; and you make yourself another. Think of your grave, woman, not ever of being beautified. All the perfumes of Arabia will not whiten this Tudor hand.

THE MAN. "All the perfumes of Arabia"! "Beautified"! "Beautified"! a poem in a single word. Can this be my Mary? *[To the Lady]* Why do you speak in a strange voice, and utter poetry for the first time? Are you ailing? You walk like the dead. Mary! Mary!

THE LADY. *[echoing him]* Mary! Mary! Who would have thought that woman to have had so much blood in her! Is it my fault that my counsellors put deeds of blood on me? Fie! If you were women you would have more wit than to stain the floor so foully. Hold not up her head so: the hair is false. I tell you yet again, Mary's buried: she cannot come out of her grave. I fear her not: these cats that dare jump into thrones though they be fit only for men's laps must be put away. Whats done cannot be undone. Out, I say. Fie! a queen, and freckled!

THE MAN. *[shaking her arm]* Mary, I say: art asleep?

The Lady wakes; starts; and nearly faints. He catches her on his arm.

THE LADY. Where am I? What art thou?

THE MAN. I cry your mercy. I have mistook your person all this while. Methought you were my Mary: my mistress.

THE LADY. *[outraged]* Profane fellow: how do you dare?

THE MAN. Be not wroth with me, lady. My mistress is a marvellous proper woman. But she does not speak so well as you. "All the perfumes of Arabia"! That was well said: spoken with good accent and excellent discretion.

THE LADY. Have I been in speech with you here?

THE MAN. Why, yes, fair lady. Have you forgot it?

THE LADY. I have walked in my sleep.

THE MAN. Walk ever in your sleep, fair one; for then your words drop like honey.

THE LADY. *[with cold majesty]* Know you to whom you speak, sir, that you dare express yourself so saucily?

THE MAN. *[unabashed]* Not I, not care neither. You are some lady of the Court, belike. To me there are but two sorts of women: those with excellent voices, sweet and low, and cackling hens that cannot make me dream. Your voice has all manner of loveliness in it. Grudge me not a short hour of its music.

THE LADY. Sir: you are overbold. Season your admiration for a while with—

THE MAN. *[holding up his hand to stop her]* "Season your admiration for a while—"

THE LADY. Fellow: do you dare mimic me to my face?

THE MAN. Tis music. Can you not hear? When a good musician sings a song, do you not sing it and sing it again till you have caught and fixed its perfect melody? Season your admiration for a while": God! the history of man's heart is in that one word admiration. Admiration! *[Taking up his tablets]* What was it? "Suspend your admiration for a space—"

THE LADY. A very vile jingle of esses. I said "Season your—"

THE MAN. *[hastily]* Season: ay, season, season, season. Plague on my memory, my wretched memory! I must een write it down. *[He begins to write, but stops, his memory failing him]*. Yet tell me which was the vile jingle? You said very justly: mine own ear caught it even as my false tongue said it.

THE LADY. You said "for a space." I said "for a while."

THE MAN. "For a while" *[he corrects it]*. Good! *[Ardently]* And now be mine neither for a space nor a while, but for ever.

THE LADY. Odds my life! Are you by chance making love to me, knave?

THE MAN. Nay: tis you who have made the love: I but pour it out at your feet. I cannot but love a lass that sets such store by an apt word. Therefore vouchsafe, divine perfection of a woman—no: I have said that before somewhere; and the wordy garment of my love for you must be fire-new—

THE LADY. You talk too much, sir. Let me warn you: I am more accustomed to be listened to than preached at.

THE MAN. The most are like that that do talk well. But though you spake with the tongues of angels, as indeed you do, yet know that I am the king of words—

THE LADY. A king, ha!

THE MAN. No less. We are poor things, we men and women—

THE LADY. Dare you call me woman?

THE MAN. What nobler name can I tender you? How else can I love you? Yet you may well shrink from the name: have I not said we are but poor things? Yet there is a power that can redeem us.

THE LADY. Gramercy for your sermon, sir. I hope I know my duty.

THE MAN. This is no sermon, but the living truth. The power I speak of is the power of immortal poesy. For know that vile as this world is, and worms as we are, you have but to invest all this vileness with a magical garment of words to transfigure us and uplift our souls til earth flowers into a million heavens.

THE LADY. You spoil your heaven with your million. You are extravagant. Observe some measure in your speech.

THE MAN. You speak now as Ben does.

THE LADY. And who, pray, is Ben?

THE MAN. A learned bricklayer who thinks that the sky is at the top of his ladder, and so takes it on him to rebuke me for flying. I tell you there is no word yet coined and no melody yet sung that is extravagant and majestical enough for the glory that lovely words can reveal. It is heresy to deny it: have you not been taught that in the beginning was the Word? that the Word was with God? nay, that the Word was God?

THE LADY. Beware, fellow, how you presume to speak of holy things. The Queen is the head of the Church.

THE MAN. You are the head of my Church when you speak as you did at first. "All the perfumes of Arabia"! Can the Queen speak thus? They say she playeth well upon the virginals. Let her play so to me; and I'll kiss her hands. But until then, you are my Queen; and I'll kiss those lips that have dropt music on my heart. *[He puts his arms about her]*.

THE LADY. Unmeasured impudence! On your life, take your hands from me.

The Dark Lady comes stooping along the terrace behind them like a running thrush. When she sees how they are employed, she rises angrily to her full height, and listens jealously.

THE MAN. *[unaware of the Dark Lady]* Then cease to make my hands tremble with the streams of life you pour through them. You hold me as the lodestar holds the iron: I cannot but cling to you. We are lost, you and I: nothing can separate us now.

THE DARK LADY. We shall see that, false lying hound, you and your filthy trull. *[With two vigorous cuffs, she knocks the pair asunder, sending the man, who is unlucky enough to receive a righthanded blow, sprawling an the flags]*. Take that, both of you!

THE CLOAKED LADY. *[in towering wrath, throwing off her cloak and turning in outraged majesty on her assailant]* High treason!

THE DARK LADY. *[recognizing her and falling on her knees in abject terror]* Will: I am lost: I have struck the Queen.

THE MAN. *[sitting up as majestically as his ignominious posture allows]* Woman: you have struck WILLIAM SHAKESPEAR.

QUEEN ELIZABETH. *[stupent]* Marry, come up!!! Struck William Shakespear quotha! And who in the name of all the sluts and jades and light-o'-loves and fly-by-nights that infest this palace of mine, may William Shakespear be?

THE DARK LADY. Madam: he is but a player. Oh, I could have my hand cut off—

QUEEN ELIZABETH. Belike you will, mistress. Have you bethought you that I am like to have your head cut off as well?

THE DARK LADY. Will: save me. Oh, save me.

ELIZABETH. Save you! A likely savior, on my royal word! I had thought this fellow at least an esquire; for I had hoped that even the vilest of my ladies would not have dishonored my Court by wantoning with a baseborn servant.

SHAKESPEAR. *[indignantly scrambling to his feet]* Base-born! I, a Shakespear of Stratford! I, whose mother was an Arden! baseborn! You forget yourself, madam.

ELIZABETH. *[furious]* S'blood! do I so? I will teach you—

THE DARK LADY. *[rising from her knees and throwing herself between them]* Will: in God's name anger her no further. It is death. Madam: do not listen to him.

SHAKESPEAR. Not were it een to save your life, Mary, not to mention mine own, will I flatter a monarch who forgets what is due to my family. I deny not that my father was brought down to be a poor bankrupt; but twas his gentle blood that was ever too generous for trade. Never did he disown his debts. Tis true he paid them not; but it is an attested truth that he gave bills for them; and twas those bills, in the hands of base hucksters, that were his undoing.

ELIZABETH. [grimly] The son of your father shall learn his place in the presence of the daughter of Harry the Eighth.

SHAKESPEAR. [swelling with intolerant importance] Name not that inordinate man in the same breath with Stratford's worthiest alderman. John Shakespear wedded but once: Harry Tudor was married six times. You should blush to utter his name.

THE DARK LADY.	Will: for pity's sake—	*crying out*
		together
ELIZABETH.	Insolent dog—	

SHAKESPEAR. [cutting them short] How know you that King Harry was indeed your father?

ELIZABETH.	Zounds! Now by—
	[she stops to grind her teeth with rage].
THE DARK LADY.	She will have me whipped through the streets. Oh God! Oh God!

SHAKESPEAR. Learn to know yourself better, madam. I am an honest gentleman of unquestioned parentage, and have already sent in my demand for the coat-of-arms that is lawfully mine. Can you say as much for yourself?

ELIZABETH. [almost beside herself] Another word; and I begin with mine own hands the work the hangman shall finish.

SHAKESPEAR. You are no true Tudor: this baggage here has as good a right to your royal seat as you. What maintains you on the throne of England? Is it your renowned wit? your wisdom that sets at naught the craftiest statesmen of the Christian world? No. Tis the mere chance that might have happened to any milkmaid, the caprice of Nature that made you the most wondrous piece of beauty the age hath seen. *[Elizabeth's raised fists, on the point of striking him, fall to her side]*. That is what hath brought all men to your feet, and founded your throne on the impregnable rock of your proud heart, a stony island in a sea of desire. There, madam, is some wholesome blunt honest speaking for you. Now do your worst.

ELIZABETH. *[with dignity]* Master Shakespear: it is well for you that I am a merciful prince. I make allowance for your rustic ignorance. But remember that there are things which be true, and are yet not seemly to be said (I will not say to a queen; for you will have it that I am none) but to a virgin.

SHAKESPEAR. *[bluntly]* It is no fault of mine that you are a virgin, madam, albeit tis my misfortune.

THE DARK LADY. *[terrified again]* In mercy, madam, hold no further discourse with him. He hath ever some lewd jest on his tongue. You hear how he useth me! calling me baggage and the like to your Majesty's face.

ELIZABETH. As for you, mistress, I have yet to demand what your business is at this hour in this place, and how you come to be so concerned with a player that you strike blindly at your sovereign in your jealousy of him.

THE DARK LADY. Madam: as I live and hope for salvation—

SHAKESPEAR. *[sardonically]* Ha!

THE DARK LADY. *[angrily]*—ay, I'm as like to be saved as thou that believest naught save some black magic of words and verses—I say, madam, as I am a living woman I came here to break with him for ever. Oh, madam, if you would know what misery is, listen to this man that is more than man and less at the same time. He will tie you down to anatomize your very soul: he will wring tears of blood from your humiliation; and then he will heal the wound with flatteries that no woman can resist.

SHAKESPEAR. Flatteries! *[Kneeling]* Oh, madam, I put my case at your royal feet. I confess to much. I have a rude tongue: I am unmannerly: I blaspheme against the holiness of anointed royalty; but oh, my royal mistress, AM I a flatterer?

ELIZABETH. I absolve you as to that. You are far too plain a dealer to please me. *[He rises gratefully]*.

THE DARK LADY. Madam: he is flattering you even as he speaks.

ELIZABETH. *[a terrible flash in her eye]* Ha! Is it so?

SHAKESPEAR. Madam: she is jealous; and, heaven help me! not without reason. Oh, you say you are a merciful prince; but that was cruel of you, that hiding of your royal dignity when you found me here. For how can I ever be content with this black-haired, black-eyed, black-avised devil again now that I have looked upon real beauty and real majesty?

THE DARK LADY. *[wounded and desperate]* He hath swore to me ten times over that the day shall come in England when black women, for all their foulness, shall be more thought on than fair ones. *[To Shakespear, scolding at him]* Deny it if thou canst. Oh, he is compact of lies and scorns. I am tired of being tossed up to heaven and dragged down to hell at every whim that takes him. I am ashamed to my very soul that I have abased myself to love one that my father would not have deemed fit to hold my stirrup—one that will talk to all the world about me—that will put my love and my shame into his plays and make me blush for myself there—that will write sonnets about me that no man of gentle strain would put his hand to. I am all disordered: I know not what I am saying to your Majesty: I am of all ladies most deject and wretched—

SHAKESPEAR. Ha! At last sorrow hath struck a note of music out of thee. "Of all ladies most deject and wretched." *[He makes a note of it]*.

THE DARK LADY. Madam: I implore you give me leave to go. I am distracted with grief and shame. I—

ELIZABETH. Go *[The Dark Lady tries to kiss her hand]*. No more. Go. *[The Dark Lady goes, convulsed]*. You have been cruel to that poor fond wretch, Master Shakespear.

SHAKESPEAR. I am not truel, madam; but you know the fable of Jupiter and Semele. I could not help my lightnings scorching her.

ELIZABETH. You have an overweening conceit of yourself, sir, that displeases your Queen.

SHAKESPEAR. Oh, madam, can I go about with the modest cough of a minor poet, belittling my inspiration and making the mightiest wonder of your reign a thing of nought? I have said that "not marble nor the gilded monuments of princes shall outlive" the words with which I make the world glorious or foolish at my will. Besides, I would have you think me great enough to grant me a boon.

ELIZABETH. I hope it is a boon that may be asked of a virgin Queen without offence, sir. I mistrust your forwardness; and I bid you remember that I do not suffer persons of your degree (if I may say so without offence to your father the alderman) to presume too far.

SHAKESPEAR. Oh, madam, I shall not forget myself again; though by my life, could I make you a serving wench, neither a queen nor a virgin should you be for so much longer as a flash of lightning might take to cross the river to the Bankside. But since you are a queen and will none of me, nor of Philip of Spain, nor of any other mortal man, I must een contain myself as best I may, and ask you only for a boon of State.

ELIZABETH. A boon of State already! You are becoming a courtier like the rest of them. You lack advancement.

SHAKESPEAR. "Lack advancement." By your Majesty's leave: a queenly phrase. *[He is about to write it down]*.

ELIZABETH. *[striking the tablets from his hand]* Your tables begin to anger me, sir. I am not here to write your plays for you.

SHAKESPEAR. You are here to inspire them, madam. For this, among the rest, were you ordained. But the boon I crave is that you do endow a great playhouse, or, if I may make bold to coin a scholarly name for it, a National Theatre, for the better instruction and gracing of your Majesty's subjects.

ELIZABETH. Why, sir, are there not theatres enow on the Bankside and in Blackfriars?

SHAKESPEAR. Madam: these are the adventures of needy and desperate men that must, to save themselves from perishing of want, give the sillier sort of people what they best like; and what they best like, God knows, is not their own betterment and instruction, as we well see by the example of the churches, which must needs compel men to frequent them, though they be open to all without charge. Only when there is a matter of a murder, or a plot, or a pretty youth in petticoats, or some naughty tale of wantonness, will your subjects pay the great cost of good players and their finery, with a little profit to boot. To prove this I will tell you that I have written two noble and excellent plays setting forth the advancement of women of high nature and fruitful industry even as your Majesty is: the one a skilful physician, the other a sister devoted to good works. I have also stole from a book of idle wanton tales two of the most damnable foolishnesses in the world, in the one of which a woman goeth in man's attire and maketh impudent love to her swain, who pleaseth the groundlings by overthrowing a wrestler; whilst, in the other, one of the same kidney sheweth her wit by saying endless naughtinesses to a gentleman as lewd as herself. I have writ these to save my friends from penury, yet shewing my scorn for such follies and for them that praise them by calling the one As You Like It, meaning that it is not as *I* like it, and the other Much Ado About Nothing, as it truly is. And now these two filthy pieces drive their nobler fellows from the stage, where indeed I cannot have my lady physician presented at all, she being too honest a woman for the taste of the town. Wherefore I humbly beg your Majesty to give order that a theatre be endowed out of the public revenue for the playing of those pieces of mine which no merchant will touch, seeing that his gain is so much greater with the worse than with the better. Thereby you shall also encourage other men to undertake the writing of plays who do now despise it and leave it wholly to those whose counsels will work little good to your realm. For this writing of plays is a great matter, forming as it does the minds and affections of men in such sort that whatsoever they see done in show on the stage, they will presently be doing in earnest in the world, which is but a larger stage. Of late, as you know, the Church taught the people by means of plays; but the people flocked only to such as were full of superstitious miracles and bloody martyrdoms; and so the Church, which also was just then brought into straits by the policy of your royal father, did abandon and discountenance the art of playing; and thus it fell into the hands of poor players and greedy merchants that had their pockets to look to and not the greatness of this your kingdom. Therefore now must your Majesty take up that good work that your Church hath abandoned, and restore the art of playing to its former use and dignity.

ELIZABETH. Master Shakespear: I will speak of this matter to the Lord Treasurer.

SHAKESPEAR. Then am I undone, madam; for there was never yet a Lord Treasurer that could find a penny for anything over and above the necessary expenses of your government, save for a war or a salary for his own nephew.

ELIZABETH. Master Shakespear: you speak sooth; yet cannot I in any wise mend it. I dare not offend my unruly Puritans by making so lewd a place as the playhouse a public charge; and there be a thousand things to be done in this London of mine before your poetry can have its penny from the general purse. I tell thee, Master Will, it will be three hundred years and more before my subjects learn that man cannot live by bread alone, but by every word that cometh from the mouth of those whom God inspires. By that time you and I will be dust beneath the feet of the horses, if indeed there be any horses then, and men be still riding instead of flying. Now it may be that by then your works will be dust also.

SHAKESPEAR. They will stand, madam: fear nor for that.

ELIZABETH. It may prove so. But of this I am certain (for I know my countrymen) that until every other country in the Christian world, even to barbarian Muscovy and the hamlets of the boorish Germans, have its playhouse at the public charge, England will never adventure. And she will adventure then only because it is her desire to be ever in the fashion, and to do humbly and dutifully whatso she seeth everybody else doing. In the meantime you must content yourself as best you can by the playing of those two pieces which you give out as the most damnable ever writ, but which your countrymen, I warn you, will swear are the best you have ever done. But this I will say, that if I could speak across the ages to our descendants, I should heartily recommend them to fulfil your wish; for the Scottish minstrel hath well said that he that maketh the songs of a nation is mightier than he that maketh its laws; and the same may well be true of plays and interludes. *[The clock chimes the first quarter. The warder returns on his round]*. And now, sir, we are upon the hour when it better beseems a virgin queen to be abed than to converse alone with the naughtiest of her subjects. Ho there! Who keeps ward on the queen's lodgings tonight?

THE WARDER. I do, an't please your majesty.

ELIZABETH. See that you keep it better in future. You have let pass a most dangerous gallant even to the very door of our royal chamber.

Lead him forth; and bring me word when he is safely locked out; for I shall scarce dare disrobe until the palace gates are between us.

SHAKESPEAR. *[kissing her hand]* My body goes through the gate into the darkness, madam; but my thoughts follow you.

ELIZABETH. How! to my bed!

SHAKESPEAR. No, madam, to your prayers, in which I beg you to remember my theatre.

ELIZABETH. That is my prayer to posterity. Forget not your own to God; and so goodnight, Master Will.

SHAKESPEAR. Goodnight, great Elizabeth. God save the Queen!

ELIZABETH. Amen.

Exeunt severally: she to her chamber: he, in custody of the warder, to the gate nearest Blackfriars.

AYOT, ST. LAWRENCE, *20th June* 1910.

MRS WARREN'S PROFESSION

With The Author's Apology (1902)

THE AUTHOR'S APOLOGY

Mrs Warren's Profession has been performed at last, after a delay of only eight years; and I have once more shared with Ibsen the triumphant amusement of startling all but the strongest-headed of the London theatre critics clean out of the practice of their profession. No author who has ever known the exultation of sending the Press into an hysterical tumult of protest, of moral panic, of involuntary and frantic confession of sin, of a horror of conscience in which the power of distinguishing between the work of art on the stage and the real life of the spectator is confused and overwhelmed, will ever care for the stereotyped compliments which every successful farce or melodrama elicits from the newspapers. Give me that critic who rushed from my play to declare furiously that Sir George Crofts ought to be kicked. What a triumph for the actor, thus to reduce a jaded London journalist to the condition of the simple sailor in the Wapping gallery, who shouts execrations at Iago and warnings to Othello not to believe him! But dearer still than such simplicity is that sense of the sudden earthquake shock to the foundations of morality which sends a pallid crowd of critics into the street shrieking that the pillars of society are cracking and the ruin of the State is at hand. Even the Ibsen champions of ten years ago remonstrate with me just as the veterans of those brave days remonstrated with them. Mr Grein, the hardy iconoclast who first launched my plays on the stage alongside Ghosts and The Wild Duck, exclaimed that I have shattered his ideals. Actually his ideals! What would Dr Relling say? And Mr William Archer himself disowns me because I "cannot touch pitch without wallowing in it". Truly my play must be more needed than I knew; and yet I thought I knew how little the others know.

Do not suppose, however, that the consternation of the Press reflects any consternation among the general public. Anybody can upset the theatre critics, in a turn of the wrist, by substituting for the romantic commonplaces of the stage the moral commonplaces of the pulpit, platform, or the library. Play Mrs Warren's Profession to an audience of clerical members of the Christian Social Union and of women well experienced in Rescue, Temperance, and Girls' Club work, and no moral panic will arise; every man and woman present will know that as long as poverty makes virtue hideous and the spare pocket-money of rich bachelordom makes vice dazzling, their daily hand-to-hand fight against prostitution with prayer and persuasion, shelters and scanty alms, will be a losing one. There was a time when they were able to urge that though "the white-lead factory where Anne Jane was poisoned" may be a far more terrible place than Mrs Warren's house, yet hell is still more dreadful. Nowadays they no longer believe in hell; and the girls among whom they are working know that they do not believe in it, and would laugh at them if they did. So well have the rescuers learnt that Mrs Warren's defence of herself and indictment of society is the thing that most needs saying, that those who know me personally reproach me, not for writing this play, but for wasting my energies on "pleasant plays" for the amusement of frivolous people, when I can build up such excellent stage sermons on their own work. Mrs Warren's Profession is the one play of mine which I could submit to a censorship without doubt of the result; only, it must not be the censorship of the minor theatre critic, nor of an innocent court official like the Lord Chamberlain's Examiner, much less of people who consciously profit by Mrs Warren's profession, or who personally make use of it, or who hold the widely whispered view that it is an indispensable safety-valve for the protection of domestic virtue, or, above all, who are smitten with a sentimental affection for our fallen sister, and would "take her up tenderly, lift her with care, fashioned so slenderly, young, and SO fair." Nor am I prepared to accept the verdict of the medical gentlemen who would compulsorily sanitate and register Mrs Warren, whilst leaving

Mrs Warren's patrons, especially her military patrons, free to destroy her health and anybody else's without fear of reprisals. But I should be quite content to have my play judged by, say, a joint committee of the Central Vigilance Society and the Salvation Army. And the sterner moralists the members of the committee were, the better.

Some of the journalists I have shocked reason so unripely that they will gather nothing from this but a confused notion that I am accusing the National Vigilance Association and the Salvation Army of complicity in my own scandalous immorality. It will seem to them that people who would stand this play would stand anything. They are quite mistaken. Such an audience as I have described would be revolted by many of our fashionable plays. They would leave the theatre convinced that the Plymouth Brother who still regards the playhouse as one of the gates of hell is perhaps the safest adviser on the subject of which he knows so little. If I do not draw the same conclusion, it is not because I am one of those who claim that art is exempt from moral obligations, and deny that the writing or performance of a play is a moral act, to be treated on exactly the same footing as theft or murder if it produces equally mischievous consequences. I am convinced that fine art is the subtlest, the most seductive, the most effective instrument of moral propaganda in the world, excepting only the example of personal conduct; and I waive even this exception in favor of the art of the stage, because it works by exhibiting examples of personal conduct made intelligible and moving to crowds of unobservant, unreflecting people to whom real life means nothing. I have pointed out again and again that the influence of the theatre in England is growing so great that whilst private conduct, religion, law, science, politics, and morals are becoming more and more theatrical, the theatre itself remains impervious to common sense, religion, science, politics, and morals. That is why I fight the theatre, not with pamphlets and sermons and treatises, but with plays; and so effective do I find the dramatic method that I have no doubt I shall at last persuade even London to take its conscience and its brains with it when it goes to the theatre, instead of leaving them at home with its prayer-book as it does at present. Consequently, I am the last man in the world to deny that if the net effect of performing Mrs Warren's Profession were an increase in the number of persons entering that profession, its performance should be dealt with accordingly.

Now let us consider how such recruiting can be encouraged by the theatre. Nothing is easier. Let the King's Reader of Plays, backed by the Press, make an unwritten but perfectly well understood regulation that members of Mrs Warren's profession shall be tolerated on the stage only when they are beautiful, exquisitely dressed, and sumptuously lodged and fed; also that they shall, at the end of the play, die of consumption to the sympathetic tears of the whole audience, or step into the next room to commit suicide, or at least be turned out by their protectors and passed on to be "redeemed" by old and faithful lovers who have adored them in spite of their levities. Naturally, the poorer girls in the gallery will believe in the beauty, in the exquisite dresses, and the luxurious living, and will see that there is no real necessity for the consumption, the suicide, or the ejectment: mere pious forms, all of them, to save the Censor's face. Even if these purely official catastrophes carried any conviction, the majority of English girls remain so poor, so dependent, so well aware that the drudgeries of such honest work as is within their reach are likely enough to lead them eventually to lung disease, premature death, and domestic desertion or brutality, that they would still see reason to prefer the primrose path to the strait path of virtue, since both, vice at worst and virtue at best, lead to the same end in poverty and overwork. It is true that the Board School mistress will tell you that only girls of a certain kind will reason in this way. But alas! that certain kind turns out on inquiry to be simply the pretty, dainty kind: that is, the only kind that gets the chance of acting on such reasoning. Read the first report of the Commission on the Housing of the Working Classes [Bluebook C 4402, 8d., 1889]; read the Report on Home Industries (sacred word, Home!) issued by the Women's Industrial Council [Home Industries of Women in London,

1897, 1s., 12 Buckingham Street, W. C.]; and ask yourself whether, if the lot in life therein described were your lot in life, you would not prefer the lot of Cleopatra, of Theodora, of the Lady of the Camellias, of Mrs Tanqueray, of Zaza, of Iris. If you can go deep enough into things to be able to say no, how many ignorant half-starved girls will believe you are speaking sincerely? To them the lot of Iris is heavenly in comparison with their own. Yet our King, like his predecessors, says to the dramatist, "Thus, and thus only, shall you present Mrs Warren's profession on the stage, or you shall starve. Witness Shaw, who told the untempting truth about it, and whom We, by the Grace of God, accordingly disallow and suppress, and do what in Us lies to silence." Fortunately, Shaw cannot be silenced. "The harlot's cry from street to street" is louder than the voices of all the kings. I am not dependent on the theatre, and cannot be starved into making my play a standing advertisement of the attractive side of Mrs Warren's business.

Here I must guard myself against a misunderstanding. It is not the fault of their authors that the long string of wanton's tragedies, from Antony and Cleopatra to Iris, are snares to poor girls, and are objected to on that account by many earnest men and women who consider Mrs Warren's Profession an excellent sermon. Mr Pinero is in no way bound to suppress the fact that his Iris is a person to be envied by millions of better women. If he made his play false to life by inventing fictitious disadvantages for her, he would be acting as unscrupulously as any tract writer. If society chooses to provide for its Irises better than for its working women, it must not expect honest playwrights to manufacture spurious evidence to save its credit. The mischief lies in the deliberate suppression of the other side of the case: the refusal to allow Mrs Warren to expose the drudgery and repulsiveness of plying for hire among coarse, tedious drunkards; the determination not to let the Parisian girl in Brieux's Les Avaries come on the stage and drive into people's minds what her diseases mean for her and for themselves. All that, says the King's Reader in effect, is horrifying, loathsome.

Precisely: what does he expect it to be? would he have us represent it as beautiful and gratifying? The answer to this question, I fear, must be a blunt Yes; for it seems impossible to root out of an Englishman's mind the notion that vice is delightful, and that abstention from it is privation. At all events, as long as the tempting side of it is kept towards the public, and softened by plenty of sentiment and sympathy, it is welcomed by our Censor, whereas the slightest attempt to place it in the light of the policeman's lantern or the Salvation Army shelter is checkmated at once as not merely disgusting, but, if you please, unnecessary.

Everybody will, I hope, admit that this state of things is intolerable; that the subject of Mrs Warren's profession must be either tapu altogether, or else exhibited with the warning side as freely displayed as the tempting side. But many persons will vote for a complete tapu, and an impartial sweep from the boards of Mrs Warren and Gretchen and the rest; in short, for banishing the sexual instincts from the stage altogether. Those who think this impossible can hardly have considered the number and importance of the subjects which are actually banished from the stage. Many plays, among them Lear, Hamlet, Macbeth, Coriolanus, Julius Caesar, have no sex complications: the thread of their action can be followed by children who could not understand a single scene of Mrs Warren's Profession or Iris. None of our plays rouse the sympathy of the audience by an exhibition of the pains of maternity, as Chinese plays constantly do. Each nation has its own particular set of tapus in addition to the common human stock; and though each of these tapus limits the scope of the dramatist, it does not make drama impossible. If the Examiner were to refuse to license plays with female characters in them, he would only be doing to the stage what our tribal customs already do to the pulpit and the bar. I have myself written a rather entertaining play with only one woman in it, and she is quite heartwhole; and I could just as easily write a play without a woman in it at all. I will even go so far as to promise the Mr Redford my support if he will introduce this limitation for part of the year, say during Lent, so as to make a close season for that dullest of stock dramatic subjects, adultery, and force our managers and authors to find out what all great dramatists find out spontaneously: to wit, that people who sacrifice every other consideration to love are as hopelessly unheroic on the stage as lunatics or dipsomaniacs. Hector is the world's hero; not Paris nor Antony.

But though I do not question the possibility of a drama in which love should be as effectively ignored as cholera is at present, there is not the slightest chance of that way out of the difficulty being taken by the Mr Redford. If he attempted it there would be a revolt in which he would be swept away in spite of my singlehanded efforts to defend him. A complete tapu is politically impossible. A complete toleration is equally impossible to Mr Redford, because his occupation would be gone if there were no tapu to enforce. He is therefore compelled to maintain the present compromise of a partial tapu, applied, to the best of his judgement, with a careful respect to persons and to public opinion. And a very sensible English solution of the difficulty, too, most readers will say. I should not dispute it if dramatic poets really were what English public opinion generally assumes them to be during their lifetime: that is, a licentiously irregular group to be kept in order in a rough and ready way by a magistrate who will stand no nonsense from them. But I cannot admit that the class represented by Eschylus, Sophocles, Aristophanes, Euripides, Shakespear, Goethe, Ibsen, and Tolstoy, not to mention our own contemporary playwrights, is as much in place in Mr Redford's office as a pickpocket is in Bow Street. Further, it is not true that the Censorship, though it certainly suppresses Ibsen and Tolstoy, and would suppress Shakespear but for the absurd rule that a play once licensed is always licensed (so that Wycherly is permitted and Shelley prohibited), also suppresses unscrupulous playwrights. I challenge Mr Redford to mention any extremity of sexual misconduct which any manager in his senses would risk presenting on the London stage that has not been presented under his license and that of his predecessor. The compromise, in fact, works out in practice in favor of loose plays as against earnest ones.

To carry conviction on this point, I will take the extreme course of narrating the plots of two plays witnessed within the last ten years by myself at London West End theatres, one licensed by the late Queen Victoria's Reader of Plays, the other by the present Reader to the King. Both plots conform to the strictest rules of the period when La Dame aux Camellias was still a forbidden play, and when The Second Mrs Tanqueray would have been tolerated only on condition that she carefully explained to the audience that when she met Captain Ardale she sinned "but in intention."

Play number one. A prince is compelled by his parents to marry the daughter of a neighboring king, but loves another maiden. The scene represents a hall in the king's palace at night. The wedding has taken place that day; and the closed door of the nuptial chamber is in view of the audience. Inside, the princess awaits her bridegroom. A duenna is in attendance. The bridegroom enters. His sole desire is to escape from a marriage which is hateful to him. An idea strikes him. He will assault the duenna, and get ignominiously expelled from the palace by his indignant father-in-law. To his horror, when he proceeds to carry out this stratagem, the duenna, far from raising an alarm, is flattered, delighted, and compliant. The assaulter becomes the assaulted. He flings her angrily to the ground, where she remains placidly. He flies. The father enters; dismisses the duenna; and listens at the keyhole of his daughter's nuptial chamber, uttering various pleasantries, and declaring, with a shiver, that a sound of kissing, which he supposes to proceed from within, makes him feel young again.

In deprecation of the scandalized astonishment with which such a story as this will be read, I can only say that it was not presented on the stage until its propriety had been certified by the chief officer of the Queen of England's household.

Story number two. A German officer finds himself in an inn with a French lady who has wounded his national vanity. He resolves to humble her by committing a rape upon her. He announces his purpose. She remonstrates, implores, flies to the doors and finds them locked, calls for help and finds none at hand, runs screaming from side to side, and, after a harrowing scene, is overpowered and faints. Nothing further being possible on the stage without actual felony, the officer then relents and leaves her. When she recovers, she believes that he has carried out his threat; and during the rest of the play she is represented as vainly vowing vengeance upon him, whilst she is really falling in love with him under the influence of his imaginary crime against her. Finally she consents to marry him; and the curtain falls on their happiness.

This story was certified by the present King's Reader, acting for the Lord Chamberlain, as void in its general tendency of "anything immoral or otherwise improper for the stage." But let nobody conclude therefore that Mr Redford is a monster, whose policy it is to deprave the theatre. As a matter of fact, both the above stories are strictly in order from the official point of view. The incidents of sex which they contain, though carried in both to the extreme point at which another step would be dealt with, not by the King's Reader, but by the police, do not involve adultery, nor any allusion to Mrs Warren's profession, nor to the fact that the children of any polyandrous group will, when they grow up, inevitably be confronted, as those of Mrs Warren's group are in my play, with the insoluble problem of their own possible consanguinity. In short, by depending wholly on the coarse humors and the physical fascination of sex, they comply with all the formulable requirements of the Censorship, whereas plays in which these humors and fascinations are discarded, and the social problems created by sex seriously faced and dealt with, inevitably ignore the official formula and are suppressed. If the old rule against the exhibition of illicit sex relations on stage were revived, and the subject absolutely barred, the only result would be that Antony and Cleopatra, Othello (because of the Bianca episode), Troilus and Cressida, Henry IV, Measure for Measure, Timon of Athens, La Dame aux Camellias, The Profligate, The Second Mrs Tanqueray, The Notorious Mrs Ebbsmith, The Gay Lord Quex, Mrs Dane's Defence, and Iris would be swept from the stage, and placed under the same ban as Tolstoy's Dominion of Darkness and Mrs Warren's Profession, whilst such plays as the two described above would have a monopoly of the theatre as far as sexual interest is concerned.

What is more, the repulsiveness of the worst of the certified plays would protect the Censorship against effective exposure and criticism. Not long ago an American Review of high standing asked me for an article on the Censorship of the English stage. I replied that such an article would involve passages too disagreeable for publication in a magazine for general family reading. The editor persisted nevertheless; but not until he had declared his readiness to face this, and had pledged himself to insert the article unaltered (the particularity of the pledge extending even to a specification of the exact number of words in the article) did I consent to the proposal. What was the result?

The editor, confronted with the two stories given above, threw his pledge to the winds, and, instead of returning the article, printed it with the illustrative examples omitted, and nothing left but the argument from political principles against the Censorship. In doing this he fired my broadside after withdrawing the cannon balls; for neither the Censor nor any other Englishman, except perhaps Mr Leslie Stephen and a few other veterans of the dwindling old guard of Benthamism, cares a dump about political principle. The ordinary Briton thinks that if every other Briton is not kept under some form of tutelage, the more childish the better, he will abuse his freedom viciously. As far as its principle is concerned, the Censorship is the most popular institution in England; and the playwright who criticizes it is slighted as a blackguard agitating for impunity. Consequently nothing can really shake the confidence of the public in the Lord Chamberlain's department except a remorseless and unbowdlerized narration of the licentious fictions which slip through its net, and are hallmarked by it with the approval of the Throne. But since these narrations cannot be made public without great difficulty, owing to the obligation an editor is under not to deal unexpectedly with matters that are not *virginibus puerisque*, the chances are heavily in favor of the Censor escaping all remonstrance. With the exception of such comments as I was able to make in my own critical articles in The World and The Saturday Review when the pieces I have described were first produced, and a few ignorant protests by churchmen against much better plays which they confessed they had not seen nor read, nothing has been said in the press that could seriously disturb the easygoing notion that the stage would be much worse than it admittedly is but for the vigilance of the King's Reader. The truth is, that no manager would dare produce on his own responsibility the pieces he can now get royal certificates for at two guineas per piece.

I hasten to add that I believe these evils to be inherent in the nature of all censorship, and not merely a consequence of the form the institution takes in London. No doubt there is a staggering absurdity in appointing an ordinary clerk to see that the leaders of European literature do not corrupt the morals of the nation, and to restrain Sir Henry Irving, as a rogue and a vagabond, from presuming to impersonate Samson or David on the stage, though any other sort of artist may daub these scriptural figures on a signboard or carve them on a tombstone without hindrance. If the General Medical Council, the Royal College of Physicians, the Royal Academy of Arts, the Incorporated Law Society, and Convocation were abolished, and their functions handed over to the Mr Redford, the Concert of Europe would presumably declare England mad, and treat her accordingly. Yet, though neither medicine nor painting nor law nor the Church moulds the character of the nation as potently as the theatre does, nothing can come on the stage unless its dimensions admit of its passing through Mr Redford's mind! Pray do not think that I question Mr Redford's honesty. I am quite sure that he sincerely thinks me a blackguard, and my play a grossly improper one, because, like Tolstoy's Dominion of Darkness, it produces, as they are both meant to produce, a very strong and very painful impression of evil. I do not doubt for a moment that the rapine play which I have described, and which he licensed, was quite incapable in manuscript of producing any particular effect on his mind at all, and that when he was once satisfied that the ill-conducted hero was a German and not an English officer, he passed the play without studying its moral tendencies. Even if he had undertaken that study, there is no more reason to suppose that he is a competent moralist than there is to suppose that I am a competent mathematician. But truly it does not matter whether he is a moralist or not. Let nobody dream for a moment that what is wrong with the Censorship is the shortcoming of the gentleman who happens at any moment to be acting as Censor. Replace him to-morrow by an Academy of Letters and an Academy of Dramatic Poetry, and the new and enlarged filter will still exclude original and epoch-making work, whilst passing conventional, old-fashioned, and vulgar work without question. The conclave which compiles the index of the Roman Catholic Church is the most august, ancient, learned, famous, and authoritative censorship in Europe. Is it more enlightened, more liberal, more tolerant that the comparatively infinitesimal office of the Lord Chamberlain? On the contrary, it has reduced itself to a degree of absurdity which makes a Catholic university a contradiction in terms. All censorships exist to prevent anyone from challenging current conceptions and existing institutions. All progress is initiated by challenging current concepts, and executed by supplanting existing institutions. Consequently the first condition of progress is the removal of censorships. There is the whole case against censorships in a nutshell.

It will be asked whether theatrical managers are to be allowed to produce what they like, without regard to the public interest. But that is not the alternative. The managers of our London music-halls are not subject to any censorship. They produce their entertainments on their own responsibility, and have no two-guinea certificates to plead if their houses are conducted viciously. They know that if they lose their character, the County Council will simply refuse to renew their license at the end of the year; and nothing in the history of popular art is more amazing than the improvement in music-halls that this simple arrangement has produced within a few years. Place the theatres on the same footing, and we shall promptly have a similar revolution: a whole class of frankly blackguardly plays, in which unscrupulous low comedians attract crowds to gaze at bevies of girls who have nothing to exhibit but their prettiness, will vanish like the obscene songs which were supposed to enliven the squalid dulness, incredible to the younger generation, of the music-halls fifteen years ago. On the other hand, plays which treat sex questions as problems for thought instead of as aphrodisiacs will be freely performed. Gentlemen of Mr Redford's way of thinking will have plenty of opportunity of protesting against them in Council; but the result will be that the Mr Redford will find his natural level; Ibsen and Tolstoy theirs; so no harm will be done.

This question of the Censorship reminds me that I have to apologize to those who went to the recent performance of Mrs Warren's Profession expecting to find it what I have just called an aphrodisiac. That was not my fault; it was Mr Redford's. After the specimens I have given of the tolerance of his department, it was natural enough for thoughtless people to infer that a play which overstepped his indulgence must be a very exciting play indeed. Accordingly, I find one critic so explicit as to the nature of his disappointment as to say candidly that "such airy talk as there is upon the matter is utterly unworthy of acceptance as being a representation of what people with blood in them think or do on such occasions." Thus am I crushed between the upper millstone of the Mr Redford, who thinks me a libertine, and the nether popular critic, who thinks me a prude. Critics of all grades and ages, middle-aged fathers of families no less than ardent young enthusiasts, are equally indignant with me. They revile me as lacking in passion, in feeling, in manhood. Some of them even sum the matter up by denying me any dramatic power: a melancholy betrayal of what dramatic power has come to mean on our stage under the Censorship! Can I be expected to refrain from laughing at the spectacle of a number of respectable gentlemen lamenting because a playwright lures them to the theatre by a promise to excite their senses in a very special and sensational manner, and then, having successfully trapped them in exceptional numbers, proceeds to ignore their senses and ruthlessly improve their minds? But I protest again that the lure was not mine. The play had been in print for four years; and I have spared no pains to make known that my plays are built to induce, not voluptuous reverie but intellectual interest, not romantic rhapsody but humane concern. Accordingly, I do not find those critics who are gifted with intellectual appetite and political conscience complaining of want of dramatic power. Rather do they protest, not altogether unjustly, against a few relapses into staginess and caricature which betray the young playwright and the old playgoer in this early work of mine.

As to the voluptuaries, I can assure them that the playwright, whether he be myself or another, will always disappoint them. The drama can do little to delight the senses: all the apparent instances to the contrary are instances of the personal fascination of the performers. The drama of pure feeling is no longer in the hands of the playwright: it has been conquered by the musician, after whose enchantments all the verbal arts seem cold and tame. Romeo and Juliet with the loveliest Juliet is dry, tedious, and rhetorical in comparison with Wagner's Tristan, even though Isolde be both fourteen stone and forty, as she often is in Germany. Indeed, it needed no Wagner to convince the public of this. The voluptuous sentimentality of Gounod's Faust and Bizet's Carmen has captured the common playgoer; and there is, flatly, no future now for any drama without music except the drama of thought. The attempt to produce a genus of opera without music (and this absurdity is what our fashionable theatres have been driving at for a long time without knowing it) is far less hopeful than my own determination to accept problem as the normal materiel of the drama.

That this determination will throw me into a long conflict with our theatre critics, and with the few playgoers who go to the theatre as often as the critics, I well know; but I am too well equipped for the strife to be deterred by it, or to bear malice towards the losing side. In trying to produce the sensuous effects of opera, the fashionable drama has become so flaccid in its sentimentality, and the intellect of its frequenters so atrophied by disuse, that the reintroduction of problem, with its remorseless logic and iron framework of fact, inevitably produces at first an overwhelming impression of coldness and inhuman rationalism. But this will soon pass away. When the intellectual muscle and moral nerve of the critics has been developed in the struggle with modern problem plays, the pettish luxuriousness of the clever ones, and the sulky sense of disadvantaged weakness in the sentimental ones, will clear away; and it will be seen that only in the problem play is there any real drama, because drama is no mere setting up of the camera to nature: it is the presentation in parable of the conflict between Man's will and his environment: in a word, of problem. The vapidness of such drama as the pseudo-operatic plays contain lies in the fact that in them animal passion, sentimentally diluted, is shewn in conflict, not with real circumstances, but with a set of conventions and assumptions half of which do not exist off the stage, whilst the other half can either be evaded by a pretence of compliance or defied with complete impunity by any reasonably strong-minded person. Nobody can feel that such conventions are really compulsory; and consequently nobody can believe in the stage pathos that accepts them as an inexorable fate, or in the genuineness of the people who indulge in such pathos. Sitting at such plays, we do not believe: we make-believe. And the habit of make-believe becomes at last so rooted that criticism of the theatre insensibly ceases to be criticism at all, and becomes more and more a chronicle of the fashionable enterprises of the only realities left on the stage: that is, the performers in their own persons. In this phase the playwright who attempts to revive genuine drama produces the disagreeable impression of the pedant who attempts to start a serious discussion at a fashionable at-home. Later on, when he has driven the tea services out and made the people who had come to use the theatre as a drawing-room understand that it is they and not the dramatist who are the intruders, he has to face the accusation that his plays ignore human

215

feeling, an illusion produced by that very resistance of fact and law to human feeling which creates drama. It is the *deus ex machina* who, by suspending that resistance, makes the fall of the curtain an immediate necessity, since drama ends exactly where resistance ends. Yet the introduction of this resistance produces so strong an impression of heartlessness nowadays that a distinguished critic has summed up the impression made on him by Mrs Warren's Profession, by declaring that "the difference between the spirit of Tolstoy and the spirit of Mr Shaw is the difference between the spirit of Christ and the spirit of Euclid." But the epigram would be as good if Tolstoy's name were put in place of mine and D'Annunzio's in place of Tolstoy. At the same time I accept the enormous compliment to my reasoning powers with sincere complacency; and I promise my flatterer that when he is sufficiently accustomed to and therefore undazzled by problem on the stage to be able to attend to the familiar factor of humanity in it as well as to the unfamiliar one of a real environment, he will both see and feel that Mrs Warren's Profession is no mere theorem, but a play of instincts and temperaments in conflict with each other and with a flinty social problem that never yields an inch to mere sentiment.

I go further than this. I declare that the real secret of the cynicism and inhumanity of which shallower critics accuse me is the unexpectedness with which my characters behave like human beings, instead of conforming to the romantic logic of the stage. The axioms and postulates of that dreary mimanthropometry are so well known that it is almost impossible for its slaves to write tolerable last acts to their plays, so conventionally do their conclusions follow from their premises. Because I have thrown this logic ruthlessly overboard, I am accused of ignoring, not stage logic, but, of all things, human feeling. People with completely theatrified imaginations tell me that no girl would treat her mother as Vivie Warren does, meaning that no stage heroine would in a popular sentimental play. They say this just as they might say that no two straight lines would enclose a space. They do not see how completely inverted their vision has become even when I throw its preposterousness in their faces, as I repeatedly do in this very play. Praed, the sentimental artist (fool that I was not to make him a theatre critic instead of an architect!) burlesques them by expecting all through the piece that the feelings of others will be logically deducible from their family relationships and from his "conventionally unconventional" social code. The sarcasm is lost on the critics: they, saturated with the same logic, only think him the sole sensible person on the stage. Thus it comes about that the more completely the dramatist is emancipated from the illusion that men and women are primarily reasonable beings, and the more powerfully he insists on the ruthless indifference of their great dramatic antagonist, the external world, to their whims and emotions, the surer he is to be denounced as blind to the very distinction on which his whole work is built. Far from ignoring idiosyncrasy, will, passion, impulse, whim, as factors in human action, I have placed them so nakedly on the stage that the elderly citizen, accustomed to see them clothed with the veil of manufactured logic about duty, and to disguise even his own impulses from himself in this way, finds the picture as unnatural as Carlyle's suggested painting of parliament sitting without its clothes.

I now come to those critics who, intellectually baffled by the problem in Mrs Warren's Profession, have made a virtue of running away from it. I will illustrate their method by quotation from Dickens, taken from the fifth chapter of Our Mutual Friend:

"Hem!" began Wegg. "This, Mr Boffin and Lady, is the first chapter of the first wollume of the Decline and Fall off—" here he looked hard at the book, and stopped.

"What's the matter, Wegg?"

"Why, it comes into my mind, do you know, sir," said Wegg with an air of insinuating frankness (having first again looked hard at the book), "that you made a little mistake this morning, which I had meant to set you right in; only something put it out of my head. I think you said Rooshan Empire, sir?"

"It is Rooshan; ain't it, Wegg?"

"No, sir. Roman. Roman."

"What's the difference, Wegg?"

"The difference, sir?" Mr Wegg was faltering and in danger of breaking down, when a bright thought flashed upon him. "The difference, sir? There you place me in a difficulty, Mr Boffin. Suffice it to observe, that the difference is best postponed to some other occasion when Mrs Boffin does not honor us with her company. In Mrs Boffin's presence, sir, we had better drop it."

Mr Wegg thus came out of his disadvantage with quite a chivalrous air, and not only that, but by dint of repeating with a manly delicacy, "In Mrs Boffin's presence, sir, we had better drop it!" turned the disadvantage on Boffin, who felt that he had committed himself in a very painful manner.

I am willing to let Mr Wegg drop it on these terms, provided I am allowed to mention here that Mrs Warren's Profession is a play for women; that it was written for women; that it has been performed and produced mainly through the determination of women that it should be performed and produced; that the enthusiasm of women made its first performance excitingly successful; and that not one of these women had any inducement to support it except their belief in the timeliness and the power of the lesson the play teaches. Those who were "surprised to see ladies present" were men; and when they proceeded to explain that the journals they represented could not possibly demoralize the public by describing such a play, their editors cruelly devoted the space saved by their delicacy to an elaborate and respectful account of the progress of a young lord's attempt to break the bank at Monte Carlo. A few days sooner Mrs Warren would have been crowded out of their papers by an exceptionally abominable police case. I do not suggest that the police case should have been suppressed; but neither do I believe that regard for public morality had anything to do with their failure to grapple with the performance by the Stage Society. And, after all, there was no need to fall back on Silas Wegg's subterfuge. Several critics saved the faces of their papers easily enough by the simple expedient of saying all they had

218

to say in the tone of a shocked governess lecturing a naughty child. To them I might plead, in Mrs Warren's words, "Well, it's only good manners to be ashamed, dearie;" but it surprises me, recollecting as I do the effect produced by Miss Fanny Brough's delivery of that line, that gentlemen who shivered like violets in a zephyr as it swept through them, should so completely miss the full width of its application as to go home and straightway make a public exhibition of mock modesty.

My old Independent Theatre manager, Mr Grein, besides that reproach to me for shattering his ideals, complains that Mrs Warren is not wicked enough, and names several romancers who would have clothed her black soul with all the terrors of tragedy. I have no doubt they would; but if you please, my dear Grein, that is just what I did not want to do. Nothing would please our sanctimonious British public more than to throw the whole guilt of Mrs Warren's profession on Mrs Warren herself. Now the whole aim of my play is to throw that guilt on the British public itself. You may remember that when you produced my first play, Widowers' Houses, exactly the same misunderstanding arose. When the virtuous young gentleman rose up in wrath against the slum landlord, the slum landlord very effectively shewed him that slums are the product, not of individual Harpagons, but of the indifference of virtuous young gentlemen to the condition of the city they live in, provided they live at the west end of it on money earned by someone else's labor. The notion that prostitution is created by the wickedness of Mrs Warren is as silly as the notion—prevalent, nevertheless, to some extent in Temperance circles—that drunkenness is created by the wickedness of the publican. Mrs Warren is not a whit a worse woman than the reputable daughter who cannot endure her. Her indifference to the ultimate social consequences of her means of making money, and her discovery of that means by the ordinary method of taking the line of least resistance to getting it, are too common in English society to call for any special remark. Her vitality, her thrift, her energy, her outspokenness, her wise care of her daughter, and the managing capacity which has enabled her and her sister to climb from the fried fish shop down by the Mint to the establishments of which she boasts, are all high English social virtues. Her defence of herself is so overwhelming that it provokes the St James Gazette to declare that "the tendency of the play is wholly evil" because "it contains one of the boldest and most specious defences of an immoral life for poor women that has ever been penned." Happily the St James Gazette here speaks in its haste. Mrs Warren's defence of herself is not only bold and specious, but valid and unanswerable. But it is no defence at all of the vice which she organizes. It is no defence of an immoral life to say that the alternative offered by society collectively to poor women is a miserable life, starved, overworked, fetid, ailing, ugly. Though it is quite natural and RIGHT for Mrs Warren to choose what is, according to her lights, the least immoral alternative, it is none the less infamous of society to offer such alternatives. For the alternatives offered are not morality and immorality, but two sorts of immorality. The man who cannot see that starvation, overwork, dirt, and disease are as anti-social as prostitution—that they are the vices and crimes of a nation, and not merely its misfortunes—is (to put it as politely as possible) a hopelessly Private Person.

The notion that Mrs Warren must be a fiend is only an example of the violence and passion which the slightest reference to sex arouses in undisciplined minds, and which makes it seem natural for our lawgivers to punish silly and negligible indecencies with a ferocity unknown in dealing with, for example, ruinous financial swindling. Had my play been titled Mr Warren's Profession, and Mr Warren been a bookmaker, nobody would have expected me to make him a villain as well. Yet gambling is a vice, and bookmaking an institution, for which there is absolutely nothing to be said. The moral and economic evil done by trying to get other people's money without working for it (and this is the essence of gambling) is not only enormous but uncompensated. There are no two sides to the question of gambling, no circumstances which force us to tolerate it lest its suppression lead to worse things, no consensus of opinion among responsible classes, such as magistrates and military commanders, that it is a necessity, no Athenian records of gambling made splendid by the talents of its professors, no contention that instead of violating morals it only violates a legal institution which is in many respects oppressive and unnatural, no possible plea that the instinct on which it is founded is a vital one. Prostitution can confuse the issue with all these excuses: gambling has none of them. Consequently, if Mrs Warren must needs be a demon, a bookmaker must be a cacodemon. Well, does anybody who knows the sporting world really believe that bookmakers are worse than their neighbors? On the contrary, they have to be a good deal better; for in that world nearly everybody whose social rank does not exclude such an occupation would be a bookmaker if he could; but the strength of character for handling large sums of money and for strict settlements and unflinching payment of losses is so rare that successful bookmakers are rare too. It may seem that at least public spirit cannot be one of a bookmaker's virtues; but I can testify from personal experience that excellent public work is done with money subscribed by bookmakers. It is true that there are abysses in bookmaking: for example, welshing. Mr Grein hints that there are abysses in Mrs Warren's profession also. So there are in every profession: the error lies in supposing that every member of them sounds these depths. I sit on a public body which prosecutes Mrs Warren zealously; and I can assure Mr Grein that she is often leniently dealt with because she has conducted her business "respectably" and held herself above its vilest branches. The degrees in infamy are as numerous and as scrupulously observed as the degrees in the peerage: the moralist's notion that there are depths at which the moral atmosphere ceases is as delusive as the rich man's notion that there are no social jealousies or snobberies among the very poor. No: had I drawn Mrs Warren as a fiend in human form, the very people who now rebuke me for flattering her would probably be the first to deride me for deducing her character logically from occupation instead of observing it accurately in society.

One critic is so enslaved by this sort of logic that he calls my portraiture of the Reverend Samuel Gardner an attack on religion.

According to this view Subaltern Iago is an attack on the army, Sir John Falstaff an attack on knighthood, and King Claudius an attack on royalty. Here again the clamor for naturalness and human feeling, raised by so many critics when they are confronted by the real thing on the stage, is really a clamor for the most mechanical and superficial sort of logic. The dramatic reason for making the clergyman what Mrs Warren calls "an old stick-in-the-mud," whose son, in spite of much capacity and charm, is a cynically worthless member of society, is to set up a mordant contrast between him and the woman of infamous profession, with her well brought-up, straightforward, hardworking daughter. The critics who have missed the contrast have doubtless observed often enough that many clergymen are in the Church through no genuine calling, but simply because, in circles which can command preferment, it is the refuge of "the fool of the family"; and that clergymen's sons are often conspicuous reactionists against the restraints imposed on them in childhood by their father's profession. These critics must know, too, from history if not from experience, that women as unscrupulous as Mrs Warren have distinguished themselves as administrators and rulers, both commercially and politically. But both observation and knowledge are left behind when journalists go to the theatre. Once in their stalls, they assume that it is "natural" for clergymen to be saintly, for soldiers to be heroic, for lawyers to be hard-hearted, for sailors to be simple and generous, for doctors to perform miracles with little bottles, and for Mrs Warren to be a beast and a demon. All this is not only not natural, but not dramatic. A man's profession only enters into the drama of his life when it comes into conflict with his nature. The result of this conflict is tragic in Mrs Warren's case, and comic in the clergyman's case (at least we are savage enough to laugh at it); but in both cases it is illogical, and in both cases natural. I repeat, the critics who accuse me of sacrificing nature to logic are so sophisticated by their profession that to them logic is nature, and nature absurdity.

Many friendly critics are too little skilled in social questions and moral discussions to be able to conceive that respectable gentlemen like themselves, who would instantly call the police to remove Mrs Warren if she ventured to canvass them personally, could possibly be in any way responsible for her proceedings. They remonstrate sincerely, asking me what good such painful exposures can possibly do. They might as well ask what good Lord Shaftesbury did by devoting his life to the exposure of evils (by no means yet remedied) compared to which the worst things brought into view or even into surmise by this play are trifles. The good of mentioning them is that you make people so extremely uncomfortable about them that they finally stop blaming "human nature" for them, and begin to support measures for their reform.

Can anything be more absurd than the copy of The Echo which contains a notice of the performance of my play? It is edited by a gentleman who, having devoted his life to work of the Shaftesbury type, exposes social evils and clamors for their reform in every column except one; and that one is occupied by the declaration of the paper's kindly theatre critic, that the performance left him "wondering what useful purpose the play was intended to serve." The balance has to be redressed by the more fashionable papers, which usually combine capable art criticism with West-End solecism on politics and sociology. It is very noteworthy, however, on comparing the press explosion produced by Mrs Warren's Profession in 1902 with that produced by Widowers' Houses about ten years earlier, that whereas in 1892 the facts were frantically denied and the persons of the drama flouted as monsters of wickedness, in 1902 the facts are admitted and the characters recognized, though it is suggested that this is exactly why no gentleman should mention them in public. Only one writer has ventured to imply this time that the poverty mentioned by Mrs Warren has since been quietly relieved, and need not have been dragged back to the footlights. I compliment him on his splendid mendacity, in which he is unsupported, save by a little plea in a theatrical paper which is innocent enough to think that ten guineas a year with board and lodging is an impossibly low wage for a barmaid. It goes on to cite Mr Charles Booth as having testified that there are many laborers' wives who are happy and contented on eighteen shillings a week. But I can go further than that myself. I have seen an Oxford agricultural laborer's wife looking cheerful on eight shillings a week; but that does not console me for the fact that agriculture in England is a ruined industry. If poverty does not matter as long as it is contented, then crime does not matter as long as it is unscrupulous. The truth is that it is only then that it does matter most desperately. Many persons are more comfortable when they are dirty than when they are clean; but that does not recommend dirt as a national policy.

Here I must for the present break off my arduous work of educating the Press. We shall resume our studies later on; but just now I am tired of playing the preceptor; and the eager thirst of my pupils for improvement does not console me for the slowness of their progress. Besides, I must reserve space to gratify my own vanity and do justice to the six artists who acted my play, by placing on record the hitherto unchronicled success of the first representation. It is not often that an author, after a couple of hours of those rare alternations of excitement and intensely attentive silence which only occur in the theatre when actors and audience are reacting on one another to the utmost, is able to step on the stage and apply the strong word genius to the representation with the certainty of eliciting an instant and overwhelming assent from the audience. That was my good fortune on the afternoon of Sunday, the fifth of January last. I was certainly extremely fortunate in my interpreters in the enterprise, and that not alone in respect of their artistic talent; for had it not been for their superhuman patience, their imperturbable good humor and good fellowship, there could have been no performance. The terror of the Censor's power gave us trouble enough to break up any ordinary commercial enterprise. Managers promised and even engaged their theatres to us after the most explicit warnings that the play was unlicensed, and at the last moment suddenly realized that Mr Redford had their livelihoods in the hollow of his hand, and backed out. Over and over again the date and place were fixed and the tickets printed, only to be canceled, until at last the desperate and overworked manager of the Stage Society could only laugh, as criminals broken on the wheel used to laugh at the second stroke. We rehearsed under great difficulties. Christmas pieces and plays for the new year were being produced in all directions; and my six actor colleagues were busy people, with engagements in these pieces in addition to their current professional work every night. On several raw winter days stages for rehearsal were unattainable even by the most distinguished applicants; and we shared corridors and saloons with them whilst the stage was given over to children in training for Boxing night. At last we had to rehearse at an hour at which no actor or actress has been out of bed within the memory of man; and we sardonically congratulated one another every morning on our rosy matutinal looks and the improvement wrought by our early rising in our health and characters. And all this, please observe, for a society without treasury or commercial prestige, for a play which was being denounced in advance as unmentionable, for an author without influence at the fashionable theatres! I victoriously challenge the West End managers to get as much done for interested motives, if they can.

Three causes made the production the most notable that has fallen to my lot. First, the veto of the Censor, which put the supporters of the play on their mettle. Second, the chivalry of the Stage Society, which, in spite of my urgent advice to the contrary, and my demonstration of the difficulties, dangers, and expenses the enterprise would cost, put my discouragements to shame and resolved to give battle at all costs to the attempt of the Censorship to suppress the play. Third, the artistic spirit of the actors, who made the play their own and carried it through triumphantly in spite of a series of disappointments and annoyances much more trying to the dramatic temperament than mere difficulties.

The acting, too, required courage and character as well as skill and intelligence. The veto of the Censor introduced quite a novel element of moral responsibility into the undertaking. And the characters were very unusual on the English stage. The younger heroine is, like her mother, an Englishwoman to the backbone, and not, like the heroines of our fashionable drama, a prima donna of Italian origin. Consequently she was sure to be denounced as unnatural and undramatic by the critics. The most vicious man in the play is not in the least a stage villain; indeed, he regards his own moral character with the sincere complacency of a hero of melodrama. The amiable devotee of romance and beauty is shewn at an age which brings out the futilization which these worships are apt to produce if they are made the staple of life instead of the sauce. The attitude of the clever young people to their elders is faithfully represented as one of pitiless ridicule and unsympathetic criticism, and forms a spectacle incredible to those who, when young, were not cleverer than their nearest elders, and painful to those sentimental parents who shrink from the cruelty of youth, which pardons nothing because it knows nothing. In short, the characters and their relations are of a kind that the routineer critic has not yet learned to place; so that their misunderstanding was a foregone conclusion. Nevertheless, there was no hesitation behind the curtain. When it went up at last, a stage much too small for the company was revealed to an auditorium much too small for the audience. But the players, though it was impossible for them to forget their own discomfort, at once made the spectators forget theirs. It certainly was a model audience, responsive from the first line to the last; and it got no less than it deserved in return.

I grieve to add that the second performance, given for the edification of the London Press and of those members of the Stage Society who cannot attend the Sunday performances, was a less inspiriting one than the first. A solid phalanx of theatre-weary journalists in an afternoon humor, most of them committed to irreconcilable disparagement of problem plays, and all of them bound by etiquette to be as undemonstrative as possible, is not exactly the sort of audience that rises at the performers and cures them of the inevitable reaction after an excitingly successful first night. The artist nature is a sensitive and therefore a vindictive one; and masterful players have a way with recalcitrant audiences of rubbing a play into them instead of delighting them with it. I should describe the second performance of Mrs Warren's Profession, especially as to its earlier stages, as decidedly a rubbed-in one. The rubbing was no doubt salutary; but it must have hurt some of the thinner skins. The charm of the lighter passages fled; and the strong scenes, though they again carried everything before them, yet discharged that duty in a grim fashion, doing execution on the enemy rather than moving them to repentance and confession. Still, to those who had not seen the first performance, the effect was sufficiently impressive; and they had the advantage of witnessing a fresh development in Mrs Warren, who, artistically jealous, as I took it, of the overwhelming effect of the end of the second act on the previous day, threw herself into the fourth act in quite a new way, and achieved the apparently impossible feat of surpassing herself. The compliments paid to Miss Fanny Brough by the critics, eulogistic as they are, are the compliments of men three-fourths duped as Partridge was duped by Garrick. By much of her acting they were so completely taken in that they did not recognize it as acting at all. Indeed, none of the six players quite escaped this consequence of their own thoroughness. There was a distinct tendency among the less experienced critics to complain of their sentiments and behavior. Naturally, the author does not share that grievance.

PICCARD'S COTTAGE, JANUARY 1902.

MRS WARREN'S PROFESSION

[Mrs Warren's Profession was performed for the first time in the theatre of the New Lyric Club, London, on the 5th and 6th January 1902, with Madge McIntosh as Vivie, Julius Knight as Praed, Fanny Brough as Mrs Warren, Charles Goodhart as Crofts, Harley Granville-Barker as Frank, and Cosmo Stuart as the Reverend Samuel Gardner.]

ACT I

[Summer afternoon in a cottage garden on the eastern slope of a hill a little south of Haslemere in Surrey. Looking up the hill, the cottage is seen in the left hand corner of the garden, with its thatched roof and porch, and a large latticed window to the left of the porch. A paling completely shuts in the garden, except for a gate on the right. The common rises uphill beyond the paling to the sky line. Some folded canvas garden chairs are leaning against the side bench in the porch. A lady's bicycle is propped against the wall, under the window. A little to the right of the porch a hammock is slung from two posts. A big canvas umbrella, stuck in the ground, keeps the sun off the hammock, in which a young lady is reading and making notes, her head towards the cottage and her feet towards the gate. In front of the hammock, and within reach of her hand, is a common kitchen chair, with a pile of serious-looking books and a supply of writing paper on it.]

[A gentleman walking on the common comes into sight from behind the cottage. He is hardly past middle age, with something of the artist about him, unconventionally but carefully dressed, and clean-shaven except for a moustache, with an eager susceptible face and very amiable and considerate manners. He has silky black hair, with waves of grey and white in it. His eyebrows are white, his moustache black. He seems not certain of his way. He looks over the palings; takes stock of the place; and sees the young lady.]

THE GENTLEMAN [taking off his hat] I beg your pardon. Can you direct me to Hindhead View—Mrs Alison's?

THE YOUNG LADY [glancing up from her book] This is Mrs Alison's. [She resumes her work].

THE GENTLEMAN. Indeed! Perhaps—may I ask are you Miss Vivie Warren?

THE YOUNG LADY [sharply, as she turns on her elbow to get a good look at him] Yes.

THE GENTLEMAN [daunted and conciliatory] I'm afraid I appear intrusive. My name is Praed. [Vivie at once throws her books upon the chair, and gets out of the hammock]. Oh, pray don't let me disturb you.

VIVIE [striding to the gate and opening it for him] Come in, Mr Praed. [He comes in]. Glad to see you. [She proffers her hand and takes his with a resolute and hearty grip. She is an attractive specimen of the sensible, able, highly-educated young middle-class Englishwoman. Age 22. Prompt, strong, confident, self-possessed. Plain business-like dress, but not dowdy. She wears a chatelaine at her belt, with a fountain pen and a paper knife among its pendants].

PRAED. Very kind of you indeed, Miss Warren. [She shuts the gate with a vigorous slam. He passes in to the middle of the garden, exercising his fingers, which are slightly numbed by her greeting]. Has your mother arrived?

VIVIE [quickly, evidently scenting aggression] Is she coming?

PRAED [surprised] Didn't you expect us?

VIVIE. No.

PRAED. Now, goodness me, I hope I've not mistaken the day. That would be just like me, you know. Your mother arranged that she was to come down from London and that I was to come over from Horsham to be introduced to you.

VIVIE [not at all pleased] Did she? Hm! My mother has rather a trick of taking me by surprise—to see how I behave myself while she's away,

I suppose. I fancy I shall take my mother very much by surprise one of these days, if she makes arrangements that concern me without consulting me beforehand. She hasnt come.

PRAED [embarrassed] I'm really very sorry.

VIVIE [throwing off her displeasure] It's not your fault, Mr Praed, is it? And I'm very glad you've come. You are the only one of my mother's friends I have ever asked her to bring to see me.

PRAED [relieved and delighted] Oh, now this is really very good of you, Miss Warren!

VIVIE. Will you come indoors; or would you rather sit out here and talk?

PRAED. It will be nicer out here, don't you think?

VIVIE. Then I'll go and get you a chair. [She goes to the porch for a garden chair].

PRAED [following her] Oh, pray, pray! Allow me. [He lays hands on the chair].

VIVIE [letting him take it] Take care of your fingers; theyre rather dodgy things, those chairs. [She goes across to the chair with the books on it; pitches them into the hammock; and brings the chair forward with one swing].

PRAED [who has just unfolded his chair] Oh, now do let me take that hard chair. I like hard chairs.

VIVIE. So do I. Sit down, Mr Praed. [This invitation she gives with a genial peremptoriness, his anxiety to please her clearly striking her as a sign of weakness of character on his part. But he does not immediately obey].

PRAED. By the way, though, hadnt we better go to the station to meet your mother?

VIVIE [coolly] Why? She knows the way.

PRAED [disconcerted] Er—I suppose she does [he sits down].

VIVIE. Do you know, you are just like what I expected. I hope you are disposed to be friends with me.

PRAED [again beaming] Thank you, my *dear* Miss Warren; thank you. Dear me! I'm so glad your mother hasnt spoilt you!

VIVIE. How?

PRAED. Well, in making you too conventional. You know, my dear Miss Warren, I am a born anarchist. I hate authority. It spoils the relations between parent and child; even between mother and daughter. Now I was always afraid that your mother would strain her authority to make you very conventional. It's such a relief to find that she hasnt.

VIVIE. Oh! have I been behaving unconventionally?

PRAED. Oh no: oh dear no. At least, not conventionally unconventionally, you understand. [She nods and sits down. He goes on, with a cordial outburst] But it was so charming of you to say that you were disposed to be friends with me! You modern young ladies are splendid: perfectly splendid!

VIVIE [dubiously] Eh? [watching him with dawning disappointment as to the quality of his brains and character].

PRAED. When I was your age, young men and women were afraid of each other: there was no good fellowship. Nothing real. Only gallantry copied out of novels, and as vulgar and affected as it could be. Maidenly reserve! gentlemanly chivalry! always saying no when you meant yes! simple purgatory for shy and sincere souls.

VIVIE. Yes, I imagine there must have been a frightful waste of time. Especially women's time.

PRAED. Oh, waste of life, waste of everything. But things are improving. Do you know, I have been in a positive state of excitement about meeting you ever since your magnificent achievements at Cambridge: a thing unheard of in my day. It was perfectly splendid, your tieing with the third wrangler. Just the right place, you know. The first wrangler is always a dreamy, morbid fellow, in whom the thing is pushed to the length of a disease.

VIVIE. It doesn't pay. I wouldn't do it again for the same money.

PRAED [aghast] The same money!

VIVIE. Yes. Fifty pounds. Perhaps you don't know how it was. Mrs Latham, my tutor at Newnham, told my mother that I could distinguish myself in the mathematical tripos if I went in for it in earnest. The papers were full just then of Phillipa Summers beating the senior wrangler. You remember about it, of course.

PRAED [shakes his head energetically] !!!

VIVIE. Well, anyhow, she did; and nothing would please my mother but that I should do the same thing. I said flatly that it was not worth my while to face the grind since I was not going in for teaching; but I offered to try for fourth wrangler or thereabouts for fifty pounds. She closed with me at that, after a little grumbling; and I was better than my bargain. But I wouldn't do it again for that. Two hundred pounds would have been nearer the mark.

PRAED [much damped] Lord bless me! Thats a very practical way of looking at it.

VIVIE. Did you expect to find me an unpractical person?

PRAED. But surely it's practical to consider not only the work these honors cost, but also the culture they bring.

VIVIE. Culture! My dear Mr Praed: do you know what the mathematical tripos means? It means grind, grind, grind for six to eight hours a day at mathematics, and nothing but mathematics.

I'm supposed to know something about science; but I know nothing except the mathematics it involves. I can make calculations for engineers, electricians, insurance companies, and so on; but I know next to nothing about engineering or electricity or insurance. I don't even know arithmetic well. Outside mathematics, lawn-tennis, eating, sleeping, cycling, and walking, I'm a more ignorant barbarian than any woman could possibly be who hadn't gone in for the tripos.

PRAED [revolted] What a monstrous, wicked, rascally system! I knew it! I felt at once that it meant destroying all that makes womanhood beautiful!

235

VIVIE. I don't object to it on that score in the least. I shall turn it to very good account, I assure you.

PRAED. Pooh! In what way?

VIVIE. I shall set up chambers in the City, and work at actuarial calculations and conveyancing. Under cover of that I shall do some law, with one eye on the Stock Exchange all the time. I've come down here by myself to read law: not for a holiday, as my mother imagines. I hate holidays.

PRAED. You make my blood run cold. Are you to have no romance, no beauty in your life?

VIVIE. I don't care for either, I assure you.

PRAED. You can't mean that.

VIVIE. Oh yes I do. I like working and getting paid for it. When I'm tired of working, I like a comfortable chair, a cigar, a little whisky, and a novel with a good detective story in it.

PRAED [rising in a frenzy of repudiation] I don't believe it. I am an artist; and I can't believe it: I refuse to believe it. It's only that you havn't discovered yet what a wonderful world art can open up to you.

VIVIE. Yes I have. Last May I spent six weeks in London with Honoria Fraser. Mamma thought we were doing a round of sightseeing together; but I was really at Honoria's chambers in Chancery Lane every day, working away at actuarial calculations for her, and helping her as well as a greenhorn could. In the evenings we smoked and talked, and never dreamt of going out except for exercise. And I never enjoyed myself more in my life.

I cleared all my expenses and got initiated into the business without a fee in the bargain.

PRAED. But bless my heart and soul, Miss Warren, do you call that discovering art?

VIVIE. Wait a bit. That wasn't the beginning. I went up to town on an invitation from some artistic people in Fitzjohn's Avenue: one of the girls was a Newnham chum. They took me to the National Gallery—

PRAED [approving] Ah!! [He sits down, much relieved].

VIVIE [continuing]—to the Opera—

PRAED [still more pleased] Good!

VIVIE.—and to a concert where the band played all the evening: Beethoven and Wagner and so on. I wouldn't go through that experience again for anything you could offer me. I held out for civility's sake until the third day; and then I said, plump out, that I couldn't stand any more of it, and went off to Chancery Lane. N o w you know the sort of perfectly splendid modern young lady I am. How do you think I shall get on with my mother?

PRAED [startled] Well, I hope—er—

VIVIE. It's not so much what you hope as what you believe, that I want to know.

PRAED. Well, frankly, I am afraid your mother will be a little disappointed. Not from any shortcoming on your part, you know: I don't mean that. But you are so different from her ideal.

VIVIE. Her what?!

PRAED. Her ideal.

VIVIE. Do you mean her ideal of ME?

PRAED. Yes.

VIVIE. What on earth is it like?

PRAED. Well, you must have observed, Miss Warren, that people who are dissatisfied with their own bringing-up generally think that the world would be all right if everybody were to be brought up quite differently. Now your mother's life has been—er—I suppose you know—

VIVIE. Don't suppose anything, Mr Praed. I hardly know my mother. Since I was a child I have lived in England, at school or at college, or with people paid to take charge of me. I have been boarded out all my life. My mother has lived in Brussels or Vienna and never let me go to her. I only see her when she visits England for a few days. I don't complain: it's been very pleasant; for people have been very good to me; and there has always been plenty of money to make things smooth. But don't imagine I know anything about my mother. I know far less than you do.

PRAED [very ill at ease] In that case—[He stops, quite at a loss. Then, with a forced attempt at gaiety] But what nonsense we are talking! Of course you and your mother will get on capitally. [He rises, and looks abroad at the view]. What a charming little place you have here!

VIVIE [unmoved] Rather a violent change of subject, Mr Praed. Why won't my mother's life bear being talked about?

PRAED. Oh, you mustn't say that. Isn't it natural that I should have a certain delicacy in talking to my old friend's daughter about her behind her back? You and she will have plenty of opportunity of talking about it when she comes.

VIVIE. No: she won't talk about it either. [Rising] However, I daresay you have good reasons for telling me nothing. Only, mind this, Mr Praed, I expect there will be a battle royal when my mother hears of my Chancery Lane project.

PRAED [ruefully] I'm afraid there will.

VIVIE. Well, I shall win because I want nothing but my fare to London to start there to-morrow earning my own living by devilling for Honoria. Besides, I have no mysteries to keep up; and it seems she has. I shall use that advantage over her if necessary.

PRAED [greatly shocked] Oh no! No, pray. Youd not do such a thing.

VIVIE. Then tell me why not.

PRAED. I really cannot. I appeal to your good feeling. [She smiles at his sentimentality]. Besides, you may be too bold. Your mother is not to be trifled with when she's angry.

VIVIE. You can't frighten me, Mr Praed. In that month at Chancery Lane I had opportunities of taking the measure of one or two women v e r y like my mother. You may back me to win. But if I hit harder in my ignorance than I need, remember it is you who refuse to enlighten me. Now, let us drop the subject. [She takes her chair and replaces it near the hammock with the same vigorous swing as before].

PRAED [taking a desperate resolution] One word, Miss Warren. I had better tell you. It's very difficult; but—

[Mrs Warren and Sir George Crofts arrive at the gate. Mrs Warren is between 40 and 50, formerly pretty, showily dressed in a brilliant hat and a gay blouse fitting tightly over her bust and flanked by fashionable sleeves. Rather spoilt and domineering, and decidedly vulgar, but, on the whole, a genial and fairly presentable old blackguard of a woman.]

[Crofts is a tall powerfully-built man of about 50, fashionably dressed in the style of a young man. Nasal voice, reedier than might be expected from his strong frame. Clean-shaven bulldog jaws, large flat ears, and thick neck: gentlemanly combination of the most brutal types of city man, sporting man, and man about town.]

VIVIE. Here they are. [Coming to them as they enter the garden] How do, mater? Mr Praed's been here this half hour, waiting for you.

MRS WARREN. Well, if you've been waiting, Praddy, it's your own fault: I thought youd have had the gumption to know I was coming by the 3.10 train. Vivie: put your hat on, dear: youll get sunburnt. Oh, I forgot to introduce you. Sir George Crofts: my little Vivie.

[Crofts advances to Vivie with his most courtly manner. She nods, but makes no motion to shake hands.]

CROFTS. May I shake hands with a young lady whom I have known by reputation very long as the daughter of one of my oldest friends?

VIVIE [who has been looking him up and down sharply] If you like.

[She takes his tenderly proferred hand and gives it a squeeze that makes him open his eyes; then turns away, and says to her mother] Will you come in, or shall I get a couple more chairs? [She goes into the porch for the chairs].

MRS WARREN. Well, George, what do you think of her?

CROFTS [ruefully] She has a powerful fist. Did you shake hands with her, Praed?

PRAED. Yes: it will pass off presently.

CROFTS. I hope so. [Vivie reappears with two more chairs. He hurries to her assistance]. Allow me.

MRS WARREN [patronizingly] Let Sir George help you with the chairs, dear.

VIVIE [pitching them into his arms] Here you are. [She dusts her hands and turns to Mrs Warren]. Youd like some tea, wouldn't you?

MRS WARREN [sitting in Praed's chair and fanning herself] I'm dying for a drop to drink.

VIVIE. I'll see about it. [She goes into the cottage].

[Sir George has by this time managed to unfold a chair and plant it by Mrs Warren, on her left. He throws the other on the grass and sits down, looking dejected and rather foolish, with the handle of his stick in his mouth. Praed, still very uneasy, fidgets around the garden on their right.]

MRS WARREN [to Praed, looking at Crofts] Just look at him, Praddy: he looks cheerful, don't he? He's been worrying my life out these three years to have that little girl of mine shewn to him; and now that Ive done it, he's quite out of countenance. [Briskly] Come! sit up, George; and take your stick out of your mouth. [Crofts sulkily obeys].

PRAED. I think, you know—if you don't mind my saying so—that we had better get out of the habit of thinking of her as a little girl. You see she has really distinguished herself; and I'm not sure, from what I have seen of her, that she is not older than any of us.

MRS WARREN [greatly amused] Only listen to him, George! Older than any of us! Well she *has* been stuffing you nicely with her importance.

PRAED. But young people are particularly sensitive about being treated in that way.

MRS WARREN. Yes; and young people have to get all that nonsense taken out of them, and good deal more besides. Don't you interfere, Praddy: I know how to treat my own child as well as you do. [Praed, with a grave shake of his head, walks up the garden with his hands behind his back. Mrs Warren pretends to laugh, but looks after him with perceptible concern. Then, she whispers to Crofts] Whats the matter with him? What does he take it like that for?

CROFTS [morosely] Youre afraid of Praed.

MRS WARREN. What! Me! Afraid of dear old Praddy! Why, a fly wouldn't be afraid of him.

CROFTS. *You're* afraid of him.

MRS WARREN [angry] I'll trouble you to mind your own business, and not try any of your sulks on me. I'm not afraid of y o u, anyhow. If you can't make yourself agreeable, youd better go home. [She gets up, and, turning her back on him, finds herself face to face with Praed]. Come, Praddy, I know it was only your tender-heartedness. Youre afraid I'll bully her.

PRAED. My dear Kitty: you think I'm offended. Don't imagine that: pray don't. But you know I often notice things that escape you; and though you never take my advice, you sometimes admit afterwards that you ought to have taken it.

MRS WARREN. Well, what do you notice now?

PRAED. Only that Vivie is a grown woman. Pray, Kitty, treat her with every respect.

MRS WARREN [with genuine amazement] Respect! Treat my own daughter with respect! What next, pray!

VIVIE [appearing at the cottage door and calling to Mrs Warren] Mother: will you come to my room before tea?

MRS WARREN. Yes, dearie. [She laughs indulgently at Praed's gravity, and pats him on the cheek as she passes him on her way to the porch]. Don't be cross, Praddy. [She follows Vivie into the cottage].

CROFTS [furtively] I say, Praed.

PRAED. Yes.

CROFTS. I want to ask you a rather particular question.

PRAED. Certainly. [He takes Mrs Warren's chair and sits close to Crofts].

CROFTS. Thats right: they might hear us from the window. Look here: did Kitty every tell you who that girl's father is?

PRAED. Never.

CROFTS. Have you any suspicion of who it might be?

PRAED. None.

CROFTS [not believing him] I know, of course, that you perhaps might feel bound not to tell if she had said anything to you. But it's very awkward to be uncertain about it now that we shall be meeting the girl every day. We don't exactly know how we ought to feel towards her.

PRAED. What difference can that make? We take her on her own merits. What does it matter who her father was?

CROFTS [suspiciously] Then you know who he was?

PRAED [with a touch of temper] I said no just now. Did you not hear me?

CROFTS. Look here, Praed. I ask you as a particular favor. If you *do* know [movement of protest from Praed]—I only say, if you know, you might at least set my mind at rest about her. The fact is, I fell attracted.

PRAED [sternly] What do you mean?

CROFTS. Oh, don't be alarmed: it's quite an innocent feeling. Thats what puzzles me about it. Why, for all I know, *I* might be her father.

PRAED. You! Impossible!

CROFTS [catching him up cunningly] You know for certain that I'm not?

PRAED. I know nothing about it, I tell you, any more than you. But really, Crofts—oh no, it's out of the question. Theres not the least resemblance.

CROFTS. As to that, theres no resemblance between her and her mother that I can see. I suppose she's not y o u r daughter, is she?

PRAED [rising indignantly] Really, Crofts—!

CROFTS. No offence, Praed. Quite allowable as between two men of the world.

PRAED [recovering himself with an effort and speaking gently and gravely] Now listen to me, my dear Crofts. [He sits down again].

I have nothing to do with that side of Mrs Warren's life, and never had. She has never spoken to me about it; and of course I have never spoken to her about it. Your delicacy will tell you that a handsome woman needs some friends who are not—well, not on that footing with her. The effect of her own beauty would become a torment to her if she could not escape from it occasionally. You are probably on much more confidential terms with Kitty than I am. Surely you can ask her the question yourself.

CROFTS. I h a v e asked her, often enough. But she's so determined to keep the child all to herself that she would deny that it ever had a father if she could. [Rising] I'm thoroughly uncomfortable about it, Praed.

PRAED [rising also] Well, as you are, at all events, old enough to be her father, I don't mind agreeing that we both regard Miss Vivie in a parental way, as a young girl who we are bound to protect and help. What do you say?

CROFTS [aggressively] I'm no older than you, if you come to that.

PRAED. Yes you are, my dear fellow: you were born old. I was born a boy: Ive never been able to feel the assurance of a grown-up man in my life. [He folds his chair and carries it to the porch].

MRS WARREN [calling from within the cottage] Prad-dee! George! Tea-ea-ea-ea!

CROFTS [hastily] She's calling us. [He hurries in].

[Praed shakes his head bodingly, and is following Crofts when he is hailed by a young gentleman who has just appeared on the common, and is making for the gate. He is pleasant, pretty, smartly dressed, cleverly good-for-nothing, not long turned 20, with a charming voice and agreeably disrespectful manners. He carries a light sporting magazine rifle.]

THE YOUNG GENTLEMAN. Hallo! Praed!

PRAED. Why, Frank Gardner! [Frank comes in and shakes hands cordially]. What on earth are you doing here?

FRANK. Staying with my father.

PRAED. The Roman father?

FRANK. He's rector here. I'm living with my people this autumn for the sake of economy. Things came to a crisis in July: the Roman father had to pay my debts. He's stony broke in consequence; and so am I. What are you up to in these parts? do you know the people here?

PRAED. Yes: I'm spending the day with a Miss Warren.

FRANK [enthusiastically] What! Do you know Vivie? Isn't she a jolly girl? I'm teaching her to shoot with this [putting down the rifle]. I'm so glad she knows you: youre just the sort of fellow she ought to know. [He smiles, and raises the charming voice almost to a singing tone as he exclaims] It's e v e r so jolly to find you here, Praed.

PRAED. I'm an old friend of her mother. Mrs Warren brought me over to make her daughter's acquaintance.

FRANK. The mother! Is *she* here?

PRAED. Yes: inside, at tea.

MRS WARREN [calling from within] Prad-dee-ee-ee-eee! The tea-cake'll be cold.

PRAED [calling] Yes, Mrs Warren. In a moment. I've just met a friend here.

MRS WARREN. A what?

PRAED [louder] A friend.

MRS WARREN. Bring him in.

PRAED. All right. [To Frank] Will you accept the invitation?

FRANK [incredulous, but immensely amused] Is that Vivie's mother?

PRAED. Yes.

FRANK. By Jove! What a lark! Do you think she'll like me?

PRAED. I've no doubt youll make yourself popular, as usual. Come in and try [moving towards the house].

FRANK. Stop a bit. [Seriously] I want to take you into my confidence.

PRAED. Pray don't. It's only some fresh folly, like the barmaid at Redhill.

FRANK. It's ever so much more serious than that. You say you've only just met Vivie for the first time?

PRAED. Yes.

FRANK [rhapsodically] Then you can have no idea what a girl she is. Such character! Such sense! And her cleverness! Oh, my eye, Praed, but I can tell you she is clever! And—need I add?—she loves me.

CROFTS [putting his head out of the window] I say, Praed: what are you about? Do come along. [He disappears].

FRANK. Hallo! Sort of chap that would take a prize at a dog show, ain't he? Who's he?

PRAED. Sir George Crofts, an old friend of Mrs Warren's. I think we had better come in.

[On their way to the porch they are interrupted by a call from the gate. Turning, they see an elderly clergyman looking over it.]

THE CLERGYMAN [calling] Frank!

FRANK. Hallo! [To Praed] The Roman father. [To the clergyman] Yes, gov'nor: all right: presently. [To Praed] Look here, Praed: youd better go in to tea. I'll join you directly.

PRAED. Very good. [He goes into the cottage].

[The clergyman remains outside the gate, with his hands on the top of it. The Rev. Samuel Gardner, a beneficed clergyman of the Established Church, is over 50. Externally he is pretentious, booming, noisy, important. Really he is that obsolescent phenomenon the fool of the family dumped on the Church by his father the patron, clamorously asserting himself as father and clergyman without being able to command respect in either capacity.]

REV. S. Well, sir. Who are your friends here, if I may ask?

FRANK. Oh, it's all right, gov'nor! Come in.

REV. S. No, sir; not until I know whose garden I am entering.

FRANK. It's all right. It's Miss Warren's.

REV. S. I have not seen her at church since she came.

FRANK. Of course not: she's a third wrangler. Ever so intellectual. Took a higher degree than you did; so why should she go to hear you preach?

REV. S. Don't be disrespectful, sir.

FRANK. Oh, it don't matter: nobody hears us. Come in. [He opens the gate, unceremoniously pulling his father with it into the garden]. I want to introduce you to her. Do you remember the advice you gave me last July, gov'nor?

REV. S. [severely] Yes. I advised you to conquer your idleness and flippancy, and to work your way into an honorable profession and live on it and not upon me.

FRANK. No: thats what you thought of afterwards. What you actually said was that since I had neither brains nor money, I'd better turn my good looks to account by marrying someone with both. Well, look here. Miss Warren has brains: you can't deny that.

REV. S. Brains are not everything.

FRANK. No, of course not: theres the money—

REV. S. [interrupting him austerely] I was not thinking of money, sir. I was speaking of higher things. Social position, for instance.

FRANK. I don't care a rap about that.

REV. S. But I do, sir.

FRANK. Well, nobody wants y o u to marry her. Anyhow, she has what amounts to a high Cambridge degree; and she seems to have as much money as she wants.

REV. S. [sinking into a feeble vein of humor] I greatly doubt whether she has as much money as y o u will want.

FRANK. Oh, come: I havn't been so very extravagant. I live ever so quietly; I don't drink; I don't bet much; and I never go regularly to the razzle-dazzle as you did when you were my age.

REV. S. [booming hollowly] Silence, sir.

FRANK. Well, you told me yourself, when I was making every such an ass of myself about the barmaid at Redhill, that you once offered a woman fifty pounds for the letters you wrote to her when—

REV. S. [terrified] Sh-sh-sh, Frank, for Heaven's sake! [He looks round apprehensively Seeing no one within earshot he plucks up courage to boom again, but more subduedly]. You are taking an ungentlemanly advantage of what I confided to you for your own good, to save you from an error you would have repented all your life long. Take warning by your father's follies, sir; and don't make them an excuse for your own.

FRANK. Did you ever hear the story of the Duke of Wellington and his letters?

REV. S. No, sir; and I don't want to hear it.

FRANK. The old Iron Duke didn't throw away fifty pounds: not he. He just wrote: "Dear Jenny: publish and be damned! Yours affectionately, Wellington." Thats what you should have done.

REV. S. [piteously] Frank, my boy: when I wrote those letters I put myself into that woman's power. When I told you about them I put myself, to some extent, I am sorry to say, in your power. She refused my money with these words, which I shall never forget. "Knowledge is power" she said; "and I never sell power."

Thats more than twenty years ago; and she has never made use of her power or caused me a moment's uneasiness. You are behaving worse to me than she did, Frank.

FRANK. Oh yes I dare say! Did you ever preach at her the way you preach at me every day?

REV. S. [wounded almost to tears] I leave you, sir. You are incorrigible. [He turns towards the gate].

FRANK [utterly unmoved] Tell them I shan't be home to tea, will you, gov'nor, like a good fellow? [He moves towards the cottage door and is met by Praed and Vivie coming out].

VIVIE [to Frank] Is that your father, Frank? I do so want to meet him.

FRANK. Certainly. [Calling after his father] Gov'nor. Youre wanted. [The parson turns at the gate, fumbling nervously at his hat. Praed crosses the garden to the opposite side, beaming in anticipation of civilities]. My father: Miss Warren.

VIVIE [going to the clergyman and shaking his hand] Very glad to see you here, Mr Gardner. [Calling to the cottage] Mother: come along: youre wanted.

[Mrs Warren appears on the threshold, and is immediately transfixed, recognizing the clergyman.]

VIVIE [continuing] Let me introduce—

MRS WARREN [swooping on the Reverend Samuel] Why it's Sam Gardner, gone into the Church! Well, I never! Don't you know us, Sam? This is George Crofts, as large as life and twice as natural. Don't you remember me?

REV. S. [very red] I really—er—

MRS WARREN. Of course you do. Why, I have a whole album of your letters still: I came across them only the other day.

REV. S. [miserably confused] Miss Vavasour, I believe.

MRS WARREN [correcting him quickly in a loud whisper] Tch! Nonsense! Mrs Warren: don't you see my daughter there?

ACT II

[Inside the cottage after nightfall. Looking eastward from within instead of westward from without, the latticed window, with its curtains drawn, is now seen in the middle of the front wall of the cottage, with the porch door to the left of it. In the left-hand side wall is the door leading to the kitchen. Farther back against the same wall is a dresser with a candle and matches on it, and Frank's rifle standing beside them, with the barrel resting in the plate-rack. In the centre a table stands with a lighted lamp on it. Vivie's books and writing materials are on a table to the right of the window, against the wall. The fireplace is on the right, with a settle: there is no fire. Two of the chairs are set right and left of the table.]

[The cottage door opens, shewing a fine starlit night without; and Mrs Warren, her shoulders wrapped in a shawl borrowed from Vivie, enters, followed by Frank, who throws his cap on the window seat. She has had enough of walking, and gives a gasp of relief as she unpins her hat; takes it off; sticks the pin through the crown; and puts it on the table.]

MRS WARREN. O Lord! I don't know which is the worst of the country, the walking or the sitting at home with nothing to do. I could do with a whisky and soda now very well, if only they had such a things in this place.

FRANK. Perhaps Vivie's got some.

MRS WARREN. Nonsense! What would a young girl like her be doing with such things! Never mind: it don't matter. I wonder how she passes her time here! I'd a good deal rather be in Vienna.

FRANK. Let me take you there. [He helps her to take off her shawl, gallantly giving her shoulders a very perceptible squeeze as he does so].

MRS WARREN. Ah! would you? I'm beginning to think youre a chip of the old block.

FRANK. Like the gov'nor, eh? [He hangs the shawl on the nearest chair, and sits down].

MRS WARREN. Never you mind. What do you know about such things?

Youre only a boy. [She goes to the hearth to be farther from temptation].

FRANK. Do come to Vienna with me? It'd be ever such larks.

MRS WARREN. No, thank you. Vienna is no place for you—at least not until youre a little older. [She nods at him to emphasize this piece of advice. He makes a mock-piteous face, belied by his laughing eyes. She looks at him; then comes back to him]. Now, look here, little boy [taking his face in her hands and turning it up to her]: I know you through and through by your likeness to your father, better than you know yourself. Don't you go taking any silly ideas into your head about me. Do you hear?

FRANK [gallantly wooing her with his voice] Can't help it, my dear Mrs Warren: it runs in the family.

[She pretends to box his ears; then looks at the pretty laughing upturned face of a moment, tempted. At last she kisses him, and immediately turns away, out of patience with herself.]

MRS WARREN. There! I shouldn't have done that. I *am* wicked. Never you mind, my dear: it's only a motherly kiss. Go and make love to Vivie.

FRANK. So I have.

MRS WARREN [turning on him with a sharp note of alarm in her voice] What!

FRANK. Vivie and I are ever such chums.

MRS WARREN. What do you mean? Now see here: I won't have any young scamp tampering with my little girl. Do you hear? I won't have it.

FRANK [quite unabashed] My dear Mrs Warren: don't you be alarmed. My intentions are honorable: ever so honorable; and your little girl is jolly well able to take care of herself. She don't need looking after half so much as her mother. She ain't so handsome, you know.

MRS WARREN [taken aback by his assurance] Well, you have got a nice healthy two inches of cheek all over you. I don't know where you got it. Not from your father, anyhow.

CROFTS [in the garden] The gipsies, I suppose?

REV. S. [replying] The broomsquires are far worse.

MRS WARREN [to Frank] S-sh! Remember! you've had your warning.

[Crofts and the Reverend Samuel Gardner come in from the garden, the clergyman continuing his conversation as he enters.]

REV. S. The perjury at the Winchester assizes is deplorable.

MRS WARREN. Well? what became of you two? And wheres Praddy and Vivie?

CROFTS [putting his hat on the settle and his stick in the chimney corner] They went up the hill. We went to the village. I wanted a drink. [He sits down on the settle, putting his legs up along the seat].

MRS WARREN. Well, she oughtn't to go off like that without telling me. [To Frank] Get your father a chair, Frank: where are your manners? [Frank springs up and gracefully offers his father his chair; then takes another from the wall and sits down at the table, in the middle, with his father on his right and Mrs Warren on his left]. George: where are you going to stay to-night? You can't stay here. And whats Praddy going to do?

CROFTS. Gardner'll put me up.

MRS WARREN. Oh, no doubt you've taken care of yourself! But what about Praddy?

CROFTS. Don't know. I suppose he can sleep at the inn.

MRS WARREN. Havn't you room for him, Sam?

REV. S. Well—er—you see, as rector here, I am not free to do as I like. Er—what is Mr Praed's social position?

MRS WARREN. Oh, he's all right: he's an architect. What an old stick-in-the-mud you are, Sam!

FRANK. Yes, it's all right, gov'nor. He built that place down in Wales for the Duke. Caernarvon Castle they call it. You must have heard of it. [He winks with lightning smartness at Mrs Warren, and regards his father blandly].

REV. S. Oh, in that case, of course we shall only be too happy. I suppose he knows the Duke personally.

FRANK. Oh, ever so intimately! We can stick him in Georgina's old room.

MRS WARREN. Well, thats settled. Now if those two would only come in and let us have supper. Theyve no right to stay out after dark like this.

CROFTS [aggressively] What harm are they doing you?

MRS WARREN. Well, harm or not, I don't like it.

FRANK. Better not wait for them, Mrs Warren. Praed will stay out as long as possible. He has never known before what it is to stray over the heath on a summer night with my Vivie.

CROFTS [sitting up in some consternation] I say, you know! Come!

REV. S. [rising, startled out of his professional manner into real force and sincerity] Frank, once and for all, it's out of the question. Mrs Warren will tell you that it's not to be thought of.

CROFTS. Of course not.

FRANK [with enchanting placidity] Is that so, Mrs Warren?

MRS WARREN [reflectively] Well, Sam, I don't know. If the girl wants to get married, no good can come of keeping her unmarried.

REV. S. [astounded] But married to *him!*—your daughter to my son! Only think: it's impossible.

CROFTS. Of course it's impossible. Don't be a fool, Kitty.

MRS WARREN [nettled] Why not? Isn't my daughter good enough for your son?

REV. S. But surely, my dear Mrs Warren, you know the reasons—

MRS WARREN [defiantly] I know no reasons. If you know any, you can tell them to the lad, or to the girl, or to your congregation, if you like.

REV. S. [collapsing helplessly into his chair] You know very well that I couldn't tell anyone the reasons. But my boy will believe me when I tell him there a r e reasons.

FRANK. Quite right, Dad: he will. But has your boy's conduct ever been influenced by your reasons?

CROFTS. You can't marry her; and thats all about it. [He gets up and stands on the hearth, with his back to the fireplace, frowning determinedly].

MRS WARREN [turning on him sharply] What have you got to do with it, pray?

FRANK [with his prettiest lyrical cadence] Precisely what I was going to ask, myself, in my own graceful fashion.

CROFTS [to Mrs Warren] I suppose you don't want to marry the girl to a man younger than herself and without either a profession or twopence to keep her on. Ask Sam, if you don't believe me. [To the parson] How much more money are you going to give him?

REV. S. Not another penny. He has had his patrimony; and he spent the last of it in July. [Mrs Warren's face falls].

CROFTS [watching her] There! I told you. [He resumes his place on the settle and puts his legs on the seat again, as if the matter were finally disposed of].

FRANK [plaintively] This is ever so mercenary. Do you suppose Miss Warren's going to marry for money? If we love one another—

MRS WARREN. Thank you. Your love's a pretty cheap commodity, my lad. If you have no means of keeping a wife, that settles it; you can't have Vivie.

FRANK [much amused] What do y o u say, gov'nor, eh?

REV. S. I agree with Mrs Warren.

FRANK. And good old Crofts has already expressed his opinion.

CROFTS [turning angrily on his elbow] Look here: I want none of your cheek.

FRANK [pointedly] I'm e v e r so sorry to surprise you, Crofts; but you allowed yourself the liberty of speaking to me like a father a moment ago. One father is enough, thank you.

CROFTS [contemptuously] Yah! [He turns away again].

FRANK [rising] Mrs Warren: I cannot give my Vivie up, even for your sake.

MRS WARREN [muttering] Young scamp!

FRANK [continuing] And as you no doubt intend to hold out other prospects to her, I shall lose no time in placing my case before her. [They stare at him; and he begins to declaim gracefully] He either fears his fate too much, Or his deserts are small, That dares not put it to the touch, To gain or lose it all.

[The cottage doors open whilst he is reciting; and Vivie and Praed come in. He breaks off. Praed puts his hat on the dresser. There is an immediate improvement in the company's behavior. Crofts takes down his legs from the settle and pulls himself together as Praed joins him at the fireplace. Mrs Warren loses her ease of manner and takes refuge in querulousness.]

MRS WARREN. Wherever have you been, Vivie?

VIVIE [taking off her hat and throwing it carelessly on the table] On the hill.

MRS WARREN. Well, you shouldn't go off like that without letting me know. How could I tell what had become of you? And night coming on too!

VIVIE [going to the door of the kitchen and opening it, ignoring her mother] Now, about supper? [All rise except Mrs Warren] We shall be rather crowded in here, I'm afraid.

MRS WARREN. Did you hear what I said, Vivie?

VIVIE [quietly] Yes, mother. [Reverting to the supper difficulty] How many are we? [Counting] One, two, three, four, five, six. Well, two will have to wait until the rest are done: Mrs Alison has only plates and knives for four.

PRAED. Oh, it doesn't matter about me. I—

VIVIE. You have had a long walk and are hungry, Mr Praed: you shall have your supper at once. I can wait myself. I want one person to wait with me. Frank: are you hungry?

FRANK. Not the least in the world. Completely off my peck, in fact.

MRS WARREN [to Crofts] Neither are you, George. You can wait.

CROFTS. Oh, hang it, I've eaten nothing since tea-time. Can't Sam do it?

FRANK. Would you starve my poor father?

REV. S. [testily] Allow me to speak for myself, sir. I am perfectly willing to wait.

VIVIE [decisively] There's no need. Only two are wanted. [She opens the door of the kitchen]. Will you take my mother in, Mr Gardner. [The parson takes Mrs Warren; and they pass into the kitchen. Praed and Crofts follow. All except Praed clearly disapprove of the arrangement, but do not know how to resist it. Vivie stands at the door looking in at them]. Can you squeeze past to that corner, Mr Praed: it's rather a tight fit. Take care of your coat against the whitewash: that right. Now, are you all comfortable?

PRAED [within] Quite, thank you.

MRS WARREN [within] Leave the door open, dearie. [Vivie frowns; but Frank checks her with a gesture, and steals to the cottage door, which he softly sets wide open]. Oh Lor, what a draught! Youd better shut it, dear.

[Vivie shuts it with a slam, and then, noting with disgust that her mother's hat and shawl are lying about, takes them tidily to the window seat, whilst Frank noiselessly shuts the cottage door.]

FRANK [exulting] Aha! Got rid of em. Well, Vivvums: what do you think of my governor?

VIVIE [preoccupied and serious] I've hardly spoken to him. He doesn't strike me as a particularly able person.

FRANK. Well, you know, the old man is not altogether such a fool as he looks. You see, he was shoved into the Church, rather; and in trying to live up to it he makes a much bigger ass of himself than he really is. I don't dislike him as much as you might expect. He means well. How do you think youll get on with him?

VIVIE [rather grimly] I don't think my future life will be much concerned with him, or with any of that old circle of my mother's, except perhaps Praed. [She sits down on the settle] What do you think of my mother?

FRANK. Really and truly?

VIVIE. Yes, really and truly.

FRANK. Well, she's ever so jolly. But she's rather a caution, isn't she? And Crofts! Oh, my eye, Crofts! [He sits beside her].

VIVIE. What a lot, Frank!

FRANK. What a crew!

VIVIE [with intense contempt for them] If I thought that *I* was like that—that I was going to be a waster, shifting along from one meal to another with no purpose, and no character, and no grit in me, I'd open an artery and bleed to death without one moment's hesitation.

FRANK. Oh no, you wouldn't. Why should they take any grind when they can afford not to? I wish I had their luck. No: what I object to is their form. It isn't the thing: it's slovenly, ever so slovenly.

VIVIE. Do you think your form will be any better when youre as old as Crofts, if you don't work?

FRANK. Of course I do. Ever so much better. Vivvums mustn't lecture: her little boy's incorrigible. [He attempts to take her face caressingly in his hands].

VIVIE [striking his hands down sharply] Off with you: Vivvums is not in a humor for petting her little boy this evening. [She rises and comes forward to the other side of the room].

FRANK [following her] How unkind!

VIVIE [stamping at him] Be serious. I'm serious.

FRANK. Good. Let us talk learnedly, Miss Warren: do you know that all the most advanced thinkers are agreed that half the diseases of modern civilization are due to starvation of the affections of the young. Now, *I*—

VIVIE [cutting him short] You are very tiresome. [She opens the inner door] Have you room for Frank there? He's complaining of starvation.

MRS WARREN [within] Of course there is [clatter of knives and glasses as she moves the things on the table]. Here! theres room now beside me. Come along, Mr Frank.

FRANK. Her little boy will be ever so even with his Vivvums for this. [He passes into the kitchen].

MRS WARREN [within] Here, Vivie: come on you too, child. You must be famished. [She enters, followed by Crofts, who holds the door open with marked deference. She goes out without looking at him; and he shuts the door after her]. Why George, you can't be done: you've eaten nothing. Is there anything wrong with you?

CROFTS. Oh, all I wanted was a drink. [He thrusts his hands in his pockets, and begins prowling about the room, restless and sulky].

MRS WARREN. Well, I like enough to eat. But a little of that cold beef and cheese and lettuce goes a long way. [With a sigh of only half repletion she sits down lazily on the settle].

CROFTS. What do you go encouraging that young pup for?

MRS WARREN [on the alert at once] Now see here, George: what are you up to about that girl? I've been watching your way of looking at her. Remember: I know you and what your looks mean.

CROFTS. Theres no harm in looking at her, is there?

MRS WARREN. I'd put you out and pack you back to London pretty soon if I saw any of your nonsense. My girl's little finger is more to me than your whole body and soul. [Crofts receives this with a sneering grin. Mrs Warren, flushing a little at her failure to impose on him in the character of a theatrically devoted mother, adds in a lower key] Make your mind easy: the young pup has no more chance than you have.

CROFTS. Maynt a man take an interest in a girl?

MRS WARREN. Not a man like you.

CROFTS. How old is she?

MRS WARREN. Never you mind how old she is.

CROFTS. Why do you make such a secret of it?

MRS WARREN. Because I choose.

CROFTS. Well, I'm not fifty yet; and my property is as good as it ever was—

MRS [interrupting him] Yes; because youre as stingy as youre vicious.

CROFTS [continuing] And a baronet isnt to be picked up every day. No other man in my position would put up with you for a mother-in-law. Why shouldnt she marry me?

MRS WARREN. You!

CROFTS. We three could live together quite comfortably. I'd die before her and leave her a bouncing widow with plenty of money. Why not? It's been growing in my mind all the time I've been walking with that fool inside there.

MRS WARREN [revolted] Yes; it's the sort of thing that *would* grow in your mind.

[He halts in his prowling; and the two look at one another, she steadfastly, with a sort of awe behind her contemptuous disgust: he stealthily, with a carnal gleam in his eye and a loose grin.]

CROFTS [suddenly becoming anxious and urgent as he sees no sign of sympathy in her] Look here, Kitty: youre a sensible woman: you needn't put on any moral airs. I'll ask no more questions; and you need answer none. I'll settle the whole property on her; and if you want a checque for yourself on the wedding day, you can name any figure you like—in reason.

MRS WARREN. So it's come to that with you, George, like all the other worn-out old creatures!

CROFTS [savagely] Damn you!

[Before she can retort the door of the kitchen is opened; and the voices of the others are heard returning. Crofts, unable to recover his presence of mind, hurries out of the cottage. The clergyman appears at the kitchen door.]

REV. S. [looking round] Where is Sir George?

MRS WARREN. Gone out to have a pipe. [The clergyman takes his hat from the table, and joins Mrs Warren at the fireside. Meanwhile, Vivie comes in, followed by Frank, who collapses into the nearest chair with an air of extreme exhaustion. Mrs Warren looks round at Vivie and says, with her affectation of maternal patronage even more forced than usual] Well, dearie: have you had a good supper?

VIVIE. You know what Mrs Alison's suppers are. [She turns to Frank and pets him] Poor Frank! was all the beef gone? did it get nothing but bread and cheese and ginger beer? [Seriously, as if she had done quite enough trifling for one evening] Her butter is really awful. I must get some down from the stores.

FRANK. Do, in Heaven's name!

[Vivie goes to the writing-table and makes a memorandum to order the butter. Praed comes in from the kitchen, putting up his handkerchief, which he has been using as a napkin.]

REV. S. Frank, my boy: it is time for us to be thinking of home. Your mother does not know yet that we have visitors.

PRAED. I'm afraid we're giving trouble.

FRANK [rising] Not the least in the world: my mother will be delighted to see you. She's a genuinely intellectual artistic woman; and she sees nobody here from one year's end to another except the gov'nor; so you can imagine how jolly dull it pans out for her. [To his father] Y o u r e not intellectual or artistic: are you pater? So take Praed home at once; and I'll stay here and entertain Mrs Warren. Youll pick up Crofts in the garden. He'll be excellent company for the bull-pup.

PRAED [taking his hat from the dresser, and coming close to Frank] Come with us, Frank. Mrs Warren has not seen Miss Vivie for a long time; and we have prevented them from having a moment together yet.

FRANK [quite softened, and looking at Praed with romantic admiration] Of course. I forgot. Ever so thanks for reminding me. Perfect gentleman, Praddy. Always were. My ideal through life. [He rises to go, but pauses a moment between the two older men, and puts his hand on Praed's shoulder]. Ah, if you had only been my father instead of this unworthy old man! [He puts his other hand on his father's shoulder].

REV. S. [blustering] Silence, sir, silence: you are profane.

MRS WARREN [laughing heartily] You should keep him in better order, Sam. Good-night. Here: take George his hat and stick with my compliments.

REV. S. [taking them] Good-night. [They shake hands. As he passes Vivie he shakes hands with her also and bids her good-night. Then, in booming command, to Frank] Come along, sir, at once. [He goes out].

MRS WARREN. Byebye, Praddy.

PRAED. Byebye, Kitty.

[They shake hands affectionately and go out together, she accompanying him to the garden gate.]

FRANK [to Vivie] Kissums?

VIVIE [fiercely] No. I hate you. [She takes a couple of books and some paper from the writing-table, and sits down with them at the middle table, at the end next the fireplace].

FRANK [grimacing] Sorry. [He goes for his cap and rifle. Mrs Warren returns. He takes her hand] Good-night, dear Mrs Warren. [He kisses her hand. She snatches it away, her lips tightening, and looks more than half disposed to box his ears. He laughs mischievously and runs off, clapping-to the door behind him].

MRS WARREN [resigning herself to an evening of boredom now that the men are gone] Did you ever in your life hear anyone rattle on so? Isn't he a tease? [She sits at the table]. Now that I think of it, dearie, don't you go encouraging him. I'm sure he's a regular good-for-nothing.

VIVIE [rising to fetch more books] I'm afraid so. Poor Frank! I shall have to get rid of him; but I shall feel sorry for him, though he's not worth it. That man Crofts does not seem to me to be good for much either: is he? [She throws the books on the table rather roughly].

MRS WARREN [galled by Vivie's indifference] What do you know of men, child, to talk that way of them? Youll have to make up your mind to see a good deal of Sir George Crofts, as he's a friend of mine.

VIVIE [quite unmoved] Why? [She sits down and opens a book]. Do you expect that we shall be much together? You and I, I mean?

MRS WARREN [staring at her] Of course: until youre married. Youre not going back to college again.

VIVIE. Do you think my way of life would suit you? I doubt it.

MRS WARREN. Y o u r way of life! What do you mean?

VIVIE [cutting a page of her book with the paper knife on her chatelaine]
Has it really never occurred to you, mother, that I have a way of life
like other people?

MRS WARREN. What nonsense is this youre trying to talk? Do you want
to shew your independence, now that youre a great little person at
school? Don't be a fool, child.

VIVIE [indulgently] Thats all you have to say on the subject, is it,
mother?

MRS WARREN [puzzled, then angry] Don't you keep on asking me
questions like that. [Violently] Hold your tongue. [Vivie works on,
losing no time, and saying nothing]. You and your way of life, indeed!
What next? [She looks at Vivie again. No reply].

Your way of life will be what I please, so it will. [Another
pause]. Ive been noticing these airs in you ever since you got that
tripos or whatever you call it. If you think I'm going to put up with
them, youre mistaken; and the sooner you find it out, the better.
[Muttering] All I have to say on the subject, indeed! [Again raising
her voice angrily] Do you know who youre speaking to, Miss?

VIVIE [looking across at her without raising her head from her book]
No. Who are you? What are you?

MRS WARREN [rising breathless] You young imp!

VIVIE. Everybody knows my reputation, my social standing, and the
profession I intend to pursue. I know nothing about you. What
is that way of life which you invite me to share with you and Sir
George Crofts, pray?

MRS WARREN. Take care. I shall do something I'll be sorry for after,
and you too.

VIVIE [putting aside her books with cool decision] Well, let us drop the
subject until you are better able to face it. [Looking critically at her
mother] You want some good walks and a little lawn tennis to set
you up. You are shockingly out of condition: you were not able to
manage twenty yards uphill today without stopping to pant; and

your wrists are mere rolls of fat. Look at mine. [She holds out her wrists].

MRS WARREN [after looking at her helplessly, begins to whimper] Vivie—

VIVIE [springing up sharply] Now pray don't begin to cry. Anything but that. I really cannot stand whimpering. I will go out of the room if you do.

MRS WARREN [piteously] Oh, my darling, how can you be so hard on me? Have I no rights over you as your mother?

VIVIE. A r e you my mother?

MRS WARREN. *Am* I your mother? Oh, Vivie!

VIVIE. Then where are our relatives? my father? our family friends? You claim the rights of a mother: the right to call me fool and child; to speak to me as no woman in authority over me at college dare speak to me; to dictate my way of life; and to force on me the acquaintance of a brute whom anyone can see to be the most vicious sort of London man about town. Before I give myself the trouble to resist such claims, I may as well find out whether they have any real existence.

MRS WARREN [distracted, throwing herself on her knees] Oh no, no. Stop, stop. I *am* your mother: I swear it. Oh, you can't mean to turn on me—my own child! it's not natural. You believe me, don't you? Say you believe me.

VIVIE. Who was my father?

MRS WARREN. You don't know what youre asking. I can't tell you.

VIVIE [determinedly] Oh yes you can, if you like. I have a right to know; and you know very well that I have that right. You can refuse to tell me if you please; but if you do, you will see the last of me tomorrow morning.

MRS WARREN. Oh, it's too horrible to hear you talk like that. You wouldn't—you *couldn't* leave me.

VIVIE [ruthlessly] Yes, without a moment's hesitation, if you trifle with me about this. [Shivering with disgust] How can I feel sure that I may not have the contaminated blood of that brutal waster in my veins?

MRS WARREN. No, no. On my oath it's not he, nor any of the rest that you have ever met. I'm certain of that, at least.

[Vivie's eyes fasten sternly on her mother as the significance of this flashes on her.]

VIVIE [slowly] You are certain of that, at *least*. Ah! You mean that that is all you are certain of. [Thoughtfully] I see. [Mrs Warren buries her face in her hands]. Don't do that, mother: you know you don't feel it a bit. [Mrs Warren takes down her hands and looks up deplorably at Vivie, who takes out her watch and says] Well, that is enough for tonight. At what hour would you like breakfast? Is half-past eight too early for you?

MRS WARREN [wildly] My God, what sort of woman are you?

VIVIE [coolly] The sort the world is mostly made of, I should hope. Otherwise I don't understand how it gets its business done. Come [taking her mother by the wrist and pulling her up pretty resolutely]: pull yourself together. Thats right.

MRS WARREN [querulously] Youre very rough with me, Vivie.

VIVIE. Nonsense. What about bed? It's past ten.

MRS WARREN [passionately] Whats the use of my going to bed? Do you think I could sleep?

VIVIE. Why not? I shall.

MRS WARREN. You! you've no heart. [She suddenly breaks out vehemently in her natural tongue—the dialect of a woman of the people—with all her affectations of maternal authority and conventional manners gone, and an overwhelming inspiration of true conviction and scorn in her] Oh, I wont bear it: I won't put up with the injustice of it. What right have you to set yourself up above me like this? You boast of what you are to me—to *me*, who gave

265

you a chance of being what you are. What chance had I? Shame on you for a bad daughter and a stuck-up prude!

VIVIE [sitting down with a shrug, no longer confident; for her replies, which have sounded sensible and strong to her so far, now begin to ring rather woodenly and even priggishly against the new tone of her mother] Don't think for a moment I set myself above you in any way. You attacked me with the conventional authority of a mother: I defended myself with the conventional superiority of a respectable woman. Frankly, I am not going to stand any of your nonsense; and when you drop it I shall not expect you to stand any of mine. I shall always respect your right to your own opinions and your own way of life.

MRS WARREN. My own opinions and my own way of life! Listen to her talking! Do you think I was brought up like you? able to pick and choose my own way of life? Do you think I did what I did because I liked it, or thought it right, or wouldn't rather have gone to college and been a lady if I'd had the chance?

VIVIE. Everybody has some choice, mother. The poorest girl alive may not be able to choose between being Queen of England or Principal of Newnham; but she can choose between ragpicking and flowerselling, according to her taste. People are always blaming circumstances for what they are. I don't believe in circumstances. The people who get on in this world are the people who get up and look for the circumstances they want, and, if they can't find them, make them.

MRS WARREN. Oh, it's easy to talk, isn't it? Here! would you like to know what *my* circumstances were?

VIVIE. Yes: you had better tell me. Won't you sit down?

MRS WARREN. Oh, I'll sit down: don't you be afraid. [She plants her chair farther forward with brazen energy, and sits down. Vivie is impressed in spite of herself]. D'you know what your gran'mother was?

VIVIE. No.

MRS WARREN. No, you don't. I do. She called herself a widow and had a fried-fish shop down by the Mint, and kept herself and four daughters out of it. Two of us were sisters: that was me and Liz; and we were both good-looking and well made. I suppose our father was a well-fed man: mother pretended he was a gentleman; but I don't know. The other two were only half sisters: undersized, ugly, starved looking, hard working, honest poor creatures: Liz and I would have half-murdered them if mother hadn't half-murdered us to keep our hands off them. They were the respectable ones. Well, what did they get by their respectability? I'll tell you. One of them worked in a whitelead factory twelve hours a day for nine shillings a week until she died of lead poisoning. She only expected to get her hands a little paralyzed; but she died. The other was always held up to us as a model because she married a Government laborer in the Deptford victualling yard, and kept his room and the three children neat and tidy on eighteen shillings a week—until he took to drink. That was worth being respectable for, wasn't it?

VIVIE [now thoughtfully attentive] Did you and your sister think so?

MRS WARREN. Liz didn't, I can tell you: she had more spirit. We both went to a church school—that was part of the ladylike airs we gave ourselves to be superior to the children that knew nothing and went nowhere—and we stayed there until Liz went out one night and never came back. I know the schoolmistress thought I'd soon follow her example; for the clergyman was always warning me that Lizzie'd end by jumping off Waterloo Bridge. Poor fool: that was all he knew about it! But I was more afraid of the whitelead factory than I was of the river; and so would you have been in my place. That clergyman got me a situation as a scullery maid in a temperance restaurant where they sent out for anything you liked. Then I was a waitress; and then I went to the bar at Waterloo station: fourteen hours a day serving drinks and washing glasses for four shillings a week and my board. That was considered a great promotion for me. Well, one cold, wretched night, when I was so tired I could hardly keep myself awake, who should come up for a half of Scotch but Lizzie, in a long fur cloak, elegant and comfortable, with a lot of sovereigns in her purse.

VIVIE [grimly] My aunt Lizzie!

MRS WARREN. Yes; and a very good aunt to have, too. She's living down at Winchester now, close to the cathedral, one of the most respectable ladies there. Chaperones girls at the country ball, if you please. No river for Liz, thank you! You remind me of Liz a little: she was a first-rate business woman—saved money from the beginning—never let herself look too like what she was—never lost her head or threw away a chance. When she saw I'd grown up good-looking she said to me across the bar "What are you doing there, you little fool? wearing out your health and your appearance for other people's profit!" Liz was saving money then to take a house for herself in Brussels; and she thought we two could save faster than one. So she lent me some money and gave me a start; and I saved steadily and first paid her back, and then went into business with her as a partner. Why shouldn't I have done it? The house in Brussels was real high class: a much better place for a woman to be in than the factory where Anne Jane got poisoned. None of the girls were ever treated as I was treated in the scullery of that temperance place, or at the Waterloo bar, or at home. Would you have had me stay in them and become a worn out old drudge before I was forty?

VIVIE [intensely interested by this time] No; but why did you choose that business? Saving money and good management will succeed in any business.

MRS WARREN. Yes, saving money. But where can a woman get the money to save in any other business? Could y o u save out of four shillings a week and keep yourself dressed as well? Not you. Of course, if youre a plain woman and can't earn anything more; or if you have a turn for music, or the stage, or newspaper-writing: thats different. But neither Liz nor I had any turn for such things at all: all we had was our appearance and our turn for pleasing men. Do you think we were such fools as to let other people trade in our good looks by employing us as shopgirls, or barmaids, or waitresses, when we could trade in them ourselves and get all the profits instead of starvation wages? Not likely.

VIVIE. You were certainly quite justified—from the business point of view.

MRS WARREN. Yes; or any other point of view. What is any respectable girl brought up to do but to catch some rich man's fancy and get the benefit of his money by marrying him?—as if a marriage ceremony could make any difference in the right or wrong of the thing! Oh, the hypocrisy of the world makes me sick! Liz and I had to work and save and calculate just like other people; elseways we should be as poor as any good-for-nothing drunken waster of a woman that thinks her luck will last for ever. [With great energy] I despise such people: theyve no character; and if theres a thing I hate in a woman, it's want of character.

VIVIE. Come now, mother: frankly! Isn't it part of what you call character in a woman that she should greatly dislike such a way of making money?

MRS WARREN. Why, of course. Everybody dislikes having to work and make money; but they have to do it all the same. I'm sure I've often pitied a poor girl, tired out and in low spirits, having to try to please some man that she doesn't care two straws for—some half-drunken fool that thinks he's making himself agreeable when he's teasing and worrying and disgusting a woman so that hardly any money could pay her for putting up with it. But she has to bear with disagreeables and take the rough with the smooth, just like a nurse in a hospital or anyone else. It's not work that any woman would do for pleasure, goodness knows; though to hear the pious people talk you would suppose it was a bed of roses.

VIVIE. Still, you consider it worth while. It pays.

MRS WARREN. Of course it's worth while to a poor girl, if she can resist temptation and is good-looking and well conducted and sensible. It's far better than any other employment open to her.

I always thought that it oughtn't to be. It *can't* be right, Vivie, that there shouldn't be better opportunities for women. I stick to that: it's wrong. But it's so, right or wrong; and a girl must make the best of it. But of course it's not worth while for a lady. If you took to it youd be a fool; but I should have been a fool if I'd taken to anything else.

VIVIE [more and more deeply moved] Mother: suppose we were both as poor as you were in those wretched old days, are you quite sure that you wouldn't advise me to try the Waterloo bar, or marry a laborer, or even go into the factory?

MRS WARREN [indignantly] Of course not. What sort of mother do you take me for! How could you keep your self-respect in such starvation and slavery? And whats a woman worth? whats life worth? without self-respect! Why am I independent and able to give my daughter a first-rate education, when other women that had just as good opportunities are in the gutter? Because I always knew how to respect myself and control myself. Why is Liz looked up to in a cathedral town? The same reason. Where would we be now if we'd minded the clergyman's foolishness? Scrubbing floors for one and sixpence a day and nothing to look forward to but the workhouse infirmary. Dont you be led astray by people who don't know the world, my girl. The only way for a woman to provide for herself decently is for her to be good to some man that can afford to be good to her. If she's in his own station of life, let her make him marry her; but if she's far beneath him she can't expect it: why should she? it wouldn't be for her own happiness. Ask any lady in London society that has daughters; and she'll tell you the same, except that I tell you straight and she'll tell you crooked. Thats all the difference.

VIVIE [fascinated, gazing at her] My dear mother: you are a wonderful woman: you are stronger than all England. And are you really and truly not one wee bit doubtful—or—or—ashamed?

MRS WARREN. Well, of course, dearie, it's only good manners to be ashamed of it: it's expected from a woman. Women have to pretend to feel a great deal that they don't feel. Liz used to be angry with me for plumping out the truth about it. She used to say that when every woman could learn enough from what was going on in the world before her eyes, there was no need to talk about it to her. But then Liz was such a perfect lady! She had the true instinct of it; while I was always a bit of a vulgarian. I used to be so pleased when you sent me your photos to see that you were growing up like Liz: you've just her ladylike, determined way. But I can't stand saying one thing when everyone knows I mean another. Whats the use in such hypocrisy? If people arrange the world that way for women, theres no good pretending it's arranged the other way. No: I never was a bit ashamed really. I consider I had a right to be proud of how we managed everything so respectably, and never had a word against us, and how the girls were so well taken care of. Some of them did very well: one of them married an ambassador. But of course now I daren't talk about such things: whatever would they think of us! [She yawns]. Oh dear! I do believe I'm getting sleepy after all. [She stretches herself lazily, thoroughly relieved by her explosion, and placidly ready for her night's rest].

VIVIE. I believe it is I who will not be able to sleep now. [She goes to the dresser and lights the candle. Then she extinguishes the lamp, darkening the room a good deal]. Better let in some fresh air before locking up. [She opens the cottage door, and finds that it is broad moonlight]. What a beautiful night! Look! [She draws the curtains of the window. The landscape is seen bathed in the radiance of the harvest moon rising over Blackdown].

MRS WARREN [with a perfunctory glance at the scene] Yes, dear; but take care you don't catch your death of cold from the night air.

VIVIE [contemptuously] Nonsense.

MRS WARREN [querulously] Oh yes: everything I say is nonsense, according to you.

VIVIE [turning to her quickly] No: really that is not so, mother. You have got completely the better of me tonight, though I intended it to be the other way. Let us be good friends now.

MRS WARREN [shaking her head a little ruefully] So it *has* been the other way. But I suppose I must give in to it. I always got the worst of it from Liz; and now I suppose it'll be the same with you.

VIVIE. Well, never mind. Come: good-night, dear old mother. [She takes her mother in her arms].

MRS WARREN [fondly] I brought you up well, didn't I, dearie?

VIVIE. You did.

MRS WARREN. And youll be good to your poor old mother for it, won't you?

VIVIE. I will, dear. [Kissing her] Good-night.

MRS WARREN [with unction] Blessings on my own dearie darling! a mother's blessing!

[She embraces her daughter protectingly, instinctively looking upward for divine sanction.]

ACT III

[In the Rectory garden next morning, with the sun shining from a cloudless sky. The garden wall has a five-barred wooden gate, wide enough to admit a carriage, in the middle. Beside the gate hangs a bell on a coiled spring, communicating with a pull outside. The carriage drive comes down the middle of the garden and then swerves to its left, where it ends in a little gravelled circus opposite the Rectory porch. Beyond the gate is seen the dusty high road, parallel with the wall, bounded on the farther side by a strip of turf and an unfenced pine wood. On the lawn, between the house and the drive, is a clipped yew tree, with a garden bench in its shade. On the opposite side the garden is shut in by a box hedge; and there is a little sundial on the turf, with an iron chair near it. A little path leads through the box hedge, behind the sundial.]

[Frank, seated on the chair near the sundial, on which he has placed the morning paper, is reading The Standard. His father comes from the house, red-eyed and shivery, and meets Frank's eye with misgiving.]

FRANK [looking at his watch] Half-past eleven. Nice your for a rector to come down to breakfast!

REV. S. Don't mock, Frank: don't mock. I am a little—er—[Shivering]—

FRANK. Off color?

REV. S. [repudiating the expression] No, sir: *unwell* this morning. Where's your mother?

FRANK. Don't be alarmed: she's not here. Gone to town by the 11.13 with Bessie. She left several messages for you. Do you feel equal to receiving them now, or shall I wait til you've breakfasted?

REV. S. I h a v e breakfasted, sir. I am surprised at your mother going to town when we have people staying with us. They'll think it very strange.

FRANK. Possibly she has considered that. At all events, if Crofts is going to stay here, and you are going to sit up every night with him until four, recalling the incidents of your fiery youth, it is clearly my mother's duty, as a prudent housekeeper, to go up to the stores and order a barrel of whisky and a few hundred siphons.

REV. S. I did not observe that Sir George drank excessively.

FRANK. You were not in a condition to, gov'nor.

REV. S. Do you mean to say that *I*—?

FRANK [calmly] I never saw a beneficed clergyman less sober. The anecdotes you told about your past career were so awful that I really don't think Praed would have passed the night under your roof if it hadnt been for the way my mother and he took to one another.

REV. S. Nonsense, sir. I am Sir George Crofts' host. I must talk to him about something; and he has only one subject. Where is Mr Praed now?

FRANK. He is driving my mother and Bessie to the station.

REV. S. Is Crofts up yet?

FRANK. Oh, long ago. He hasn't turned a hair: he's in much better practice than you. Has kept it up ever since, probably. He's taken himself off somewhere to smoke.

[Frank resumes his paper. The parson turns disconsolately towards the gate; then comes back irresolutely.]

REV. S. Er—Frank.

FRANK. Yes.

REV. S. Do you think the Warrens will expect to be asked here after yesterday afternoon?

FRANK. Theyve been asked already.

REV. S. [appalled] What!!!

FRANK. Crofts informed us at breakfast that you told him to bring Mrs Warren and Vivie over here to-day, and to invite them to make this house their home. My mother then found she must go to town by the 11.13 train.

REV. S. [with despairing vehemence] I never gave any such invitation. I never thought of such a thing.

FRANK [compassionately] How do you know, gov'nor, what you said and thought last night?

PRAED [coming in through the hedge] Good morning.

REV. S. Good morning. I must apologize for not having met you at breakfast. I have a touch of—of—

FRANK. Clergyman's sore throat, Praed. Fortunately not chronic.

PRAED [changing the subject] Well I must say your house is in a charming spot here. Really most charming.

REV. S. Yes: it is indeed. Frank will take you for a walk, Mr Praed, if you like. I'll ask you to excuse me: I must take the opportunity to write my sermon while Mrs Gardner is away and you are all amusing yourselves. You won't mind, will you?

PRAED. Certainly not. Don't stand on the slightest ceremony with me.

REV. S. Thank you. I'll—er—er—[He stammers his way to the porch and vanishes into the house].

PRAED. Curious thing it must be writing a sermon every week.

FRANK. Ever so curious, if he did it. He buys em. He's gone for some soda water.

PRAED. My dear boy: I wish you would be more respectful to your father. You know you can be so nice when you like.

FRANK. My dear Praddy: you forget that I have to live with the governor. When two people live together—it don't matter whether theyre father

275

and son or husband and wife or brother and sister—they can't keep up the polite humbug thats so easy for ten minutes on an afternoon call. Now the governor, who unites to many admirable domestic qualities the irresoluteness of a sheep and the pompousness and aggressiveness of a jackass—

PRAED. No, pray, pray, my dear Frank, remember! He is your father.

FRANK. I give him due credit for that. [Rising and flinging down his paper] But just imagine his telling Crofts to bring the Warrens over here! He must have been ever so drunk. You know, my dear Praddy, my mother wouldn't stand Mrs Warren for a moment. Vivie mustn't come here until she's gone back to town.

PRAED. But your mother doesn't know anything about Mrs Warren, does she? [He picks up the paper and sits down to read it].

FRANK. I don't know. Her journey to town looks as if she did. Not that my mother would mind in the ordinary way: she has stuck like a brick to lots of women who had got into trouble. But they were all nice women. Thats what makes the real difference. Mrs Warren, no doubt, has her merits; but she's ever so rowdy; and my mother simply wouldn't put up with her. So—hallo! [This exclamation is provoked by the reappearance of the clergyman, who comes out of the house in haste and dismay].

REV. S. Frank: Mrs Warren and her daughter are coming across the heath with Crofts: I saw them from the study windows. What *am* I to say about your mother?

FRANK. Stick on your hat and go out and say how delighted you are to see them; and that Frank's in the garden; and that mother and Bessie have been called to the bedside of a sick relative, and were ever so sorry they couldn't stop; and that you hope Mrs Warren slept well; and—and—say any blessed thing except the truth, and leave the rest to Providence.

REV. S. But how are we to get rid of them afterwards?

FRANK. Theres no time to think of that now. Here! [He bounds into the house].

REV. S. He's so impetuous. I don't know what to do with him, Mr Praed.

FRANK [returning with a clerical felt hat, which he claps on his father's head]. Now: off with you. [Rushing him through the gate]. Praed and I'll wait here, to give the thing an unpremeditated air. [The clergyman, dazed but obedient, hurries off].

FRANK. We must get the old girl back to town somehow, Praed. Come! Honestly, dear Praddy, do you like seeing them together?

PRAED. Oh, why not?

FRANK [his teeth on edge] Don't it make your flesh creep ever so little? that wicked old devil, up to every villainy under the sun, I'll swear, and Vivie—ugh!

PRAED. Hush, pray. Theyre coming.

[The clergyman and Crofts are seen coming along the road, followed by Mrs Warren and Vivie walking affectionately together.]

FRANK. Look: she actually has her arm round the old woman's waist. It's her right arm: she began it. She's gone sentimental, by God! Ugh! ugh! Now do you feel the creeps? [The clergyman opens the gate: and Mrs Warren and Vivie pass him and stand in the middle of the garden looking at the house. Frank, in an ecstasy of dissimulation, turns gaily to Mrs Warren, exclaiming] Ever so delighted to see you, Mrs Warren. This quiet old rectory garden becomes you perfectly.

MRS WARREN. Well, I never! Did you hear that, George? He says I look well in a quiet old rectory garden.

REV. S. [still holding the gate for Crofts, who loafs through it, heavily bored] You look well everywhere, Mrs Warren.

FRANK. Bravo, gov'nor! Now look here: lets have a treat before lunch. First lets see the church. Everyone has to do that. It's a regular old thirteenth century church, you know: the gov'nor's ever so fond of it, because he got up a restoration fund and had it completely rebuilt six years ago. Praed will be able to shew its points.

PRAED [rising] Certainly, if the restoration has left any to shew.

REV. S. [mooning hospitably at them] I shall be pleased, I'm sure, if Sir George and Mrs Warren really care about it.

MRS WARREN. Oh, come along and get it over.

CROFTS [turning back toward the gate] I've no objection.

REV. S. Not that way. We go through the fields, if you don't mind. Round here. [He leads the way by the little path through the box hedge].

CROFTS. Oh, all right. [He goes with the parson].

[Praed follows with Mrs Warren. Vivie does not stir: she watches them until they have gone, with all the lines of purpose in her face marking it strongly.]

FRANK. Ain't you coming?

VIVIE. No. I want to give you a warning, Frank. You were making fun of my mother just now when you said that about the rectory garden. That is barred in the future. Please treat my mother with as much respect as you treat your own.

FRANK. My dear Viv: she wouldn't appreciate it: the two cases require different treatment. But what on earth has happened to you? Last night we were perfectly agreed as to your mother and her set. This morning I find you attitudinizing sentimentally with your arm around your parent's waist.

VIVIE [flushing] Attitudinizing!

FRANK. That was how it struck me. First time I ever saw you do a second-rate thing.

VIVIE [controlling herself] Yes, Frank: there has been a change: but I don't think it a change for the worse. Yesterday I was a little prig.

FRANK. And today?

VIVIE [wincing; then looking at him steadily] Today I know my mother better than you do.

FRANK. Heaven forbid!

VIVIE. What do you mean?

FRANK. Viv: theres a freemasonry among thoroughly immoral people that you know nothing of. You've too much character. *That's* the bond between your mother and me: that's why I know her better than youll ever know her.

VIVIE. You are wrong: you know nothing about her. If you knew the circumstances against which my mother had to struggle—

FRANK [adroitly finishing the sentence for her] I should know why she is what she is, shouldn't I? What difference would that make?

Circumstances or no circumstances, Viv, you won't be able to stand your mother.

VIVIE [very angry] Why not?

FRANK. Because she's an old wretch, Viv. If you ever put your arm around her waist in my presence again, I'll shoot myself there and then as a protest against an exhibition which revolts me.

VIVIE. Must I choose between dropping your acquaintance and dropping my mother's?

FRANK [gracefully] That would put the old lady at ever such a disadvantage. No, Viv: your infatuated little boy will have to stick to you in any case. But he's all the more anxious that you shouldn't make mistakes. It's no use, Viv: your mother's impossible. She may be a good sort; but she's a bad lot, a very bad lot.

VIVIE [hotly] Frank—! [He stands his ground. She turns away and sits down on the bench under the yew tree, struggling to recover her self-command. Then she says] Is she to be deserted by the world because she's what you call a bad lot? Has she no right to live?

FRANK. No fear of that, Viv: *she* won't ever be deserted. [He sits on the bench beside her].

VIVIE. But I am to desert her, I suppose.

FRANK [babyishly, lulling her and making love to her with his voice]
Mustn't go live with her. Little family group of mother and daughter
wouldn't be a success. Spoil o u r little group.

VIVIE [falling under the spell] What little group?

FRANK. The babes in the wood: Vivie and little Frank. [He nestles against
her like a weary child]. Lets go and get covered up with leaves.

VIVIE [rhythmically, rocking him like a nurse] Fast asleep, hand in hand,
under the trees.

FRANK. The wise little girl with her silly little boy.

VIVIE. The dead little boy with his dowdy little girl.

FRANK. Ever so peaceful, and relieved from the imbecility of the little
boy's father and the questionableness of the little girl's—

VIVIE [smothering the word against her breast] Sh-sh-sh-sh! little girl
wants to forget all about her mother. [They are silent for some
moments, rocking one another. Then Vivie wakes up with a shock,
exclaiming] What a pair of fools we are! Come: sit up. Gracious!
your hair. [She smooths it]. I wonder do all grown up people play in
that childish way when nobody is looking.

I never did it when I was a child.

FRANK. Neither did I. You are my first playmate. [He catches her hand
to kiss it, but checks himself to look around first. Very unexpectedly,
he sees Crofts emerging from the box hedge]. Oh damn!

VIVIE. Why damn, dear?

FRANK [whispering] Sh! Here's this brute Crofts. [He sits farther away
from her with an unconcerned air].

CROFTS. Could I have a few words with you, Miss Vivie?

VIVIE. Certainly.

CROFTS [to Frank] Youll excuse me, Gardner. Theyre waiting for you in
the church, if you don't mind.

FRANK [rising] Anything to oblige you, Crofts—except church. If you
should happen to want me, Vivvums, ring the gate bell. [He goes
into the house with unruffled suavity].

CROFTS [watching him with a crafty air as he disappears, and speaking to Vivie with an assumption of being on privileged terms with her] Pleasant young fellow that, Miss Vivie. Pity he has no money, isn't it?

VIVIE. Do you think so?

CROFTS. Well, whats he to do? No profession. No property. Whats he good for?

VIVIE. I realize his disadvantages, Sir George.

CROFTS [a little taken aback at being so precisely interpreted] Oh, it's not that. But while we're in this world we're in it; and money's money. [Vivie does not answer]. Nice day, isn't it?

VIVIE [with scarcely veiled contempt for this effort at conversation] Very.

CROFTS [with brutal good humor, as if he liked her pluck] Well thats not what I came to say. [Sitting down beside her] Now listen, Miss Vivie. I'm quite aware that I'm not a young lady's man.

VIVIE. Indeed, Sir George?

CROFTS. No; and to tell you the honest truth I don't want to be either. But when I say a thing I mean it; and when I feel a sentiment I feel it in earnest; and what I value I pay hard money for. Thats the sort of man I am.

VIVIE. It does you great credit, I'm sure.

CROFTS. Oh, I don't mean to praise myself. I have my faults, Heaven knows: no man is more sensible of that than I am. I know I'm not perfect: thats one of the advantages of being a middle-aged man; for I'm not a young man, and I know it. But my code is a simple one, and, I think, a good one. Honor between man and man; fidelity between man and woman; and no can't about this religion or that religion, but an honest belief that things are making for good on the whole.

VIVIE [with biting irony] "A power, not ourselves, that makes for righteousness," eh?

CROFTS [taking her seriously] Oh certainly. Not ourselves, of course. Y o u understand what I mean. Well, now as to practical matters. You may have an idea that I've flung my money about; but I havn't: I'm richer today than when I first came into the property. I've used my knowledge of the world to invest my money in ways that other men have overlooked; and whatever else I may be, I'm a safe man from the money point of view.

VIVIE. It's very kind of you to tell me all this.

CROFTS. Oh well, come, Miss Vivie: you needn't pretend you don't see what I'm driving at. I want to settle down with a Lady Crofts. I suppose you think me very blunt, eh?

VIVIE. Not at all: I am very much obliged to you for being so definite and business-like. I quite appreciate the offer: the money, the position, *Lady Crofts*, and so on. But I think I will say no, if you don't mind, I'd rather not. [She rises, and strolls across to the sundial to get out of his immediate neighborhood].

CROFTS [not at all discouraged, and taking advantage of the additional room left him on the seat to spread himself comfortably, as if a few preliminary refusals were part of the inevitable routine of courtship] I'm in no hurry. It was only just to let you know in case young Gardner should try to trap you. Leave the question open.

VIVIE [sharply] My no is final. I won't go back from it.

[Crofts is not impressed. He grins; leans forward with his elbows on his knees to prod with his stick at some unfortunate insect in the grass; and looks cunningly at her. She turns away impatiently.]

CROFTS. I'm a good deal older than you. Twenty-five years: quarter of a century. I shan't live for ever; and I'll take care that you shall be well off when I'm gone.

VIVIE. I am proof against even that inducement, Sir George. Don't you think youd better take your answer? There is not the slightest chance of my altering it.

CROFTS [rising, after a final slash at a daisy, and coming nearer to her] Well, no matter. I could tell you some things that would change your mind fast enough; but I wont, because I'd rather win you by honest affection. I was a good friend to your mother: ask her whether I wasn't. She'd never have make the money that paid for your education if it hadnt been for my advice and help, not to mention the money I advanced her. There are not many men who would have stood by her as I have. I put not less than forty thousand pounds into it, from first to last.

VIVIE [staring at him] Do you mean to say that you were my mother's business partner?

CROFTS. Yes. Now just think of all the trouble and the explanations it would save if we were to keep the whole thing in the family, so to speak. Ask your mother whether she'd like to have to explain all her affairs to a perfect stranger.

VIVIE. I see no difficulty, since I understand that the business is wound up, and the money invested.

CROFTS [stopping short, amazed] Wound up! Wind up a business thats paying 35 per cent in the worst years! Not likely. Who told you that?

VIVIE [her color quite gone] Do you mean that it is still—? [She stops abruptly, and puts her hand on the sundial to support herself. Then she gets quickly to the iron chair and sits down].

What business are you talking about?

CROFTS. Well, the fact is it's not what would considered exactly a high-class business in my set—the country set, you know—o u r set it will be if you think better of my offer. Not that theres any mystery about it: don't think that. Of course you know by your mother's being in it that it's perfectly straight and honest. I've known her for many years; and I can say of her that she'd cut off her hands sooner than touch anything that was not what it ought to be. I'll tell you all about it if you like. I don't know whether you've found in travelling how hard it is to find a really comfortable private hotel.

VIVIE [sickened, averting her face] Yes: go on.

CROFTS. Well, thats all it is. Your mother has got a genius for managing such things. We've got two in Brussels, one in Ostend, one in Vienna, and two in Budapest. Of course there are others besides ourselves in it; but we hold most of the capital; and your mother's indispensable as managing director. You've noticed, I daresay, that she travels a good deal. But you see you can't mention such things in society. Once let out the word hotel and everybody thinks you keep a public-house. You wouldn't like people to say that of your mother, would you? Thats why we're so reserved about it. By the way, youll keep it to yourself, won't you? Since it's been a secret so long, it had better remain so.

VIVIE. And this is the business you invite me to join you in?

CROFTS. Oh no. My wife shan't be troubled with business. Youll not be in it more than you've always been.

VIVIE. *I* always been! What do you mean?

CROFTS. Only that you've always lived on it. It paid for your education and the dress you have on your back. Don't turn up your nose at business, Miss Vivie: where would your Newnhams and Girtons be without it?

VIVIE [rising, almost beside herself] Take care. I know what this business is.

CROFTS [starting, with a suppressed oath] Who told you?

VIVIE. Your partner. My mother.

CROFTS [black with rage] The old—

VIVIE. Just so.

[He swallows the epithet and stands for a moment swearing and raging foully to himself. But he knows that his cue is to be sympathetic. He takes refuge in generous indignation.]

CROFTS. She ought to have had more consideration for you. *I'd* never have told you.

VIVIE. I think you would probably have told me when we were married: it would have been a convenient weapon to break me in with.

CROFTS [quite sincerely] I never intended that. On my word as a gentleman I didn't.

[Vivie wonders at him. Her sense of the irony of his protest cools and braces her. She replies with contemptuous self-possession.]

VIVIE. It does not matter. I suppose you understand that when we leave here today our acquaintance ceases.

CROFTS. Why? Is it for helping your mother?

VIVIE. My mother was a very poor woman who had no reasonable choice but to do as she did. You were a rich gentleman; and you did the same for the sake of 35 per cent. You are a pretty common sort of scoundrel, I think. That is my opinion of you.

CROFTS [after a stare: not at all displeased, and much more at his ease on these frank terms than on their former ceremonious ones] Ha! ha! ha! ha! Go it, little missie, go it: it doesn't hurt me and it amuses you. Why the devil shouldn't I invest my money that way? I take the interest on my capital like other people: I hope you don't think I dirty my own hands with the work.

Come! you wouldn't refuse the acquaintance of my mother's cousin the Duke of Belgravia because some of the rents he gets are earned in queer ways. You wouldn't cut the Archbishop of Canterbury, I suppose, because the Ecclesiastical Commissioners have a few publicans and sinners among their tenants. Do you remember your Crofts scholarship at Newnham? Well, that was founded by my brother the M.P. He gets his 22 per cent out of a factory with 600 girls in it, and not one of them getting wages enough to live on.

How d'ye suppose they manage when they have no family to fall back on? Ask your mother. And do you expect me to turn my back on 35 per cent when all the rest are pocketing what they can, like sensible men? No such fool! If youre going to pick and choose your acquaintances on moral principles, youd better clear out of this country, unless you want to cut yourself out of all decent society.

VIVIE [conscience stricken] You might go on to point out that I myself never asked where the money I spent came from. I believe I am just as bad as you.

CROFTS [greatly reassured] Of course you are; and a very good thing too! What harm does it do after all? [Rallying her jocularly] So you don't think me such a scoundrel now you come to think it over. Eh?

VIVIE. I have shared profits with you: and I admitted you just now to the familiarity of knowing what I think of you.

CROFTS [with serious friendliness] To be sure you did. You won't find me a bad sort: I don't go in for being superfine intellectually; but Ive plenty of honest human feeling; and the old Crofts breed comes out in a sort of instinctive hatred of anything low, in which I'm sure youll sympathize with me. Believe me, Miss Vivie, the world isn't such a bad place as the croakers make out. As long as you don't fly openly in the face of society, society doesn't ask any inconvenient questions; and it makes precious short work of the cads who do. There are no secrets better kept than the secrets everybody guesses. In the class of people I can introduce you to, no lady or gentleman would so far forget themselves as to discuss my business affairs or your mothers. No man can offer you a safer position.

VIVIE [studying him curiously] I suppose you really think youre getting on famously with me.

CROFTS. Well, I hope I may flatter myself that you think better of me than you did at first.

VIVIE [quietly] I hardly find you worth thinking about at all now. When I think of the society that tolerates you, and the laws that protect you! when I think of how helpless nine out of ten young girls would be in the hands of you and my mother! the unmentionable woman and her capitalist bully—

CROFTS [livid] Damn you!

VIVIE. You need not. I feel among the damned already.

[She raises the latch of the gate to open it and go out. He follows her and puts his hand heavily on the top bar to prevent its opening.]

CROFTS [panting with fury] Do you think I'll put up with this from you, you young devil?

VIVIE [unmoved] Be quiet. Some one will answer the bell. [Without flinching a step she strikes the bell with the back of her hand. It clangs harshly; and he starts back involuntarily. Almost immediately Frank appears at the porch with his rifle].

FRANK [with cheerful politeness] Will you have the rifle, Viv; or shall I operate?

VIVIE. Frank: have you been listening?

FRANK [coming down into the garden] Only for the bell, I assure you; so that you shouldn't have to wait. I think I shewed great insight into your character, Crofts.

CROFTS. For two pins I'd take that gun from you and break it across your head.

FRANK [stalking him cautiously] Pray don't. I'm ever so careless in handling firearms. Sure to be a fatal accident, with a reprimand from the coroner's jury for my negligence.

VIVIE. Put the rifle away, Frank: it's quite unnecessary.

FRANK. Quite right, Viv. Much more sportsmanlike to catch him in a trap. [Crofts, understanding the insult, makes a threatening movement].

Crofts: there are fifteen cartridges in the magazine here; and I am a dead shot at the present distance and at an object of your size.

CROFTS. Oh, you needn't be afraid. I'm not going to touch you.

FRANK. Ever so magnanimous of you under the circumstances! Thank you.

CROFTS. I'll just tell you this before I go. It may interest you, since youre so fond of one another. Allow me, Mister Frank, to introduce you to your half-sister, the eldest daughter of the Reverend Samuel Gardner. Miss Vivie: you half-brother. Good morning! [He goes out through the gate and along the road].

FRANK [after a pause of stupefaction, raising the rifle] Youll testify before the coroner that it's an accident, Viv. [He takes aim at the retreating figure of Crofts. Vivie seizes the muzzle and pulls it round against her breast].

VIVIE. Fire now. You may.

FRANK [dropping his end of the rifle hastily] Stop! take care. [She lets it go. It falls on the turf]. Oh, you've given your little boy such a turn. Suppose it had gone off! ugh! [He sinks on the garden seat, overcome].

VIVIE. Suppose it had: do you think it would not have been a relief to have some sharp physical pain tearing through me?

FRANK [coaxingly] Take it ever so easy, dear Viv. Remember: even if the rifle scared that fellow into telling the truth for the first time in his life, that only makes us the babes in the woods in earnest. [He holds out his arms to her]. Come and be covered up with leaves again.

VIVIE [with a cry of disgust] Ah, not that, not that. You make all my flesh creep.

FRANK. Why, whats the matter?

VIVIE. Goodbye. [She makes for the gate].

FRANK [jumping up] Hallo! Stop! Viv! Viv! [She turns in the gateway] Where are you going to? Where shall we find you?

VIVIE. At Honoria Fraser's chambers, 67 Chancery Lane, for the rest of my life. [She goes off quickly in the opposite direction to that taken by Crofts].

FRANK. But I say—wait—dash it! [He runs after her].

ACT IV

[Honoria Fraser's chambers in Chancery Lane. An office at the top of New Stone Buildings, with a plate-glass window, distempered walls, electric light, and a patent stove. Saturday afternoon. The chimneys of Lincoln's Inn and the western sky beyond are seen through the window. There is a double writing table in the middle of the room, with a cigar box, ash pans, and a portable electric reading lamp almost snowed up in heaps of papers and books. This table has knee holes and chairs right and left and is very untidy. The clerk's desk, closed and tidy, with its high stool, is against the wall, near a door communicating with the inner rooms. In the opposite wall is the door leading to the public corridor. Its upper panel is of opaque glass, lettered in black on the outside, FRASER AND WARREN. A baize screen hides the corner between this door and the window.]

[Frank, in a fashionable light-colored coaching suit, with his stick, gloves, and white hat in his hands, is pacing up and down in the office. Somebody tries the door with a key.]

FRANK [calling] Come in. It's not locked.

[Vivie comes in, in her hat and jacket. She stops and stares at him.]

VIVIE [sternly] What are you doing here?
FRANK. Waiting to see you. I've been here for hours. Is this the way you attend to your business? [He puts his hat and stick on the table, and

perches himself with a vault on the clerk's stool, looking at her with every appearance of being in a specially restless, teasing, flippant mood].

VIVIE. I've been away exactly twenty minutes for a cup of tea. [She takes off her hat and jacket and hangs them behind the screen]. How did you get in?

FRANK. The staff had not left when I arrived. He's gone to play cricket on Primrose Hill. Why don't you employ a woman, and give your sex a chance?

VIVIE. What have you come for?

FRANK [springing off the stool and coming close to her] Viv: lets go and enjoy the Saturday half-holiday somewhere, like the staff. What do you say to Richmond, and then a music hall, and a jolly supper?

VIVIE. Can't afford it. I shall put in another six hours work before I go to bed.

FRANK. Can't afford it, can't we? Aha! Look here. [He takes out a handful of sovereigns and makes them chink]. Gold, Viv: gold!

VIVIE. Where did you get it?

FRANK. Gambling, Viv: gambling. Poker.

VIVIE. Pah! It's meaner than stealing it. No: I'm not coming. [She sits down to work at the table, with her back to the glass door, and begins turning over the papers].

FRANK [remonstrating piteously] But, my dear Viv, I want to talk to you ever so seriously.

VIVIE. Very well: sit down in Honoria's chair and talk here. I like ten minutes chat after tea. [He murmurs]. No use groaning: I'm inexorable. [He takes the opposite seat disconsolately]. Pass that cigar box, will you?

FRANK [pushing the cigar box across] Nasty womanly habit. Nice men don't do it any longer.

VIVIE. Yes: they object to the smell in the office; and we've had to take to cigarets. See! [She opens the box and takes out a cigaret, which she lights. She offers him one; but he shakes his head with a wry face. She settles herself comfortably in her chair, smoking]. Go ahead.

FRANK. Well, I want to know what you've done—what arrangements you've made.

VIVIE. Everything was settled twenty minutes after I arrived here. Honoria has found the business too much for her this year; and she was on the point of sending for me and proposing a partnership when I walked in and told her I hadn't a farthing in the world. So I installed myself and packed her off for a fortnight's holiday. What happened at Haslemere when I left?

FRANK. Nothing at all. I said youd gone to town on particular business.

VIVIE. Well?

FRANK. Well, either they were too flabbergasted to say anything, or else Crofts had prepared your mother. Anyhow, she didn't say anything; and Crofts didn't say anything; and Praddy only stared. After tea they got up and went; and I've not seen them since.

VIVIE [nodding placidly with one eye on a wreath of smoke] Thats all right.

FRANK [looking round disparagingly] Do you intend to stick in this confounded place?

VIVIE [blowing the wreath decisively away, and sitting straight up] Yes. These two days have given me back all my strength and self-possession. I will never take a holiday again as long as I live.

FRANK [with a very wry face] Mps! You look quite happy. And as hard as nails.

VIVIE [grimly] Well for me that I am!

FRANK [rising] Look here, Viv: we must have an explanation. We parted the other day under a complete misunderstanding. [He sits on the table, close to her].

VIVIE [putting away the cigaret] Well: clear it up.

FRANK. You remember what Crofts said.

VIVIE. Yes.

FRANK. That revelation was supposed to bring about a complete change in the nature of our feeling for one another. It placed us on the footing of brother and sister.

VIVIE. Yes.

FRANK. Have you ever had a brother?

VIVIE. No.

FRANK. Then you don't know what being brother and sister feels like? Now I have lots of sisters; and the fraternal feeling is quite familiar to me. I assure you my feeling for you is not the least in the world like it. The girls will go *their* way; I will go mine; and we shan't care if we never see one another again. Thats brother and sister. But as to you, I can't be easy if I have to pass a week without seeing you. Thats not brother and sister. Its exactly what I felt an hour before Crofts made his revelation. In short, dear Viv, it's love's young dream.

VIVIE [bitingly] The same feeling, Frank, that brought your father to my mother's feet. Is that it?

FRANK [so revolted that he slips off the table for a moment] I very strongly object, Viv, to have my feelings compared to any which the Reverend Samuel is capable of harboring; and I object still more to a comparison of you to your mother. [Resuming his perch] Besides, I don't believe the story. I have taxed my father with it, and obtained from him what I consider tantamount to a denial.

VIVIE. What did he say?

FRANK. He said he was sure there must be some mistake.

VIVIE. Do you believe him?

FRANK. I am prepared to take his word against Crofts'.

VIVIE. Does it make any difference? I mean in your imagination or conscience; for of course it makes no real difference.

FRANK [shaking his head] None whatever to *me*.

VIVIE. Nor to me.

FRANK [staring] But this is ever so surprising! [He goes back to his chair]. I thought our whole relations were altered in your imagination and conscience, as you put it, the moment those words were out of that brute's muzzle.

VIVIE. No: it was not that. I didn't believe him. I only wish I could.

FRANK. Eh?

VIVIE. I think brother and sister would be a very suitable relation for us.

FRANK. You really mean that?

VIVIE. Yes. It's the only relation I care for, even if we could afford any other. I mean that.

FRANK [raising his eyebrows like one on whom a new light has dawned, and rising with quite an effusion of chivalrous sentiment] My dear Viv: why didn't you say so before? I am ever so sorry for persecuting you. I understand, of course.

VIVIE [puzzled] Understand what?

FRANK. Oh, I'm not a fool in the ordinary sense: only in the Scriptural sense of doing all the things the wise man declared to be folly, after trying them himself on the most extensive scale. I see I am no longer Vivvums's little boy. Don't be alarmed: I shall never call you Vivvums again—at least unless you get tired of your new little boy, whoever he may be.

VIVIE. My new little boy!

FRANK [with conviction] Must be a new little boy. Always happens that way. No other way, in fact.

VIVIE. None that you know of, fortunately for you.

[Someone knocks at the door.]

FRANK. My curse upon yon caller, whoe'er he be!

VIVIE. It's Praed. He's going to Italy and wants to say goodbye. I asked him to call this afternoon. Go and let him in.

FRANK. We can continue our conversation after his departure for Italy. I'll stay him out. [He goes to the door and opens it]. How are you, Praddy? Delighted to see you. Come in.

[Praed, dressed for travelling, comes in, in high spirits.]

PRAED. How do you do, Miss Warren? [She presses his hand cordially, though a certain sentimentality in his high spirits jars upon her]. I start in an hour from Holborn Viaduct. I wish I could persuade you to try Italy.

VIVIE. What for?

PRAED. Why, to saturate yourself with beauty and romance, of course.

[Vivie, with a shudder, turns her chair to the table, as if the work waiting for her there were a support to her. Praed sits opposite to her. Frank places a chair near Vivie, and drops lazily and carelessly into it, talking at her over his shoulder.]

FRANK. No use, Praddy. Viv is a little Philistine. She is indifferent to *my* romance, and insensible to *my* beauty.

VIVIE. Mr Praed: once for all, there is no beauty and no romance in life for me. Life is what it is; and I am prepared to take it as it is.

PRAED [enthusiastically] You will not say that if you come with me to Verona and on to Venice. You will cry with delight at living in such a beautiful world.

FRANK. This is most eloquent, Praddy. Keep it up.

PRAED. Oh, I assure you *I* have cried—I shall cry again, I hope—at fifty! At your age, Miss Warren, you would not need to go so far as Verona. Your spirits would absolutely fly up at the mere sight of Ostend. You would be charmed with the gaiety, the vivacity, the happy air of Brussels.

VIVIE [springing up with an exclamation of loathing] Agh!

PRAED [rising] Whats the matter?

FRANK [rising] Hallo, Viv!

VIVIE [to Praed, with deep reproach] Can you find no better example of your beauty and romance than Brussels to talk to me about?

PRAED [puzzled] Of course it's very different from Verona. I don't suggest for a moment that—

VIVIE [bitterly] Probably the beauty and romance come to much the same in both places.

PRAED [completely sobered and much concerned] My dear Miss Warren: I—[looking enquiringly at Frank] Is anything the matter?

FRANK. She thinks your enthusiasm frivolous, Praddy. She's had ever such a serious call.

VIVIE [sharply] Hold your tongue, Frank. Don't be silly.

FRANK [sitting down] Do you call this good manners, Praed?

PRAED [anxious and considerate] Shall I take him away, Miss Warren? I feel sure we have disturbed you at your work.

VIVIE. Sit down: I'm not ready to go back to work yet. [Praed sits]. You both think I have an attack of nerves. Not a bit of it. But there are two subjects I want dropped, if you don't mind.

One of them [to Frank] is love's young dream in any shape or form: the other [to Praed] is the romance and beauty of life, especially Ostend and the gaiety of Brussels. You are welcome to any illusions you may have left on these subjects: I have none. If we three are to remain friends, I must be treated as a woman of business, permanently single [to Frank] and permanently unromantic [to Praed].

FRANK. I also shall remain permanently single until you change your mind. Praddy: change the subject. Be eloquent about something else.

PRAED [diffidently] I'm afraid theres nothing else in the world that I *can* talk about. The Gospel of Art is the only one I can preach. I know Miss Warren is a great devotee of the Gospel of Getting On; but we can't discuss that without hurting your feelings, Frank, since you are determined not to get on.

FRANK. Oh, don't mind my feelings. Give me some improving advice by all means: it does me ever so much good. Have another try to make a successful man of me, Viv. Come: lets have it all: energy, thrift, foresight, self-respect, character. Don't you hate people who have no character, Viv?

VIVIE [wincing] Oh, stop, stop. Let us have no more of that horrible cant. Mr Praed: if there are really only those two gospels in the world, we had better all kill ourselves; for the same taint is in both, through and through.

FRANK [looking critically at her] There is a touch of poetry about you today, Viv, which has hitherto been lacking.

PRAED [remonstrating] My dear Frank: aren't you a little unsympathetic?

VIVIE [merciless to herself] No: it's good for me. It keeps me from being sentimental.

FRANK [bantering her] Checks your strong natural propensity that way, don't it?

VIVIE [almost hysterically] Oh yes: go on: don't spare me. I was sentimental for one moment in my life—beautifully sentimental—by moonlight; and now—

FRANK [quickly] I say, Viv: take care. Don't give yourself away.

VIVIE. Oh, do you think Mr Praed does not know all about my mother? [Turning on Praed] You had better have told me that morning, Mr Praed. You are very old fashioned in your delicacies, after all.

PRAED. Surely it is you who are a little old fashioned in your prejudices, Miss Warren. I feel bound to tell you, speaking as an artist, and believing that the most intimate human relationships are far beyond and above the scope of the law, that though I know that your mother is an unmarried woman, I do not respect her the less on that account. I respect her more.

FRANK [airily] Hear! hear!

VIVIE [staring at him] Is that *all* you know?

PRAED. Certainly that is all.

VIVIE. Then you neither of you know anything. Your guesses are innocence itself compared with the truth.

PRAED [rising, startled and indignant, and preserving his politeness with an effort] I hope not. [More emphatically] I hope not, Miss Warren.

FRANK [whistles] Whew!

VIVIE. You are not making it easy for me to tell you, Mr Praed.

PRAED [his chivalry drooping before their conviction] If there is anything worse—that is, anything else—are you sure you are right to tell us, Miss Warren?

VIVIE. I am sure that if I had the courage I should spend the rest of my life in telling everybody—stamping and branding it into them until they all felt their part in its abomination as I feel mine. There is nothing I despise more than the wicked convention that protects these things by forbidding a woman to mention them. And yet I can't tell you. The two infamous words that describe what my mother is are ringing in my ears and struggling on my tongue; but I can't utter them: the shame of them is too horrible for me. [She buries her face in her hands. The two men, astonished, stare at one another and then at her. She raises her head again desperately and snatches a sheet of paper and a pen]. Here: let me draft you a prospectus.

FRANK. Oh, she's mad. Do you hear, Viv? mad. Come! pull yourself together.

VIVIE. You shall see. [She writes]. "Paid up capital: not less than forty thousand pounds standing in the name of Sir George Crofts, Baronet, the chief shareholder. Premises at Brussels, Ostend, Vienna, and Budapest. Managing director: Mrs Warren"; and now don't let us forget h e r qualifications: the two words. [She writes the words and pushes the paper to them]. There! Oh no: don't read it: don't! [She snatches it back and tears it to pieces; then seizes her head in her hands and hides her face on the table].

[Frank, who has watched the writing over her shoulder, and opened his eyes very widely at it, takes a card from his pocket; scribbles the two words on it; and silently hands it to Praed, who reads it with amazement, and hides it hastily in his pocket.]

FRANK [whispering tenderly] Viv, dear: thats all right. I read what you wrote: so did Praddy. We understand. And we remain, as this leaves us at present, yours ever so devotedly.

PRAED. We do indeed, Miss Warren. I declare you are the most splendidly courageous woman I ever met.

[This sentimental compliment braces Vivie. She throws it away from her with an impatient shake, and forces herself to stand up, though not without some support from the table.]

FRANK. Don't stir, Viv, if you don't want to. Take it easy.

VIVIE. Thank you. You an always depend on me for two things: not to cry and not to faint. [She moves a few steps towards the door of the inner room, and stops close to Praed to say] I shall need much more courage than that when I tell my mother that we have come to a parting of the ways. Now I must go into the next room for a moment to make myself neat again, if you don't mind.

PRAED. Shall we go away?

VIVIE. No: I'll be back presently. Only for a moment. [She goes into the other room, Praed opening the door for her].

PRAED. What an amazing revelation! I'm extremely disappointed in Crofts: I am indeed.

FRANK. I'm not in the least. I feel he's perfectly accounted for at last. But what a facer for me, Praddy! I can't marry her now.

PRAED [sternly] Frank! [The two look at one another, Frank unruffled, Praed deeply indignant]. Let me tell you, Gardner, that if you desert her now you will behave very despicably.

FRANK. Good old Praddy! Ever chivalrous! But you mistake: it's not the moral aspect of the case: it's the money aspect. I really can't bring myself to touch the old woman's money now.

PRAED. And was that what you were going to marry on?

FRANK. What else? *I* havn't any money, nor the smallest turn for making it. If I married Viv now she would have to support me; and I should cost her more than I am worth.

PRAED. But surely a clever bright fellow like you can make something by your own brains.

FRANK. Oh yes, a little. [He takes out his money again]. I made all that yesterday in an hour and a half. But I made it in a highly speculative business. No, dear Praddy: even if Bessie and Georgina marry millionaires and the governor dies after cutting them off with a shilling, I shall have only four hundred a year. And he won't die until he's three score and ten: he hasn't originality enough. I shall be on short allowance for the next twenty years. No short allowance for Viv, if I can help it. I withdraw gracefully and leave the field to the gilded youth of England. So that settled. I shan't worry her about it: I'll just send her a little note after we're gone. She'll understand.

PRAED [grasping his hand] Good fellow, Frank! I heartily beg your pardon. But must you never see her again?

FRANK. Never see her again! Hang it all, be reasonable. I shall come along as often as possible, and be her brother. I can *not* understand the absurd consequences you romantic people expect from the most ordinary transactions. [A knock at the door]. I wonder who this is. Would you mind opening the door? If it's a client it will look more respectable than if I appeared.

PRAED. Certainly. [He goes to the door and opens it. Frank sits down in Vivie's chair to scribble a note]. My dear Kitty: come in: come in.

[Mrs Warren comes in, looking apprehensively around for Vivie. She has done her best to make herself matronly and dignified. The brilliant hat is replaced by a sober bonnet, and the gay blouse covered by a costly black silk mantle. She is pitiably anxious and ill at ease: evidently panic-stricken.]

MRS WARREN [to Frank] What! Y o u r e here, are you?

FRANK [turning in his chair from his writing, but not rising] Here, and charmed to see you. You come like a breath of spring.

MRS WARREN. Oh, get out with your nonsense. [In a low voice] Where's Vivie?

[Frank points expressively to the door of the inner room, but says nothing.]

MRS WARREN [sitting down suddenly and almost beginning to cry] Praddy: won't she see me, don't you think?

PRAED. My dear Kitty: don't distress yourself. Why should she not?

MRS WARREN. Oh, you never can see why not: youre too innocent. Mr Frank: did she say anything to you?

FRANK [folding his note] She *must* see you, if [very expressively] you wait til she comes in.

MRS WARREN [frightened] Why shouldn't I wait?

[Frank looks quizzically at her; puts his note carefully on the ink-bottle, so that Vivie cannot fail to find it when next she dips her pen; then rises and devotes his attention entirely to her.]

FRANK. My dear Mrs Warren: suppose you were a sparrow—ever so tiny and pretty a sparrow hopping in the roadway—and you saw a steam roller coming in your direction, would you wait for it?

MRS WARREN. Oh, don't bother me with your sparrows. What did she run away from Haslemere like that for?

FRANK. I'm afraid she'll tell you if you rashly await her return.

MRS WARREN. Do you want me to go away?

FRANK. No: I always want you to stay. But I *advise* you to go away.

MRS WARREN. What! And never see her again!

FRANK. Precisely.

MRS WARREN [crying again] Praddy: don't let him be cruel to me. [She hastily checks her tears and wipes her eyes]. She'll be so angry if she sees I've been crying.

FRANK [with a touch of real compassion in his airy tenderness] You know that Praddy is the soul of kindness, Mrs Warren. Praddy: what do you say? Go or stay?

PRAED [to Mrs Warren] I really should be very sorry to cause you unnecessary pain; but I think perhaps you had better not wait. The fact is—[Vivie is heard at the inner door].

FRANK. Sh! Too late. She's coming.

MRS WARREN. Don't tell her I was crying. [Vivie comes in. She stops gravely on seeing Mrs Warren, who greets her with hysterical cheerfulness]. Well, dearie. So here you are at last.

VIVIE. I am glad you have come: I want to speak to you. You said you were going, Frank, I think.

FRANK. Yes. Will you come with me, Mrs Warren? What do you say to a trip to Richmond, and the theatre in the evening? There is safety in Richmond. No steam roller there.

VIVIE. Nonsense, Frank. My mother will stay here.

MRS WARREN [scared] I don't know: perhaps I'd better go. We're disturbing you at your work.

VIVIE [with quiet decision] Mr Praed: please take Frank away. Sit down, mother. [Mrs Warren obeys helplessly].

PRAED. Come, Frank. Goodbye, Miss Vivie.

VIVIE [shaking hands] Goodbye. A pleasant trip.

PRAED. Thank you: thank you. I hope so.

FRANK [to Mrs Warren] Goodbye: youd ever so much better have taken my advice. [He shakes hands with her. Then airily to Vivie] Byebye, Viv.

VIVIE. Goodbye. [He goes out gaily without shaking hands with her].

PRAED [sadly] Goodbye, Kitty.

MRS WARREN [snivelling]—oobye!

[Praed goes. Vivie, composed and extremely grave, sits down in Honoria's chair, and waits for her mother to speak. Mrs Warren, dreading a pause, loses no time in beginning.]

MRS WARREN. Well, Vivie, what did you go away like that for without saying a word to me! How could you do such a thing! And what have you done to poor George? I wanted him to come with me; but he shuffled out of it. I could see that he was quite afraid of you. Only fancy: he wanted me not to come. As if [trembling] I should be afraid of you, dearie. [Vivie's gravity deepens]. But of course I told him it was all settled and comfortable between us, and that we were on the best of terms. [She breaks down]. Vivie: whats the meaning of this? [She produces a commercial envelope, and fumbles at the enclosure with trembling fingers]. I got it from the bank this morning.

VIVIE. It is my month's allowance. They sent it to me as usual the other day. I simply sent it back to be placed to your credit, and asked them to send you the lodgment receipt. In future I shall support myself.

MRS WARREN [not daring to understand] Wasn't it enough? Why didn't you tell me? [With a cunning gleam in her eye] I'll double it: I was intending to double it. Only let me know how much you want.

VIVIE. You know very well that that has nothing to do with it. From this time I go my own way in my own business and among my own friends. And you will go yours. [She rises]. Goodbye.

MRS WARREN [rising, appalled] Goodbye?

VIVIE. Yes: goodbye. Come: don't let us make a useless scene: you understand perfectly well. Sir George Crofts has told me the whole business.

MRS WARREN [angrily] Silly old—[She swallows an epithet, and then turns white at the narrowness of her escape from uttering it].

VIVIE. Just so.

MRS WARREN. He ought to have his tongue cut out. But I thought it was ended: you said you didn't mind.

VIVIE [steadfastly] Excuse me: I *do* mind.

MRS WARREN. But I explained—

VIVIE. You explained how it came about. You did not tell me that it is still going on [She sits].

[Mrs Warren, silenced for a moment, looks forlornly at Vivie, who waits, secretly hoping that the combat is over. But the cunning expression comes back into Mrs Warren's face; and she bends across the table, sly and urgent, half whispering.]

MRS WARREN. Vivie: do you know how rich I am?

VIVIE. I have no doubt you are very rich.

MRS WARREN. But you don't know all that that means; youre too young. It means a new dress every day; it means theatres and balls every night; it means having the pick of all the gentlemen in Europe at your feet; it means a lovely house and plenty of servants; it means the choicest of eating and drinking; it means everything you like, everything you want, everything you can think of. And what are you here? A mere drudge, toiling and moiling early and late for your bare living and two cheap dresses a year. Think over it. [Soothingly] Youre shocked, I know. I can enter into your feelings; and I think they do you credit; but trust me, nobody will blame you: you may take my word for that. I know what young girls are; and I know youll think better of it when you've turned it over in your mind.

VIVIE. So that's how it is done, is it? You must have said all that to many a woman, to have it so pat.

MRS WARREN [passionately] What harm am I asking you to do? [Vivie turns away contemptuously. Mrs Warren continues desperately] Vivie: listen to me: you don't understand: you were taught wrong on purpose: you don't know what the world is really like.

VIVIE [arrested] Taught wrong on purpose! What do you mean?

MRS WARREN. I mean that youre throwing away all your chances for nothing. You think that people are what they pretend to be: that the way you were taught at school and college to think right and proper is the way things really are. But it's not: it's all only a pretence, to keep the cowardly slavish common run of people quiet. Do you want to find that out, like other women, at forty, when you've thrown yourself away and lost your chances; or won't you take it in good time now from your own mother, that loves you and swears to you that it's truth: gospel truth? [Urgently] Vivie: the big people, the clever people, the managing people, all know it. They do as I do, and think what I think. I know plenty of them. I know them to speak to, to introduce you to, to make friends of for you. I don't mean anything wrong: thats what you don't understand: your head is full of ignorant ideas about me. What do the people that taught you know about life or about people like me? When did they ever meet me, or speak to me, or let anyone tell them about me? the fools! Would they ever have done anything for you if I hadn't paid them? Havn't I told you that I want you to be respectable? Havn't I brought you up to be respectable? And how can you keep it up without my money and my influence and Lizzie's friends? Can't you see that youre cutting your own throat as well as breaking my heart in turning your back on me?

VIVIE. I recognize the Crofts philosophy of life, mother. I heard it all from him that day at the Gardners'.

MRS WARREN. You think I want to force that played-out old sot on you! I don't, Vivie: on my oath I don't.

VIVIE. It would not matter if you did: you would not succeed. [Mrs Warren winces, deeply hurt by the implied indifference towards her affectionate intention. Vivie, neither understanding this nor concerning herself about it, goes on calmly] Mother: you don't at all know the sort of person I am. I don't object to Crofts more than to any other coarsely built man of his class. To tell you the truth, I rather admire him for being strongminded enough to enjoy himself in his own way and make plenty of money instead of living the usual shooting, hunting, dining-out, tailoring, loafing life of his set merely because all the rest do it. And I'm perfectly aware that if

I'd been in the same circumstances as my aunt Liz, I'd have done exactly what she did.

I don't think I'm more prejudiced or straitlaced than you: I think I'm less. I'm certain I'm less sentimental. I know very well that fashionable morality is all a pretence, and that if I took your money and devoted the rest of my life to spending it fashionably, I might be as worthless and vicious as the silliest woman could possibly be without having a word said to me about it. But I don't want to be worthless. I shouldn't enjoy trotting about the park to advertize my dressmaker and carriage builder, or being bored at the opera to shew off a shopwindowful of diamonds.

MRS WARREN [bewildered] But—

VIVIE. Wait a moment: I've not done. Tell me why you continue your business now that you are independent of it. Your sister, you told me, has left all that behind her. Why don't you do the same?

MRS WARREN. Oh, it's all very easy for Liz: she likes good society, and has the air of being a lady. Imagine *me* in a cathedral town! Why, the very rooks in the trees would find me out even if I could stand the dulness of it. I must have work and excitement, or I should go melancholy mad. And what else is there for me to do? The life suits me: I'm fit for it and not for anything else. If I didn't do it somebody else would; so I don't do any real harm by it. And then it brings in money; and I like making money. No: it's no use: I can't give it up—not for anybody. But what need you know about it? I'll never mention it. I'll keep Crofts away. I'll not trouble you much: you see I have to be constantly running about from one place to another. Youll be quit of me altogether when I die.

VIVIE. No: I am my mother's daughter. I am like you: I must have work, and must make more money than I spend. But my work is not your work, and my way is not your way. We must part. It will not make much difference to us: instead of meeting one another for perhaps a few months in twenty years, we shall never meet: thats all.

MRS WARREN [her voice stifled in tears] Vivie: I meant to have been more with you: I did indeed.

VIVIE. It's no use, mother: I am not to be changed by a few cheap tears and entreaties any more than you are, I daresay.

MRS WARREN [wildly] Oh, you call a mother's tears cheap.

VIVIE. They cost you nothing; and you ask me to give you the peace and quietness of my whole life in exchange for them. What use would my company be to you if you could get it? What have we two in common that could make either of us happy together?

MRS WARREN [lapsing recklessly into her dialect] We're mother and daughter. I want my daughter. I've a right to you. Who is to care for me when I'm old? Plenty of girls have taken to me like daughters and cried at leaving me; but I let them all go because I had you to look forward to. I kept myself lonely for you. You've no right to turn on me now and refuse to do your duty as a daughter.

VIVIE [jarred and antagonized by the echo of the slums in her mother's voice] My duty as a daughter! I thought we should come to that presently. Now once for all, mother, you want a daughter and Frank wants a wife. I don't want a mother; and I don't want a husband. I have spared neither Frank nor myself in sending him about his business. Do you think I will spare you?

MRS WARREN [violently] Oh, I know the sort you are: no mercy for yourself or anyone else. _I_ know. My experience has done that for me anyhow: I can tell the pious, canting, hard, selfish woman when I meet her. Well, keep yourself to yourself: _I_ don't want you. But listen to this. Do you know what I would do with you if you were a baby again? aye, as sure as there's a Heaven above us.

VIVIE. Strangle me, perhaps.

MRS WARREN. No: I'd bring you up to be a real daughter to me, and not what you are now, with your pride and your prejudices and the college education you stole from me: yes, stole: deny it if you can: what was it but stealing? I'd bring you up in my own house, I would.

VIVIE [quietly] In one of your own houses.

MRS WARREN [screaming] Listen to her! listen to how she spits on her mother's grey hairs! Oh, may you live to have your own daughter tear and trample on you as you have trampled on me. And you will: you will. No woman ever had luck with a mother's curse on her.

VIVIE. I wish you wouldn't rant, mother. It only hardens me. Come: I suppose I am the only young woman you ever had in your power that you did good to. Don't spoil it all now.

MRS WARREN. Yes, Heaven forgive me, it's true; and you are the only one that ever turned on me. Oh, the injustice of it! the injustice! the injustice! I always wanted to be a good woman. I tried honest work; and I was slave-driven until I cursed the day I ever heard of honest work. I was a good mother; and because I made my daughter a good woman she turns me out as if I were a leper. Oh, if I only had my life to live over again! I'd talk to that lying clergyman in the school. From this time forth, so help me Heaven in my last hour, I'll do wrong and nothing but wrong. And I'll prosper on it.

VIVIE. Yes: it's better to choose your line and go through with it. If I had been you, mother, I might have done as you did; but I should not have lived one life and believed in another. You are a conventional woman at heart. That is why I am bidding you goodbye now. I am right, am I not?

MRS WARREN [taken aback] Right to throw away all my money!

VIVIE. No: right to get rid of you? I should be a fool not to. Isn't that so?

MRS WARREN [sulkily] Oh well, yes, if you come to that, I suppose you are. But Lord help the world if everybody took to doing the right thing! And now I'd better go than stay where I'm not wanted. [She turns to the door].

VIVIE [kindly] Won't you shake hands?

MRS WARREN [after looking at her fiercely for a moment with a savage impulse to strike her] No, thank you. Goodbye.

VIVIE [matter-of-factly] Goodbye. [Mrs Warren goes out, slamming the door behind her. The strain on Vivie's face relaxes; her grave expression breaks up into one of joyous content; her breath goes out in a half sob, half laugh of intense relief. She goes buoyantly to her place at the writing table; pushes the electric lamp out of the way; pulls over a great sheaf of papers; and is in the act of dipping her pen in the ink when she finds Frank's note. She opens it unconcernedly and reads it quickly, giving a little laugh at some quaint turn of expression in it]. And goodbye, Frank. [She tears the note up and tosses the pieces into the wastepaper basket without a second thought. Then she goes at her work with a plunge, and soon becomes absorbed in its figures].

YOU NEVER CAN TELL

ACT I

In a dentist's operating room on a fine August morning in 1896. Not the usual tiny London den, but the best sitting room of a furnished lodging in a terrace on the sea front at a fashionable watering place. The operating chair, with a gas pump and cylinder beside it, is half way between the centre of the room and one of the corners. If you look into the room through the window which lights it, you will see the fireplace in the middle of the wall opposite you, with the door beside it to your left; an M.R.C.S. diploma in a frame hung on the chimneypiece; an easy chair covered in black leather on the hearth; a neat stool and bench, with vice, tools, and a mortar and pestle in the corner to the right. Near this bench stands a slender machine like a whip provided with a stand, a pedal, and an exaggerated winch. Recognising this as a dental drill, you shudder and look away to your left, where you can see another window, underneath which stands a writing table, with a blotter and a diary on it, and a chair. Next the writing table, towards the door, is a leather covered sofa. The opposite wall, close on your right, is occupied mostly by a bookcase. The operating chair is under your nose, facing you, with the cabinet of instruments handy to it on your left. You observe that the professional furniture and apparatus are new, and that the wall paper, designed, with the taste of an undertaker, in festoons and urns, the carpet with its symmetrical plans of rich, cabbagy nosegays, the glass gasalier with lustres; the ornamental gilt rimmed blue candlesticks on the ends of the mantelshelf, also glass- draped with lustres, and the ormolu clock under a glass-cover in the middle between them, its uselessness emphasized by a cheap American clock disrespectfully placed beside it and now indicating

313

12 o'clock noon, all combine with the black marble which gives the fireplace the air of a miniature family vault, to suggest early Victorian commercial respectability, belief in money, Bible fetishism, fear of hell always at war with fear of poverty, instinctive horror of the passionate character of art, love and Roman Catholic religion, and all the first fruits of plutocracy in the early generations of the industrial revolution.

There is no shadow of this on the two persons who are occupying the room just now. One of them, a very pretty woman in miniature, her tiny figure dressed with the daintiest gaiety, is of a later generation, being hardly eighteen yet. This darling little creature clearly does not belong to the room, or even to the country; for her complexion, though very delicate, has been burnt biscuit color by some warmer sun than England's; and yet there is, for a very subtle observer, a link between them. For she has a glass of water in her hand, and a rapidly clearing cloud of Spartan obstinacy on her tiny firm set mouth and quaintly squared eyebrows. If the least line of conscience could be traced between those eyebrows, an Evangelical might cherish some faint hope of finding her a sheep in wolf's clothing—for her frock is recklessly pretty—but as the cloud vanishes it leaves her frontal sinus as smoothly free from conviction of sin as a kitten's.

The dentist, contemplating her with the self-satisfaction of a successful operator, is a young man of thirty or thereabouts. He does not give the impression of being much of a workman: his professional manner evidently strikes him as being a joke, and is underlain by a thoughtless pleasantry which betrays the young gentleman still unsettled and in search of amusing adventures, behind the newly set-up dentist in search of patients. He is not without gravity of demeanor; but the strained nostrils stamp it as the gravity of the humorist. His eyes are clear, alert, of sceptically moderate size, and yet a little rash; his forehead is an excellent one, with plenty of room behind it; his nose and chin cavalierly handsome. On the whole, an attractive, noticeable beginner, of whose prospects a man of business might form a tolerably favorable estimate.

THE YOUNG LADY (handing him the glass). Thank you. (In spite of the biscuit complexion she has not the slightest foreign accent.)

THE DENTIST (putting it down on the ledge of his cabinet of instruments). That was my first tooth.

THE YOUNG LADY (aghast). Your first! Do you mean to say that you began practising on me?

THE DENTIST. Every dentist has to begin on somebody.

THE YOUNG LADY. Yes: somebody in a hospital, not people who pay.

THE DENTIST (laughing). Oh, the hospital doesn't count. I only meant my first tooth in private practice. Why didn't you let me give you gas?

THE YOUNG LADY. Because you said it would be five shillings extra.

THE DENTIST (shocked). Oh, don't say that. It makes me feel as if I had hurt you for the sake of five shillings.

THE YOUNG LADY (with cool insolence). Well, so you have! (She gets up.) Why shouldn't you? it's your business to hurt people. (It amuses him to be treated in this fashion: he chuckles secretly as he proceeds to clean and replace his instruments. She shakes her dress into order; looks inquisitively about her; and goes to the window.) You have a good view of the sea from these rooms! Are they expensive?

THE DENTIST. Yes.

THE YOUNG LADY. You don't own the whole house, do you?

THE DENTIST. No.

THE YOUNG LADY (taking the chair which stands at the writing-table and looking critically at it as she spins it round on one leg.) Your furniture isn't quite the latest thing, is it?

THE DENTIST. It's my landlord's.

THE YOUNG LADY. Does he own that nice comfortable Bath chair? (pointing to the operating chair.)

THE DENTIST. No: I have that on the hire-purchase system.

THE YOUNG LADY (disparagingly). I thought so. (Looking about her again in search of further conclusions.) I suppose you haven't been here long?

THE DENTIST. Six weeks. Is there anything else you would like to know?

THE YOUNG LADY (the hint quite lost on her). Any family?

THE DENTIST. I am not married.

THE YOUNG LADY. Of course not: anybody can see that. I meant sisters and mother and that sort of thing.

THE DENTIST. Not on the premises.

THE YOUNG LADY. Hm! If you've been here six weeks, and mine was your first tooth, the practice can't be very large, can it?

THE DENTIST. Not as yet. (He shuts the cabinet, having tidied up everything.)

THE YOUNG LADY. Well, good luck! (She takes our her purse.) Five shillings, you said it would be?

THE DENTIST. Five shillings.

THE YOUNG LADY (producing a crown piece). Do you charge five shillings for everything?

THE DENTIST. Yes.

THE YOUNG LADY. Why?

THE DENTIST. It's my system. I'm what's called a five shilling dentist.

THE YOUNG LADY. How nice! Well, here! (holding up the crown piece) a nice new five shilling piece! your first fee! Make a hole in it with the thing you drill people's teeth with and wear it on your watch-chain.

THE DENTIST. Thank you.

THE PARLOR MAID (appearing at the door). The young lady's brother, sir.

A handsome man in miniature, obviously the young lady's twin, comes in eagerly. He wears a suit of terra-cotta cashmere, the elegantly cut frock coat lined in brown silk, and carries in his hand a brown tall hat and tan gloves to match. He has his sister's delicate biscuit complexion, and is built on the same small scale; but he is elastic and strong in muscle, decisive in movement, unexpectedly deeptoned and trenchant in speech, and with perfect manners and a finished personal style which might be envied by a man twice his age. Suavity and self- possession are points of honor with him; and though this, rightly considered, is only the modern mode of boyish self-consciousness, its effect is none the less staggering to his elders, and would be insufferable in a less prepossessing youth. He is promptitude itself, and has a question ready the moment he enters.

THE YOUNG GENTLEMAN. Am I on time?

THE YOUNG LADY. No: it's all over.

THE YOUNG GENTLEMAN. Did you howl?

THE YOUNG LADY. Oh, something awful. Mr. Valentine: this is my brother Phil. Phil: this is Mr. Valentine, our new dentist. (Valentine and Phil bow to one another. She proceeds, all in one breath.) He's only been here six weeks; and he's a bachelor. The house isn't his; and the furniture is the landlord's; but the professional plant is hired. He got my tooth out beautifully at the first go; and he and I are great friends.

PHILIP. Been asking a lot of questions?

THE YOUNG LADY (as if incapable of doing such a thing). Oh, no.

PHILIP. Glad to hear it. (To Valentine.) So good of you not to mind us, Mr. Valentine. The fact is, we've never been in England before; and our mother tells us that the people here simply won't stand us. Come and lunch with us. (Valentine, bewildered by the leaps and bounds with which their acquaintanceship is proceeding, gasps; but he has no opportunity of speaking, as the conversation of the twins is swift and continuous.)

THE YOUNG LADY. Oh, do, Mr. Valentine.

PHILIP. At the Marine Hotel—half past one.

THE YOUNG LADY. We shall be able to tell mamma that a respectable Englishman has promised to lunch with us.

PHILIP. Say no more, Mr. Valentine: you'll come.

VALENTINE. Say no more! I haven't said anything. May I ask whom I have the pleasure of entertaining? It's really quite impossible for me to lunch at the Marine Hotel with two perfect strangers.

THE YOUNG LADY (flippantly). Ooooh! what bosh! One patient in six weeks! What difference does it make to you?

PHILIP (maturely). No, Dolly: my knowledge of human nature confirms Mr. Valentine's judgment. He is right. Let me introduce Miss Dorothy Clandon, commonly called Dolly. (Valentine bows to Dolly. She nods to him.) I'm Philip Clandon. We're from Madeira, but perfectly respectable, so far.

VALENTINE. Clandon! Are you related to—

DOLLY (unexpectedly crying out in despair). Yes, we are.

VALENTINE (astonished). I beg your pardon?

DOLLY. Oh, we are, we are. It's all over, Phil: they know all about us in England. (To Valentine.) Oh, you can't think how maddening it is to be related to a celebrated person, and never be valued anywhere for our own sakes.

VALENTINE. But excuse me: the gentleman I was thinking of is not celebrated.

DOLLY (staring at him). Gentleman! (Phil is also puzzled.)

VALENTINE. Yes. I was going to ask whether you were by any chance a daughter of Mr. Densmore Clandon of Newbury Hall.

DOLLY (vacantly). No.

PHILIP. Well come, Dolly: how do you know you're not?

DOLLY (cheered). Oh, I forgot. Of course. Perhaps I am.

VALENTINE. Don't you know?

PHILIP. Not in the least.

DOLLY. It's a wise child—

PHILIP (cutting her short). Sh! (Valentine starts nervously; for the sound made by Philip, though but momentary, is like cutting a sheet of silk in two with a flash of lightning. It is the result of long practice in checking Dolly's indiscretions.) The fact is, Mr. Valentine, we are the children of the celebrated Mrs. Lanfrey Clandon, an authoress of great repute—in Madeira. No household is complete without her works. We came to England to get away from them. The are called the Twentieth Century Treatises.

DOLLY. Twentieth Century Cooking.

PHILIP. Twentieth Century Creeds.

DOLLY. Twentieth Century Clothing.

PHILIP. Twentieth Century Conduct.

DOLLY. Twentieth Century Children.

PHILIP. Twentieth Century Parents.

DOLLY. Cloth limp, half a dollar.

PHILIP. Or mounted on linen for hard family use, two dollars. No family should be without them. Read them, Mr. Valentine: they'll improve your mind.

DOLLY. But not till we've gone, please.

PHILIP. Quite so: we prefer people with unimproved minds. Our own minds are in that fresh and unspoiled condition.

VALENTINE (dubiously). Hm!

DOLLY (echoing him inquiringly). Hm? Phil: he prefers people whose minds are improved.

PHILIP. In that case we shall have to introduce him to the other member of the family: the Woman of the Twentieth Century; our sister Gloria!

DOLLY (dithyrambically). Nature's masterpiece!

PHILIP. Learning's daughter!

DOLLY. Madeira's pride!

PHILIP. Beauty's paragon!

DOLLY (suddenly descending to prose). Bosh! No complexion.

VALENTINE (desperately). May I have a word?

PHILIP (politely). Excuse us. Go ahead.

DOLLY (very nicely). So sorry.

VALENTINE (attempting to take them paternally). I really must give a hint to you young people—

DOLLY (breaking out again). Oh, come: I like that. How old are you?

PHILIP. Over thirty.

DOLLY. He's not.

PHILIP (confidently). He is.

DOLLY (emphatically). Twenty-seven.

PHILIP (imperturbably). Thirty-three.

DOLLY. Stuff!

PHILIP (to Valentine). I appeal to you, Mr. Valentine.

VALENTINE (remonstrating). Well, really—(resigning himself.) Thirty-one.

PHILIP (to Dolly). You were wrong.

DOLLY. So were you.

PHILIP (suddenly conscientious). We're forgetting our manners, Dolly.

DOLLY (remorseful). Yes, so we are.

PHILIP (apologetic). We interrupted you, Mr. Valentine.

DOLLY. You were going to improve our minds, I think.

VALENTINE. The fact is, your—

PHILIP (anticipating him). Our appearance?

DOLLY. Our manners?

VALENTINE (ad misericordiam). Oh, do let me speak.

DOLLY. The old story. We talk too much.

PHILIP. We do. Shut up, both. (He seats himself on the arm of the opposing chair.)

DOLLY. Mum! (She sits down in the writing-table chair, and closes her lips tight with the tips of her fingers.)

VALENTINE. Thank you. (He brings the stool from the bench in the corner; places it between them; and sits down with a judicial air. They attend to him with extreme gravity. He addresses himself first to Dolly.) Now may I ask, to begin with, have you ever been in an English seaside resort before? (She shakes her head slowly and solemnly. He turns to Phil, who shakes his head quickly and expressively.) I thought so. Well, Mr. Clandon, our acquaintance has been short; but it has been voluble; and I have gathered enough to convince me that you are neither of you capable of conceiving what life in an English seaside resort is. Believe me, it's not a question of manners and appearance. In those respects we enjoy a freedom unknown in Madeira. (Dolly shakes her head vehemently.) Oh, yes, I assure you. Lord de Cresci's sister bicycles in knickerbockers; and the rector's wife advocates dress reform and wears hygienic boots. (Dolly furtively looks at her own shoe: Valentine catches her in the act, and deftly adds) No, that's not the sort of boot I mean. (Dolly's shoe vanishes.) We don't bother much about dress and manners in England, because, as a nation we don't dress well and we've no manners. But—and now will you excuse my frankness? (They nod.) Thank you. Well, in a seaside resort there's one thing you must have before anybody can afford to be seen going about with you; and that's a father, alive or dead. (He looks at them alternately, with emphasis. They meet his gaze like martyrs.) Am I to infer that you have omitted that indispensable part of your social equipment? (They confirm him by melancholy nods.) Them I'm sorry to say that if you are going to stay here for any length of time, it will be impossible for me to accept your kind invitation to lunch. (He rises with an air of finality, and replaces the stool by the bench.)

PHILIP (rising with grave politeness). Come, Dolly. (He gives her his arm.)

DOLLY. Good morning. (They go together to the door with perfect dignity.)

VALENTINE (overwhelmed with remorse). Oh, stop, stop. (They halt and turn, arm in arm.) You make me feel a perfect beast.

DOLLY. That's your conscience: not us.

VALENTINE (energetically, throwing off all pretence of a professional manner). My conscience! My conscience has been my ruin. Listen to me. Twice before I have set up as a respectable medical practitioner in various parts of England. On both occasions I acted conscientiously, and told my patients the brute truth instead of what they wanted to be told. Result, ruin. Now I've set up as a dentist, a five shilling dentist; and I've done with conscience forever. This is my last chance. I spent my last sovereign on moving in; and I haven't paid a shilling of rent yet. I'm eating and drinking on credit; my landlord is as rich as a Jew and as hard as nails; and I've made five shillings in six weeks. If I swerve by a hair's breadth from the straight line of the most rigid respectability, I'm done for. Under such a circumstance, is it fair to ask me to lunch with you when you don't know your own father?

DOLLY. After all, our grandfather is a canon of Lincoln Cathedral.

VALENTINE (like a castaway mariner who sees a sail on the horizon). What! Have you a grandfather?

DOLLY. Only one.

VALENTINE. My dear, good young friends, why on earth didn't you tell me that before? A cannon of Lincoln! That makes it all right, of course. Just excuse me while I change my coat. (He reaches the door in a bound and vanishes. Dolly and Phil stare after him, and then stare at one another. Missing their audience, they droop and become commonplace at once.)

PHILIP (throwing away Dolly's arm and coming ill-humoredly towards the operating chair). That wretched bankrupt ivory snatcher makes a compliment of allowing us to stand him a lunch—probably the first square meal he has had for months. (He gives the chair a kick, as if it were Valentine.)

DOLLY. It's too beastly. I won't stand it any longer, Phil. Here in England everybody asks whether you have a father the very first thing.

PHILIP. I won't stand it either. Mamma must tell us who he was.

DOLLY. Or who he is. He may be alive.

PHILIP. I hope not. No man alive shall father me.

DOLLY. He might have a lot of money, though.

PHILIP. I doubt it. My knowledge of human nature leads me to believe that if he had a lot of money he wouldn't have got rid of his affectionate family so easily. Anyhow, let's look at the bright side of things. Depend on it, he's dead. (He goes to the hearth and stands with his back to the fireplace, spreading himself. The parlor maid appears. The twins, under observation, instantly shine out again with their former brilliancy.)

THE PARLOR MAID. Two ladies for you, miss. Your mother and sister, miss, I think.

Mrs. Clandon and Gloria come in. Mrs. Clandon is between forty and fifty, with a slight tendency to soft, sedentary fat, and a fair remainder of good looks, none the worse preserved because she has evidently followed the old tribal matronly fashion of making no pretension in that direction after her marriage, and might almost be suspected of wearing a cap at home. She carries herself artificially well, as women were taught to do as a part of good manners by dancing masters and reclining boards before these were superseded by the modern artistic cult of beauty and health. Her hair, a flaxen hazel fading into white, is crimped, and parted in the middle with the ends plaited and made into a knot, from which observant people of a certain age infer that Mrs. Clandon had sufficient individuality and good taste to stand out resolutely against the now forgotten chignon in her girlhood. In short, she is distinctly old fashioned for her age in dress and manners. But she belongs to the forefront of her own period (say 1860-80) in a jealously assertive attitude of character and intellect, and in being a woman of cultivated interests rather than passionately developed personal affections. Her voice and ways are entirely kindly and humane; and she lends herself conscientiously to the occasional demonstrations of fondness by which her children mark their esteem for her; but displays of personal sentiment secretly embarrass her: passion in her is humanitarian rather than human: she feels strongly about social questions and principles, not about persons. Only, one observes that this reasonableness and intense personal privacy, which leaves her relations with Gloria and Phil much as they might be between her and the children of any other woman, breaks down in the case of Dolly. Though almost every word she addresses to her is necessarily in the nature of a remonstrance for some breach of decorum, the tenderness in her voice is unmistakable; and it is not surprising that years of such remonstrance have left Dolly hopelessly spoiled.

Gloria, who is hardly past twenty, is a much more formidable person than her mother. She is the incarnation of haughty highmindedness, raging with the impatience of an impetuous, dominative character paralyzed by the impotence of her youth, and unwillingly disciplined by the constant danger of ridicule from her lighter-handed juniors. Unlike her mother, she is all passion; and the conflict of her passion with her obstinate pride and intense fastidiousness results in a freezing coldness of manner. In an ugly woman all this would be repulsive; but Gloria is an attractive woman. Her deep chestnut hair, olive brown skin, long eyelashes, shaded grey eyes that often flash like stars, delicately turned full lips, and compact and supple, but muscularly plump figure appeal with disdainful frankness to the senses and imagination. A very dangerous girl, one would say, if the moral passions were not also marked, and even nobly marked, in a fine brow. Her tailor-made skirt-and-jacket dress of saffron brown cloth, seems conventional when her back is turned; but it displays in front a blouse of sea-green silk which upsets its conventionality with one stroke, and sets her apart as effectually as the twins from the ordinary run of fashionable seaside humanity.

Mrs. Clandon comes a little way into the room, looking round to see who is present. Gloria, who studiously avoids encouraging the twins by betraying any interest in them, wanders to the window and looks out with her thoughts far away. The parlor maid, instead of withdrawing, shuts the door and waits at it.

MRS. CLANDON. Well, children? How is the toothache, Dolly?

DOLLY. Cured, thank Heaven. I've had it out. (She sits down on the step of the operating chair. Mrs. Clandon takes the writing-table chair.)

PHILIP (striking in gravely from the hearth). And the dentist, a first-rate professional man of the highest standing, is coming to lunch with us.

MRS. CLANDON (looking round apprehensively at the servant). Phil!

THE PARLOR MAID. Beg pardon, ma'am. I'm waiting for Mr. Valentine. I have a message for him.

DOLLY. Who from?

MRS. CLANDON (shocked). Dolly! (Dolly catches her lips with her finger tips, suppressing a little splutter of mirth.)

THE PARLOR MAID. Only the landlord, ma'am.

Valentine, in a blue serge suit, with a straw hat in his hand, comes back in high spirits, out of breath with the haste he has made. Gloria turns from the window and studies him with freezing attention.

PHILIP. Let me introduce you, Mr. Valentine. My mother, Mrs. Lanfrey Clandon. (Mrs. Clandon bows. Valentine bows, self-possessed and quite equal to the occasion.) My sister Gloria. (Gloria bows with cold dignity and sits down on the sofa. Valentine falls in love at first sight and is miserably confused. He fingers his hat nervously, and makes her a sneaking bow.)

MRS. CLANDON. I understand that we are to have the pleasure of seeing you at luncheon to-day, Mr. Valentine.

VALENTINE. Thank you—er—if you don't mind—I mean if you will be so kind—(to the parlor maid testily) What is it?

THE PARLOR MAID. The landlord, sir, wishes to speak to you before you go out.

VALENTINE. Oh, tell him I have four patients here. (The Clandons look surprised, except Phil, who is imperturbable.) If he wouldn't mind waiting just two minutes, I—I'll slip down and see him for a moment. (Throwing himself confidentially on her sense of the position.) Say I'm busy, but that I want to see him.

THE PARLOR MAID (reassuringly). Yes, sir. (She goes.)

MRS. CLANDON (on the point of rising). We are detaining you, I am afraid.

VALENTINE. Not at all, not at all. Your presence here will be the greatest help to me. The fact is, I owe six week's rent; and I've had no patients until to-day. My interview with my landlord will be considerably smoothed by the apparent boom in my business.

DOLLY (vexed). Oh, how tiresome of you to let it all out! And we've just been pretending that you were a respectable professional man in a first-rate position.

MRS. CLANDON (horrified). Oh, Dolly, Dolly! My dearest, how can you be so rude? (To Valentine.) Will you excuse these barbarian children of mine, Mr. Valentine?

VALENTINE. Thank you, I'm used to them. Would it be too much to ask you to wait five minutes while I get rid of my landlord downstairs?

DOLLY. Don't be long. We're hungry.

MRS. CLANDON (again remonstrating). Dolly, dear!

VALENTINE (to Dolly). All right. (To Mrs. Clandon.) Thank you: I shan't be long. (He steals a look at Gloria as he turns to go. She is looking gravely at him. He falls into confusion.) I—er—er—yes—

thank you (he succeeds at last in blundering himself out of the room; but the exhibition is a pitiful one).

PHILIP. Did you observe? (Pointing to Gloria.) Love at first sight. You can add his scalp to your collection, Gloria.

MRS. CLANDON. Sh—sh, pray, Phil. He may have heard you.

PHILIP. Not he. (Bracing himself for a scene.) And now look here, mamma. (He takes the stool from the bench; and seats himself majestically in the middle of the room, taking a leaf out of Valentine's book. Dolly, feeling that her position on the step of the operating chair is unworthy of the dignity of the occasion, rises, looking important and determined; crosses to the window; and stands with her back to the end of the writing-table, her hands behind her and on the table. Mrs. Clandon looks at them, wondering what is coming. Gloria becomes attentive. Philip straightens his back; places his knuckles symmetrically on his knees; and opens his case.) Dolly and I have been talking over things a good deal lately; and I don't think, judging from my knowledge of human nature—we don't think that you (speaking very staccato, with the words detached) quite appreciate the fact—

DOLLY (seating herself on the end of the table with a spring). That we've grown up.

MRS. CLANDON. Indeed? In what way have I given you any reason to complain?

PHILIP. Well, there are certain matters upon which we are beginning to feel that you might take us a little more into your confidence.

MRS. CLANDON (rising, with all the placidity of her age suddenly broken up; and a curious hard excitement, dignified but dogged, ladylike but implacable—the manner of the Old Guard of the Women's Rights movement—coming upon her). Phil: take care. Remember what I have always taught you. There are two sorts of family life, Phil; and your experience of human nature only extends, so far, to one of them. (Rhetorically.) The sort you know is based on mutual respect, on recognition of the right of every member of the household to independence and privacy (her emphasis on "privacy" is intense) in their personal concerns. And because you have always enjoyed that, it seems such a matter of course to you that you don't value it. But (with biting acrimony) there is another sort of family life: a life in which husbands open their wives' letters, and call on them to account for every farthing of their expenditure and every moment of their time; in which women do the same to their children; in which no room is private and no hour sacred; in which duty, obedience, affection, home, morality and religion are detestable tyrannies, and life is a vulgar round of punishments and lies, coercion and rebellion, jealousy, suspicion, recrimination—Oh! I cannot describe it to you: fortunately for you, you know nothing about it. (She sits down, panting. Gloria has listened to her with flashing eyes, sharing all her indignation.)

DOLLY (inaccessible to rhetoric). See Twentieth Century Parents, chapter on Liberty, passim.

MRS. CLANDON (touching her shoulder affectionately, soothed even by a gibe from her). My dear Dolly: if you only knew how glad I am that it is nothing but a joke to you, though it is such bitter earnest to me. (More resolutely, turning to Philip.) Phil, I never ask you questions about your private concerns. You are not going to question me, are you?

PHILIP. I think it due to ourselves to say that the question we wanted to ask is as much our business as yours.

DOLLY. Besides, it can't be good to keep a lot of questions bottled up inside you. You did it, mamma; but see how awfully it's broken out again in me.

MRS. CLANDON. I see you want to ask your question. Ask it.

DOLLY AND PHILIP (beginning simultaneously). Who—(They stop.)

PHILIP. Now look here, Dolly: am I going to conduct this business or are you?

DOLLY. You.

PHILIP. Then hold your mouth. (Dolly does so literally.) The question is a simple one. When the ivory snatcher—

MRS. CLANDON (remonstrating). Phil!

PHILIP. Dentist is an ugly word. The man of ivory and gold asked us whether we were the children of Mr. Densmore Clandon of Newbury Hall. In pursuance of the precepts in your treatise on Twentieth Century Conduct, and your repeated personal exhortations to us to curtail the number of unnecessary lies we tell, we replied truthfully the we didn't know.

DOLLY. Neither did we.

PHILIP. Sh! The result was that the gum architect made considerable difficulties about accepting our invitation to lunch, although I doubt if he has had anything but tea and bread and butter for a fortnight past. Now my knowledge of human nature leads me to believe that we had a father, and that you probably know who he was.

MRS. CLANDON (her agitation returning). Stop, Phil. Your father is nothing to you, nor to me (vehemently). That is enough. (The twins are silenced, but not satisfied. Their faces fall. But Gloria, who has been following the altercation attentively, suddenly intervenes.)

GLORIA (advancing). Mother: we have a right to know.

MRS. CLANDON (rising and facing her). Gloria! "We!" Who is "we"?

GLORIA (steadfastly). We three. (Her tone is unmistakable: she is pitting her strength against her mother for the first time. The twins instantly go over to the enemy.)

MRS. CLANDON (wounded). In your mouth "we" used to mean you and I, Gloria.

PHILIP (rising decisively and putting away the stool). We're hurting you: let's drop it. We didn't think you'd mind. I don't want to know.

DOLLY (coming off the table). I'm sure I don't. Oh, don't look like that, mamma. (She looks angrily at Gloria.)

MRS. CLANDON (touching her eyes hastily with her handkerchief and sitting down again). Thank you, my dear. Thanks, Phil.

GLORIA (inexorably). We have a right to know, mother.

MRS. CLANDON (indignantly). Ah! You insist.

GLORIA. Do you intend that we shall never know?

DOLLY. Oh, Gloria, don't. It's barbarous.

GLORIA (with quiet scorn). What is the use of being weak? You see what has happened with this gentleman here, mother. The same thing has happened to me.

MRS. CLANDON	}	(all	{ What do you mean?
DOLLY	}	together).	{ Oh, tell us.
PHILIP	}		{ What happened to you?

GLORIA. Oh, nothing of any consequence. (She turns away from them and goes up to the easy chair at the fireplace, where she sits down, almost with her back to them. As they wait expectantly, she adds, over her shoulder, with studied indifference.) On board the steamer the first officer did me the honor to propose to me.

DOLLY. No, it was to me.

MRS. CLANDON. The first officer! Are you serious, Gloria? What did you say to him? (correcting herself) Excuse me: I have no right to ask that.

GLORIA. The answer is pretty obvious. A woman who does not know who her father was cannot accept such an offer.

MRS. CLANDON. Surely you did not want to accept it?

GLORIA (turning a little and raising her voice). No; but suppose I had wanted to!

PHILIP. Did that difficulty strike you, Dolly?

DOLLY. No, I accepted him.

GLORIA	}	(all crying	{ Accepted him!
MRS. CLANDON	}	out	{ Dolly!
PHILIP	}	together)	{ Oh, I say!

DOLLY (naively). He did look such a fool!

MRS. CLANDON. But why did you do such a thing, Dolly?

DOLLY. For fun, I suppose. He had to measure my finger for a ring. You'd have done the same thing yourself.

MRS. CLANDON. No, Dolly, I would not. As a matter of fact the first officer did propose to me; and I told him to keep that sort of thing for women were young enough to be amused by it. He appears to have acted on my advice. (She rises and goes to the hearth.) Gloria: I am sorry you think me weak; but I cannot tell you what you want. You are all too young.

PHILIP. This is rather a startling departure from Twentieth Century principles.

DOLLY (quoting). "Answer all your children's questions, and answer them truthfully, as soon as they are old enough to ask them." See Twentieth Century Motherhood—

PHILIP. Page one—

DOLLY. Chapter one—

PHILIP. Sentence one.

MRS. CLANDON. My dears: I did not say that you were too young to know. I said you were too young to be taken into my confidence. You are very bright children, all of you; but I am glad for your sakes that you are still very inexperienced and consequently very unsympathetic. There are some experiences of mine that I cannot bear to speak of except to those who have gone through what I have gone through. I hope you will never be qualified for such confidences. But I will take care that you shall learn all you want to know. Will that satisfy you?

PHILIP. Another grievance, Dolly.

DOLLY. We're not sympathetic.

GLORIA (leaning forward in her chair and looking earnestly up at her mother). Mother: I did not mean to be unsympathetic.

MRS. CLANDON (affectionately). Of course not, dear. Do you think I don't understand?

GLORIA (rising). But, mother—

MRS. CLANDON (drawing back a little). Yes?

GLORIA (obstinately). It is nonsense to tell us that our father is nothing to us.

MRS. CLANDON (provoked to sudden resolution). Do you remember your father?

GLORIA (meditatively, as if the recollection were a tender one). I am not quite sure. I think so.

MRS. CLANDON (grimly). You are not sure?

GLORIA. No.

MRS. CLANDON (with quiet force). Gloria: if I had ever struck you— (Gloria recoils: Philip and Dolly are disagreeably shocked; all three start at her, revolted as she continues)—struck you purposely, deliberately, with the intention of hurting you, with a whip bought for the purpose! Would you remember that, do you think? (Gloria utters an exclamation of indignant repulsion.) That would have been your last recollection of your father, Gloria, if I had not taken you away from him. I have kept him out of your life: keep him now out of mine by never mentioning him to me again. (Gloria, with a shudder, covers her face with her hands, until, hearing someone at the door, she turns away and pretends to occupy herself looking at the names of the books in the bookcase. Mrs. Clandon sits down on the sofa. Valentine returns.).

VALENTINE. I hope I've not kept you waiting. That landlord of mine is really an extraordinary old character.

DOLLY (eagerly). Oh, tell us. How long has he given you to pay?

MRS. CLANDON (distracted by her child's bad manners). Dolly, Dolly, Dolly dear! You must not ask questions.

DOLLY (demurely). So sorry. You'll tell us, won't you, Mr. Valentine?

VALENTINE. He doesn't want his rent at all. He's broken his tooth on a Brazil nut; and he wants me to look at it and to lunch with him afterwards.

DOLLY. Then have him up and pull his tooth out at once; and we'll bring him to lunch, too. Tell the maid to fetch him along. (She runs to the bell and rings it vigorously. Then, with a sudden doubt she turns to Valentine and adds) I suppose he's respectable—really respectable.

VALENTINE. Perfectly. Not like me.

DOLLY. Honest Injun? (Mrs. Clandon gasps faintly; but her powers of remonstrance are exhausted.)

VALENTINE. Honest Injun!

DOLLY. Then off with you and bring him up.

VALENTINE (looking dubiously at Mrs. Clandon). I daresay he'd be delighted if—er—?

MRS. CLANDON (rising and looking at her watch). I shall be happy to see your friend at lunch, if you can persuade him to come; but I can't wait to see him now: I have an appointment at the hotel at a quarter to one with an old friend whom I have not seen since I left England eighteen years ago. Will you excuse me?

VALENTINE. Certainly, Mrs. Clandon.

GLORIA. Shall I come?

MRS. CLANDON. No, dear. I want to be alone. (She goes out, evidently still a good deal troubled. Valentine opens the door for her and follows her out.)

PHILIP (significantly—to Dolly). Hmhm!

DOLLY (significantly to Philip). Ahah! (The parlor maid answers the bell.)

DOLLY. Show the old gentleman up.

THE PARLOR MAID (puzzled). Madam?

DOLLY. The old gentleman with the toothache.

PHILIP. The landlord.

THE PARLOR MAID. Mr. Crampton, Sir?

PHILIP. Is his name Crampton?

DOLLY (to Philip). Sounds rheumaticky, doesn't it?

PHILIP. Chalkstones, probably.

DOLLY (over her shoulder, to the parlor maid). Show Mr. Crampstones up. (Goes R. to writing-table chair).

THE PARLOR MAID (correcting her). Mr. Crampton, miss. (She goes.)

DOLLY (repeating it to herself like a lesson). Crampton, Crampton, Crampton, Crampton, Crampton. (She sits down studiously at the writing- table.) I must get that name right, or Heaven knows what I shall call him.

GLORIA. Phil: can you believe such a horrible thing as that about our father—what mother said just now?

PHILIP. Oh, there are lots of people of that kind. Old Chalice used to thrash his wife and daughters with a cartwhip.

DOLLY (contemptuously). Yes, a Portuguese!

PHILIP. When you come to men who are brutes, there is much in common between the Portuguese and the English variety, Doll. Trust my knowledge of human nature. (He resumes his position on the hearthrug with an elderly and responsible air.)

GLORIA (with angered remorse). I don't think we shall ever play again at our old game of guessing what our father was to be like. Dolly: are you sorry for your father—the father with lots of money?

DOLLY. Oh, come! What about your father—the lonely old man with the tender aching heart? He's pretty well burst up, I think.

PHILIP. There can be no doubt that the governor is an exploded superstition. (Valentine is heard talking to somebody outside the door.) But hark: he comes.

GLORIA (nervously). Who?

DOLLY. Chalkstones.

PHILIP. Sh! Attention. (They put on their best manners. Philip adds in a lower voice to Gloria) If he's good enough for the lunch, I'll nod to Dolly; and if she nods to you, invite him straight away.

(Valentine comes back with his landlord. Mr. Fergus Crampton is a man of about sixty, tall, hard and stringy, with an atrociously obstinate, ill tempered, grasping mouth, and a querulously dogmatic voice. Withal he is highly nervous and sensitive, judging by his thin transparent skin marked with multitudinous lines, and his slender fingers. His consequent capacity for suffering acutely from all the dislike that his temper and obstinacy can bring upon him is proved by his wistful, wounded eyes, by a plaintive note in his voice, a painful want of confidence in his welcome, and a constant but indifferently successful effort to correct his natural incivility of manner and proneness to take offence. By his keen brows and forehead he is clearly a shrewd man; and there is no sign of straitened means or commercial diffidence about him: he is well dressed, and would be classed at a guess as a prosperous master manufacturer in a business inherited from an old family in the aristocracy of trade. His navy blue coat is not of the usual fashionable pattern. It is not exactly a pilot's coat; but it is cut that way, double breasted, and with stout buttons and broad lappels, a coat for a shipyard rather than a counting house. He has taken a fancy to Valentine, who cares nothing for his crossness of grain and treats him with a sort of disrespectful humanity, for which he is secretly grateful.)

VALENTINE. May I introduce—this is Mr. Crampton—Miss Dorothy Clandon, Mr. Philip Clandon, Miss Clandon. (Crampton stands nervously bowing. They all bow.) Sit down, Mr. Crampton.

DOLLY (pointing to the operating chair). That is the most comfortable chair, Mr. Ch—crampton.

CRAMPTON. Thank you; but won't this young lady—(indicating Gloria, who is close to the chair)?

GLORIA. Thank you, Mr. Crampton: we are just going.

VALENTINE (bustling him across to the chair with good-humored peremptoriness). Sit down, sit down. You're tired.

CRAMPTON. Well, perhaps as I am considerably the oldest person present, I—(He finishes the sentence by sitting down a little rheumatically in the operating chair. Meanwhile, Philip, having studied him critically during his passage across the room, nods to Dolly; and Dolly nods to Gloria.)

GLORIA. Mr. Crampton: we understand that we are preventing Mr. Valentine from lunching with you by taking him away ourselves. My mother would be very glad, indeed, if you would come too.

CRAMPTON (gratefully, after looking at her earnestly for a moment). Thank you. I will come with pleasure.

GLORIA } (politely   { Thank you very much—er—
DOLLY } murmuring)   { So glad—er—
PHILIP }   { Delighted, I'm sure—er—

(The conversation drops. Gloria and Dolly look at one another; then at Valentine and Philip. Valentine and Philip, unequal to the occasion, look away from them at one another, and are instantly so disconcerted by catching one another's eye, that they look back again and catch the eyes of Gloria and Dolly. Thus, catching one another all round, they all look at nothing and are quite at a loss. Crampton looks about him, waiting for them to begin. The silence becomes unbearable.)

DOLLY (suddenly, to keep things going). How old are you, Mr. Crampton?

GLORIA (hastily). I am afraid we must be going, Mr. Valentine. It is understood, then, that we meet at half past one. (She makes for the door. Philip goes with her. Valentine retreats to the bell.)

VALENTINE. Half past one. (He rings the bell.) Many thanks. (He follows Gloria and Philip to the door, and goes out with them.)

DOLLY (who has meanwhile stolen across to Crampton). Make him give you gas. It's five shillings extra: but it's worth it.

CRAMPTON (amused). Very well. (Looking more earnestly at her.) So you want to know my age, do you? I'm fifty-seven.

DOLLY (with conviction). You look it.

CRAMPTON (grimly). I dare say I do.

DOLLY. What are you looking at me so hard for? Anything wrong? (She feels whether her hat is right.)

CRAMPTON. You're like somebody.

DOLLY. Who?

CRAMPTON. Well, you have a curious look of my mother.

DOLLY (incredulously). Your mother!!! Quite sure you don't mean your daughter?

CRAMPTON (suddenly blackening with hate). Yes: I'm quite sure I don't mean my daughter.

DOLLY (sympathetically). Tooth bad?

CRAMPTON. No, no: nothing. A twinge of memory, Miss Clandon, not of toothache.

DOLLY. Have it out. "Pluck from the memory a rooted sorrow:" with gas, five shillings extra.

CRAMPTON (vindicatively). No, not a sorrow. An injury that was done me once: that's all. I don't forget injuries; and I don't want to forget them. (His features settle into an implacable frown.)

(re-enter Philip: to look for Dolly. He comes down behind her unobserved.)

DOLLY (looking critically at Crampton's expression). I don't think we shall like you when you are brooding over your sorrows.

PHILIP (who has entered the room unobserved, and stolen behind her). My sister means well, Mr. Crampton: but she is indiscreet. Now Dolly, outside! (He takes her towards the door.)

DOLLY (in a perfectly audible undertone). He says he's only fifty- seven; and he thinks me the image of his mother; and he hates his daughter; and—(She is interrupted by the return of Valentine.)

VALENTINE. Miss Clandon has gone on.

PHILIP. Don't forget half past one.

DOLLY. Mind you leave Mr. Crampton with enough teeth to eat with. (They go out. Valentine comes down to his cabinet, and opens it.)

CRAMPTON. That's a spoiled child, Mr. Valentine. That's one of your modern products. When I was her age, I had many a good hiding fresh in my memory to teach me manners.

VALENTINE (taking up his dental mirror and probe from the shelf in front of the cabinet). What did you think of her sister?

CRAMPTON. You liked her better, eh?

VALENTINE (rhapsodically). She struck me as being—(He checks himself, and adds, prosaically) However, that's not business. (He places himself behind Crampton's right shoulder and assumes his professional tone.) Open, please. (Crampton opens his mouth. Valentine puts the mirror in, and examines his teeth.) Hm! You have broken that one. What a pity to spoil such a splendid set of teeth! Why do you crack nuts with them? (He withdraws the mirror, and comes forward to converse with Crampton.)

CRAMPTON. I've always cracked nuts with them: what else are they for? (Dogmatically.) The proper way to keep teeth good is to give them plenty of use on bones and nuts, and wash them every day with soap—plain yellow soap.

VALENTINE. Soap! Why soap?

CRAMPTON. I began using it as a boy because I was made to; and I've used it ever since. And I never had toothache in my life.

VALENTINE. Don't you find it rather nasty?

CRAMPTON. I found that most things that were good for me were nasty. But I was taught to put up with them, and made to put up with them. I'm used to it now: in fact, I like the taste when the soap is really good.

VALENTINE (making a wry face in spite of himself). You seem to have been very carefully educated, Mr. Crampton.

CRAMPTON (grimly). I wasn't spoiled, at all events.

VALENTINE (smiling a little to himself). Are you quite sure?

CRAMPTON. What d'y' mean?

VALENTINE. Well, your teeth are good, I admit. But I've seen just as good in very self-indulgent mouths. (He goes to the ledge of cabinet and changes the probe for another one.)

CRAMPTON. It's not the effect on the teeth: it's the effect on the character.

VALENTINE (placably). Oh, the character, I see. (He recommences operations.) A little wider, please. Hm! That one will have to come out: it's past saving. (He withdraws the probe and again comes to the side of the chair to converse.) Don't be alarmed: you shan't feel anything. I'll give you gas.

CRAMPTON. Rubbish, man: I want none of your gas. Out with it. People were taught to bear necessary pain in my day.

VALENTINE. Oh, if you like being hurt, all right. I'll hurt you as much as you like, without any extra charge for the beneficial effect on your character.

CRAMPTON (rising and glaring at him). Young man: you owe me six weeks' rent.

VALENTINE. I do.

CRAMPTON. Can you pay me?

VALENTINE. No.

CRAMPTON (satisfied with his advantage). I thought not. How soon d'y' think you'll be able to pay me if you have no better manners than to make game of your patients? (He sits down again.)

VALENTINE. My good sir: my patients haven't all formed their characters on kitchen soap.

CRAMPTON (suddenly gripping him by the arm as he turns away again to the cabinet). So much the worse for them. I tell you you don't understand my character. If I could spare all my teeth, I'd make you pull them all out one after another to shew you what a properly hardened man can go through with when he's made up his mind to do it. (He nods at him to enforce the effect of this declaration, and releases him.)

VALENTINE (his careless pleasantry quite unruffled). And you want to be more hardened, do you?

CRAMPTON. Yes.

VALENTINE (strolling away to the bell). Well, you're quite hard enough for me already—as a landlord. (Crampton receives this with a growl of grim humor. Valentine rings the bell, and remarks in a cheerful, casual way, whilst waiting for it to be answered.) Why did you never get married, Mr. Crampton? A wife and children would have taken some of the hardness out of you.

CRAMPTON (with unexpected ferocity). What the devil is that to you? (The parlor maid appears at the door.)

VALENTINE (politely). Some warm water, please. (She retires: and Valentine comes back to the cabinet, not at all put out by Crampton's rudeness, and carries on the conversation whilst he selects a forceps and places it ready to his hand with a gag and a drinking glass.) You were asking me what the devil that was to me. Well, I have an idea of getting married myself.

CRAMPTON (with grumbling irony). Naturally, sir, naturally. When a young man has come to his last farthing, and is within twenty-four hours of having his furniture distrained upon by his landlord, he marries. I've noticed that before. Well, marry; and be miserable.

VALENTINE. Oh, come, what do you know about it?

CRAMPTON. I'm not a bachelor.

VALENTINE. Then there is a Mrs. Crampton?

CRAMPTON (wincing with a pang of resentment). Yes—damn her!

VALENTINE (unperturbed). Hm! A father, too, perhaps, as well as a husband, Mr. Crampton?

CRAMPTON. Three children.

VALENTINE (politely). Damn them?—eh?

CRAMPTON (jealously). No, sir: the children are as much mine as hers. (The parlor maid brings in a jug of hot water.)

VALENTINE. Thank you. (He takes the jug from her, and brings it to the cabinet, continuing in the same idle strain) I really should like to know your family, Mr. Crampton. (The parlor maid goes out: and he pours some hot water into the drinking glass.)

CRAMPTON. Sorry I can't introduce you, sir. I'm happy to say that I don't know where they are, and don't care, so long as they keep out of my way. (Valentine, with a hitch of his eyebrows and shoulders, drops the forceps with a clink into the glass of hot water.) You needn't warm that thing to use on me. I'm not afraid of the cold steel. (Valentine stoops to arrange the gas pump and cylinder beside the chair.) What's that heavy thing?

VALENTINE. Oh, never mind. Something to put my foot on, to get the necessary purchase for a good pull. (Crampton looks alarmed in spite of himself. Valentine stands upright and places the glass with the forceps in it ready to his hand, chatting on with provoking indifference.) And so you advise me not to get married, Mr. Crampton? (He stoops to fit the handle on the apparatus by which the chair is raised and lowered.)

CRAMPTON (irritably). I advise you to get my tooth out and have done reminding me of my wife. Come along, man. (He grips the arms of the chair and braces himself.)

VALENTINE (pausing, with his hand on the lever, to look up at him and say). What do you bet that I don't get that tooth out without your feeling it?

CRAMPTON. Your six week's rent, young man. Don't you gammon me.

VALENTINE (jumping at the bet and winding him aloft vigorously). Done! Are you ready? (Crampton, who has lost his grip of the chair in his alarm at its sudden ascent, folds his arms: sits stiffly upright: and prepares for the worst. Valentine lets down the back of the chair to an obtuse angle.)

CRAMPTON (clutching at the arms of the chair as he falls back). Take care man. I'm quite helpless in this po—

VALENTINE (deftly stopping him with the gag, and snatching up the mouthpiece of the gas machine). You'll be more helpless presently. (He presses the mouthpiece over Crampton's mouth and nose, leaning over his chest so as to hold his head and shoulders well down on the chair. Crampton makes an inarticulate sound in the mouthpiece and tries to lay hands on Valentine, whom he supposes to be in front of him. After a moment his arms wave aimlessly, then subside and drop. He is quite insensible. Valentine, with an exclamation of somewhat preoccupied triumph, throws aside the mouthpiece quickly: picks up the forceps adroitly from the glass: and—the curtain falls.)

END OF ACT I.

ACT II

On the terrace at the Marine Hotel. It is a square flagged platform, with a parapet of heavy oil jar pilasters supporting a broad stone coping on the outer edge, which stands up over the sea like a cliff. The head waiter of the establishment, busy laying napkins on a luncheon table with his back to the sea, has the hotel on his right, and on his left, in the corner nearest the sea, the flight of steps leading down to the beach.

When he looks down the terrace in front of him he sees a little to his left a solitary guest, a middle-aged gentleman sitting on a chair of iron laths at a little iron table with a bowl of lump sugar and three wasps on it, reading the Standard, with his umbrella up to defend him from the sun, which, in August and at less than an hour after noon, is toasting his protended insteps. Just opposite him, at the hotel side of the terrace, there is a garden seat of the ordinary esplanade pattern. Access to the hotel for visitors is by an entrance in the middle of its facade, reached by a couple of steps on a broad square of raised pavement. Nearer the parapet there lurks a way to the kitchen, masked by a little trellis porch. The table at which the waiter is occupied is a long one, set across the terrace with covers and chairs for five, two at each side and one at the end next the hotel. Against the parapet another table is prepared as a buffet to serve from.

The waiter is a remarkable person in his way. A silky old man, white-haired and delicate looking, but so cheerful and contented that in his encouraging presence ambition stands rebuked as vulgarity, and imagination as treason to the abounding sufficiency and interest of the actual. He has a certain expression peculiar to men who have been extraordinarily successful in their calling, and who, whilst aware of the vanity of success, are untouched by envy.

The gentleman at the iron table is not dressed for the seaside. He wears his London frock coat and gloves; and his tall silk hat is on the table beside the sugar bowl. The excellent condition and quality of these garments, the gold-rimmed folding spectacles through which he is reading the Standard, and the Times at his elbow overlaying the local paper, all testify to his respectability. He is about fifty, clean shaven, and close-cropped, with the corners of his mouth turned down purposely, as if he suspected them of wanting to turn up, and was determined not to let them have their way. He has large expansive ears, cod colored eyes, and a brow kept resolutely wide open, as if, again, he had resolved in his youth to be truthful, magnanimous, and incorruptible, but had never succeeded in making that habit of mind automatic and unconscious. Still, he is by no means to be laughed at. There is no sign of stupidity or infirmity of will about him: on the contrary, he would pass anywhere at sight as a man of more than average professional capacity and responsibility. Just at present he is enjoying the weather and the sea too much to be out of patience; but he has exhausted all the news in his papers and is at present reduced to the advertisements, which are not sufficiently succulent to induce him to persevere with them.

THE GENTLEMAN (yawning and giving up the paper as a bad job).
    Waiter!
WAITER. Sir? (coming down C.)
THE GENTLEMAN. Are you quite sure Mrs. Clandon is coming back
    before lunch?
WAITER. Quite sure, sir. She expects you at a quarter to one, sir. (The
    gentleman, soothed at once by the waiter's voice, looks at him with
    a lazy smile. It is a quiet voice, with a gentle melody in it that gives
    sympathetic interest to his most commonplace remark; and he

speaks with the sweetest propriety, neither dropping his aitches nor misplacing them, nor committing any other vulgarism. He looks at his watch as he continues) Not that yet, sir, is it? 12:43, sir. Only two minutes more to wait, sir. Nice morning, sir?

THE GENTLEMAN. Yes: very fresh after London.

WAITER. Yes, sir: so all our visitors say, sir. Very nice family, Mrs. Clandon's, sir.

THE GENTLEMAN. You like them, do you?

WAITER. Yes, sir. They have a free way with them that is very taking, sir, very taking indeed, sir: especially the young lady and gentleman.

THE GENTLEMAN. Miss Dorothea and Mr. Philip, I suppose.

WAITER. Yes, sir. The young lady, in giving an order, or the like of that, will say, "Remember, William, we came to this hotel on your account, having heard what a perfect waiter you are." The young gentleman will tell me that I remind him strongly of his father (the gentleman starts at this) and that he expects me to act by him as such. (Soothing, sunny cadence.) Oh, very peasant, sir, very affable and pleasant indeed!

THE GENTLEMAN. You like his father! (He laughs at the notion.)

WAITER. Oh, we must not take what they say too seriously, sir. Of course, sir, if it were true, the young lady would have seen the resemblance, too, sir.

THE GENTLEMAN. Did she?

WAITER. No, sir. She thought me like the bust of Shakespear in Stratford Church, sir. That is why she calls me William, sir. My real name is Walter, sir. (He turns to go back to the table, and sees Mrs. Clandon coming up to the terrace from the beach by the steps.) Here is Mrs. Clandon, sir. (To Mrs. Clandon, in an unobtrusively confidential tone) Gentleman for you, ma'am.

MRS. CLANDON. We shall have two more gentlemen at lunch, William.

WAITER. Right, ma'am. Thank you, ma'am. (He withdraws into the hotel. Mrs. Clandon comes forward looking round for her visitor, but passes over the gentleman without any sign of recognition.)

THE GENTLEMAN (peering at her quaintly from under the umbrella). Don't you know me?

MRS. CLANDON (incredulously, looking hard at him) Are you Finch McComas?

McCOMAS. Can't you guess? (He shuts the umbrella; puts it aside; and jocularly plants himself with his hands on his hips to be inspected.)

MRS. CLANDON. I believe you are. (She gives him her hand. The shake that ensues is that of old friends after a long separation.) Where's your beard?

McCOMAS (with humorous solemnity). Would you employ a solicitor with a beard?

MRS. CLANDON (pointing to the silk hat on the table). Is that your hat?

McCOMAS. Would you employ a solicitor with a sombrero?

MRS. CLANDON. I have thought of you all these eighteen years with the beard and the sombrero. (She sits down on the garden seat. McComas takes his chair again.) Do you go to the meetings of the Dialectical Society still?

McCOMAS (gravely). I do not frequent meetings now.

MRS. CLANDON. Finch: I see what has happened. You have become respectable.

McCOMAS. Haven't you?

MRS. CLANDON. Not a bit.

McCOMAS. You hold to your old opinions still?

MRS. CLANDON. As firmly as ever.

McCOMAS. Bless me! And you are still ready to make speeches in public, in spite of your sex (Mrs. Clandon nods); to insist on a married woman's right to her own separate property (she nods again); to champion Darwin's view of the origin of species and John Stuart Mill's essay on Liberty (nod); to read Huxley, Tyndall and George Eliot (three nods); and to demand University degrees, the opening of the professions, and the parliamentary franchise for women as well as men?

MRS. CLANDON (resolutely). Yes: I have not gone back one inch; and I have educated Gloria to take up my work where I left it. That is what has brought me back to England: I felt that I had no right to bury her alive in Madeira—my St. Helena, Finch. I suppose she will be howled at as I was; but she is prepared for that.

McCOMAS. Howled at! My dear good lady: there is nothing in any of those views now-a-days to prevent her from marrying a bishop. You reproached me just now for having become respectable. You were wrong: I hold to our old opinions as strongly as ever. I don't go to church; and I don't pretend I do. I call myself what I am: a Philosophic Radical, standing for liberty and the rights of the individual, as I learnt to do from my master Herbert Spencer. Am I howled at? No: I'm indulged as an old fogey. I'm out of everything, because I've refused to bow the knee to Socialism.

MRS. CLANDON (shocked). Socialism.

McCOMAS. Yes, Socialism. That's what Miss Gloria will be up to her ears in before the end of the month if you let her loose here.

MRS. CLANDON (emphatically). But I can prove to her that Socialism is a fallacy.

McCOMAS (touchingly). It is by proving that, Mrs. Clandon, that I have lost all my young disciples. Be careful what you do: let her go her own way. (With some bitterness.) We're old-fashioned: the world thinks it has left us behind. There is only one place in all England where your opinions would still pass as advanced.

MRS. CLANDON (scornfully unconvinced). The Church, perhaps?

McCOMAS. No, the theatre. And now to business! Why have you made me come down here?

MRS. CLANDON. Well, partly because I wanted to see you—

McCOMAS (with good-humored irony). Thanks.

MRS. CLANDON.—and partly because I want you to explain everything to the children. They know nothing; and now that we have come back to England, it is impossible to leave them in ignorance any longer. (Agitated.) Finch: I cannot bring myself to tell them. I—(She is interrupted by the twins and Gloria. Dolly comes tearing up the steps, racing Philip, who combines a terrific speed with unhurried propriety of bearing which, however, costs him the race, as Dolly reaches her mother first and almost upsets the garden seat by the precipitancy of her arrival.)

DOLLY (breathless). It's all right, mamma. The dentist is coming; and he's bringing his old man.

MRS. CLANDON. Dolly, dear: don't you see Mr. McComas? (Mr. McComas rises, smilingly.)

DOLLY (her face falling with the most disparagingly obvious disappointment). This! Where are the flowing locks?

PHILIP (seconding her warmly). Where the beard?—the cloak?—the poetic exterior?

DOLLY. Oh, Mr. McComas, you've gone and spoiled yourself. Why didn't you wait till we'd seen you?

McCOMAS (taken aback, but rallying his humor to meet the emergency). Because eighteen years is too long for a solicitor to go without having his hair cut.

GLORIA (at the other side of McComas). How do you do, Mr. McComas? (He turns; and she takes his hand and presses it, with a frank straight look into his eyes.) We are glad to meet you at last.

McCOMAS. Miss Gloria, I presume? (Gloria smiles assent, and releases his hand after a final pressure. She then retires behind the garden seat, leaning over the back beside Mrs. Clandon.) And this young gentleman?

PHILIP. I was christened in a comparatively prosaic mood. My name is—

DOLLY (completing his sentence for him declamatorily). "Norval. On the Grampian hills"—

PHILIP (declaiming gravely). "My father feeds his flock, a frugal swain"—

MRS. CLANDON (remonstrating). Dear, dear children: don't be silly. Everything is so new to them here, Finch, that they are in the wildest spirits. They think every Englishman they meet is a joke.

DOLLY. Well, so he is: it's not our fault.

PHILIP. My knowledge of human nature is fairly extensive, Mr. McComas; but I find it impossible to take the inhabitants of this island seriously.

McCOMAS. I presume, sir, you are Master Philip (offering his hand)?

PHILIP (taking McComas's hand and looking solemnly at him). I was Master Philip—was so for many years; just as you were once Master Finch. (He gives his hand a single shake and drops it; then turns away, exclaiming meditatively) How strange it is to look back on our boyhood! (McComas stares after him, not at all pleased.)

DOLLY (to Mrs. Clandon). Has Finch had a drink?

MRS. CLANDON (remonstrating). Dearest: Mr. McComas will lunch with us.

DOLLY. Have you ordered for seven? Don't forget the old gentleman.

MRS. CLANDON. I have not forgotten him, dear. What is his name?

DOLLY. Chalkstones. He'll be here at half past one. (To McComas.) Are we like what you expected?

MRS. CLANDON (changing her tone to a more earnest one). Dolly: Mr. McComas has something more serious than that to tell you. Children: I have asked my old friend to answer the question you asked this morning. He is your father's friend as well as mine: and he will tell you the story more fairly than I could. (Turning her head from them to Gloria.) Gloria: are you satisfied?

349

GLORIA (gravely attentive). Mr. McComas is very kind.

McCOMAS (nervously). Not at all, my dear young lady: not at all. At the same time, this is rather sudden. I was hardly prepared—er—

DOLLY (suspiciously). Oh, we don't want anything prepared.

PHILIP (exhorting him). Tell us the truth.

DOLLY (emphatically). Bald headed.

McCOMAS (nettled). I hope you intend to take what I have to say seriously.

PHILIP (with profound mock gravity). I hope it will deserve it, Mr. McComas. My knowledge of human nature teaches me not to expect too much.

MRS. CLANDON (remonstrating). Phil—

PHILIP. Yes, mother, all right. I beg your pardon, Mr. McComas: don't mind us.

DOLLY (in conciliation). We mean well.

PHILIP. Shut up, both.

(Dolly holds her lips. McComas takes a chair from the luncheon table; places it between the little table and the garden seat with Dolly on his right and Philip on his left; and settles himself in it with the air of a man about to begin a long communication. The Clandons match him expectantly.)

McCOMAS. Ahem! Your father—

DOLLY (interrupting). How old is he?

PHILIP. Sh!

MRS. CLANDON (softly). Dear Dolly: don't let us interrupt Mr. McComas.

McCOMAS (emphatically). Thank you, Mrs. Clandon. Thank you. (To Dolly.) Your father is fifty-seven.

DOLLY (with a bound, startled and excited). Fifty-seven! Where does he live?

MRS. CLANDON (remonstrating). Dolly, Dolly!

McCOMAS (stopping her). Let me answer that, Mrs. Clandon. The answer will surprise you considerably. He lives in this town. (Mrs. Clandon rises. She and Gloria look at one another in the greatest consternation.)

DOLLY (with conviction). I knew it! Phil: Chalkstones is our father.

McCOMAS. Chalkstones!

DOLLY. Oh, Crampstones, or whatever it is. He said I was like his mother. I knew he must mean his daughter.

PHILIP (very seriously). Mr. McComas: I desire to consider your feelings in every possible way: but I warn you that if you stretch the long arm of coincidence to the length of telling me that Mr. Crampton of this town is my father, I shall decline to entertain the information for a moment.

McCOMAS. And pray why?

PHILIP. Because I have seen the gentleman; and he is entirely unfit to be my father, or Dolly's father, or Gloria's father, or my mother's husband.

McCOMAS. Oh, indeed! Well, sir, let me tell you that whether you like it or not, he is your father, and your sister' father, and Mrs. Clandon's husband. Now! What have you to say to that!

DOLLY (whimpering). You needn't be so cross. Crampton isn't your father.

PHILIP. Mr. McComas: your conduct is heartless. Here you find a family enjoying the unspeakable peace and freedom of being orphans. We have never seen the face of a relative—never known a claim except the claim of freely chosen friendship. And now you wish to thrust into the most intimate relationship with us a man whom we don't know—

DOLLY (vehemently). An awful old man! (reproachfully) And you began as if you had quite a nice father for us.

McCOMAS (angrily). How do you know that he is not nice? And what right have you to choose your own father? (raising his voice.) Let me tell you, Miss Clandon, that you are too young to—

DOLLY (interrupting him suddenly and eagerly). Stop, I forgot! Has he any money?

McCOMAS. He has a great deal of money.

DOLLY (delighted). Oh, what did I always say, Phil?

PHILIP. Dolly: we have perhaps been condemning the old man too hastily. Proceed, Mr. McComas.

McCOMAS. I shall not proceed, sir. I am too hurt, too shocked, to proceed.

MRS. CLANDON (urgently). Finch: do you realize what is happening? Do you understand that my children have invited that man to lunch, and that he will be here in a few moments?

McCOMAS (completely upset). What! do you mean—am I to understand——is it—

PHILIP (impressively). Steady, Finch. Think it out slowly and carefully. He's coming—coming to lunch.

GLORIA. Which of us is to tell him the truth? Have you thought of that?

MRS. CLANDON. Finch: you must tell him.

DOLLY Oh, Finch is no good at telling things. Look at the mess he has made of telling us.

McCOMAS. I have not been allowed to speak. I protest against this.

DOLLY (taking his arm coaxingly). Dear Finch: don't be cross.

MRS. CLANDON. Gloria: let us go in. He may arrive at any moment.

GLORIA (proudly). Do not stir, mother. I shall not stir. We must not run away.

MRS. CLANDON (delicately rebuking her). My dear: we cannot sit down to lunch just as we are. We shall come back again. We must have no bravado. (Gloria winces, and goes into the hotel without a word.) Come, Dolly. (As she goes into the hotel door, the waiter comes out with plates, etc., for two additional covers on a tray.)

WAITER. Gentlemen come yet, ma'am?

MRS. CLANDON. Two more to come yet, thank you. They will be here, immediately. (She goes into the hotel. The waiter takes his tray to the service table.)

PHILIP. I have an idea. Mr. McComas: this communication should be made, should it not, by a man of infinite tact?

McCOMAS. It will require tact, certainly.

PHILIP Good! Dolly: whose tact were you noticing only this morning?

DOLLY (seizing the idea with rapture). Oh, yes, I declare! William!

PHILIP. The very man! (Calling) William!

WAITER. Coming, sir.

McCOMAS (horrified). The waiter! Stop, stop! I will not permit this. I—

WAITER (presenting himself between Philip and McComas). Yes, sir. (McComas's complexion fades into stone grey; and all movement and expression desert his eyes. He sits down stupefied.)

PHILIP. William: you remember my request to you to regard me as your son?

WAITER (with respectful indulgence). Yes, sir. Anything you please, sir.

PHILIP. William: at the very outset of your career as my father, a rival has appeared on the scene.

WAITER. Your real father, sir? Well, that was to be expected, sooner or later, sir, wasn't it? (Turning with a happy smile to McComas.) Is it you, sir?

McCOMAS (renerved by indignation). Certainly not. My children know how to behave themselves.

PHILIP. No, William: this gentleman was very nearly my father: he wooed my mother, but wooed her in vain.

McCOMAS (outraged). Well, of all the—

PHILIP. Sh! Consequently, he is only our solicitor. Do you know one Crampton, of this town?

WAITER. Cock-eyed Crampton, sir, of the Crooked Billet, is it?

PHILIP. I don't know. Finch: does he keep a public house?

McCOMAS (rising scandalized). No, no, no. Your father, sir, is a well-known yacht builder, an eminent man here.

WAITER (impressed). Oh, beg pardon, sir, I'm sure. A son of Mr. Crampton's! Dear me!

PHILIP. Mr. Crampton is coming to lunch with us.

WAITER (puzzled). Yes, sir. (Diplomatically.) Don't usually lunch with his family, perhaps, sir?

PHILIP (impressively). William: he does not know that we are his family. He has not seen us for eighteen years. He won't know us. (To emphasize the communication he seats himself on the iron table with a spring, and looks at the waiter with his lips compressed and his legs swinging.)

DOLLY. We want you to break the news to him, William.

WAITER. But I should think he'd guess when he sees your mother, miss. (Philip's legs become motionless at this elucidation. He contemplates the waiter raptly.)

DOLLY (dazzled). I never thought of that.

PHILIP. Nor I. (Coming off the table and turning reproachfully on McComas.) Nor you.

DOLLY. And you a solicitor!

PHILIP. Finch: Your professional incompetence is appalling. William: your sagacity puts us all to shame.

DOLLY You really are like Shakespear, William.

WAITER. Not at all, sir. Don't mention it, miss. Most happy, I'm sure, sir. (Goes back modestly to the luncheon table and lays the two additional covers, one at the end next the steps, and the other so as to make a third on the side furthest from the balustrade.)

PHILIP (abruptly). Finch: come and wash your hands. (Seizes his arm and leads him toward the hotel.)

McCOMAS. I am thoroughly vexed and hurt, Mr. Clandon—

PHILIP (interrupting him). You will get used to us. Come, Dolly. (McComas shakes him off and marches into the hotel. Philip follows with unruffled composure.)

DOLLY (turning for a moment on the steps as she follows them). Keep your wits about you, William. There will be fire-works.

WAITER. Right, miss. You may depend on me, miss. (She goes into the hotel.)

(Valentine comes lightly up the steps from the beach, followed doggedly by Crampton. Valentine carries a walking stick. Crampton, either because he is old and chilly, or with some idea of extenuating the unfashionableness of his reefer jacket, wears a light overcoat. He stops at the chair left by McComas in the middle of the terrace, and steadies himself for a moment by placing his hand on the back of it.)

CRAMPTON. Those steps make me giddy. (He passes his hand over his forehead.) I have not got over that infernal gas yet.

(He goes to the iron chair, so that he can lean his elbows on the little table to prop his head as he sits. He soon recovers, and begins to unbutton his overcoat. Meanwhile Valentine interviews the waiter.)

VALENTINE. Waiter!

WAITER (coming forward between them). Yes, sir.

VALENTINE. Mrs. Lanfrey Clandon.

WAITER (with a sweet smile of welcome). Yes, sir. We're expecting you, sir. That is your table, sir. Mrs. Clandon will be down presently, sir. The young lady and young gentleman were just talking about your friend, sir.

VALENTINE. Indeed!

WAITER (smoothly melodious). Yes, sire. Great flow of spirits, sir. A vein of pleasantry, as you might say, sir. (Quickly, to Crampton, who has risen to get the overcoat off.) Beg pardon, sir, but if you'll allow me (helping him to get the overcoat off and taking it from him). Thank you, sir. (Crampton sits down again; and the waiter resumes

355

the broken melody.) The young gentleman's latest is that you're his father, sir.

CRAMPTON. What!

WAITER. Only his joke, sir, his favourite joke. Yesterday, I was to be his father. To-day, as soon as he knew you were coming, sir, he tried to put it up on me that you were his father, his long lost father——not seen you for eighteen years, he said.

CRAMPTON (startled). Eighteen years!

WAITER. Yes, sir. (With gentle archness.) But I was up to his tricks, sir. I saw the idea coming into his head as he stood there, thinking what new joke he'd have with me. Yes, sir: that's the sort he is: very pleasant, ve——ry off hand and affable indeed, sir. (Again changing his tempo to say to Valentine, who is putting his stick down against the corner of the garden seat) If you'll allow me, sir? (Taking Valentine's stick.) Thank you, sir. (Valentine strolls up to the luncheon table and looks at the menu. The waiter turns to Crampton and resumes his lay.) Even the solicitor took up the joke, although he was in a manner of speaking in my confidence about the young gentleman, sir. Yes, sir, I assure you, sir. You would never imagine what respectable professional gentlemen from London will do on an outing, when the sea air takes them, sir.

CRAMPTON. Oh, there's a solicitor with them, is there?

WAITER. The family solicitor, sir—yes, sir. Name of McComas, sir. (He goes towards hotel entrance with coat and stick, happily unconscious of the bomblike effect the name has produced on Crampton.)

CRAMPTON (rising in angry alarm). McComas! (Calls to Valentine.) Valentine! (Again, fiercely.) Valentine!! (Valentine turns.) This is a plant, a conspiracy. This is my family—my children—my infernal wife.

VALENTINE (coolly). On, indeed! Interesting meeting! (He resumes his study of the menu.)

CRAMPTON. Meeting! Not for me. Let me out of this. (Calling to the waiter.) Give me that coat.

WAITER. Yes, sir. (He comes back, puts Valentine's stick carefully down against the luncheon table; and delicately shakes the coat out and holds it for Crampton to put on.) I seem to have done the young gentleman an injustice, sir, haven't I, sir.

CRAMPTON. Rrrh! (He stops on the point of putting his arms into the sleeves, and turns to Valentine with sudden suspicion.) Valentine: you are in this. You made this plot. You—

VALENTINE (decisively). Bosh! (He throws the menu down and goes round the table to look out unconcernedly over the parapet.)

CRAMPTON (angrily). What d'ye—(McComas, followed by Philip and Dolly, comes out. He vacillates for a moment on seeing Crampton.)

WAITER (softly—interrupting Crampton). Steady, sir. Here they come, sir. (He takes up the stick and makes for the hotel, throwing the coat across his arm. McComas turns the corners of his mouth resolutely down and crosses to Crampton, who draws back and glares, with his hands behind him. McComas, with his brow opener than ever, confronts him in the majesty of a spotless conscience.)

WAITER (aside, as he passes Philip on his way out). I've broke it to him, sir.

PHILIP. Invaluable William! (He passes on to the table.)

DOLLY (aside to the waiter). How did he take it?

WAITER (aside to her). Startled at first, miss; but resigned—very resigned, indeed, miss. (He takes the stick and coat into the hotel.)

McCOMAS (having stared Crampton out of countenance). So here you are, Mr. Crampton.

CRAMPTON. Yes, here—caught in a trap—a mean trap. Are those my children?

PHILIP (with deadly politeness). Is this our father, Mr. McComas?

McCOMAS. Yes—er—(He loses countenance himself and stops.)

DOLLY (conventionally). Pleased to meet you again. (She wanders idly round the table, exchanging a smile and a word of greeting with Valentine on the way.)

357

PHILIP. Allow me to discharge my first duty as host by ordering your wine. (He takes the wine list from the table. His polite attention, and Dolly's unconcerned indifference, leave Crampton on the footing of the casual acquaintance picked up that morning at the dentist's. The consciousness of it goes through the father with so keen a pang that he trembles all over; his brow becomes wet; and he stares dumbly at his son, who, just conscious enough of his own callousness to intensely enjoy the humor and adroitness of it, proceeds pleasantly.) Finch: some crusted old port for you, as a respectable family solicitor, eh?

McCOMAS (firmly). Apollinaris only. I prefer to take nothing heating. (He walks away to the side of the terrace, like a man putting temptation behind him.)

PHILIP. Valentine—?

VALENTINE. Would Lager be considered vulgar?

PHILIP. Probably. We'll order some. Dolly takes it. (Turning to Crampton with cheerful politeness.) And now, Mr. Crampton, what can we do for you?

CRAMPTON. What d'ye mean, boy?

PHILIP. Boy! (Very solemnly.) Whose fault is it that I am a boy?

(Crampton snatches the wine list rudely from him and irresolutely pretends to read it. Philip abandons it to him with perfect politeness.)

DOLLY (looking over Crampton's right shoulder). The whisky's on the last page but one.

CRAMPTON. Let me alone, child.

DOLLY. Child! No, no: you may call me Dolly if you like; but you mustn't call me child. (She slips her arm through Philip's; and the two stand looking at Crampton as if he were some eccentric stranger.)

CRAMPTON (mopping his brow in rage and agony, and yet relieved even by their playing with him). McComas: we are—ha!—going to have a pleasant meal.

McCOMAS (pusillanimously). There is no reason why it should not be pleasant. (He looks abjectly gloomy.)

PHILIP. Finch's face is a feast in itself. (Mrs. Clandon and Gloria come from the hotel. Mrs. Clandon advances with courageous self-possession and marked dignity of manner. She stops at the foot of the steps to address Valentine, who is in her path. Gloria also stops, looking at Crampton with a certain repulsion.)

MRS. CLANDON. Glad to see you again, Mr. Valentine. (He smiles. She passes on and confronts Crampton, intending to address him with perfect composure; but his aspect shakes her. She stops suddenly and says anxiously, with a touch of remorse.) Fergus: you are greatly changed.

CRAMPTON (grimly). I daresay. A man does change in eighteen years.

MRS. CLANDON (troubled). I—I did not mean that. I hope your health is good.

CRAMPTON. Thank you. No: it's not my health. It's my happiness: that's the change you meant, I think. (Breaking out suddenly.) Look at her, McComas! Look at her; and look at me! (He utters a half laugh, half sob.)

PHILIP. Sh! (Pointing to the hotel entrance, where the waiter has just appeared.) Order before William!

DOLLY (touching Crampton's arm warningly with her finger). Ahem! (The waiter goes to the service table and beckons to the kitchen entrance, whence issue a young waiter with soup plates, and a cook, in white apron and cap, with the soup tureen. The young waiter remains and serves: the cook goes out, and reappears from time to time bringing in the courses. He carves, but does not serve. The waiter comes to the end of the luncheon table next the steps.)

MRS. CLANDON (as they all assemble about the table). I think you have all met one another already to-day. Oh, no, excuse me. (Introducing) Mr. Valentine: Mr. McComas. (She goes to the end of the table

359

nearest the hotel.) Fergus: will you take the head of the table, please.

CRAMPTON. Ha! (Bitterly.) The head of the table!

WAITER (holding the chair for him with inoffensive encouragement). This end, sir. (Crampton submits, and takes his seat.) Thank you, sir.

MRS. CLANDON. Mr. Valentine: will you take that side (indicating the side nearest the parapet) with Gloria? (Valentine and Gloria take their places, Gloria next Crampton and Valentine next Mrs. Clandon.) Finch: I must put you on this side, between Dolly and Phil. You must protect yourself as best you can. (The three take the remaining side of the table, Dolly next her mother, Phil next his father, and McComas between them. Soup is served.)

WAITER (to Crampton). Thick or clear, sir?

CRAMPTON (to Mrs. Clandon). Does nobody ask a blessing in this household?

PHILIP (interposing smartly). Let us first settle what we are about to receive. William!

WAITER. Yes, sir. (He glides swiftly round the table to Phil's left elbow. On his way he whispers to the young waiter) Thick.

PHILIP. Two small Lagers for the children as usual, William; and one large for this gentleman (indicating Valentine). Large Apollinaris for Mr. McComas.

WAITER. Yes, sir.

DOLLY. Have a six of Irish in it, Finch?

McCOMAS (scandalized). No—no, thank you.

PHILIP. Number 413 for my mother and Miss Gloria as before; and— (turning enquiringly to Crampton) Eh?

CRAMPTON (scowling and about to reply offensively). I—

WAITER (striking in mellifluously). All right, sir. We know what Mr. Crampton likes here, sir. (He goes into the hotel.)

PHILIP (looking gravely at his father). You frequent bars. Bad habit! (The cook, accompanied by a waiter with a supply of hot plates, brings in the fish from the kitchen to the service table, and begins slicing it.)

CRAMPTON. You have learnt your lesson from your mother, I see.

MRS. CLANDON. Phil: will you please remember that your jokes are apt to irritate people who are not accustomed to us, and that your father is our guest to-day.

CRAMPTON (bitterly). Yes, a guest at the head of my own table. (The soup plates are removed.)

DOLLY (sympathetically). Yes: it's embarrassing, isn't it? It's just as bad for us, you know.

PHILIP. Sh! Dolly: we are both wanting in tact. (To Crampton.) We mean well, Mr. Crampton; but we are not yet strong in the filial line. (The waiter returns from the hotel with the drinks.) William: come and restore good feeling.

WAITER (cheerfully). Yes, sir. Certainly, sir. Small Lager for you, sir. (To Crampton.) Seltzer and Irish, sir. (To McComas.) Apollinaris, sir. (To Dolly.) Small Lager, miss. (To Mrs. Clandon, pouring out wine.) 413, madam. (To Valentine.) Large Lager for you, sir. (To Gloria.) 413, miss.

DOLLY (drinking). To the family!

PHILIP. (drinking). Hearth and Home! (Fish is served.)

McCOMAS (with an obviously forced attempt at cheerful domesticity). We are getting on very nicely after all.

DOLLY (critically). After all! After all what, Finch?

CRAMPTON (sarcastically). He means that you are getting on very nicely in spite of the presence of your father. Do I take your point rightly, Mr. McComas?

McCOMAS (disconcerted). No, no. I only said "after all" to round off the sentence. I—er—er—er—

WAITER (tactfully). Turbot, sir?

McCOMAS (intensely grateful for the interruption). Thank you, waiter: thank you.

WAITER (sotto voce). Don't mention it, sir. (He returns to the service table.)

CRAMPTON (to Phil). Have you thought of choosing a profession yet?

PHILIP. I am keeping my mind open on that subject. William!

WAITER. Yes, sir.

PHILIP. How long do you think it would take me to learn to be a really smart waiter?

WAITER. Can't be learnt, sir. It's in the character, sir. (Confidentially to Valentine, who is looking about for something.) Bread for the lady, sir? yes, sir. (He serves bread to Gloria, and resumes at his former pitch.) Very few are born to it, sir.

PHILIP. You don't happen to have such a thing as a son, yourself, have you?

WAITER. Yes, sir: oh, yes, sir. (To Gloria, again dropping his voice.) A little more fish, miss? you won't care for the joint in the middle of the day.

GLORIA. No, thank you. (The fish plates are removed.)

DOLLY. Is your son a waiter, too, William?

WAITER (serving Gloria with fowl). Oh, no, miss, he's too impetuous. He's at the Bar.

McCOMAS (patronizingly). A potman, eh?

WAITER (with a touch of melancholy, as if recalling a disappointment softened by time). No, sir: the other bar—your profession, sir. A Q.C., sir.

McCOMAS (embarrassed). I'm sure I beg your pardon.

WAITER. Not at all, sir. Very natural mistake, I'm sure, sir. I've often wished he was a potman, sir. Would have been off my hands ever so much sooner, sir. (Aside to Valentine, who is again in difficulties.) Salt at your elbow, sir. (Resuming.) Yes, sir: had to support him until he was thirty-seven, sir. But doing well now, sir: very satisfactory indeed, sir. Nothing less than fifty guineas, sir.

McCOMAS. Democracy, Crampton!—modern democracy!

WAITER (calmly). No, sir, not democracy: only education, sir. Scholarships, sir. Cambridge Local, sir. Sidney Sussex College, sir. (Dolly plucks his sleeve and whispers as he bends down.) Stone ginger, miss? Right, miss. (To McComas.) Very good thing for him, sir: he never had any turn for real work, sir. (He goes into the hotel, leaving the company somewhat overwhelmed by his son's eminence.)

VALENTINE. Which of us dare give that man an order again!

DOLLY. I hope he won't mind my sending him for ginger-beer.

CRAMPTON (doggedly). While he's a waiter it's his business to wait. If you had treated him as a waiter ought to be treated, he'd have held his tongue.

DOLLY. What a loss that would have been! Perhaps he'll give us an introduction to his son and get us into London society. (The waiter reappears with the ginger-beer.)

CRAMPTON (growling contemptuously). London society! London society!! You're not fit for any society, child.

DOLLY (losing her temper). Now look here, Mr. Crampton. If you think—

WAITER (softly, at her elbow). Stone ginger, miss.

DOLLY (taken aback, recovers her good humor after a long breath and says sweetly). Thank you, dear William. You were just in time. (She drinks.)

McCOMAS (making a fresh effort to lead the conversation into dispassionate regions). If I may be allowed to change the subject, Miss Clandon, what is the established religion in Madeira?

GLORIA. I suppose the Portuguese religion. I never inquired.

DOLLY. The servants come in Lent and kneel down before you and confess all the things they've done: and you have to pretend to forgive them. Do they do that in England, William?

WAITER. Not usually, miss. They may in some parts: but it has not come under my notice, miss. (Catching Mrs. Clandon's eye as the young waiter offers her the salad bowl.) You like it without dressing, ma'am: yes, ma'am, I have some for you. (To his young colleague, motioning him to serve Gloria.) This side, Jo. (He takes a special portion of salad from the service table and puts it beside Mrs. Clandon's plate. In doing so he observes that Dolly is making a wry face.) Only a bit of watercress, miss, got in by mistake. (He takes her salad away.) Thank you, miss. (To the young waiter, admonishing him to serve Dolly afresh.) Jo. (Resuming.) Mostly members of the Church of England, miss.

DOLLY. Members of the Church of England! What's the subscription?

CRAMPTON (rising violently amid general consternation). You see how my children have been brought up, McComas. You see it; you hear it. I call all of you to witness—(He becomes inarticulate, and is about to strike his fist recklessly on the table when the waiter considerately takes away his plate.)

MRS. CLANDON (firmly). Sit down, Fergus. There is no occasion at all for this outburst. You must remember that Dolly is just like a foreigner here. Pray sit down.

CRAMPTON (subsiding unwillingly). I doubt whether I ought to sit here and countenance all this. I doubt it.

WAITER. Cheese, sir; or would you like a cold sweet?

CRAMPTON (take aback). What? Oh!—cheese, cheese.

DOLLY. Bring a box of cigarets, William.

WAITER. All ready, miss. (He takes a box of cigarets from the service table and places them before Dolly, who selects one and prepares to smoke. He then returns to his table for a box of vestas.)

CRAMPTON (staring aghast at Dolly). Does she smoke?

DOLLY (out of patience). Really, Mr. Crampton, I'm afraid I'm spoiling your lunch. I'll go and have my cigaret on the beach. (She leaves the table with petulant suddenness and goes down the steps. The waiter attempts to give her the matches; but she is gone before he can reach her.)

CRAMPTON (furiously). Margaret: call that girl back. Call her back, I say.

McCOMAS (trying to make peace). Come, Crampton: never mind. She's her father's daughter: that's all.

MRS. CLANDON (with deep resentment). I hope not, Finch. (She rises: they all rise a little.) Mr. Valentine: will you excuse me: I am afraid Dolly is hurt and put out by what has passed. I must go to her.

CRAMPTON. To take her part against me, you mean.

MRS. CLANDON (ignoring him). Gloria: will you take my place whilst I am away, dear. (She crosses to the steps. Crampton's eyes follow her with bitter hatred. The rest watch her in embarrassed silence, feeling the incident to be a very painful one.)

WAITER (intercepting her at the top of the steps and offering her a box of vestas). Young lady forgot the matches, ma'am. If you would be so good, ma'am.

MRS. CLANDON (surprised into grateful politeness by the witchery of his sweet and cheerful tones). Thank you very much. (She takes the matches and goes down to the beach. The waiter shepherds his assistant along with him into the hotel by the kitchen entrance, leaving the luncheon party to themselves.)

CRAMPTON (throwing himself back in his chair). There's a mother for you, McComas! There's a mother for you!

GLORIA (steadfastly). Yes: a good mother.

CRAMPTON. And a bad father? That's what you mean, eh?

VALENTINE (rising indignantly and addressing Gloria). Miss Clandon: I—

CRAMPTON (turning on him). That girl's name is Crampton, Mr. Valentine, not Clandon. Do you wish to join them in insulting me?

VALENTINE (ignoring him). I'm overwhelmed, Miss Clandon. It's all my fault: I brought him here: I'm responsible for him. And I'm ashamed of him.

CRAMPTON. What d'y' mean?

GLORIA (rising coldly). No harm has been done, Mr. Valentine. We have all been a little childish, I am afraid. Our party has been a failure: let us break it up and have done with it. (She puts her chair aside and turns to the steps, adding, with slighting composure, as she passes Crampton.) Good-bye, father.

(She descends the steps with cold, disgusted indifference. They all look after her, and so do not notice the return of the waiter from the hotel, laden with Crampton's coat, Valentine's stick, a couple of shawls and parasols, a white canvas umbrella, and some camp stools.)

CRAMPTON (to himself, staring after Gloria with a ghastly expression). Father! Father!! (He strikes his fist violently on the table.) Now—

WAITER (offering the coat). This is yours, sir, I think, sir. (Crampton glares at him; then snatches it rudely and comes down the terrace towards the garden seat, struggling with the coat in his angry efforts to put it on. McComas rises and goes to his assistance; then takes his hat and umbrella from the little iron table, and turns towards the steps. Meanwhile the waiter, after thanking Crampton with unruffled sweetness for taking the coat, offers some of his burden to Phil.) The ladies' sunshades, sir. Nasty glare off the sea to-day, sir: very trying to the complexion, sir. I shall carry down the camp stools myself, sir.

PHILIP. You are old, Father William; but you are the most considerate of men. No: keep the sunshades and give me the camp stools (taking them).

WAITER (with flattering gratitude). Thank you, sir.

PHILIP. Finch: share with me (giving him a couple). Come along. (They go down the steps together.)

VALENTINE (to the waiter). Leave me something to bring down—one of these. (Offering to take a sunshade.)

WAITER (discreetly). That's the younger lady's, sir. (Valentine lets it go.) Thank you, sir. If you'll allow me, sir, I think you had better have this. (He puts down the sunshades on Crampton's chair, and produces from the tail pocket of his dress coat, a book with a lady's handkerchief between the leaves, marking the page.) The eldest young lady is reading it at present. (Valentine takes it eagerly.) Thank you, sir. Schopenhauer, sir, you see. (He takes up the sunshades again.) Very interesting author, sir: especially on the subject of ladies, sir. (He goes down the steps. Valentine, about to follow him, recollects Crampton and changes his mind.)

VALENTINE (coming rather excitedly to Crampton). Now look here, Crampton: are you at all ashamed of yourself?

CRAMPTON (pugnaciously). Ashamed of myself! What for?

VALENTINE. For behaving like a bear. What will your daughter think of me for having brought you here?

CRAMPTON. I was not thinking of what my daughter was thinking of you.

VALENTINE. No, you were thinking of yourself. You're a perfect maniac.

CRAMPTON (heartrent). She told you what I am—a father—a father robbed of his children. What are the hearts of this generation like? Am I to come here after all these years—to see what my children are for the first time! to hear their voices!—and carry it all off like a fashionable visitor; drop in to lunch; be Mr. Crampton—M i s t e r Crampton! What right have they to talk to me like that? I'm their father: do they deny that? I'm a man, with the feelings of our common humanity: have I no rights, no claims? In all these years who have I had round me? Servants, clerks, business acquaintances. I've had respect from them—aye, kindness. Would one of them have spoken to me as that girl spoke?—would one of them have laughed at me as that boy was laughing at me all the time? (Frantically.) My own children! M i s t e r Crampton! My—

VALENTINE. Come, come: they're only children. The only one of them that's worth anything called you father.

CRAMPTON (wildly). Yes: "good-bye, father." Oh, yes: she got at my feelings—with a stab!

VALENTINE (taking this in very bad part). Now look here, Crampton: you just let her alone: she's treated you very well. I had a much worse time of it at lunch than you.

CRAMPTON. You!

VALENTINE (with growing impetuosity). Yes: I. I sat next to her; and I never said a single thing to her the whole time—couldn't think of a blessed word. And not a word did she say to me.

CRAMPTON. Well?

VALENTINE. Well? Well??? (Tackling him very seriously and talking faster and faster.) Crampton: do you know what's been the matter with me to-day? You don't suppose, do you, that I'm in the habit of playing such tricks on my patients as I played on you?

CRAMPTON. I hope not.

VALENTINE. The explanation is that I'm stark mad, or rather that I've never been in my real senses before. I'm capable of anything: I've grown up at last: I'm a Man; and it's your daughter that's made a man of me.

CRAMPTON (incredulously). Are you in love with my daughter?

VALENTINE (his words now coming in a perfect torrent). Love! Nonsense: it's something far above and beyond that. It's life, it's faith, it's strength, certainty, paradise—

CRAMPTON (interrupting him with acrid contempt). Rubbish, man! What have you to keep a wife on? You can't marry her.

VALENTINE. Who wants to marry her? I'll kiss her hands; I'll kneel at her feet; I'll live for her; I'll die for her; and that'll be enough for me. Look at her book! See! (He kisses the handkerchief.) If you offered me all your money for this excuse for going down to the beach and speaking to her again, I'd only laugh at you. (He rushes buoyantly off to the steps, where he bounces right into the arms of the waiter, who is coming up form the beach. The two save themselves from falling by clutching one another tightly round the waist and whirling one another around.)

WAITER (delicately). Steady, sir, steady.

VALENTINE (shocked at his own violence). I beg your pardon.

WAITER. Not at all, sir, not at all. Very natural, sir, I'm sure, sir, at your age. The lady has sent me for her book, sir. Might I take the liberty of asking you to let her have it at once, sir?

VALENTINE. With pleasure. And if you will allow me to present you with a professional man's earnings for six weeks—(offering him Dolly's crown piece.)

WAITER (as if the sum were beyond his utmost expectations). Thank you, sir: much obliged. (Valentine dashes down the steps.) Very high- spirited young gentleman, sir: very manly and straight set up.

CRAMPTON (in grumbling disparagement). And making his fortune in a hurry, no doubt. I know what his six weeks' earnings come to. (He crosses the terrace to the iron table, and sits down.)

WAITER (philosophically). Well, sir, you never can tell. That's a principle in life with me, sir, if you'll excuse my having such a thing, sir. (Delicately sinking the philosopher in the waiter for a moment.) Perhaps you haven't noticed that you hadn't touched that seltzer and Irish, sir, when the party broke up. (He takes the tumbler from the luncheon table, and sets if before Crampton.) Yes, sir, you never can tell. There was my son, sir! who ever thought that he would rise to wear a silk gown, sir? And yet to-day, sir, nothing less than fifty guineas, sir. What a lesson, sir!

CRAMPTON. Well, I hope he is grateful to you, and recognizes what he owes you.

WAITER. We get on together very well, very well indeed, sir, considering the difference in our stations. (With another of his irresistible transitions.) A small lump of sugar, sir, will take the flatness out of the seltzer without noticeably sweetening the drink, sir. Allow me, sir. (He drops a lump of sugar into the tumbler.) But as I say to him, where's the difference after all? If I must put on a dress coat to show what I am, sir, he must put on a wig and gown to show what he is. If my income is mostly tips, and there's a pretence that I don't get them, why, his income is mostly fees, sir; and I understand there's a pretence that he don't get them! If he likes society, and his profession brings him into contact with all ranks, so does mine, too, sir. If it's a little against a barrister to have a waiter for his father, sir, it's a little against a waiter to have a barrister for a son: many people consider it a great liberty, sir, I assure you, sir. Can I get you anything else, sir?

CRAMPTON. No, thank you. (With bitter humility.) I suppose that's no objection to my sitting here for a while: I can't disturb the party on the beach here.

WAITER (with emotion). Very kind of you, sir, to put it as if it was not a compliment and an honour to us, Mr. Crampton, very kind indeed. The more you are at home here, sir, the better for us.

CRAMPTON (in poignant irony). Home!

WAITER (reflectively). Well, yes, sir: that's a way of looking at it, too, sir. I have always said that the great advantage of a hotel is that it's a refuge from home life, sir.

CRAMPTON. I missed that advantage to-day, I think.

WAITER. You did, sir, you did. Dear me! It's the unexpected that always happens, isn't it? (Shaking his head.) You never can tell, sir: you never can tell. (He goes into the hotel.)

CRAMPTON (his eyes shining hardly as he props his drawn, miserable face on his hands). Home! Home!! (He drops his arms on the table and bows his head on them, but presently hears someone approaching and hastily sits bolt upright. It is Gloria, who has come up the steps alone, with her sunshade and her book in her hands. He looks defiantly at her, with the brutal obstinacy of his mouth and the wistfulness of his eyes contradicting each other pathetically. She comes to the corner of the garden seat and stands with her back to it, leaning against the end of it, and looking down at him as if wondering at his weakness: too curious about him to be cold, but supremely indifferent to their kinship.) Well?

GLORIA. I want to speak with you for a moment.

CRAMPTON (looking steadily at her). Indeed? That's surprising. You meet your father after eighteen years; and you actually want to speak to him for a moment! That's touching: isn't it? (He rests his head on his hands, and looks down and away from her, in gloomy reflection.)

GLORIA. All that is what seems to me so nonsensical, so uncalled for. What do you expect us to feel for you—to do for you? What is it you want? Why are you less civil to us than other people are? You are evidently not very fond of us—why should you be? But surely we can meet without quarrelling.

CRAMPTON (a dreadful grey shade passing over his face). Do you realize that I am your father?

GLORIA. Perfectly.

CRAMPTON. Do you know what is due to me as your father?

GLORIA. For instance—?

CRAMPTON (rising as if to combat a monster). For instance! For instance!! For instance, duty, affection, respect, obedience—

GLORIA (quitting her careless leaning attitude and confronting him promptly and proudly). I obey nothing but my sense of what is right. I respect nothing that is not noble. That is my duty. (She adds, less firmly) As to affection, it is not within my control. I am not sure that I quite know what affection means. (She turns away with an evident distaste for that part of the subject, and goes to the luncheon table for a comfortable chair, putting down her book and sunshade.)

CRAMPTON (following her with his eyes). Do you really mean what you are saying?

GLORIA (turning on him quickly and severely). Excuse me: that is an uncivil question. I am speaking seriously to you; and I expect you to take me seriously. (She takes one of the luncheon chairs; turns it away from the table; and sits down a little wearily, saying) Can you not discuss this matter coolly and rationally?

CRAMPTON. Coolly and rationally! No, I can't. Do you understand that? I can't.

GLORIA (emphatically). No. That I c a n n o t understand. I have no sympathy with—

CRAMPTON (shrinking nervously). Stop! Don't say anything more yet; you don't know what you're doing. Do you want to drive me mad? (She frowns, finding such petulance intolerable. He adds hastily) No: I'm not angry: indeed I'm not. Wait, wait: give me a little time to think. (He stands for a moment, screwing and clinching his brows and hands in his perplexity; then takes the end chair from the luncheon table and sits down beside her, saying, with a touching effort to be gentle and patient) Now, I think I have it. At least I'll try.

GLORIA (firmly). You see! Everything comes right if we only think it resolutely out.

CRAMPTON (in sudden dread). No: don't think. I want you to feel: that's the only thing that can help us. Listen! Do you—but first—I forgot. What's your name? I mean you pet name. They can't very well call you Sophronia.

GLORIA (with astonished disgust). Sophronia! My name is Gloria. I am always called by it.

CRAMPTON (his temper rising again). Your name is Sophronia, girl: you were called after your aunt Sophronia, my sister: she gave you your first Bible with your name written in it.

GLORIA. Then my mother gave me a new name.

CRAMPTON (angrily). She had no right to do it. I will not allow this.

GLORIA. You had no right to give me your sister's name. I don't know her.

CRAMPTON. You're talking nonsense. There are bounds to what I will put up with. I will not have it. Do you hear that?

GLORIA (rising warningly). Are you resolved to quarrel?

CRAMPTON (terrified, pleading). No, no: sit down. Sit down, won't you? (She looks at him, keeping him in suspense. He forces himself to utter the obnoxious name.) Gloria. (She marks her satisfaction with a slight tightening of the lips, and sits down.) There! You see I only want to shew you that I am your father, my—my dear child. (The endearment is so plaintively inept that she smiles in spite of herself, and resigns herself to indulge him a little.) Listen now. What I want to ask you is this. Don't you remember me at all? You were only a tiny child when you were taken away from me; but you took plenty of notice of things. Can't you remember someone whom you loved, or (shyly) at least liked in a childish way? Come! someone who let you stay in his study and look at his toy boats, as you thought them? (He looks anxiously into her face for some response, and continues less hopefully and more urgently) Someone who let you do as you liked there and never said a word to you except to tell you that you must sit still and not speak? Someone who was something that no one else was to you—who was your father.

GLORIA (unmoved). If you describe things to me, no doubt I shall presently imagine that I remember them. But I really remember nothing.

CRAMPTON (wistfully). Has your mother never told you anything about me?

GLORIA. She has never mentioned your name to me. (He groans involuntarily. She looks at him rather contemptuously and continues) Except once; and then she did remind me of something I had forgotten.

CRAMPTON (looking up hopefully). What was that?

GLORIA (mercilessly). The whip you bought to beat me with.

CRAMPTON (gnashing his teeth). Oh! To bring that up against me! To turn from me! When you need never have known. (Under a grinding, agonized breath.) Curse her!

GLORIA (springing up). You wretch! (With intense emphasis.) You wretch!! You dare curse my mother!

CRAMPTON. Stop; or you'll be sorry afterwards. I'm your father.

GLORIA. How I hate the name! How I love the name of mother! You had better go.

CRAMPTON. I—I'm choking. You want to kill me. Some—I—(His voice stifles: he is almost in a fit.)

GLORIA (going up to the balustrade with cool, quick resourcefulness, and calling over to the beach). Mr. Valentine!

VALENTINE (answering from below). Yes.

GLORIA. Come here a moment, please. Mr. Crampton wants you. (She returns to the table and pours out a glass of water.)

CRAMPTON (recovering his speech). No: let me alone. I don't want him. I'm all right, I tell you. I need neither his help nor yours. (He rises and pulls himself together.) As you say, I had better go. (He puts on his hat.) Is that your last word?

GLORIA. I hope so. (He looks stubbornly at her for a moment; nods grimly, as if he agreed to that; and goes into the hotel. She looks at him with equal steadiness until he disappears, when she makes a gesture of relief, and turns to speak to Valentine, who comes running up the steps.)

VALENTINE (panting). What's the matter? (Looking round.) Where's Crampton?

GLORIA. Gone. (Valentine's face lights up with sudden joy, dread, and mischief. He has just realized that he is alone with Gloria. She continues indifferently) I thought he was ill; but he recovered himself. He wouldn't wait for you. I am sorry. (She goes for her book and parasol.)

VALENTINE. So much the better. He gets on my nerves after a while. (Pretending to forget himself.) How could that man have so beautiful a daughter!

GLORIA (taken aback for a moment; then answering him with polite but intentional contempt). That seems to be an attempt at what is called a pretty speech. Let me say at once, Mr. Valentine, that pretty speeches make very sickly conversation. Pray let us be friends, if we are to be friends, in a sensible and wholesome way. I have no intention of getting married; and unless you are content to accept that state of things, we had much better not cultivate each other's acquaintance.

VALENTINE (cautiously). I see. May I ask just this one question? Is your objection an objection to marriage as an institution, or merely an objection to marrying me personally?

GLORIA. I do not know you well enough, Mr. Valentine, to have any opinion on the subject of your personal merits. (She turns away from him with infinite indifference, and sits down with her book on the garden seat.) I do not think the conditions of marriage at present are such as any self-respecting woman can accept.

VALENTINE (instantly changing his tone for one of cordial sincerity, as if he frankly accepted her terms and was delighted and reassured by her principles). Oh, then that's a point of sympathy between us already. I quite agree with you: the conditions are most unfair. (He takes off his hat and throws it gaily on the iron table.) No: what I want is to get rid of all that nonsense. (He sits down beside her, so naturally that she does not think of objecting, and proceeds, with enthusiasm) Don't you think it a horrible thing that a man and a woman can hardly know one another without being supposed to have designs of that kind? As if there were no other interests—

no other subjects of conversation—as if women were capable of nothing better!

GLORIA (interested). Ah, now you are beginning to talk humanly and sensibly, Mr. Valentine.

VALENTINE (with a gleam in his eye at the success of his hunter's guile). Of course!—two intelligent people like us. Isn't it pleasant, in this stupid, convention-ridden world, to meet with someone on the same plane—someone with an unprejudiced, enlightened mind?

GLORIA (earnestly). I hope to meet many such people in England.

VALENTINE (dubiously). Hm! There are a good many people here— nearly forty millions. They're not all consumptive members of the highly educated classes like the people in Madeira.

GLORIA (now full of her subject). Oh, everybody is stupid and prejudiced in Madeira—weak, sentimental creatures! I hate weakness; and I hate sentiment.

VALENTINE. That's what makes you so inspiring.

GLORIA (with a slight laugh). Am I inspiring?

VALENTINE Yes. Strength's infectious.

GLORIA. Weakness is, I know.

VALENTINE (with conviction). Y o u're strong. Do you know that you changed the world for me this morning? I was in the dumps, thinking of my unpaid rent, frightened about the future. When you came in, I was dazzled. (Her brow clouds a little. He goes on quickly.) That was silly, of course; but really and truly something happened to me. Explain it how you will, my blood got—(he hesitates, trying to think of a sufficiently unimpassioned word)—oxygenated: my muscles braced; my mind cleared; my courage rose. That's odd, isn't it? considering that I am not at all a sentimental man.

GLORIA (uneasily, rising). Let us go back to the beach.

VALENTINE (darkly—looking up at her). What! you feel it, too?

GLORIA. Feel what?

VALENTINE. Dread.

GLORIA. Dread!

VALENTINE. As if something were going to happen. It came over me suddenly just before you proposed that we should run away to the others.

GLORIA (amazed). That's strange—very strange! I had the same presentiment.

VALENTINE. How extraordinary! (Rising.) Well: shall we run away?

GLORIA. Run away! Oh, no: that would be childish. (She sits down again. He resumes his seat beside her, and watches her with a gravely sympathetic air. She is thoughtful and a little troubled as she adds) I wonder what is the scientific explanation of those fancies that cross us occasionally!

VALENTINE. Ah, I wonder! It's a curiously helpless sensation: isn't it?

GLORIA (rebelling against the word). Helpless?

VALENTINE. Yes. As if Nature, after allowing us to belong to ourselves and do what we judged right and reasonable for all these years, were suddenly lifting her great hand to take us—her two little children— by the scruff's of our little necks, and use us, in spite of ourselves, for her own purposes, in her own way.

GLORIA. Isn't that rather fanciful?

VALENTINE (with a new and startling transition to a tone of utter recklessness). I don't know. I don't care. (Bursting out reproachfully.) Oh, Miss Clandon, Miss Clandon: how could you?

GLORIA. What have I done?

VALENTINE. Thrown this enchantment on me. I'm honestly trying to be sensible—scientific—everything that you wish me to be. But—but—oh, don't you see what you have set to work in my imagination?

GLORIA (with indignant, scornful sternness). I hope you are not going to be so foolish—so vulgar—as to say love.

VALENTINE (with ironical haste to disclaim such a weakness). No, no, no. Not love: we know better than that. Let's call it chemistry. You can't deny that there is such a thing as chemical action, chemical affinity, chemical combination—the most irresistible of all natural forces. Well, you're attracting me irresistibly—chemically.

GLORIA (contemptuously). Nonsense!

VALENTINE. Of course it's nonsense, you stupid girl. (Gloria recoils in outraged surprise.) Yes, stupid girl: t h a t's a scientific fact, anyhow. You're a prig—a feminine prig: that's what you are. (Rising.) Now I suppose you've done with me for ever. (He goes to the iron table and takes up his hat.)

GLORIA (with elaborate calm, sitting up like a High-school-mistress posing to be photographed). That shows how very little you understand my real character. I am not in the least offended. (He pauses and puts his hat down again.) I am always willing to be told of my own defects, Mr. Valentine, by my friends, even when they are as absurdly mistaken about me as you are. I have many faults—very serious faults—of character and temper; but if there is one thing that I am not, it is what you call a prig. (She closes her lips trimly and looks steadily and challengingly at him as she sits more collectedly than ever.)

VALENTINE (returning to the end of the garden seat to confront her more emphatically). Oh, yes, you are. My reason tells me so: my knowledge tells me so: my experience tells me so.

GLORIA. Excuse my reminding you that your reason and your knowledge and your experience are not infallible. At least I hope not.

VALENTINE. I must believe them. Unless you wish me to believe my eyes, my heart, my instincts, my imagination, which are all telling me the most monstrous lies about you.

GLORIA (the collectedness beginning to relax). Lies!

VALENTINE (obstinately). Yes, lies. (He sits down again beside her.) Do you expect me to believe that you are the most beautiful woman in the world?

GLORIA. That is ridiculous, and rather personal.

VALENTINE. Of course it's ridiculous. Well, that's what my eyes tell me. (Gloria makes a movement of contemptuous protest.) No: I'm not flattering. I tell you I don't believe it. (She is ashamed to find that this does not quite please her either.) Do you think that if you were to turn away in disgust from my weakness, I should sit down here and cry like a child?

GLORIA (beginning to find that she must speak shortly and pointedly to keep her voice steady). Why should you, pray?

VALENTINE (with a stir of feeling beginning to agitate his voice). Of course not: I'm not such an idiot. And yet my heart tells me I should—my fool of a heart. But I'll argue with my heart and bring it to reason. If I loved you a thousand times, I'll force myself to look the truth steadily in the face. After all, it's easy to be sensible: the facts are the facts. What's this place? it's not heaven: it's the Marine Hotel. What's the time? it's not eternity: it's about half past one in the afternoon. What am I? a dentist—a five shilling dentist!

GLORIA. And I am a feminine prig.

VALENTINE. (passionately). No, no: I can't face that: I must have one illusion left—the illusion about you. I love you. (He turns towards her as if the impulse to touch her were ungovernable: she rises and stands on her guard wrathfully. He springs up impatiently and retreats a step.) Oh, what a fool I am!—an idiot! You don't understand: I might as well talk to the stones on the beach. (He turns away, discouraged.)

GLORIA (reassured by his withdrawal, and a little remorseful). I am sorry. I do not mean to be unsympathetic, Mr. Valentine; but what can I say?

VALENTINE (returning to her with all his recklessness of manner replaced by an engaging and chivalrous respect). You can say nothing, Miss Clandon. I beg your pardon: it was my own fault, or rather my own bad luck. You see, it all depended on your naturally liking me.

(She is about to speak: he stops her deprecatingly.) Oh, I know you
    mustn't tell me whether you like me or not; but—

GLORIA (her principles up in arms at once). Must not! Why not? I am
    a free woman: why should I not tell you?

VALENTINE (pleading in terror, and retreating). Don't. I'm afraid to
    hear.

GLORIA (no longer scornful). You need not be afraid. I think you are
    sentimental, and a little foolish; but I like you.

VALENTINE (dropping into the iron chair as if crushed). Then it's all
    over. (He becomes the picture of despair.)

GLORIA (puzzled, approaching him). But why?

VALENTINE. Because liking is not enough. Now that I think down into
    it seriously, I don't know whether I like you or not.

GLORIA (looking down at him with wondering concern). I'm sorry.

VALENTINE (in an agony of restrained passion). Oh, don't pity me.
    Your voice is tearing my heart to pieces. Let me alone, Gloria. You
    go down into the very depths of me, troubling and stirring me—I
    can't struggle with it—I can't tell you—

GLORIA (breaking down suddenly). Oh, stop telling me what you feel:
    I can't bear it.

VALENTINE (springing up triumphantly, the agonized voice now solid,
    ringing, and jubilant). Ah, it's come at last—my moment of courage.
    (He seizes her hands: she looks at him in terror.) Our moment of
    courage! (He draws her to him; kisses her with impetuous strength;
    and laughs boyishly.) Now you've done it, Gloria. It's all over: we're
    in love with one another. (She can only gasp at him.) But what a
    dragon you were! And how hideously afraid I was!

PHILIP'S VOICE (calling from the beach). Valentine!

DOLLY'S VOICE. Mr. Valentine!

VALENTINE. Good-bye. Forgive me. (He rapidly kisses her hands, and
    runs away to the steps, where he meets Mrs. Clandon, ascending.
    Gloria, quite lost, can only start after him.)

MRS. CLANDON. The children want you, Mr. Valentine. (She looks anxiously around.) Is he gone?

VALENTINE (puzzled). He? (Recollecting.) Oh, Crampton. Gone this long time, Mrs. Clandon. (He runs off buoyantly down the steps.)

GLORIA (sinking upon the seat). Mother!

MRS. CLANDON (hurrying to her in alarm). What is it, dear?

GLORIA (with heartfelt, appealing reproach). Why didn't you educate me properly?

MRS. CLANDON (amazed). My child: I did my best.

GLORIA. Oh, you taught me nothing—nothing.

MRS. CLANDON. What is the matter with you?

GLORIA (with the most intense expression). Only shame—shame—shame. (Blushing unendurably, she covers her face with her hands and turns away from her mother.)

END OF ACT II.

ACT III

The Clandon's sitting room in the hotel. An expensive apartment on the ground floor, with a French window leading to the gardens. In the centre of the room is a substantial table, surrounded by chairs, and draped with a maroon cloth on which opulently bound hotel and railway guides are displayed. A visitor entering through the window and coming down to this central table would have the fireplace on his left, and a writing table against the wall on his right, next the door, which is further down. He would, if his taste lay that way, admire the wall decoration of Lincrusta Walton in plum color and bronze lacquer, with dado and cornice; the ormolu consoles in the corners; the vases on pillar pedestals of veined marble with bases of polished black wood, one on each side of the window; the ornamental cabinet next the vase on the side nearest the fireplace, its centre compartment closed by an inlaid door, and its corners rounded off with curved panes of glass protecting shelves of cheap blue and white pottery; the bamboo tea table, with folding shelves, in the corresponding space on the other side of the window; the pictures of ocean steamers and Landseer's dogs; the saddlebag ottoman in line with the door but on the other side of the room; the two comfortable seats of the same pattern on the hearthrug; and finally, on turning round and looking up, the massive brass pole above the window, sustaining a pair of maroon rep curtains with decorated borders of staid green. Altogether, a room well arranged to flatter the occupant's sense of importance, and reconcile him to a charge of a pound a day for its use.

Mrs. Clandon sits at the writing table, correcting proofs. Gloria is standing at the window, looking out in a tormented revery.

The clock on the mantelpiece strikes five with a sickly clink, the bell being unable to bear up against the black marble cenotaph in which it is immured.

MRS. CLANDON. Five! I don't think we need wait any longer for the children. The are sure to get tea somewhere.

GLORIA (wearily). Shall I ring?

MRS. CLANDON. Do, my dear. (Gloria goes to the hearth and rings.) I have finished these proofs at last, thank goodness!

GLORIA (strolling listlessly across the room and coming behind her mother's chair). What proofs?

MRS. CLANDON The new edition of Twentieth Century Women.

GLORIA (with a bitter smile). There's a chapter missing.

MRS. CLANDON (beginning to hunt among her proofs). Is there? Surely not.

GLORIA. I mean an unwritten one. Perhaps I shall write it for you—-when I know the end of it. (She goes back to the window.)

MRS. CLANDON. Gloria! More enigmas!

GLORIA. Oh, no. The same enigma.

MRS. CLANDON (puzzled and rather troubled; after watching her for a moment). My dear.

GLORIA (returning). Yes.

MRS. CLANDON. You know I never ask questions.

GLORIA (kneeling beside her chair). I know, I know. (She suddenly throws her arms about her mother and embraces her almost passionately.)

MRS. CLANDON. (gently, smiling but embarrassed). My dear: you are getting quite sentimental

GLORIA (recoiling). Ah, no, no. Oh, don't say that. Oh! (She rises and turns away with a gesture as if tearing herself.)

MRS. CLANDON (mildly). My dear: what is the matter? What—(The waiter enters with the tea tray.)

WAITER (balmily). This was what you rang for, ma'am, I hope?

MRS. CLANDON. Thank you, yes. (She turns her chair away from the writing table, and sits down again. Gloria crosses to the hearth and sits crouching there with her face averted.)

WAITER (placing the tray temporarily on the centre table). I thought so, ma'am. Curious how the nerves seem to give out in the afternoon without a cup of tea. (He fetches the tea table and places it in front of Mrs. Cladon, conversing meanwhile.) the young lady and gentleman have just come back, ma'am: they have been out in a boat, ma'am. Very pleasant on a fine afternoon like this—very pleasant and invigorating indeed. (He takes the tray from the centre table and puts it on the tea table.) Mr. McComas will not come to tea, ma'am: he has gone to call upon Mr. Crampton. (He takes a couple of chairs and sets one at each end of the tea table.)

GLORIA (looking round with an impulse of terror). And the other gentleman?

WAITER (reassuringly, as he unconsciously drops for a moment into the measure of "I've been roaming," which he sang as a boy.) Oh, he's coming, miss, he's coming. He has been rowing the boat, miss, and has just run down the road to the chemist's for something to put on the blisters. But he will be here directly, miss—directly. (Gloria, in ungovernable apprehension, rises and hurries towards the door.)

MRS. CLANDON. (half rising). Glo—(Gloria goes out. Mrs. Clandon looks perplexedly at the waiter, whose composure is unruffled.)

WAITER (cheerfully). Anything more, ma'am?

MRS. CLANDON. Nothing, thank you.

WAITER. Thank you, ma'am. (As he withdraws, Phil and Dolly, in the highest spirits, come tearing in. He holds the door open for them; then goes out and closes it.)

DOLLY (ravenously). Oh, give me some tea. (Mrs. Clandon pours out a cup for her.) We've been out in a boat. Valentine will be here presently.

PHILIP. He is unaccustomed to navigation. Where's Gloria?

MRS. CLANDON (anxiously, as she pours out his tea). Phil: there is something the matter with Gloria. Has anything happened? (Phil and Dolly look at one another and stifle a laugh.) What is it?

PHILIP (sitting down on her left). Romeo—

DOLLY (sitting down on her right).—and Juliet.

PHILIP (taking his cup of tea from Mrs. Clandon). Yes, my dear mother: the old, old story. Dolly: don't take all the milk. (He deftly takes the jug from her.) Yes: in the spring—

DOLLY.—a young man's fancy—

PHILIP.—lightly turns to—thank you (to Mrs. Clandon, who has passed the biscuits)—thoughts of love. It also occurs in the autumn. The young man in this case is—

DOLLY. Valentine.

PHILIP. And his fancy has turned to Gloria to the extent of—

DOLLY. —kissing her—

PHILIP.—on the terrace—

DOLLY (correcting him).—on the lips, before everybody.

MRS. CLANDON (incredulously). Phil! Dolly! Are you joking? (They shake their heads.) Did she allow it?

PHILIP. We waited to see him struck to earth by the lightning of her scorn;—

DOLLY.—but he wasn't.

PHILIP. She appeared to like it.

DOLLY. As far as we could judge. (Stopping Phil, who is about to pour out another cup.) No: you've sworn off two cups.

MRS. CLANDON (much troubled). Children: you must not be here when Mr. Valentine comes. I must speak very seriously to him about this.

PHILIP. To ask him his intentions? What a violation of Twentieth Century principles!

DOLLY. Quite right, mamma: bring him to book. Make the most of the nineteenth century while it lasts.

PHILIP. Sh! Here he is. (Valentine comes in.)

VALENTINE Very sorry to be late for tea, Mrs. Clandon. (She takes up the tea-pot.) No, thank you: I never take any. No doubt Miss Dolly and Phil have explained what happened to me.

PHILIP (momentously rising). Yes, Valentine: we have explained.

DOLLY (significantly, also rising). We have explained very thoroughly.

PHILIP. It was our duty. (Very seriously.) Come, Dolly. (He offers Dolly his arm, which she takes. They look sadly at him, and go out gravely, arm in arm. Valentine stares after them, puzzled; then looks at Mrs. Clandon for an explanation.)

MRS. CLANDON (rising and leaving the tea table). Will you sit down, Mr. Valentine. I want to speak to you a little, if you will allow me. (Valentine sits down slowly on the ottoman, his conscience presaging a bad quarter of an hour. Mrs. Clandon takes Phil's chair, and seats herself deliberately at a convenient distance from him.) I must begin by throwing myself somewhat at your consideration. I am going to speak of a subject of which I know very little—perhaps nothing. I mean love.

VALENTINE. Love!

MRS. CLANDON. Yes, love. Oh, you need not look so alarmed as that, Mr. Valentine: I am not in love with you.

VALENTINE (overwhelmed). Oh, really, Mrs.—(Recovering himself.) I should be only too proud if you were.

MRS. CLANDON. Thank you, Mr. Valentine. But I am too old to begin.

VALENTINE. Begin! Have you never—?

MRS. CLANDON. Never. My case is a very common one, Mr. Valentine. I married before I was old enough to know what I was doing. As you have seen for yourself, the result was a bitter disappointment for both my husband and myself. So you see, though I am a married woman, I have never been in love; I have never had a love affair; and to be quite frank with you, Mr. Valentine, what I have seen of the love affairs of other people has not led me to regret that deficiency in my experience. (Valentine, looking very glum, glances sceptically at her, and says nothing. Her color rises a little; and she adds, with restrained anger) You do not believe me?

VALENTINE (confused at having his thought read). Oh, why not? Why not?

MRS. CLANDON. Let me tell you, Mr. Valentine, that a life devoted to the Cause of Humanity has enthusiasms and passions to offer which far transcend the selfish personal infatuations and sentimentalities of romance. Those are not your enthusiasms and passions, I take it? (Valentine, quite aware that she despises him for it, answers in the negative with a melancholy shake of the head.) I thought not. Well, I am equally at a disadvantage in discussing those so-called affairs of the heart in which you appear to be an expert.

VALENTINE (restlessly). What are you driving at, Mrs. Clandon?

MRS. CLANDON. I think you know.

VALENTINE. Gloria?

MRS. CLANDON. Yes. Gloria.

VALENTINE (surrendering). Well, yes: I'm in love with Gloria. (Interposing as she is about to speak.) I know what you're going to say: I've no money.

MRS. CLANDON. I care very little about money, Mr. Valentine.

VALENTINE. Then you're very different to all the other mothers who have interviewed me.

MRS. CLANDON. Ah, now we are coming to it, Mr. Valentine. You are an old hand at this. (He opens his mouth to protest: she cuts him short with some indignation.) Oh, do you think, little as I understand these matters, that I have not common sense enough to know that a man who could make as much way in one interview with such a woman as my daughter, can hardly be a novice!

VALENTINE. I assure you—

MRS. CLANDON (stopping him). I am not blaming you, Mr. Valentine. It is Gloria's business to take care of herself; and you have a right to amuse yourself as you please. But—

VALENTINE (protesting). Amuse myself! Oh, Mrs. Clandon!

MRS. CLANDON (relentlessly). On your honor, Mr. Valentine, are you in earnest?

VALENTINE (desperately). On my honor I am in earnest. (She looks searchingly at him. His sense of humor gets the better of him; and he adds quaintly) Only, I always have been in earnest; and yet—here I am, you see!

MRS. CLANDON. This is just what I suspected. (Severely.) Mr. Valentine: you are one of those men who play with women's affections.

VALENTINE. Well, why not, if the Cause of Humanity is the only thing worth being serious about? However, I understand. (Rising and taking his hat with formal politeness.) You wish me to discontinue my visits.

MRS. CLANDON. No: I am sensible enough to be well aware that Gloria's best chance of escape from you now is to become better acquainted with you.

VALENTINE (unaffectedly alarmed). Oh, don't say that, Mrs. Clandon. You don't think that, do you?

MRS. CLANDON. I have great faith, Mr. Valentine, in the sound training Gloria's mind has had since she was a child.

VALENTINE (amazingly relieved). O-oh! Oh, that's all right. (He sits down again and throws his hat flippantly aside with the air of a man who has no longer anything to fear.)

MRS. CLANDON (indignant at his assurance). What do you mean?

VALENTINE (turning confidentially to her). Come: shall I teach you something, Mrs. Clandon?

MRS. CLANDON (stiffly). I am always willing to learn.

VALENTINE. Have you ever studied the subject of gunnery—artillery—cannons and war-ships and so on?

MRS. CLANDON. Has gunnery anything to do with Gloria?

VALENTINE. A great deal—by way of illustration. During this whole century, my dear Mrs. Clandon, the progress of artillery has been a duel between the maker of cannons and the maker of armor plates to keep the cannon balls out. You build a ship proof against the best gun known: somebody makes a better gun and sinks your ship. You build a heavier ship, proof against that gun: somebody makes a heavier gun and sinks you again. And so on. Well, the duel of sex is just like that.

MRS. CLANDON. The duel of sex!

VALENTINE. Yes: you've heard of the duel of sex, haven't you? Oh, I forgot: you've been in Madeira: the expression has come up since your time. Need I explain it?

MRS. CLANDON (contemptuously). No.

VALENTINE. Of course not. Now what happens in the duel of sex? The old fashioned mother received an old fashioned education to protect her against the wiles of man. Well, you know the result: the old fashioned man got round her. The old fashioned woman resolved to protect her daughter more effectually—to find some armor too strong for the old fashioned man. So she gave her daughter a scientific education—your plan. That was a corker for the old fashioned man: he said it wasn't fair—unwomanly and all the rest of it. But that didn't do him any good. So he had to give up his old fashioned plan of attack—you know——going down on his knees and swearing to love, honor and obey, and so on.

MRS. CLANDON. Excuse me: that was what the woman swore.

VALENTINE. Was it? Ah, perhaps you're right—yes: of course it was. Well, what did the man do? Just what the artillery man does—went one better than the woman—educated himself scientifically and beat her at that game just as he had beaten her at the old game. I learnt how to circumvent the Women's Rights woman before I was twenty- three: it's all been found out long ago. You see, my methods are thoroughly modern.

MRS. CLANDON (with quiet disgust). No doubt.

VALENTINE. But for that very reason there's one sort of girl against whom they are of no use.

MRS. CLANDON. Pray which sort?

VALENTINE. The thoroughly old fashioned girl. If you had brought up Gloria in the old way, it would have taken me eighteen months to get to the point I got to this afternoon in eighteen minutes. Yes, Mrs. Clandon: the Higher Education of Women delivered Gloria into my hands; and it was you who taught her to believe in the Higher Education of Women.

MRS. CLANDON (rising). Mr. Valentine: you are very clever.

VALENTINE (rising also). Oh, Mrs. Clandon!

MRS. CLANDON And you have taught me n o t h i n g. Good-bye.

VALENTINE (horrified). Good-bye! Oh, mayn't I see her before I go?

MRS. CLANDON. I am afraid she will not return until you have gone Mr. Valentine. She left the room expressly to avoid you.

VALENTINE (thoughtfully). That's a good sign. Good-bye. (He bows and makes for the door, apparently well satisfied.)

MRS. CLANDON (alarmed). Why do you think it a good sign?

VALENTINE (turning near the door). Because I am mortally afraid of her; and it looks as if she were mortally afraid of me. (He turns to go and finds himself face to face with Gloria, who has just entered. She looks steadfastly at him. He stares helplessly at her; then round at Mrs. Clandon; then at Gloria again, completely at a loss.)

GLORIA (white, and controlling herself with difficulty). Mother: is what Dolly told me true?

MRS. CLANDON. What did she tell you, dear?

GLORIA. That you have been speaking about me to this gentleman.

VALENTINE (murmuring). This gentleman! Oh!

390

MRS. CLANDON (sharply). Mr. Valentine: can you hold your tongue for a moment? (He looks piteously at them; then, with a despairing shrug, goes back to the ottoman and throws his hat on it.)

GLORIA (confronting her mother, with deep reproach). Mother: what right had you to do it?

MRS. CLANDON. I don't think I have said anything I have no right to say, Gloria.

VALENTINE (confirming her officiously). Nothing. Nothing whatever. (Gloria looks at him with unspeakable indignation.) I beg your pardon. (He sits down ignominiously on the ottoman.)

GLORIA. I cannot believe that any one has any right even to think about things that concern me only. (She turns away from them to conceal a painful struggle with her emotion.)

MRS. CLANDON. My dear, if I have wounded your pride—

GLORIA (turning on them for a moment). My p r i d e! My pride!! Oh, it's gone: I have learnt now that I have no strength to be proud of. (Turning away again.) But if a woman cannot protect herself, no one can protect her. No one has any right to try—not even her mother. I know I have lost your confidence, just as I have lost this man's respect;—(She stops to master a sob.)

VALENTINE (under his breath). This man! (Murmuring again.) Oh!

MRS. CLANDON (in an undertone). Pray be silent, sir.

GLORIA (continuing).—but I have at least the right to be left alone in my disgrace. I am one of those weak creatures born to be mastered by the first man whose eye is caught by them; and I must fulfill my destiny, I suppose. At least spare me the humiliation of trying to save me. (She sits down, with her handkerchief to her eyes, at the farther end of the table.)

VALENTINE (jumping up). Look here—

MRS. CLANDON. Mr. Va—

VALENTINE (recklessly). No: I will speak: I've been silent for nearly thirty seconds. (He goes up to Gloria.) Miss Clandon—

GLORIA (bitterly). Oh, not Miss Clandon: you have found that it is quite safe to call me Gloria.

VALENTINE. No, I won't: you'll throw it in my teeth afterwards and accuse me of disrespect. I say it's a heartbreaking falsehood that I don't respect you. It's true that I didn't respect your old pride: why should I? It was nothing but cowardice. I didn't respect your intellect: I've a better one myself: it's a masculine specialty. But when the depths stirred!—when my moment came!—when you made me brave!—ah, then, then, t h e n!

GLORIA. Then you respected me, I suppose.

VALENTINE. No, I didn't: I adored you. (She rises quickly and turns her back on him.) And you can never take that moment away from me. So now I don't care what happens. (He comes down the room addressing a cheerful explanation to nobody in particular.) I'm perfectly aware that I'm talking nonsense. I can't help it. (To Mrs. Clandon.) I love Gloria; and there's an end of it.

MRS. CLANDON (emphatically). Mr. Valentine: you are a most dangerous man. Gloria: come here. (Gloria, wondering a little at the command, obeys, and stands, with drooping head, on her mother's right hand, Valentine being on the opposite side. Mrs. Clandon then begins, with intense scorn.) Ask this man whom you have inspired and made brave, how many women have inspired him before (Gloria looks up suddenly with a flash of jealous anger and amazement); how many times he has laid the trap in which he has caught you; how often he has baited it with the same speeches; how much practice it has taken to make him perfect in his chosen part in life as the Duellist of Sex.

VALENTINE. This isn't fair. You're abusing my confidence, Mrs. Clandon.

MRS. CLANDON. Ask him, Gloria.

GLORIA (in a flush of rage, going over to him with her fists clenched). Is that true?

VALENTINE. Don't be angry—

GLORIA (interrupting him implacably). Is it true? Did you ever say that before? Did you ever feel that before—for another woman?

VALENTINE (bluntly). Yes. (Gloria raises her clenched hands.)

MRS. CLANDON (horrified, springing to her side and catching her uplifted arm). Gloria!! My dear! You're forgetting yourself. (Gloria, with a deep expiration, slowly relaxes her threatening attitude.)

VALENTINE. Remember: a man's power of love and admiration is like any other of his powers: he has to throw it away many times before he learns what is really worthy of it.

MRS. CLANDON. Another of the old speeches, Gloria. Take care.

VALENTINE (remonstrating). Oh!

GLORIA (to Mrs. Clandon, with contemptuous self-possession). Do you think I need to be warned now? (To Valentine.) You have tried to make me love you.

VALENTINE. I have.

GLORIA. Well, you have succeeded in making me hate you—passionately.

VALENTINE (philosophically). It's surprising how little difference there is between the two. (Gloria turns indignantly away from him. He continues, to Mrs. Clandon) I know men whose wives love them; and they go on exactly like that.

MRS. CLANDON. Excuse me, Mr. Valentine; but had you not better go?

GLORIA. You need not send him away on my account, mother. He is nothing to me now; and he will amuse Dolly and Phil. (She sits down with slighting indifference, at the end of the table nearest the window.)

VALENTINE (gaily). Of course: that's the sensible way of looking at it. Come, Mrs. Clandon: you can't quarrel with a mere butterfly like me.

MRS. CLANDON. I very greatly mistrust you, Mr. Valentine. But I do not like to think that your unfortunate levity of disposition is mere shamelessness and worthlessness;—

GLORIA (to herself, but aloud). It is shameless; and it is worthless.

MRS. CLANDON.—so perhaps we had better send for Phil and Dolly and allow you to end your visit in the ordinary way.

VALENTINE (as if she had paid him the highest compliment). You overwhelm me, Mrs. Clandon. Thank you. (The waiter enters.)

WAITER. Mr. McComas, ma'am.

MRS. CLANDON. Oh, certainly. Bring him in.

WAITER. He wishes to see you in the reception-room, ma'am.

MRS. CLANDON. Why not here?

WAITER. Well, if you will excuse my mentioning it, ma'am, I think Mr. McComas feels that he would get fairer play if he could speak to you away from the younger members of your family, ma'am.

MRS. CLANDON. Tell him they are not here.

WAITER. They are within sight of the door, ma'am; and very watchful, for some reason or other.

MRS. CLANDON (going). Oh, very well: I'll go to him.

WAITER (holding the door open for her). Thank you, ma'am. (She goes out. He comes back into the room, and meets the eye of Valentine, who wants him to go.) All right, sir. Only the tea-things, sir. (Taking the tray.) Excuse me, sir. Thank you sir. (He goes out.)

VALENTINE (to Gloria). Look here. You will forgive me, sooner or later. Forgive me now.

GLORIA (rising to level the declaration more intensely at him). Never! While grass grows or water runs, never, never, never!!!

VALENTINE (unabashed). Well, I don't care. I can't be unhappy about anything. I shall never be unhappy again, never, never, never, while grass grows or water runs. The thought of you will always make me wild with joy. (Some quick taunt is on her lips: he interposes swiftly.) No: I never said that before: that's new.

GLORIA. It will not be new when you say it to the next woman.

VALENTINE. Oh, don't, Gloria, don't. (He kneels at her feet.)

GLORIA. Get up. Get up! How dare you? (Phil and Dolly, racing, as usual, for first place, burst into the room. They check themselves on seeing what is passing. Valentine springs up.)

PHILIP (discreetly). I beg your pardon. Come, Dolly. (He turns to go.)

GLORIA (annoyed). Mother will be back in a moment, Phil. (Severely.) Please wait here for her. (She turns away to the window, where she stands looking out with her back to them.)

PHILIP (significantly). Oh, indeed. Hmhm!

DOLLY. Ahah!

PHILIP. You seem in excellent spirits, Valentine.

VALENTINE. I am. (Comes between them.) Now look here. You both know what's going on, don't you? (Gloria turns quickly, as if anticipating some fresh outrage.)

DOLLY. Perfectly.

VALENTINE. Well, it's all over. I've been refused—scorned. I'm only here on sufferance. You understand: it's all over. Your sister is in no sense entertaining my addresses, or condescending to interest herself in me in any way. (Gloria, satisfied, turns back contemptuously to the window.) Is that clear?

DOLLY. Serve you right. You were in too great a hurry.

PHILIP (patting him on the shoulder). Never mind: you'd never have been able to call your soul your own if she'd married you. You can now begin a new chapter in your life.

DOLLY. Chapter seventeen or thereabouts, I should imagine.

VALENTINE (much put out by this pleasantry). No: don't say things like that. That's just the sort of thoughtless remark that makes a lot of mischief.

DOLLY. Oh, indeed. Hmhm!

PHILIP. Ahah! (He goes to the hearth and plants himself there in his best head-of-the-family attitude.)

McComas, looking very serious, comes in quickly with Mrs. Clandon, whose first anxiety is about Gloria. She looks round to see where she is, and is going to join her at the window when Gloria comes down to meet her with a marked air of trust and affection. Finally, Mrs. Clandon takes her former seat, and Gloria posts herself behind it. McComas, on his way to the ottoman, is hailed by Dolly.

DOLLY. What cheer, Finch?

McCOMAS (sternly). Very serious news from your father, Miss Clandon. Very serious news indeed. (He crosses to the ottoman, and sits down. Dolly, looking deeply impressed, follows him and sits beside him on his right.)

VALENTINE. Perhaps I had better go.

McCOMAS. By no means, Mr. Valentine. You are deeply concerned in this. (Valentine takes a chair from the table and sits astride of it, leaning over the back, near the ottoman.) Mrs. Clandon: your husband demands the custody of his two younger children, who are not of age. (Mrs. Clandon, in quick alarm, looks instinctively to see if Dolly is safe.)

DOLLY (touched). Oh, how nice of him! He likes us, mamma.

McCOMAS. I am sorry to have to disabuse you of any such idea, Miss Dorothea.

DOLLY (cooing ecstatically). Dorothee-ee-ee-a! (Nestling against his shoulder, quite overcome.) Oh, Finch!

McCOMAS (nervously, moving away). No, no, no, no!

MRS. CLANDON (remonstrating). D e a r e s t Dolly! (To McComas.) The deed of separation gives me the custody of the children.

McCOMAS. It also contains a covenant that you are not to approach or molest him in any way.

MRS. CLANDON. Well, have I done so?

McCOMAS. Whether the behavior of your younger children amounts to legal molestation is a question on which it may be necessary to take counsel's opinion. At all events, Mr. Crampton not only claims to have been molested; but he believes that he was brought here by a plot in which Mr. Valentine acted as your agent.

VALENTINE. What's that? Eh?

McCOMAS. He alleges that you drugged him, Mr. Valentine.

VALENTINE. So I did. (They are astonished.)

McCOMAS. But what did you do that for?

DOLLY. Five shillings extra.

McCOMAS (to Dolly, short-temperedly). I must really ask you, Miss Clandon, not to interrupt this very serious conversation with irrelevant interjections. (Vehemently.) I insist on having earnest matters earnestly and reverently discussed. (This outburst produces an apologetic silence, and puts McComas himself out of countenance. He coughs, and starts afresh, addressing himself to Gloria.) Miss Clandon: it is my duty to tell you that your father has also persuaded himself that Mr. Valentine wishes to marry you—

VALENTINE (interposing adroitly). I do.

McCOMAS (offended). In that case, sir, you must not be surprised to find yourself regarded by the young lady's father as a fortune hunter.

VALENTINE. So I am. Do you expect my wife to live on what I earn? ten-pence a week!

McCOMAS (revolted). I have nothing more to say, sir. I shall return and tell Mr. Crampton that this family is no place for a father. (He makes for the door.)

MRS. CLANDON (with quiet authority). Finch! (He halts.) If Mr. Valentine cannot be serious, you can. Sit down. (McComas, after a brief struggle between his dignity and his friendship, succumbs, seating himself this time midway between Dolly and Mrs. Clandon.) You know that all this is a made up case—that Fergus does not believe in it any more than you do. Now give me your real advice—your sincere, friendly advice: you know I have always trusted your judgment. I promise you the children will be quiet.

McCOMAS (resigning himself). Well, well! What I want to say is this. In the old arrangement with your husband, Mrs. Clandon, you had him at a terrible disadvantage.

MRS. CLANDON. How so, pray?

McCOMAS. Well, you were an advanced woman, accustomed to defy public opinion, and with no regard for what the world might say of you.

MRS. CLANDON (proud of it). Yes: that is true. (Gloria, behind the chair, stoops and kisses her mother's hair, a demonstration which disconcerts her extremely.)

McCOMAS. On the other hand, Mrs. Clandon, your husband had a great horror of anything getting into the papers. There was his business to be considered, as well as the prejudices of an old-fashioned family.

MRS. CLANDON. Not to mention his own prejudices.

McCOMAS. Now no doubt he behaved badly, Mrs. Clandon—

MRS. CLANDON (scornfully). No doubt.

McCOMAS. But was it altogether his fault?

MRS. CLANDON. Was it mine?

McCOMAS (hastily). No. Of course not.

GLORIA (observing him attentively). You do not mean that, Mr. McComas.

McCOMAS. My dear young lady, you pick me up very sharply. But let me just put this to you. When a man makes an unsuitable marriage (nobody's fault, you know, but purely accidental incompatibility of tastes); when he is deprived by that misfortune of the domestic sympathy which, I take it, is what a man marries for; when in short, his wife is rather worse than no wife at all (through no fault of his own, of course), is it to be wondered at if he makes matters worse at first by blaming her, and even, in his desperation, by occasionally drinking himself into a violent condition or seeking sympathy elsewhere?

MRS. CLANDON. I did not blame him: I simply rescued myself and the children from him.

McCOMAS. Yes: but you made hard terms, Mrs. Clandon. You had him at your mercy: you brought him to his knees when you threatened to make the matter public by applying to the Courts for a judicial separation. Suppose he had had that power over you, and used it to take your children away from you and bring them up in ignorance of your very name, how would you feel? what would you do? Well, won't you make some allowance for his feelings?—in common humanity.

MRS. CLANDON. I never discovered his feelings. I discovered his temper, and his—(she shivers) the rest of his common humanity.

McCOMAS (wistfully). Women can be very hard, Mrs. Clandon.

VALENTINE. That's true.

GLORIA (angrily). Be silent. (He subsides.)

McCOMAS (rallying all his forces). Let me make one last appeal. Mrs. Clandon: believe me, there are men who have a good deal of feeling, and kind feeling, too, which they are not able to express. What you miss in Crampton is that mere veneer of civilization, the art of shewing worthless attentions and paying insincere compliments in a kindly, charming way. If you lived in London, where the whole system is one of false good-fellowship, and you may know a man for twenty years without finding out that he hates you like poison, you would soon have your eyes opened. There we do unkind things in a kind way: we say bitter things in a sweet voice: we always give our friends chloroform when we tear them to pieces. But think of the other side of it! Think of the people who do kind things in an unkind way—people whose touch hurts, whose voices jar, whose tempers play them false, who wound and worry the people they love in the very act of trying to conciliate them, and yet who need affection as much as the rest of us. Crampton has an abominable temper, I admit. He has no manners, no tact, no grace. He'll never be able to gain anyone's affection unless they will take his desire for it on trust. Is he to have none—not even pity—from his own flesh and blood?

DOLLY (quite melted). Oh, how beautiful, Finch! How nice of you!

PHILIP (with conviction). Finch: this is eloquence—positive eloquence.

DOLLY. Oh, mamma, let us give him another chance. Let us have him to dinner.

MRS. CLANDON (unmoved). No, Dolly: I hardly got any lunch. My dear Finch: there is not the least use in talking to me about Fergus. You have never been married to him: I have.

McCOMAS (to Gloria). Miss Clandon: I have hitherto refrained from appealing to you, because, if what Mr. Crampton told me to be true, you have been more merciless even than your mother.

GLORIA (defiantly). You appeal from her strength to my weakness!

McCOMAS. Not your weakness, Miss Clandon. I appeal from her intellect to your heart.

GLORIA. I have learnt to mistrust my heart. (With an angry glance at Valentine.) I would tear my heart and throw it away if I could. My answer to you is my mother's answer. (She goes to Mrs. Clandon, and stands with her arm about her; but Mrs. Clandon, unable to endure this sort of demonstrativeness, disengages herself as soon as she can without hurting Gloria's feelings.)

McCOMAS (defeated). Well, I am very sorry—very sorry. I have done my best. (He rises and prepares to go, deeply dissatisfied.)

MRS. CLANDON. But what did you expect, Finch? What do you want us to do?

McCOMAS. The first step for both you and Crampton is to obtain counsel's opinion as to whether he is bound by the deed of separation or not. Now why not obtain this opinion at once, and have a friendly meeting (her face hardens)—or shall we say a neutral meeting?—to settle the difficulty—here—in this hotel—to-night? What do you say?

MRS. CLANDON. But where is the counsel's opinion to come from?

McCOMAS. It has dropped down on us out of the clouds. On my way back here from Crampton's I met a most eminent Q.C., a man whom I briefed in the case that made his name for him. He has come down here from Saturday to Monday for the sea air, and to visit a relative of his who lives here. He has been good enough to say that if I can arrange a meeting of the parties he will come and help us with his opinion. Now do let us seize this chance of a quiet friendly family adjustment. Let me bring my friend here and try to persuade Crampton to come, too. Come: consent.

MRS. CLANDON (rather ominously, after a moment's consideration). Finch: I don't want counsel's opinion, because I intend to be guided by my own opinion. I don't want to meet Fergus again, because I don't like him, and don't believe the meeting will do any good. However (rising), you have persuaded the children that he is not quite hopeless. Do as you please.

McCOMAS (taking her hand and shaking it). Thank you, Mrs. Clandon. Will nine o'clock suit you?

MRS. CLANDON. Perfectly. Phil: will you ring, please. (Phil rings the bell.) But if I am to be accused of conspiring with Mr. Valentine, I think he had better be present.

VALENTINE (rising). I quite agree with you. I think it's most important.

McCOMAS. There can be no objection to that, I think. I have the greatest hopes of a happy settlement. Good-bye for the present. (He goes out, meeting the waiter; who holds the door for him to pass through.)

MRS. CLANDON. We expect some visitors at nine, William. Can we have dinner at seven instead of half-past?

WAITER (at the door). Seven, ma'am? Certainly, ma'am. It will be a convenience to us this busy evening, ma'am. There will be the band and the arranging of the fairy lights and one thing or another, ma'am.

DOLLY. The fairy lights!

PHILIP. The band! William: what mean you?

WAITER. The fancy ball, miss—

DOLLY and PHILIP (simultaneously rushing to him). Fancy ball!

WAITER. Oh, yes, sir. Given by the regatta committee for the benefit of the Life-boat, sir. (To Mrs. Clandon.) We often have them, ma'am: Chinese lanterns in the garden, ma'am: very bright and pleasant, very gay and innocent indeed. (To Phil.) Tickets downstairs at the office, sir, five shillings: ladies half price if accompanied by a gentleman.

PHILIP (seizing his arm to drag him off). To the office, William!

DOLLY (breathlessly, seizing his other arm). Quick, before they're all sold. (They rush him out of the room between them.)

MRS. CLANDON. What on earth are they going to do? (Going out.) I really must go and stop this—(She follows them, speaking as she disappears. Gloria stares coolly at Valentine, and then deliberately looks at her watch.)

VALENTINE. I understand. I've stayed too long. I'm going.

GLORIA (with disdainful punctiliousness). I owe you some apology, Mr. Valentine. I am conscious of having spoken somewhat sharply— perhaps rudely—to you.

VALENTINE. Not at all.

GLORIA. My only excuse is that it is very difficult to give consideration and respect when there is no dignity of character on the other side to command it.

VALENTINE (prosaically). How is a man to look dignified when he's infatuated?

GLORIA (effectually unstilted). Don't say those things to me. I forbid you. They are insults.

VALENTINE. No: they're only follies. I can't help them.

GLORIA. If you were really in love, it would not make you foolish: it would give you dignity—earnestness—even beauty.

VALENTINE. Do you really think it would make me beautiful? (She turns her back on him with the coldest contempt.) Ah, you see you're not in earnest. Love can't give any man new gifts. It can only heighten the gifts he was born with.

GLORIA (sweeping round at him again). What gifts were you born with, pray?

VALENTINE. Lightness of heart.

GLORIA. And lightness of head, and lightness of faith, and lightness of everything that makes a man.

VALENTINE. Yes, the whole world is like a feather dancing in the light now; and Gloria is the sun. (She rears her head angrily.) I beg your pardon: I'm off. Back at nine. Good-bye. (He runs off gaily, leaving her standing in the middle of the room staring after him.)

END OF ACT III

ACT IV

The same room. Nine o'clock. Nobody present. The lamps are lighted; but the curtains are not drawn. The window stands wide open; and strings of Chinese lanterns are glowing among the trees outside, with the starry sky beyond. The band is playing dance-music in the garden, drowning the sound of the sea.

The waiter enters, shewing in Crampton and McComas. Crampton looks cowed and anxious. He sits down wearily and timidly on the ottoman.

WAITER. The ladies have gone for a turn through the grounds to see the fancy dresses, sir. If you will be so good as to take seats, gentlemen, I shall tell them. (He is about to go into the garden through the window when McComas stops him.)

McCOMAS. One moment. If another gentleman comes, shew him in without any delay: we are expecting him.

WAITER. Right, sir. What name, sir?

McCOMAS. Boon. Mr. Boon. He is a stranger to Mrs. Clandon; so he may give you a card. If so, the name is spelt B.O.H.U.N. You will not forget.

WAITER (smiling). You may depend on me for that, sir. My own name is Boon, sir, though I am best known down here as Balmy Walters, sir. By rights I should spell it with the aitch you, sir; but I think it best not to take that liberty, sir. There is Norman blood in it, sir; and Norman blood is not a recommendation to a waiter.

McCOMAS. Well, well: "True hearts are more than coronets, and simple faith than Norman blood."

WAITER. That depends a good deal on one's station in life, sir. If you were a waiter, sir, you'd find that simple faith would leave you just as short as Norman blood. I find it best to spell myself B. double-O.N., and to keep my wits pretty sharp about me. But I'm taking up your time, sir. You'll excuse me, sir: your own fault for being so affable, sir. I'll tell the ladies you're here, sir. (He goes out into the garden through the window.)

McCOMAS. Crampton: I can depend on you, can't I?

CRAMPTON. Yes, yes. I'll be quiet. I'll be patient. I'll do my best.

McCOMAS. Remember: I've not given you away. I've told them it was all their fault.

CRAMPTON. You told me that it was all my fault.

McCOMAS. I told you the truth.

CRAMPTON (plaintively). If they will only be fair to me!

McCOMAS. My dear Crampton, they won't be fair to you: it's not to be expected from them at their age. If you're going to make impossible conditions of this kind, we may as well go back home at once.

CRAMPTON. But surely I have a right—

McCOMAS (intolerantly). You won't get your rights. Now, once for all, Crampton, did your promises of good behavior only mean that you won't complain if there's nothing to complain of? Because, if so— (He moves as if to go.)

CRAMPTON (miserably). No, no: let me alone, can't you? I've been bullied enough: I've been tormented enough. I tell you I'll do my best. But if that girl begins to talk to me like that and to look at me like—(He breaks off and buries his head in his hands.)

McCOMAS (relenting). There, there: it'll be all right, if you will only bear and forbear. Come, pull yourself together: there's someone coming. (Crampton, too dejected to care much, hardly changes his attitude. Gloria enters from the garden; McComas goes to meet her

405

at the window; so that he can speak to her without being heard by Crampton.) There he is, Miss Clandon. Be kind to him. I'll leave you with him for a moment. (He goes into the garden. Gloria comes in and strolls coolly down the middle of the room.)

CRAMPTON (looking round in alarm). Where's McComas?

GLORIA (listlessly, but not unsympathetically). Gone out—to leave us together. Delicacy on his part, I suppose. (She stops beside him and looks quaintly down at him.) Well, father?

CRAMPTON (a quaint jocosity breaking through his forlornness). Well, daughter? (They look at one another for a moment, with a melancholy sense of humor.)

GLORIA. Shake hands. (They shake hands.)

CRAMPTON (holding her hand). My dear: I'm afraid I spoke very improperly of your mother this afternoon.

GLORIA. Oh, don't apologize. I was very high and mighty myself; but I've come down since: oh, yes: I've been brought down. (She sits on the floor beside his chair.)

CRAMPTON. What has happened to you, my child?

GLORIA. Oh, never mind. I was playing the part of my mother's daughter then; but I'm not: I'm my father's daughter. (Looking at him funnily.) That's a come down, isn't it?

CRAMPTON (angry). What! (Her odd expression does not alter. He surrenders.) Well, yes, my dear: I suppose it is, I suppose it is. (She nods sympathetically.) I'm afraid I'm sometimes a little irritable; but I know what's right and reasonable all the time, even when I don't act on it. Can you believe that?

GLORIA. Believe it! Why, that's myself—myself all over. I know what's right and dignified and strong and noble, just as well as she does; but oh, the things I do! the things I do! the things I let other people do!!

CRAMPTON (a little grudgingly in spite of himself). As well as she does? You mean your mother?

406

GLORIA (quickly). Yes, mother. (She turns to him on her knees and seizes his hands.) Now listen. No treason to her: no word, no thought against her. She is our superior—yours and mine—high heavens above us. Is that agreed?

CRAMPTON. Yes, yes. Just as you please, my dear.

GLORIA (not satisfied, letting go his hands and drawing back from him). You don't like her?

CRAMPTON. My child: you haven't been married to her. I have. (She raises herself slowly to her feet, looking at him with growing coldness.) She did me a great wrong in marrying me without really caring for me. But after that, the wrong was all on my side, I dare say. (He offers her his hand again.)

GLORIA (taking it firmly and warningly). Take care. That's a dangerous subject. My feelings—my miserable, cowardly, womanly feelings—may be on your side; but my conscience is on hers.

CRAMPTON. I'm very well content with that division, my dear. Thank you. (Valentine arrives. Gloria immediately becomes deliberately haughty.)

VALENTINE. Excuse me; but it's impossible to find a servant to announce one: even the never failing William seems to be at the ball. I should have gone myself; only I haven't five shillings to buy a ticket. How are you getting on, Crampton? Better, eh?

CRAMPTON. I am myself again, Mr. Valentine, no thanks to you.

VALENTINE. Look at this ungrateful parent of yours, Miss Clandon! I saved him from an excruciating pang; and he reviles me!

GLORIA (coldly). I am sorry my mother is not here to receive you, Mr. Valentine. It is not quite nine o'clock; and the gentleman of whom Mr. McComas spoke, the lawyer, is not yet come.

VALENTINE. Oh, yes, he is. I've met him and talked to him. (With gay malice.) You'll like him, Miss Clandon: he's the very incarnation of intellect. You can hear his mind working.

GLORIA (ignoring the jibe). Where is he?

VALENTINE. Bought a false nose and gone into the fancy ball.

CRAMPTON (crustily, looking at his watch). It seems that everybody has gone to this fancy ball instead of keeping to our appointment here.

VALENTINE. Oh, he'll come all right enough: that was half an hour ago. I didn't like to borrow five shillings from him and go in with him; so I joined the mob and looked through the railings until Miss Clandon disappeared into the hotel through the window.

GLORIA. So it has come to this, that you follow me about in public to stare at me.

VALENTINE. Yes: somebody ought to chain me up.

Gloria turns her back on him and goes to the fireplace. He takes the snub very philosophically, and goes to the opposite side of the room. The waiter appears at the window, ushering in Mrs. Clandon and McComas.

MRS. CLANDON (hurrying in). I am so sorry to have kept you waiting.

A grotesquely majestic stranger, in a domino and false nose, with goggles, appears at the window.

WAITER (to the stranger). Beg pardon, sir; but this is a private apartment, sir. If you will allow me, sir, I will shew you to the American bar and supper rooms, sir. This way, sir.

He goes into the gardens, leading the way under the impression that the stranger is following him. The majestic one, however, comes straight into the room to the end of the table, where, with impressive deliberation, he takes off the false nose and then the domino, rolling up the nose into the domino and throwing the bundle on the table like a champion throwing down his glove. He is now seen to be a stout, tall man between forty and fifty, clean shaven, with a midnight oil pallor emphasized by stiff black hair, cropped short and oiled, and eyebrows like early Victorian horsehair upholstery. Physically and spiritually, a coarsened man: in cunning and logic, a ruthlessly sharpened one. His bearing as he enters is sufficiently imposing and disquieting; but when he speaks, his powerful, menacing voice, impressively articulated speech, strong inexorable manner, and a terrifying power of intensely critical listening raise the impression produced by him to absolute tremendousness.

THE STRANGER. My name is Bohun. (General awe.) Have I the honor of addressing Mrs. Clandon? (Mrs. Clandon bows. Bohun bows.) Miss Clandon? (Gloria bows. Bohun bows.) Mr. Clandon?

CRAMPTON (insisting on his rightful name as angrily as he dares). My name is Crampton, sir.

BOHUN. Oh, indeed. (Passing him over without further notice and turning to Valentine.) Are you Mr. Clandon?

VALENTINE (making it a point of honor not to be impressed by him). Do I look like it? My name is Valentine. I did the drugging.

BOHUN. Ah, quite so. Then Mr. Clandon has not yet arrived?

WAITER (entering anxiously through the window). Beg pardon, ma'am; but can you tell me what became of that—(He recognizes Bohun, and loses all his self-possession. Bohun waits rigidly for him to pull himself together. After a pathetic exhibition of confusion, he recovers himself sufficiently to address Bohun weakly but coherently.) Beg pardon, sir, I'm sure, sir. Was—was it you, sir?

BOHUN (ruthlessly). It was I.

WAITER (brokenly). Yes, sir. (Unable to restrain his tears.) You in a false nose, Walter! (He sinks faintly into a chair at the table.) I beg pardon, ma'am, I'm sure. A little giddiness—

BOHUN (commandingly). You will excuse him, Mrs. Clandon, when I inform you that he is my father.

WAITER (heartbroken). Oh, no, no, Walter. A waiter for your father on the top of a false nose! What will they think of you?

MRS. CLANDON (going to the waiter's chair in her kindest manner). I am delighted to hear it, Mr. Bohun. Your father has been an excellent friend to us since we came here. (Bohun bows gravely.)

WAITER (shaking his head). Oh, no, ma'am. It's very kind of you—very ladylike and affable indeed, ma'am; but I should feel at a great disadvantage off my own proper footing. Never mind my being the gentleman's father, ma'am: it is only the accident of birth after all, ma'am. (He gets up feebly.) You'll all excuse me, I'm sure, having interrupted your business. (He begins to make his way along the table, supporting himself from chair to chair, with his eye on the door.)

BOHUN. One moment. (The waiter stops, with a sinking heart.) My father was a witness of what passed to-day, was he not, Mrs. Clandon?

MRS. CLANDON. Yes, most of it, I think.

BOHUN. In that case we shall want him.

WAITER (pleading). I hope it may not be necessary, sir. Busy evening for me, sir, with that ball: very busy evening indeed, sir.

BOHUN (inexorably). We shall want you.

MRS. CLANDON (politely). Sit down, won't you?

WAITER (earnestly). Oh, if you please, ma'am, I really must draw the line at sitting down. I couldn't let myself be seen doing such a thing, ma'am: thank you, I am sure, all the same. (He looks round from face to face wretchedly, with an expression that would melt a heart of stone.)

GLORIA. Don't let us waste time. William only wants to go on taking care of us. I should like a cup of coffee.

WAITER (brightening perceptibly). Coffee, miss? (He gives a little gasp of hope.) Certainly, miss. Thank you, miss: very timely, miss, very thoughtful and considerate indeed. (To Mrs. Clandon, timidly but expectantly.) Anything for you, ma'am?

MRS. CLANDON Er—oh, yes: it's so hot, I think we might have a jug of claret cup.

WAITER (beaming). Claret cup, ma'am! Certainly, ma'am.

GLORIA Oh, well I'll have a claret cup instead of coffee. Put some cucumber in it.

WAITER (delighted). Cucumber, miss! yes, miss. (To Bohun.) Anything special for you, sir? You don't like cucumber, sir.

BOHUN. If Mrs. Clandon will allow me—syphon—Scotch.

WAITER. Right, sir. (To Crampton.) Irish for you, sir, I think, sir? (Crampton assents with a grunt. The waiter looks enquiringly at Valentine.)

VALENTINE. I like the cucumber.

WAITER. Right, sir. (Summing up.) Claret cup, syphon, one Scotch and one Irish?

MRS. CLANDON. I think that's right.

WAITER (perfectly happy). Right, ma'am. Directly, ma'am. Thank you. (He ambles off through the window, having sounded the whole gamut of human happiness, from the bottom to the top, in a little over two minutes.)

McCOMAS. We can begin now, I suppose?

BOHUN. We had better wait until Mrs. Clandon's husband arrives.

CRAMPTON. What d'y' mean? I'm her husband.

BOHUN (instantly pouncing on the inconsistency between this and his previous statement). You said just now your name was Crampton.

CRAMPTON. So it is.

MRS. CLANDON	}	(all four	{ I—
GLORIA	}	speaking	{ My—
McCOMAS	}	simul-	{ Mrs.—
VALENTINE	}	taneously).	{ You—

BOHUN (drowning them in two thunderous words). One moment. (Dead silence.) Pray allow me. Sit down everybody. (They obey humbly. Gloria takes the saddle-bag chair on the hearth. Valentine slips around to her side of the room and sits on the ottoman facing the window, so that he can look at her. Crampton sits on the ottoman with his back to Valentine's. Mrs. Clandon, who has all along kept at the opposite side of the room in order to avoid Crampton as much as possible, sits near the door, with McComas beside her on her left. Bohun places himself magisterially in the centre of the group, near the corner of the table on Mrs. Clandon's side. When they are settled, he fixes Crampton with his eye, and begins.) In this family, it appears, the husband's name is Crampton: the wife's Clandon. Thus we have on the very threshold of the case an element of confusion.

VALENTINE (getting up and speaking across to him with one knee on the ottoman). But it's perfectly simple.

BOHUN (annihilating him with a vocal thunderbolt). It is. Mrs. Clandon has adopted another name. That is the obvious explanation which you feared I could not find out for myself. You mistrust my intelligence, Mr. Valentine—(Stopping him as he is about to protest.) No: I don't want you to answer that: I want you to think over it when you feel your next impulse to interrupt me.

VALENTINE (dazed). This is simply breaking a butterfly on a wheel. What does it matter? (He sits down again.)

BOHUN. I will tell you what it matters, sir. It matters that if this family difference is to be smoothed over as we all hope it may be, Mrs. Clandon, as a matter of social convenience and decency, will have to resume her husband's name. (Mrs. Clandon assumes an expression of the most determined obstinacy.) Or else Mr. Crampton will have to call himself Mr. Clandon. (Crampton looks indomitably resolved to do nothing of the sort.) No doubt you think that an easy matter, Mr. Valentine. (He looks pointedly at Mrs. Clandon, then at Crampton.) I differ from you. (He throws himself back in his chair, frowning heavily.)

McCOMAS (timidly). I think, Bohun, we had perhaps better dispose of the important questions first.

BOHUN. McComas: there will be no difficulty about the important questions. There never is. It is the trifles that will wreck you at the harbor mouth. (McComas looks as if he considered this a paradox.) You don't agree with me, eh?

McCOMAS (flatteringly). If I did—

BOHUN (interrupting him). If you did, you would be me, instead of being what you are.

McCOMAS (fawning on him). Of course, Bohun, your specialty—

BOHUN (again interrupting him). My specialty is being right when other people are wrong. If you agreed with me I should be of no use here. (He nods at him to drive the point home; then turns suddenly and forcibly on Crampton.) Now you, Mr. Crampton: what point in this business have you most at heart?

CRAMPTON (beginning slowly). I wish to put all considerations of self aside in this matter—

BOHUN (interrupting him). So do we all, Mr. Crampton. (To Mrs. Clandon.) Y o u wish to put self aside, Mrs. Clandon?

MRS. CLANDON. Yes: I am not consulting my own feelings in being here.

BOHUN. So do you, Miss Clandon?

GLORIA. Yes.

BOHUN. I thought so. We all do.

VALENTINE. Except me. My aims are selfish.

BOHUN. That's because you think an impression of sincerity will produce a better effect on Miss Clandon than an impression of disinterestedness. (Valentine, utterly dismantled and destroyed by this just remark, takes refuge in a feeble, speechless smile. Bohun, satisfied at having now effectually crushed all rebellion, throws himself back in his chair, with an air of being prepared to listen tolerantly to their grievances.) Now, Mr. Crampton, go on. It's understood that self is put aside. Human nature always begins by saying that.

CRAMPTON. But I mean it, sir.

BOHUN. Quite so. Now for your point.

CRAMPTON. Every reasonable person will admit that it's an unselfish one—the children.

BOHUN. Well? What about the children?

CRAMPTON (with emotion). They have—

BOHUN (pouncing forward again). Stop. You're going to tell me about your feelings, Mr. Crampton. Don't: I sympathize with them; but they're not my business. Tell us exactly what you want: that's what we have to get at.

CRAMPTON (uneasily). It's a very difficult question to answer, Mr. Bohun.

BOHUN. Come: I'll help you out. What do you object to in the present circumstances of the children?

CRAMPTON. I object to the way they have been brought up.

BOHUN. How do you propose to alter that now?

CRAMPTON. I think they ought to dress more quietly.

VALENTINE. Nonsense.

BOHUN (instantly flinging himself back in his chair, outraged by the interruption). When you are done, Mr. Valentine—when you are quite done.

VALENTINE. What's wrong with Miss Clandon's dress?

CRAMPTON (hotly to Valentine). My opinion is as good as yours.

GLORIA (warningly). Father!

CRAMPTON (subsiding piteously). I didn't mean you, my dear. (Pleading earnestly to Bohun.) But the two younger ones! you have not seen them, Mr. Bohun; and indeed I think you would agree with me that there is something very noticeable, something almost gay and frivolous in their style of dressing.

MRS. CLANDON (impatiently). Do you suppose I choose their clothes for them? Really this is childish.

CRAMPTON (furious, rising). Childish! (Mrs. Clandon rises indignantly.)

McCOMAS	}	(all ris-	}	Crampton, you promised—
VALENTINE	}	ing and	}	Ridiculous. They dress
	}	speaking	}	charmingly.
GLORIA	}	together).	}	Pray let us behave reasonably.

414

Tumult. Suddenly they hear a chime of glasses in the room behind them. They turn in silent surprise and find that the waiter has just come back from the bar in the garden, and is jingling his tray warningly as he comes softly to the table with it.

WAITER (to Crampton, setting a tumbler apart on the table). Irish for you, sir. (Crampton sits down a little shamefacedly. The waiter sets another tumbler and a syphon apart, saying to Bohun) Scotch and syphon for you, sir. (Bohun waves his hand impatiently. The waiter places a large glass jug in the middle.) And claret cup. (All subside into their seats. Peace reigns.)

MRS. CLANDON (humbly to Bohun). I am afraid we interrupted you, Mr. Bohun.

BOHUN (calmly). You did. (To the waiter, who is going out.) Just wait a bit.

WAITER. Yes, sir. Certainly, sir. (He takes his stand behind Bohun's chair.)

MRS. CLANDON (to the waiter). You don't mind our detaining you, I hope. Mr. Bohun wishes it.

WAITER (now quite at his ease). Oh, no, ma'am, not at all, ma'am. It is a pleasure to me to watch the working of his trained and powerful mind—very stimulating, very entertaining and instructive indeed, ma'am.

BOHUN (resuming command of the proceedings). Now, Mr. Crampton: we are waiting for you. Do you give up your objection to the dressing, or do you stick to it?

CRAMPTON (pleading). Mr. Bohun: consider my position for a moment. I haven't got myself alone to consider: there's my sister Sophronia and my brother-in-law and all their circle. They have a great horror of anything that is at all—at all—well—

BOHUN. Out with it. Fast? Loud? Gay?

CRAMPTON. Not in any unprincipled sense of course; but—but—(blurting it out desperately) those two children would shock them.

They're not fit to mix with their own people. That's what I complain of.

MRS. CLANDON (with suppressed impatience). Mr. Valentine: do you think there is anything fast or loud about Phil and Dolly?

VALENTINE. Certainly not. It's utter bosh. Nothing can be in better taste.

CRAMPTON. Oh, yes: of course you say so.

MRS. CLANDON. William: you see a great deal of good English society. Are my children overdressed?

WAITER (reassuringly). Oh, dear, no, ma'am. (Persuasively.) Oh, no, sir, not at all. A little pretty and tasty no doubt; but very choice and classy—very genteel and high toned indeed. Might be the son and daughter of a Dean, sir, I assure you, sir. You have only to look at them, sir, to—(At this moment a harlequin and columbine, dancing to the music of the band in the garden, which has just reached the coda of a waltz, whirl one another into the room. The harlequin's dress is made of lozenges, an inch square, of turquoise blue silk and gold alternately. His hat is gilt and his mask turned up. The columbine's petticoats are the epitome of a harvest field, golden orange and poppy crimson, with a tiny velvet jacket for the poppy stamens. They pass, an exquisite and dazzling apparition, between McComas and Bohun, and then back in a circle to the end of the table, where, as the final chord of the waltz is struck, they make a tableau in the middle of the company, the harlequin down on his left knee, and the columbine standing on his right knee, with her arms curved over her head. Unlike their dancing, which is charmingly graceful, their attitudinizing is hardly a success, and threatens to end in a catastrophe.)

THE COLUMBINE (screaming). Lift me down, somebody: I'm going to fall. Papa: lift me down.

CRAMPTON (anxiously running to her and taking her hands). My child!

DOLLY (jumping down with his help). Thanks: so nice of you. (Phil, putting his hat into his belt, sits on the side of the table and pours out some claret cup. Crampton returns to his place on the ottoman in great perplexity.) Oh, what fun! Oh, dear. (She seats herself with a vault on the front edge of the table, panting.) Oh, claret cup! (She drinks.)

BOHUN (in powerful tones). This is the younger lady, is it?

DOLLY (slipping down off the table in alarm at his formidable voice and manner). Yes, sir. Please, who are you?

MRS. CLANDON. This is Mr. Bohun, Dolly, who has very kindly come to help us this evening.

DOLLY. Oh, then he comes as a boon and a blessing—

PHILIP. Sh!

CRAMPTON. Mr. Bohun—McComas: I appeal to you. Is this right? Would you blame my sister's family for objecting to this?

DOLLY (flushing ominously). Have you begun again?

CRAMPTON (propitiating her). No, no. It's perhaps natural at your age.

DOLLY (obstinately). Never mind my age. Is it pretty?

CRAMPTON. Yes, dear, yes. (He sits down in token of submission.)

DOLLY (following him insistently). Do you like it?

CRAMPTON. My child: how can you expect me to like it or to approve of it?

DOLLY (determined not to let him off). How can you think it pretty and not like it?

McCOMAS (rising, angry and scandalized). Really I must say—(Bohun, who has listened to Dolly with the highest approval, is down on him instantly.)

BOHUN. No: don't interrupt, McComas. The young lady's method is right. (To Dolly, with tremendous emphasis.) Press your questions, Miss Clandon: press your questions.

DOLLY (rising). Oh, dear, you are a regular overwhelmer! Do you always go on like this?

BOHUN (rising). Yes. Don't you try to put me out of countenance, young lady: you're too young to do it. (He takes McComas's chair from beside Mrs. Clandon's and sets it beside his own.) Sit down. (Dolly, fascinated, obeys; and Bohun sits down again. McComas, robbed of his seat, takes a chair on the other side between the table and the ottoman.) Now, Mr. Crampton, the facts are before you—both of them. You think you'd like to have your two youngest children to live with you. Well, you wouldn't—(Crampton tries to protest; but Bohun will not have it on any terms.) No, you wouldn't: you think you would; but I know better than you. You'd want this young lady here to give up dressing like a stage columbine in the evening and like a fashionable columbine in the morning. Well, she won't—never. She thinks she will; but—

DOLLY (interrupting him). No I don't. (Resolutely.) I'll n e v e r give up dressing prettily. Never. As Gloria said to that man in Madeira, never, never, never while grass grows or water runs.

VALENTINE (rising in the wildest agitation). What! What! (Beginning to speak very fast.) When did she say that? Who did she say that to?

BOHUN (throwing himself back with massive, pitying remonstrance). Mr. Valentine—

VALENTINE (pepperily). Don't you interrupt me, sir: this is something really serious. I i n s i s t on knowing who Miss Clandon said that to.

DOLLY. Perhaps Phil remembers. Which was it, Phil? number three or number five?

VALENTINE. Number five!!!

PHILIP. Courage, Valentine. It wasn't number five: it was only a tame naval lieutenant that was always on hand—the most patient and harmless of mortals.

GLORIA (coldly). What are we discussing now, pray?

VALENTINE (very red). Excuse me: I am sorry I interrupted. I shall intrude no further, Mrs. Clandon. (He bows to Mrs. Clandon and marches away into the garden, boiling with suppressed rage.)

DOLLY. Hmhm!

PHILIP. Ahah!

GLORIA. Please go on, Mr. Bohun.

DOLLY (striking in as Bohun, frowning formidably, collects himself for a fresh grapple with the case). You're going to bully us, Mr. Bohun.

BOHUN. I—

DOLLY (interrupting him). Oh, yes, you are: you think you're not; but you are. I know by your eyebrows.

BOHUN (capitulating). Mrs. Clandon: these are clever children—clear headed, well brought up children. I make that admission deliberately. Can you, in return, point out to me any way of inducting them to hold their tongues?

MRS. CLANDON. Dolly, dearest—!

PHILIP. Our old failing, Dolly. Silence! (Dolly holds her mouth.)

MRS. CLANDON. Now, Mr. Bohun, before they begin again—

WAITER (softer). Be quick, sir: be quick.

DOLLY (beaming at him). Dear William!

PHILIP. Sh!

BOHUN (unexpectedly beginning by hurling a question straight at Dolly). Have you any intention of getting married?

DOLLY. I! Well, Finch calls me by my Christian name.

McCOMAS. I will not have this. Mr. Bohun: I use the young lady's Christian name naturally as an old friend of her mother's.

DOLLY. Yes, you call me Dolly as an old friend of my mother's. But what about Dorothee-ee-a? (McComas rises indignantly.)

CRAMPTON (anxiously, rising to restrain him). Keep your temper, McComas. Don't let us quarrel. Be patient.

McCOMAS. I will not be patient. You are shewing the most wretched weakness of character, Crampton. I say this is monstrous.

DOLLY. Mr. Bohun: please bully Finch for us.

BOHUN. I will. McComas: you're making yourself ridiculous. Sit down.

McCOMAS. I—

BOHUN (waving him down imperiously). No: sit down, sit down. (McComas sits down sulkily; and Crampton, much relieved, follows his example.)

DOLLY (to Bohun, meekly). Thank you.

BOHUN. Now, listen to me, all of you. I give no opinion, McComas, as to how far you may or may not have committed yourself in the direction indicated by this young lady. (McComas is about to protest.) No: don't interrupt me: if she doesn't marry you she will marry somebody else. That is the solution of the difficulty as to her not bearing her father's name. The other lady intends to get married.

GLORIA (flushing). Mr. Bohun!

BOHUN. Oh, yes, you do: you don't know it; but you do.

GLORIA (rising). Stop. I warn you, Mr. Bohun, not to answer for my intentions.

BOHUN (rising). It's no use, Miss Clandon: you can't put me down. I tell you your name will soon be neither Clandon nor Crampton; and I could tell you what it will be if I chose. (He goes to the other end of the table, where he unrolls his domino, and puts the false nose on the table. When he moves they all rise; and Phil goes to the window. Bohun, with a gesture, summons the waiter to help him in robing.) Mr. Crampton: your notion of going to law is all nonsense: your children will be of age before you could get the point decided. (Allowing the waiter to put the domino on his shoulders.) You can do nothing but make a friendly arrangement. If you want your family more than they want you, you'll get the worse of the arrangement: if they want you more than you want them, you'll get the better of it. (He shakes the domino into becoming folds and takes up the false nose. Dolly gazes admiringly at him.) The strength of their position lies in their being very agreeable people personally. The strength of your position lies in your income. (He claps on the false nose, and is again grotesquely transfigured.)

DOLLY (running to him). Oh, now you look quite like a human being. Mayn't I have just one dance with you? C a n you dance? (Phil, resuming his part of harlequin, waves his hat as if casting a spell on them.)

BOHUN (thunderously). Yes: you think I can't; but I can. Come along. (He seizes her and dances off with her through the window in a most powerful manner, but with studied propriety and grace. The waiter is meanwhile busy putting the chairs back in their customary places.)

PHILIP. "On with the dance: let joy be unconfined." William!

WAITER. Yes, sir.

PHILIP. Can you procure a couple of dominos and false noses for my father and Mr. McComas?

McCOMAS. Most certainly not. I protest—

CRAMPTON. No, no. What harm will it do, just for once, McComas? Don't let us be spoil-sports.

McCOMAS. Crampton: you are not the man I took you for. (Pointedly.) Bullies are always cowards. (He goes disgustedly towards the window.)

CRAMPTON (following him). Well, never mind. We must indulge them a little. Can you get us something to wear, waiter?

WAITER. Certainly, sir. (He precedes them to the window, and stands aside there to let them pass out before him.) This way, sir. Dominos and noses, sir?

McCOMAS (angrily, on his way out). I shall wear my own nose.

WAITER (suavely). Oh, dear, yes, sir: the false one will fit over it quite easily, sir: plenty of room, sir, plenty of room. (He goes out after McComas.)

CRAMPTON (turning at the window to Phil with an attempt at genial fatherliness). Come along, my boy, come along. (He goes.)

PHILIP (cheerily, following him). Coming, dad, coming. (On the window threshold, he stops; looking after Crampton; then turns fantastically with his bat bent into a halo round his head, and says with a lowered voice to Mrs. Clandon and Gloria) Did you feel the pathos of that? (He vanishes.)

MRS. CLANDON (left alone with Gloria). Why did Mr. Valentine go away so suddenly, I wonder?

GLORIA (petulantly). I don't know. Yes, I d o know. Let us go and see the dancing. (They go towards the window, and are met by Valentine, who comes in from the garden walking quickly, with his face set and sulky.)

VALENTINE (stiffly). Excuse me. I thought the party had quite broken up.

GLORIA (nagging). Then why did you come back?

VALENTINE. I came back because I am penniless. I can't get out that way without a five shilling ticket.

MRS. CLANDON. Has anything annoyed you, Mr. Valentine?

GLORIA. Never mind him, mother. This is a fresh insult to me: that is all.

MRS. CLANDON (hardly able to realize that Gloria is deliberately provoking an altercation). Gloria!

VALENTINE. Mrs. Clandon: have I said anything insulting? Have I done anything insulting?

GLORIA. you have implied that my past has been like yours. That is the worst of insults.

VALENTINE. I imply nothing of the sort. I declare that my past has been blameless in comparison with yours.

MRS. CLANDON (most indignantly). Mr. Valentine!

VALENTINE. Well, what am I to think when I learn that Miss Clandon has made exactly the same speeches to other men that she has made to me—when I hear of at least five former lovers, with a tame naval lieutenant thrown in? Oh, it's too bad.

MRS. CLANDON. But you surely do not believe that these affairs—mere jokes of the children's—were serious, Mr. Valentine?

VALENTINE. Not to you—not to her, perhaps. But I know what the men felt. (With ludicrously genuine earnestness.) Have you ever thought of the wrecked lives, the marriages contracted in the recklessness of despair, the suicides, the—the—the—

GLORIA (interrupting him contemptuously). Mother: this man is a sentimental idiot. (She sweeps away to the fireplace.)

MRS. CLANDON (shocked). Oh, my d e a r e s t Gloria, Mr. Valentine will think that rude.

VALENTINE. I am not a sentimental idiot. I am cured of sentiment for ever. (He sits down in dudgeon.)

MRS. CLANDON. Mr. Valentine: you must excuse us all. Women have to unlearn the false good manners of their slavery before they acquire the genuine good manners of their freedom. Don't think Gloria vulgar (Gloria turns, astonished): she is not really so.

GLORIA. Mother! You apologize for me to h i m!

MRS. CLANDON. My dear: you have some of the faults of youth as well as its qualities; and Mr. Valentine seems rather too old fashioned in his ideas about his own sex to like being called an idiot. And now had we not better go and see what Dolly is doing? (She goes towards the window. Valentine rises.)

GLORIA. Do you go, mother. I wish to speak to Mr. Valentine alone.

MRS. CLANDON (startled into a remonstrance). My dear! (Recollecting herself.) I beg your pardon, Gloria. Certainly, if you wish. (She bows to Valentine and goes out.)

VALENTINE. Oh, if your mother were only a widow! She's worth six of you.

GLORIA. That is the first thing I have heard you say that does you honor.

VALENTINE. Stuff! Come: say what you want to say and let me go.

GLORIA. I have only this to say. You dragged me down to your level for a moment this afternoon. Do you think, if that had ever happened before, that I should not have been on my guard—that I should not have known what was coming, and known my own miserable weakness?

VALENTINE (scolding at her passionately). Don't talk of it in that way. What do I care for anything in you but your weakness, as you call it? You thought yourself very safe, didn't you, behind your advanced ideas! I amused myself by upsetting t h e m pretty easily.

GLORIA (insolently, feeling that now she can do as she likes with him). Indeed!

VALENTINE. But why did I do it? Because I was being tempted to awaken your heart—to stir the depths in you. Why was I tempted? Because Nature was in deadly earnest with me when I was in jest with her. When the great moment came, who was awakened? who was stirred? in whom did the depths break up? In myself—m y s e l f: I was transported: you were only offended—shocked. You were only an ordinary young lady, too ordinary to allow tame lieutenants to go as far as I went. That's all. I shall not trouble you with conventional apologies. Good-bye. (He makes resolutely for the door.)

GLORIA. Stop. (He hesitates.) Oh, will you understand, if I tell you the truth, that I am not making an advance to you?

VALENTINE. Pooh! I know what you're going to say. You think you're not ordinary—that I was right—that you really have those depths in your nature. It flatters you to believe it. (She recoils.) Well, I grant that you are not ordinary in some ways: you are a clever girl (Gloria stifles an exclamation of rage, and takes a threatening step towards

424

him); but you've not been awakened yet. You didn't care: you don't care. It was my tragedy, not yours. Good-bye. (He turns to the door. She watches him, appalled to see him slipping from her grasp. As he turns the handle, he pauses; then turns again to her, offering his hand.) Let us part kindly.

GLORIA (enormously relieved, and immediately turning her back on him deliberately.) Good-bye. I trust you will soon recover from the wound.

VALENTINE (brightening up as it flashes on him that he is master of the situation after all). I shall recover: such wounds heal more than they harm. After all, I still have my own Gloria.

GLORIA (facing him quickly). What do you mean?

VALENTINE. The Gloria of my imagination.

GLORIA (proudly). Keep your own Gloria—the Gloria of your imagination. (Her emotion begins to break through her pride.) The real Gloria—the Gloria who was shocked, offended, horrified—oh, yes, quite truly—who was driven almost mad with shame by the feeling that all her power over herself had been broken down at her first real encounter with—with—(The color rushes over her face again. She covers it with her left hand, and puts her right on his left arm to support herself.)

VALENTINE. Take care. I'm losing my senses again. (Summoning all her courage, she takes away her hand from her face and puts it on his right shoulder, turning him towards her and looking him straight in the eyes. He begins to protest agitatedly.) Gloria: be sensible: it's no use: I haven't a penny in the world.

GLORIA. Can't you earn one? Other people do.

VALENTINE (half delighted, half frightened). I never could—you'd be unhappy—My dearest love: I should be the merest fortune-hunting adventurer if—(Her grip on his arms tightens; and she kisses him.) Oh, Lord! (Breathless.) Oh, I—(He gasps.) I don't know anything about women: twelve years' experience is not enough. (In a gust of jealousy she throws him away from her; and he reels her back into the chair like a leaf before the wind, as Dolly dances in, waltzing with the waiter, followed by Mrs. Clandon and Finch, also waltzing, and Phil pirouetting by himself.)

DOLLY (sinking on the chair at the writing-table). Oh, I'm out of breath. How beautifully you waltz, William!

MRS. CLANDON (sinking on the saddlebag seat on the hearth). Oh, how could you make me do such a silly thing, Finch! I haven't danced since the soiree at South Place twenty years ago.

GLORIA (peremptorily at Valentine). Get up. (Valentine gets up abjectly.) Now let us have no false delicacy. Tell my mother that we have agreed to marry one another. (A silence of stupefaction ensues. Valentine, dumb with panic, looks at them with an obvious impulse to run away.)

DOLLY (breaking the silence). Number Six!

PHILIP. Sh!

DOLLY (tumultuously). Oh, my feelings! I want to kiss somebody; and we bar it in the family. Where's Finch?

McCOMAS (starting violently). No, positively—(Crampton appears in the window.)

DOLLY (running to Crampton). Oh, you're just in time. (She kisses him.) Now (leading him forward) bless them.

GLORIA. No. I will have no such thing, even in jest. When I need a blessing, I shall ask my mother's.

CRAMPTON (to Gloria, with deep disappointment). Am I to understand that you have engaged yourself to this young gentleman?

GLORIA (resolutely). Yes. Do you intend to be our friend or—

DOLLY (interposing).—or our father?

CRAMPTON. I should like to be both, my child. But surely—! Mr. Valentine: I appeal to your sense of honor.

VALENTINE. You're quite right. It's perfect madness. If we go out to dance together I shall have to borrow five shillings from her for a ticket. Gloria: don't be rash: you're throwing yourself away. I'd much better clear straight out of this, and never see any of you again. I shan't commit suicide: I shan't even be unhappy. It'll be a relief to me: I—I'm frightened, I'm positively frightened; and that's the plain truth.

GLORIA (determinedly). You shall not go.

VALENTINE (quailing). No, dearest: of course not. But—oh, will somebody only talk sense for a moment and bring us all to reason! I can't. Where's Bohun? Bohun's the man. Phil: go and summon Bohun—

PHILIP. From the vastly deep. I go. (He makes his bat quiver in the air and darts away through the window.)

WAITER (harmoniously to Valentine). If you will excuse my putting in a word, sir, do not let a matter of five shillings stand between you and your happiness, sir. We shall be only too pleased to put the ticket down to you: and you can settle at your convenience. Very glad to meet you in any way, very happy and pleased indeed, sir.

PHILIP (re-appearing). He comes. (He waves his bat over the window. Bohun comes in, taking off his false nose and throwing it on the table in passing as he comes between Gloria and Valentine.)

VALENTINE. The point is, Mr. Bohun—

McCOMAS (interrupting from the hearthrug). Excuse me, sir: the point must be put to him by a solicitor. The question is one of an engagement between these two young people. The lady has some property, and (looking at Crampton) will probably have a good deal more.

CRAMPTON. Possibly. I hope so.

VALENTINE. And the gentleman hasn't a rap.

BOHUN (nailing Valentine to the point instantly). Then insist on a settlement. That shocks your delicacy: most sensible precautions do. But you ask my advice; and I give it to you. Have a settlement.

GLORIA (proudly). He shall have a settlement.

VALENTINE. My good sir, I don't want advice for myself. Give h e r some advice.

BOHUN. She won't take it. When you're married, she won't take yours either—(turning suddenly on Gloria) oh, no, you won't: you think you will; but you won't. He'll set to work and earn his living—(turning suddenly to Valentine) oh, yes, you will: you think you won't; but you will. She'll make you.

CRAMPTON (only half persuaded). Then, Mr. Bohun, you don't think this match an unwise one?

BOHUN. Yes, I do: all matches are unwise. It's unwise to be born; it's unwise to be married; it's unwise to live; and it's unwise to die.

WAITER (insinuating himself between Crampton and Valentine). Then, if I may respectfully put in a word in, sir, so much the worse for wisdom! (To Valentine, benignly.) Cheer up, sir, cheer up: every man is frightened of marriage when it comes to the point; but it often turns out very comfortable, very enjoyable and happy indeed, sir—from time to time. I never was master in my own house, sir: my wife was like your young lady: she was of a commanding and masterful disposition, which my son has inherited. But if I had my life to live twice over, I'd do it again, I'd do it again, I assure you. You never can tell, sir: you never can tell.

PHILIP. Allow me to remark that if Gloria has made up her mind—

DOLLY. The matter's settled and Valentine's done for. And we're missing all the dances.

VALENTINE (to Gloria, gallantly making the best of it). May I have a dance—

BOHUN (interposing in his grandest diapason). Excuse me: I claim that privilege as counsel's fee. May I have the honor—thank you. (He dances away with Gloria and disappears among the lanterns, leaving Valentine gasping.)

VALENTINE (recovering his breath). Dolly: may I—(offering himself as her partner)?

DOLLY. Nonsense! (Eluding him and running round the table to the fireplace.) Finch—my Finch! (She pounces on McComas and makes him dance.)

McCOMAS (protesting). Pray restrain—really—(He is borne off dancing through the window.)

VALENTINE (making a last effort). Mrs. Clandon: may I—

PHILIP (forestalling him). Come, mother. (He seizes his mother and whirls her away.)

MRS. CLANDON (remonstrating). Phil, Phil—(She shares McComas's fate.)

CRAMPTON (following them with senile glee). Ho! ho! He! he! he! (He goes into the garden chuckling at the fun.)

VALENTINE (collapsing on the ottoman and staring at the waiter). I might as well be a married man already. (The waiter contemplates the captured Duellist of Sex with affectionate commiseration, shaking his head slowly.)

CURTAIN.

BIBLIOBAZAAR

The essential book market!

Did you know that you can get any of our titles in large print?

Did you know that we have an ever-growing collection of books in many languages?

Order online:
www.bibliobazaar.com

Find all of your favorite classic books!

Stay up to date with the latest government reports!

At BiblioBazaar, we aim to make knowledge more accessible by making thousands of titles available to you- *quickly and affordably*.

Contact us:
BiblioBazaar
PO Box 21206
Charleston, SC 29413

LaVergne, TN USA
05 April 2011
222980LV00001B/6/A